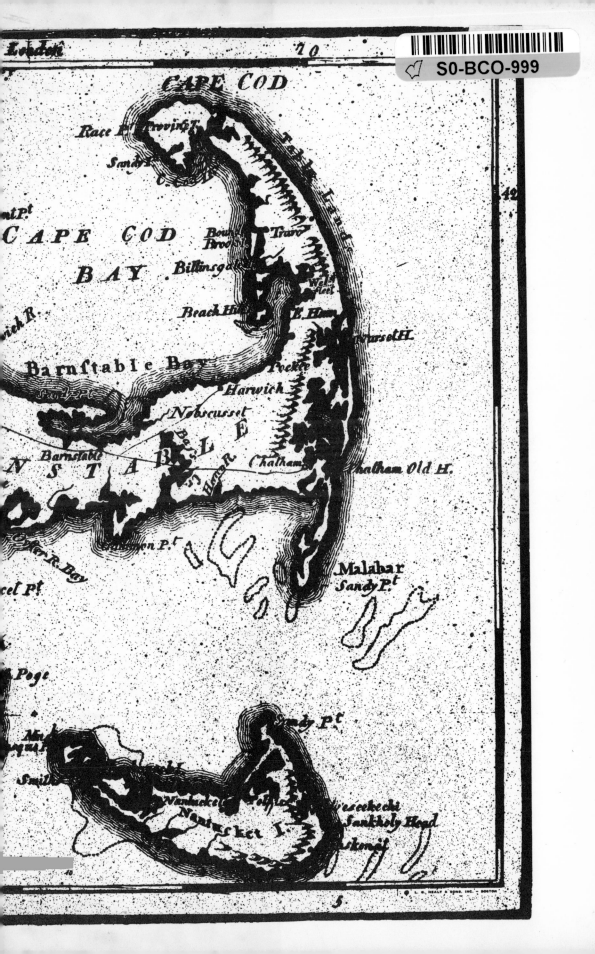

Yesterday's Cape Cod

EVELYN LAWSON

Yesterday's
CAPE COD

with a foreword by Kurt Vonnegut, Jr.

Seemann's Historic Cities Series No. 11

E. A. Seemann Publishing, Inc.
Miami, Florida

The author offers sincere appreciation to all who have so generously contributed photographs and keepsakes to this book. They are acknowledged (in abbreviated form) at the end of each caption:

AA	Provincetown Art Association
CC	Cape Cod Chamber of Commerce
CCST	*Cape Cod Standard Times*
CL	Cotuit Library
Cook	Dorothy Cook of Provincetown
Elks	Benevolent and Protective Order of Elks, Hyannis Lodge
Euler	Reeves Euler of Provincetown
Godoy	Susan Godoy of Hyannis
Gunther	Edna Gunther of Provincetown
Hastings	Martha Hastings of Hyannis
Howes	Barbara Taylor Howes of Cummaquid
Kelsey	Richard C. Kelsey of Chatham
MacLean	Marguerite B. MacLean of Centerville
NBST	*New Bedford Standard Times*
NSP	Cape Cod National Seashore Park
Palmer	Robert Palmer of Falmouth
Paulman	Dorothy Alexander Paulman of Provincetown
PMM	Plymouth Monument Museum
Poisson	Hugh G. Poisson of Falmouth
RJB	Red Jacket Beach Motor Inn
Russell	Barbara Russell of Sandwich
Seaman	Carrie Seaman of Provincetown
SGM	Sandwich Glass Museum
Smith	William L. Smith of Hyannis
Snow	Norma Snow of Truro
Tales	"Tales of Cape Cod," Inc.
Veterino	Jack Veterino of Barnstable
Vorse	Heaton Vorse of Provincetown
Williams	Percy Williams of the *Barnstable Patriot*

Jacket Photograph: Richard C. Kelsey

Library of Congress Cataloging in Publication Data

Lawson, Evelyn.
  Yesterday's Cape Cod.

  (Seemann's historic cities series ; no. 11)
  1. Cape Cod--History. I. Title.
F72.C3L35   974.4'92   74-81528
ISBN 0-912458-45-3

COPYRIGHT © 1975 by Evelyn Lawson

ISBN 0-912458-45-3

Library of Congress Catalog Card Number: 74-81528

Manufactured in the United States of America

This book is gratefully dedicated to
Arthur J. D'Elia, M.D.
of Harwich, my friend and physician.

Contents

Foreword

by Kurt Vonnegut, Jr.

EVELYN LAWSON is the only realistic lover of Cape Cod I ever knew. All the other lovers have been sentimentalists, looking at this or that beauty spot narrowly—as though through a mailing tube. There is no harm in such affectionate narrowness, God knows. But there isn't much truth about what is beloved in it, either. And Evelyn, with her Elizabethan gusto for all things human, investigates and celebrates the actual lives which have been lived on the Cape. Most people love the body of the Cape—its houses and gardens and woods and beaches and ponds. Evelyn loves not only the body, but the mind and the soul.

I lived on the Cape for many years, and so was a microscopic part of its soul, even with a name as un-Yankee as mine. Evelyn was one of the few close friends I made. I was particularly attracted to her, since she always talked about the Cape as a human habitation rather than as a museum. This made me more real to myself. Before meeting her, I was a sort of temporary ghost in a very permanent old house on a much-admired old lane.

After meeting her, I could stop wondering when my new shingles would turn the only acceptable shade of gray. I could devote my attention to altogether more amusing and instructive matters, to subjects which composed the core of human conversations everywhere else—the passionate, hilarious, erratic, tragic, noble, and ridiculous lives our neighbors led.

Good for Evelyn.

THIS BIRD'S-EYE VIEW of Chatham of 1890 was an official, accredited survey, drawn by an artist in a balloon. On returning to his base, he would check landmarks to be sure of his accuracy. (Kelsey)

Westward Ho!

THE VIKINGS were the first, some thousand years ago, to record pleasurable visits to Cape Cod. And, like all who have come later, they loved the place.

Norse sagas written in runic letters, preserved in Iceland, Greenland, and Scandinavia, describe the Cape as the "Long Land" with mild winters, abundant fish and game, much wood for ship repairs, shelter, and fire, and vines bearing fruit. These were some of the Cape's attractions that lured Vikings ashore to rest from the rigors of the North Atlantic and repair their dragon ships. They made many visits to the New England coast, and an abortive attempt to establish a colony is recorded. Finally, encounters with hostile Indians discouraged further exploration.

The swirling fogs of myth and legend have masked the history of these ancient times. But it is said that Thorwold, the leader of the last Vikings landing party, was mortally wounded by an Indian arrow. His dying request was to be buried on the "fair land" overlooking the sea, where he had hoped to spend his life.

For almost five hundred years, the Cape was left to its bronze-skinned caretakers. Only the tide and an occasional canoe visited its beaches.

In Europe, in the early 1500s, a new strain of bold, adventurous men emerged who were navigators and explorers, men not afraid to challenge uncharted seas or meet the dangers of unknown lands beyond. Their ships and equipment, primitive by today's standards, represented technical advances new to seamanship. The adventurers came from many countries, driven by dreams of prestige and wealth. They hoped to claim new territories for their sovereigns, and discover riches for themselves.

VIKINGS REPAIRING their dragon ship on a Cape Cod beach around the year 1000: At the head of the Cape a rock carving in runic letters is translated to read, "God Gives Up Light Abundantly." Solid evidence of early Norse exploration, which agrees with Icelandic records, also exists on the lower Cape.

Cape Cod lay right in the path of these early explorers who lost no time in charting Cape waters and mapping the peninsula. They soon found that the Cape's unique features begin with its geography.

The early surveyors mapped a seventy-mile peninsula, shaped like a bent arm extending out into the Atlantic Ocean. The upper arm near the shoulder was some twenty miles wide, gradually tapering to an average width of six miles as the arm thrust itself out to sea. The land ended in a cupped hand at the Cape tip. And, just before the hand-like formation, the wrist of the arm narrowed to less than a half-mile from sea to sea.

The Cape is a hook, a curlicue. To follow it from the mainland to the tip leads to a spiral course, known to sailors as boxing the compass.

The explorers were amazed to find numerous fresh-water, spring-fed lakes in beautiful sylvan settings up and down the whole land. Some were found only a few yards inland from the ocean's brine. The bay side was bordered by inlets, marshes, and potential harbor sites.

The ocean side of the Cape was not so hospitable. Swift currents raced around the Cape tip. Dangerous shoals and uncharted bars lay in wait for the unsuspecting mariner, in waters soon to be known as the "graveyard of the Atlantic."

From 1579 to 1601, French fishermen cruised Cape waters. The explorer Samuel Champlain visited the Cape tip in 1605 and called the land "Cap Blanc" because of the white sand and dunes. Dutch navigators named the peninsula "Staaten Hoeck." Capt. John Smith tried unsuccessfully to have it named "Cape James" for his king and benefactor. But it was another Englishman, Bartholomew Gosnold, who landed his ship *Sparrow Hawk* on the lower Cape and called the place "Cape Cod" because of the quantity of codfish caught by his crew. Then, in 1624, Sir William Alexander published a new maritime guide in which Cape Cod first appeared on published charts.

By the second decade of the seventeenth century, the stage had been set for the beginning of American history. The curtain rose on November 9, 1620, when the *Mayflower* with its 102 passengers dropped anchor in what is now the Provincetown harbor, and Cape Cod became the gateway to the new world.

The *Mayflower* and its passengers spent a month in the Provincetown harbor, and an eventful month it was. On November 11, the colonists crowded into the ship's cabin where they wrote and signed the Mayflower Compact. This was the first charter providing for government by democratic principles. This assembly of the "Founding Fathers" is known as the first town meeting.

Aboard ship on the same day, Peregrine White was born to Susanna Fuller White and thus became the first native-born New Englander. During the same time, Dorothy Bradford, wife of Governor Bradford, fell overboard and was drowned. Her death was recorded as accidental.

Landing parties exploring this narrow portion of the Cape did encounter small bands of Indians. Reports conflict on the temper of the Indians; while the meetings were apparently peaceful, the Indians seemed sensitive and hostile.

After an exploring party from the *Mayflower* found that the terrain on the headlands of the coast in the Plymouth area was more suitable for farming

[13]

MAYFLOWER II sails the Atlantic into Provincetown harbor in 1957. An accurate replica of the ship which brought the Pilgrims to America in 1620, it was built in England by naval architect William A. Baker who closely followed Governor Bradford's description of the one-hundred-eighty-ton vessel. *Mayflower II* is on permanent display in Plymouth harbor.

The Mayflower Compact

"In the name of God, Amen. We whose names are underwritten, the loyal subjects of our dread sovereign Lord, King James, by the grace of God, of Great Britain, France and Ireland King, defender of the faith, etc., having undertaken, for the Glory of God, and advancement of the Christian faith, and honor of our King and country, a voyage to plant the first colony in the northern parts of Virginia, do by these presents solemnly and mutually in the presence of God, and of one another, covenant and combine ourselves together into a civil body politic, for our better ordering and preservation and furtherance of the ends aforesaid; and by virtue hereof to enact, constitute and frame such just and equal laws, ordinances, acts, constitutions and offices from time to time, as shall be thought most meet and convenient for the general good of the colony, unto which we promise all due submission and obedience. In witness whereof, we have hereunder subscribed our names at Cape Cod, the 11th of November, in the year of the reign of our sovereign Lord, King James of England, France and Ireland the eighteenth, and of Scotland, the fifty-fourth. Anno Domini, 1620."

John Carver	John Billington	Thomas Williams	John Rigdale
William Bradford	Moses Fletcher	Gilbert Winslow	Edward Fuller
Edward Winslow	John Goodman	Edmund Margeson	Richard Clark
William Brewster	Samuel Fuller	Peter Brown	Richard Gardiner
Isaac Allerton	Christopher Martin	Richard Britterige	John Allerton
Myles Standish	William Mullins	George Soule	Thomas English
John Alden	William White	Edward Tilley	Edward Doty
John Turner	Richard Warren	John Tilley	Edward Leister
Frances Eaton	John Howland	Francis Cooke	
James Chilton	Stephen Hopkins	Thomas Rogers	
John Crakston	Degory Priest	Thomas Tinker	

than the sandy lower Cape, the Elders decided to leave the Cape harbor and establish their permanent colony at Plymouth.

At first, untold hardships, severe winters, and an appalling lack of knowledge of the ways of the wilderness reduced the little settlement to half its population. But the colony survived, and by 1630 three hundred colonists inhabited Plymouth.

[14]

That same year—only ten years after their landing—the Pilgrim's governor, William Bradford, was granted a patent (charter) putting all of Cape Cod under the jurisdiction of the Plymouth establishment. This opened the Cape for permanent settlement. Land was free for the clearing, and the rush began.

By now, many shiploads of pioneers had landed along the coast, some destined for New England. These newcomers found the choice acreage in the Plymouth area already allotted to the first settlers, and so the Cape was the answer for them.

A CLASSICAL SALTBOX, the Hoxie house in Sandwich, built in 1637, is the oldest house on Cape Cod. It was named for Capt. Abraham Hoxie, a whaling captain who made it his home in the 1880s. (Russell)

There were also a few in the Plymouth settlement who were not too happy living under the critical eyes of the Town Fathers. They longed for a less socially rigid lifestyle. They resolved to establish more liberal communities on the Cape.

Thus, the settlement of the Cape came rapidly, and three towns were established in 1639 alone.

Sandwich was the first. Edmund and Elizabeth Freeman, an enterprising couple, are credited with being the leaders that inspired the founding of this community, the first to last to this day on the Cape. Its site, then called Monomet by the Indians, was high on the upper Cape (the shoulder or head) only twenty miles from the parent Plymouth.

Next down the line came Barnstable, followed by Yarmouth, both also founded in 1639. Eastham on the lower Cape came into being in 1649. For many years, these four settlements alone were responsible for taming the wilderness that was Cape Cod.

The first Cape Codders, those who left the established colony at Plymouth to claim a portion of the sandy, narrow land, were hearty and brave, a description that might fit all pioneers facing an unknown continent. Yet it took special fortitude to leave the protection of the stockade and the small but real comfort of being privileged to share the community supplies, for by now the hazards of the wilderness were well-known and respected. Early Cape settlers were prepared to face savages who might be hostile, wolves and other predators, as well as the uncertainty of obtaining land suitable for agriculture.

Besides being hearty and brave, the men and women headed for Cape Cod were also nonconformist. The tight behavior patterns established by the first comers did not journey to Cape Cod where a more casual lifestyle developed. The tavern invariably became the village center. This is not to say that loose living or those of suspicious character went unnoticed—but undesirables were warned to leave town, rather than detained and punished.

Two basic characteristics set Cape people apart from their contemporaries—then and now. First, the people who settled Cape Cod had a strong empathy for the sea. They identified with a maritime environment and were willing to sacrfice much to live in one.

The second trait common to most Cape Codders is not so easily explained: From the earliest times it would seem as though Cape Codders were bent on asserting their individuality, and this urge to be singular is reflected in the startling differences between the towns on the Cape, for no two of the fifteen towns are in any way alike—in appearance or social climate—despite their close proximity.

It has been suggested by twentieth-century visitors that the Cape is much like a little continent composed of many small countries, with only a language in common.

Western view of Sandwich, (central part).

North western view of the Barnstable Court-House, and other build[ings]

Eastern view of Yarmouth.

South-eastern view of Brewster, (central part).

North-western view in Chatham.

SEVERAL TOWNS on Cape Cod are shown in woodcuts of the late 1700s or early 1800s. Going down-Cape, they are as follows: Sandwich, Barnstable, Yarmouth, Brewster, Chatham, and Provincetown.

View in the Village of Provincetown.

NORTH-EASTERN VIEW OF PROVINCETOWN

For more than a century, each Cape settlement was a self-sustaining, isolated community. Miles of wild country separated towns. Communications were limited to the infrequent visits of Indian runners who were able to follow trails obscure to the white man. So the towns of the Cape developed individually according to the tastes of their inhabitants, uninfluenced by the mores of their neighbors.

Indian legend and lore was a strong influence during Cape Cod's infancy. At first, the towns and the lands surrounding them retained their Indian names. Even today many Cape areas and almost all of the lakes and rivers are known by their original Indian names.

Two of the largest and most beautiful spring-fed lakes are Wequaquet in Centerville and Scargo Lake in Dennis. The latter was filled, according to a charming legend, by the tears of a beautiful Indian princess. Such legends abound on the Cape.

Indian names common to the peninsula, starting at the head of the Cape, are Sagamore, Mashpee, Cataumet, Pocasset, Cotuit, Wianno, and Santuit. Mattacheese is associated with the Barnstable area, Cummaquid is a residential section nearby; Monomoy, Tonset, and Nauset are found on the lower Cape as is the Pamet river and region.

These Indian names are familiar to all who have ever called Cape Cod home. They serve as a constant reminder of the Cape's Indian heritage and the generous help the "Natives of the Narrow Land" gave the early settlers of Cape Cod.

Cape Indians belonged to the Wampanoag Federation which inhabited the eastern areas of Massachusetts and Rhode Island. The Wampanoags were affiliated with the powerful Algonquin Nation. At least five, probably six Wampanoag tribes were living in the Cape area when the first settlers arrived. Each tribe had its own chief, but the leader of all the Wampanoags was the Great Sachem Massasoit who was ever friendly to the pioneers. He signed a peace treaty with the Pilgrims in 1621, which he faithfully observed. On Massasoit's death in 1661, his son, known as King Philip, became chieftain. The new sachem did not share his father's lenient attitude toward the settlers, and for a while bloody wars and massacres raged throughout southeastern New England.

But Cape Codders seem to have handled their Indian neighbors with diplomacy. During the most inflammatory periods of the King Philip wars, the settlers and the local Indians remained on friendly terms, and the Cape towns and their people flourished.

In the center section of the peninsula, the soil was richer and more productive than had been anticipated. Whales, stranded in countless numbers on Cape beaches, became a real source of revenue. And if the whales were slow to beach themselves, Cape Codders quickly became skilled at herding them ashore to the trying vats.

Cape affluence soon attracted the attention of the governing Pilgrim Fathers in Plymouth who kept a sharp eye on all the settlements that came within their jurisdiction. Soon, a portion of the oil rendered from each whale was taxed for the town, the colony, and the Crown. Whaling, nevertheless, was a pleasant diversion from farming—and far more profitable. It expanded into the Cape's prime industry.

The early government was simple, strict, and scrupulously honest. The governor was the highest authority in the land. He was elected annually by "freemen," members of the church who had land under cultivation. Two deputies were also elected from each town to join the governor and his assistants to form the General Court, the first legislature.

Cape Cod came into its own in 1657, when the executive power in Plymouth moved to the Cape, and Thomas Prence of Eastham was elected governor, with Thomas Hinckley of Barnstable as his lieutenant. In 1680, Hinckley became governor and steered Cape Cod successfully through its growing pains.

It wasn't until 1727, however, that the Cape tip became incorporated under the name of Provincetown. The first settlers had drifted down to the end of the Cape in 1680, and it was noted that, for all the Cape's many coves and inlets, only Provincetown provided a harbor for ocean-going vessels.

In the late 1600s, the British government made two mistakes that strained colonial relations, especially in the vicinity of Cape Cod. Sir Edmond Andros, an inefficient and personally unpleasant man, arrived to take over the management of the colony—after sixty years of home rule, just as the Cape Cod administration was getting underway. The new taste of democracy had wetted the colonists' appetite for more, and the appointment of Andros only served to remind them that they were still dependent on the whims of the Crown. Fortunately, Andros' reign was short-lived. He was recalled after James II was deposed and William III came to the throne in 1689.

Two years later, the English delivered another severe blow. They forced the consolidation of Plymouth, Massachusetts Bay, Maine, and Nova Scotia into one province, naming it the Massachusetts Bay Colony. Local pride was injured beyond repair, but the merger eased government expenses and tightened the bonds between all early settlers of New England.

The dawn of the eighteenth century saw a prosperous and growing Cape Cod, although the French and Indian wars were in full cry as they would be for more than half a century to come. The men of Cape Cod were expected to make their contribution to the British armed forces; many of them served with great distinction.

A Barnstable family named Gorham contributed three generations of colonels to the English forces, and, oddly enough, they were distinguished for sea duty. It seems that the French in Canada had settled away from the coast on inland rivers as protection against attack by British warships, but the small whaling vessels manned by Cape Codders could easily negotiate the shallow rivers and harass French villages.

It was not the Cape Cod way to shoulder a musket and train in formal war patterns that proved so ineffective in the wilds of America. But sea duty was different, and Cape Codders served the Crown loyally during the interminable French and Indian wars.

During colonial days, the Cape was home to many famous and infamous residents, one of the most distinguished of them being Richard Bourne, for whom the town of Bourne at the head of the Cape was named. An evangelist and a very strong and righteous man, he loved the Indians, and the Indians loved him. Among his many enduring good deeds was the founding of the Aptuxcet Trading Post, where fair trade for both Indians and settlers was strictly enforced. He obtained legislation to procure and secure for the Indians some fifty acres of land, the village of Mashpee, which would forever remain in the hands of its original owners, and he presided over the first Christian church for Indians in the United States. It is important to note that all of his endeavors have survived to present days.

Although Richard Bourne was a godly man, he was no prude, and he was not adverse to enjoying a few harmless nips in a friendly tavern after a hard day of doing good. It was during such a moment of relaxation that the Reverend Bourne encountered the Devil who, at the time, was a frequent visitor to the Cape, and had noticed Bourne's many successful projects. He planned to put an end to that plethora of goodness.

Bourne was a champion wrestler, and the Devil, who was as strong and supple as a pine tree, challenged Bourne to a wrestling match, with the stake being Dick Bourne's soul. Although the Devil was gifted with cunning as well as superhuman strength, Bourne had God on his side, and the Devil could never throw him.

The Devil met and challenged Bourne many times; the minister always accepted the challenge, and always won. After a while, the Devil gave up and left the upper Cape—and Bourne country—to build a home in Provincetown, overlooking the wild and treacherous shoals of the backshore. For he intended to cut himself in on the "mooncusser" action, the illegal salvaging flourishing on the lower Cape. Where there were lost ships, there were lost souls.

More than a hundred years passed before His Satanic Majesty returned to the upper Cape to argue with America's greatest solon, Daniel Webster, in the tap room of the Fessendon Inn (now Daniel Webster Inn) in Sandwich.

During the seventeenth and eighteenth centuries, witches were not only tolerated on Cape Cod, but accepted as part of the community. Almost every town had at least one witch whose activities were so conspicuous that they were recorded in the chronicles of the times. Up and down the Cape there were "green hollows" near burial places where witches met to celebrate their sabbaths.

Ould Betty was one who lived on the old Plymouth Road at the head of the Cape. She was said to have looked young and beautiful for over one hundred years.

Twin witches lived on the shore of Buzzards Bay and haunted the beaches looking for sailors who had deserted them. Debbie lived in "Bourne country." She was an expert weaver and had customers as far down-Cape as Barnstable. She hated children and often did them mischief.

Liza Tower Hill was the most famous Barnstable witch. She learned some of her craft from "bad Indians" who were gifted in magic. She bewitched those who rode by night in the area and was much feared. She was said to be a sharp trader. Liza had a devoted husband who was a respected farmer.

Goodie Hallett of Eastham and Wellfleet was probably the most famous of all Cape witches. People came from all over the colony for her charms and spells. She was associated with the local doctor, and was the life-long sweetheart of Black Bellamy, the infamous pirate.

And at the Cape tip, the Red Witch of Truro fell in love with the respectable Captain Sylvester, thereby leading his ship to destruction.

Contrary to the classical fairy-tale concept, Cape witches were not toothless old hags, but retained their youth and beauty long after it was proper to do so.

The bloody exploits of two pirates associated with the Cape, Sam (Black) Bellamy and Captain Kidd, have made naval history.

Sam Bellamy was running a profitable packet line from Yarmouth to the lower Cape, when he and several other Cape Codders were shanghaied from their local tavern. He was engaged to a comely serving girl at the time. When the Cape sailors awoke from the effect of their drugged drinks, they found themselves in irons aboard a British man-of-war well out at sea. The Americans bided their time by feigning obedience. But soon Bellamy organized the captives, and together they slaughtered every officer on board the ship, and hoisted the Jolly Roger. Bellamy and his crew acquired a fleet of vessels and plundered all ships that came within sight of their glass for more than twenty years. They roamed the Atlantic from Jamaica to Nova Scotia and were never apprehended. Bellamy's luxuriant black beard prompted his nickname.

While still in his prime, the pirate captain retired to the Cape. He sold his ships and divided the spoils with his crew. He found and married his old sweetheart, who was none other than Goodie Hallett. Black Bellamy covered Goodie with jewels and built a handsome house on the bluffs around Race Point. But their happiness was short-lived, for alert British customs officials were able to trace Bellamy through his crew who were indiscreetly squandering their loot in Boston taverns. Sam Bellamy and Goodie Hallett were both hung in the Boston Commons, for high piracy and witchcraft, respectively.

Although Captain Kidd was an Englishman, Cape Cod was his favorite rendezvous throughout his notorious career. The Chatham and Orleans area, especially in the vicinity of Pleasant Bay, was associated with this buccaneer who is said to have buried his hoard in the last decade of the seventeenth century on Hog Island in Pleasant Bay, or very near the shore of the Bay.

Like Bellamy, Kidd was nabbed by Boston customs officials, returned to London, and subsequently hung for piracy.

Cutthroats and rascals they undoubtedly were, but pirates also were the most competent sailors on the high seas. Their fiscal arrangements were democratic and simple. One third of the loot went to the owner or captain of the vessel; one third for the ship's maintenance; and one third was equally divided among the crew. There is much unaccounted-for pirate's booty buried on the Eastern seaboard—some perhaps on Cape Cod?

Let the naval historians argue whether Marblehead or Beverly (the north shore of Massachusetts) or the waters off Rhode Island gave birth to the Navy, but many years before the Revolution, the men of Cape Cod can take the credit for siring the Merchant Marine—and this service was to develop and establish American leadership in world commerce.

The "coastal packets" came into being early in the Cape's history, and their contribution to transportation, freight shipping, and communications is a neglected page in American history. The packets were instigated and manned by Cape Codders. Their original purpose had been to tie together the towns on the Cape, but the lines spread and expanded to include the Eastern seaboard. Cape Cod men commanded this profitable service as America's first shipping merchants, and those who became masters of the great American clipper ships owed their renowned seamanship to early service with the coastal packets.

When the fires of the Revolution first began to smolder, Cape people were were almost equally divided in sentiment. The younger ones supported the Patriots, joined activist groups, and prepared themselves to fight for the cause. The older, conservative folk represented the Tory faction in favor of "letting well enough alone," but their feelings were short-lived. Before the first shot was fired, the Patriots had won most of Cape Cod to their side.

In 1761, James Otis, a young lawyer from Barnstable, ignited the first sparks of war. He delivered a fiery address before the superior court of Massachusetts against the use of "Writs of Assistance" by British customs officers. The following year, Otis published his first political pamphlet, "A Vindication of the Conduct of the House of Representatives of the Province

THE AMERICAN CLIPPER SHIP *Red Jacket*, commanded by Capt. Asa Eldridge of Yarmouth, was the pride of the merchant fleet, shown here in an Antarctic ice floe off Cape Horn on her second voyage from Australia to Liverpool in 1854. Her maiden voyage that year from New York to Liverpool broke all records for speed and remained unrivaled for sailing vessels. She left New York on January 11, braving the fearsome winter gales of the North Atlantic while carrying her full complement of canvas. The Cape Cod captain dropped anchor in Liverpool in 13 days, 1 hour, and 25 minutes, a smashing victory for American-built ships and American seamanship. The *Red Jacket* was 251 feet overall, 2305 tons, with a draft of 31 feet. Designed by Samuel H. Pook and built by George Thomas of Rockland, Maine, she was named for a Seneca Indian chief, Sagoyewatha, who fought with the Patriots during the Revolution. (He had habitually worn a bright red jacket given him by a British officer, and the figurehead was a carving of him in his red coat.) The *Red Jacket* under Captain Eldridge could log 413 nautical miles in twenty-four hours. Her close rivals, also skippered by Cape Codders, were *Flying Cloud, Great Republic, Donald McKay, Lightning, James Bains,* and *Sovereign of the Seas.* All these clippers could log 400 miles a day, but the *Red Jacket* was the undisputed queen of the seas. (RJB)

of Massachusetts Bay," (in contest with the governor), and another one in 1764, "The Rights of the British Colonies Asserted and Proved." Both tracts were widely read and did much to strengthen the Patriots' cause.

Cape Codders identified with the Otis protests. The invasion of their privacy, homes, and properties had long become a festering sore to Cape Codders. When the men of Lexington and Concord moved, a substantial militia from the Cape joined the revolutionary forces.

The war was intensely real to the lower Cape. In 1775, Provincetown Harbor was a rendezvous for British men-of-war. The waters around the Cape tip had been designated as neutral territory, and the British took full advantage of the situation. They confiscated supplies from the inhabitants and, when short-handed, forced the town men to serve on their ships. Some of these men ended up in English prisons.

Throughout the hostilities, the shoals and treacherous sand bars and currents on the backside, or seaside, of the lower Cape were natural defenses and favored the Americans. The British ships were heavy and unwieldy, and their captains were unfamiliar with the tricky Cape waters. When wrecks occurred, as they did, they were called a "Providence of God." Experienced as the town folk were in salvaging, they showed the beached enemy vessels and their crews no mercy. Prisoners were taken and sent to Boston, and every scrap of supplies and usable materials was stripped from the wrecked ships.

One ship, the *Somerset*, wrecked on Peaked Hill Bars at the very tip of the Cape, proved to be one of the most profitable and also practical salvaging operations of the time, as the salvagers were able to drag the ship's cannon and other armaments ashore, to be used for the town's fortifications.

Triumphant as the freedom-loving Cape Codders were at the close of the war, it had been a costly victory. The British blockade had kept Cape vessels long idle. The wharves, along with the ships, accessories, and equipment for farming and seafaring had deteriorated beyond use, and no funds were available for repairs or replacements. Cape people could muster only scant resources on which to rebuild their economic structure.

CAPT. WILLIAM HOWES BURGESS of Brewster and his wife, Hannah Rebecca Crowell Burgess of West Sandwich, sat for portraits in 1852 at the time the couple married and were waiting for him to take command of the clipper *Whirlwind*. He was twenty-two and his bride eighteen. Hannah voyaged with her husband, and in their first four years together she crossed the equator eleven times. In 1856, Captain Burgess was in command of the *Challenger* when disaster struck while returning from a sail around Cape Horn to San Francisco. He had become seriously ill, the nearest port and doctor was twenty-two days away in Valparaiso, Chile, and the mate couldn't get his bearings. Resourceful and brave, Hannah took command and navigated the ship to Valparaiso, only to see her husband die shortly after reaching port. He was only twenty-seven years old. (SGM)

THIS SHINGLED WINDMILL at Eastham, one of several now cherished as landmarks, is a fine example of those that were the prime source of energy all over the Cape through the 1800s. (CCST)

THE DANIEL WEBSTER INN at Sandwich reminds all who warm themselves at the fireplace in the taproom that the Rev. Benjamin Fessenden built it originally in 1694 as part of his home. When he and his family left the Cape after the Revolution, the mansion became an inn. During the 1850s it was headquarters for Daniel Webster when the great lawyer tried cases in the Barnstable Court House and was the legal negotiator for the Boston and Sandwich Glass Company. This was where he confronted the Devil in Stephen Vincent Benet's famous story, "The Devil and Daniel Webster." At Webster's death, the inn took his name. It is still a popular Cape hostelry today.

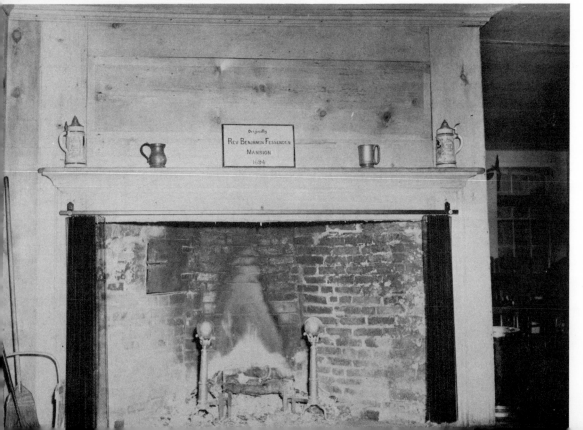

Yankee ingenuity came to the fore in these lean times. Neighbor helped neighbor rebuild. Meager supplies were shared. Funds were pooled to buy equipment which could be used by the community. The struggle for economic rebirth was shared by all.

When the nineteenth century opened, Cape Cod was well on its way to recovery, but a frugal way of life was to be the heritage of these postwar years that has never quite left the consciousness of the true Cape Codder. This reputation for being tight-fisted and sharp traders proved to be a recommendation for mastering the great merchant ships that were soon to grace the seas.

Just as the sails of Cape Cod's budding merchant fleet hit the breeze, and small industries began to take root, the War of 1812 broke out, threatening all reconstruction efforts. But Cape Codders were not to be impoverished a second time. They were not sympathetic to the 1812 conflict, judging it a mistake of an inept administration.

They ran the blockades successfully and went about their business of organizing and operating packet lines, trading, fishing, and whaling. The more adventurous sailors had already turned their eyes and imagination toward the West Indies and the far-off Pacific.

Meanwhile back on the shore, farming became profitable, for the packets could be depended on to sell and deliver produce; the manufacture of salt was becoming an industry; and boat yards and shops catering to marine activities were flourishing.

The days of Cape Cod's greatest glory were at hand.

The American clipper ships were the undisputed queens of the high seas. They put the new republic on the world map, and gave the country leadership in world trade. Their short reign began in the 1820s and lasted until steam defeated their speed at the close of the 1860s.

These great ships originated in Baltimore, but Donald McKay, a naval architect in Boston, perfected them. He designed *Flying Cloud, Glory of the Seas,* and *Lightning,* three of the most famous sailing ships in maritime history.

The clippers were berthed in Baltimore, New York, and Boston, all of which had the necessary deep-water harbors. The builders, backers, and owners maintained their business headquarters in these cities.

But what manner of men were capable of commanding these vessels built to ride the seas of the world? Not only was extraordinary seamanship required, but the clipper captain's background had to include proven business acumen to insure the investment of the owners.

Only Cape Cod men could fill the requirement, it seems. To captain a clipper was the most-coveted honor, and the Cape skippers were worthy of it. They had attracted the attention of the clipper owners with their expertise in handling the coastal packet lines.

Although no clipper ship was ever seen in the harbors of Cape Cod, more than forty clipper captains resided at Yarmouth Port in sumptuous homes along King's Highway, now Route 6A, not counting the skippers who lived in Sandwich and other Cape towns.

Captain Eldridge commanded the *Red Jacket,* and Captain Hallett's ship was the *Phantom.* Both captains were from Yarmouth. The *Northern Light* was skippered by Captain Hatch of Eastham, Captain Sears from Dennis sailed *Wild Hunter,* and Brewster's Captain Dillingham was the master of *Snow Squall.* These are just a few of the captains who steered the American clipper ships into the ports of the world.

The story is told of a Cape visitor driving through Dennis who inquired of an "old salt" along the road how to get to Chatham. The sailor was unable to give the visitor directions, since, while having been to China several times, he just never had had any business in Chatham.

At the outbreak of the Civil War, Cape Codders readily responded to the call to arms, although slavery was not unknown on the Cape. At least five slaves owned by prominent local families are recorded. But seafaring men had nothing but contempt for slavery and the stinking slave ships they encountered on their voyages.

The Civil War, the advent of the railroads, and the development of the steam engine all combined to bring to a sudden close the exciting saga of the Yankee clipper. Whaling also declined after the war, but coastal shipping made a brave stand against the competition of the railroads, and survived to a limited extent for many years.

Fishing as an industry became an important part of the Cape's economy. Since the clipper days, the Portuguese, a welcome and colorful minority, had been drifting from Portugal and the Azores to Cape Cod. Many of the early arrivals had sailed with the clipper captains, and all of them were as sea-oriented as the land they had chosen for their new home. The Portuguese population in Provincetown grew to become an important factor in the fishing industry.

The salt works and the curing of fish played a small part in the postwar economy and continued for a time, and the cultivation of cranberries had started.

On the upper Cape in Sandwich, a thriving industry had been established. Deming Jarves opened the Sandwich Manufactory in 1825 for the making of glass. Sandwich was chosen as the site because Cape beaches were thought to offer an inexhaustible supply of sand necessary in the manufacturing of flint glass. Jarvis engaged master glass blowers from all over the world who soon found the sand of Cape Cod unsuitable for the glassmaking process. The alternative was to import a fine white sand from the Berkshires. The factory

flourished despite this handicap. Boston partners and fresh capital changed the firm's name to Boston and Sandwich Glass Company, and the exquisite and prolific output of the company made Sandwich the most important glass center of the nineteenth century. Jarvis kept control of the company until 1858, when he resigned to set up the Cape Cod factory. Jarvis died ten years later, with the new factory producing glassware of the highest artistic quality. The industry died in 1888, when the firms could not sustain a strike for higher wages, and they closed down.

Cape Cod had much to show for its fat years. Churches, schools, fraternal lodges, as well as many stately Victorian homes had been built. Roads connecting the towns had been constructed. New jetties and piers pushed into the water. Truck gardens and flower gardens were diligently cultivated, and beautification programs for the towns were put in action.

The Cape had given birth to fifteen towns in Barnstable County, which extends from Buzzards Bay at the head of the Cape to Provincetown at its tip. Barnstable Village was chosen as the county seat, and the prosperous towns of Hyannis and Falmouth became trade centers.

The people of Cape Cod now had assets on which to build, but as the twentieth century approached, they faced again an uncertain economy.

Traditionally, they had looked to the sea for support, only to find that their greatest equity lay in the unique natural beauty of the land itself. They began to recognize the economic value of the recreational diversions the Cape had to offer.

Wealthy residents of the Eastern urban areas were quick to appreciate the Cape's new open-house policy, and the transition from a rural, seafaring community to a prime vacation land started. Blue-water sailors manned charter boats; ship brokers of pleasure craft opened shop; ship chandlers turned into antique dealers; and more than just a few captains' homes became inns, with the captain himself playing "mine host."

GLASSMAKING was one of the Cape's earliest industries, requiring artistic talent and the skill of master craftsmen. Here, the Boston & Sandwich Glass Company is shown after Deming Jarves, its owner, expanded it, taking in capital and partners from Boston but retaining controlling interest. (SGM)

[29]

DEMING JARVES (1790-1869) founded the glass factory in Sandwich in 1825. The firm prospered despite the added expense of hauling sand from western Massachusetts because the sand of the Cape proved unsuitable. He was the leading figure in glass manufacturing for forty-four years. (SGM)

GRANDFATHER of the Coast Guard, the Life Saving Service was first established around the early 1880s at Wychmere Harbor by Capt. S. L. Ellis, pictured in the bow of the dory. Although the Coast Guard, founded in 1790, manned revenue cutters to serve the Treasury Department, their stations on Cape Cod did not function until 1875. The Life Saving Service added a new dimension to the Coast Guard when they joined forces in 1890.

THE TOWN HALL in Provincetown was built almost one hundred years ago, in 1878, after fire destroyed the original one in 1877. The first floor is devoted to town business and courtrooms. The second floor houses an auditorium seating 600 which is used for town meetings, balls, pageants, and social and civic functions. The police department and local jail occupy the basement. (Cook)

ABANDONED GLASS FACTORY: In 1888, the Boston & Sandwich Glass Company allowed its furnaces to die, and the company was dissolved. A never-settled strike was blamed. Today, glass objects manufactured in Sandwich between 1825 and 1888 are collectors' items, some worth their weight in gold. (SGM)

ACRES OF FISH drying was a common sight on Cape Cod before and after 1900, because the dried and salted fish sold very well in those days without electric refrigeration. When this picture was taken in 1888, the fishing fleet was still under sail. (Howes)

TWO CAPTAINS NAMED CROSBY, from Brewster, and one captain from England (center), shared a serious mood the day they posed as landlubbers in the early 1890s. The original photograph was taken with a glass plate. (Tales)

PATENT MEDICINES and "nature cures" for the ever-present ailments of mankind were for many years sold without license and often from wagons. Orleans Center was on the route of these vendors of Red Sea Balsam one cold day in 1890. Note the fur blanket covering their knees. (Tales)

NO ONE CAN REMEMBER when Provincetown did not have an official town crier. Walter Smith began the job in the 1890s and cried until the early twenties. Even on the hottest days of summer he wore his colonial costume and cried the length of Commercial Street, telling the news with added paid commercials from eating places, guest houses, entertainment places, and various services.

THE FIRST HYANNIS YACHT CLUB was an impressive Eastern-style summer house, built before the turn of the century at the foot of Pleasant Street for the Petow family. In 1932, it became a cultured-pearl factory, and a new home for the yacht club went up along the harbor further from the center of the growing town. (Williams)

OYSTER PLANTING was done by seeding in quiet waters. These oystermen are putting the seed into barrels outside their shacks located in Provincetown for later planting in the harbors off Wellfleet and Cotuit where the oyster industry was well established before the turn of the century.

[33]

WHALE ASHORE! This sperm whale which ran ashore on Nantasket Beach in February 1893 was a business asset to Capt. Sal Rich who bought the blubber and rendered it into five hundred gallons of oil. Cape whalers continued hunting to a limited degree until about 1910. (Howes)

WRECKS WERE SO FREQUENT along the Cape coast that the residents became expert at salvaging legally, or "mooncussing" illegally. Here are two views of the *Katie J. Barrett,* run ashore by a winter storm at Nauset Beach on February 24, 1890. By April 4, all masts and the rigging were gone. (Tales)

NAUSET BEACH had more than its share of ships cast ashore by winter storms. Here is the *Kate Harding* beached on December 5, 1892. Between the winters of 1890 to 1895, the *Chattanooga, Katie J. Barrett, Kate Harding, Messenger,* and the *Charles A. Campbell* were wrecked here, among others. (Tales)

[34]

SUMMER WEATHER PERMITTING, excursion boats from Boston made the run to Provincetown. The train here in 1890 is on a spur of the New York, New Haven & Hartford line, a service available by 1840 to every town on the Cape from Buzzards Bay to Provincetown. In the center background is the horse-drawn "accommodation" that met all trains and steamers. (Snow)

TRAIN TIME in the 1890s meant new visitors in the summer months. Provincetown was the last stop. Heading east on Commercial Street here is the faithful "accommodation" driving the arrivals to the various guest houses. (Snow)

THESE WINDMILLS, wind-tattered themselves, were used in the production of salt in East Dennis in 1892. Sea water was pumped by wind power into vats for evaporation in the sun. More than three hundred gallons of water made a bushel of salt, which was worth eight dollars in 1873. Gradually, salt making declined on the Cape because salt from the West and foreign countries was cheaper. There are still places on Cape Cod built from boards once used in the vats of the old salt works at Wing Island, Brewster. (Tales)

[36]

LIKE LITTLE HOUSES, many of the sea-water vats at Cape Cod salt works had peaked roofs that were designed to protect the evaporation process from rain. (Tales)

The Turn of the Century

AS THE CENTURY TURNED, Cape Cod opened its land and its heart to the world. No longer was the "Narrow Land" a lonely strip of sand extending out into the sea, remote from its continent. Its towns, once isolated fishing villages, were developing into prosperous communities.

The opening of the Cape Cod Canal in 1914, planned years before, beckoned to international mercantile traffic, and the new bridges accompanying it were welcome hyphens connecting the Cape to the mainland. Train transportation had now become dependable.

Sea-related industries continued to grow and prosper. Farms flourished.

Better transportation and the natural beauty of the Cape attracted summer visitors, laying the foundation of a healthy tourist industry. Urban families of means sought second homes on the Cape, and real estate values boomed.

Almost accidentally, a few distinguished artists, writers, and dramatists discovered that the Cape provided a climate conducive to creative work, and the lower Cape got its start as a world-renowned cultural center.

World War I had the effect of solidifying Cape interests with the rest of the country, so that by the start of the 1920s, Cape Cod had taken its place as one of New England's most prosperous communities, and a prime resort area.

CHATHAM, its coast, and Pleasant Bay were photographed from a balloon just prior to 1900. At left are the Chatham Bars, the most dangerous stretch of coast on the Eastern seaboard. Old sailors knew it as the "graveyard of the Atlantic." A beautiful residential area bordered Pleasant Bay at right, and the long buildings in the center foreground were part of a dairy farm. Chatham was to become the richest town per capita in the state of Massachusetts. (Kelsey)

"FROZEN FOOD—FISH—ALSO BAIT" described the wares of the Consolidated Weir Company (*right*), a fish-processing, packing, and shipping firm which opened in 1900. It was a new idea to pack Cape Cod fish in ice in freight cars so that it could be sold as far west as Montana. The company's wharf was busy every day as fishermen landed their catch here (*above*). The concrete cold-storage plant is in the background. (Paulman)

THE FLEET UNLOADS: The early years of the new century saw fishing at the height of prosperity. Cape waters were abundantly productive and the industry was unhampered by foreign competition which helped in later years to deplete the fishing grounds. (Howes)

THE FIRST BRICK BUILDING of any size to be built on the Cape housed Hyannis Normal School which opened in the fall of 1900 with seventy-three students. It was the first institution of higher learning on Cape Cod. Main Street is to the left, and the Hyannis waterfront is in the far background. (Williams)

THE HYANNIS WATERFRONT at Lewis Bay was pierced with inlets which provided shore frontage for many palatial homes and the setting for the most highly priced real estate on Cape Cod. This scene with Nantucket Sound in the background was taken in 1900 before development.

NO BIKINIS THIS YEAR! In 1904, those visiting the Hyannis-Craigville area frequented Craigville beach, where clubs offered deluxe bathhouses for members. Craigville was and still is the Cape's most select watering spot. (MacLean)

SUMMER VISITORS liked to explore old wrecks beached on the Cape tip in the early 1900s when this picture was taken at high tide. At low tide, it was a favorite picnic spot for many years. (Cook)

WADING ON THE BACK SHORE, or ocean side, in 1900 was often intimidating because of the rough surf—but it was fun, too! (Cook)

POST OFFICE SQUARE at North Truro, the least populated settlement at the turn of the century, looks more like country than town. Between Provincetown and Wellfleet, Truro occupies the most narrow portion of the Cape. At some points only a half-mile of sand dunes separates Cape Cod Bay from the sea. (Snow)

BACK TO BOSTON in 1901: Vacation is over for these young ladies who wait for the train at the Truro station at the end of August. Two trains were scheduled daily from Boston to the Cape tip and return, stopping at each town along the way, so that they were used as "locals" by residents and tourists alike. (Snow)

[42]

DESOLATE SAND DUNES surround the old Methodist Church at Truro *(left)*. It was built in 1827, and the parsonage *(below)* in 1902. (Snow)

RECREATION GROUNDS IN TRURO: In 1903, Isaiah Snow turned Sea Breeze Hill at the rear of his farm into a recreation center for townspeople and visitors. It was used for picnics, outdoor musicales, and games. Swings and sand piles were provided for the children. The elevated platform afforded a breathtaking view of the lower Cape. (Snow)

LADIES' COSTUMES were as elaborate as their Victorian homes in the early part of the century. Mrs. C. W. Snow, a charming hostess of the lower Cape, was a bride in 1900 when this portrait was taken. (Snow)

LADY CYCLISTS were a common sight in 1902 when this picture was taken in one of the short lanes connecting Commercial Street to Bradford in Provincetown. Bicycles could easily navigate the town's narrow cross streets, and almost everyone but the very old or very young rode them. (Cook)

THIS PARTY OF FOUR stalked the meadows and marshes of the Wellfleet-Truro area in the fall of 1905, when game of all kinds was plentiful. The Pamet River runs between grassland in the background. (Cook)

[44]

CHILDREN PLAYING on the frozen harbor of Provincetown often bored holes in the ice to sink fishing lines. Old-timers contend that Cape Cod no longer has winters "like they usta." This picture of 1902 showing Provincetown's salt-water harbor under layers of ice, seems to agree. From 1940 on, no one can remember when the Cape's salt harbors with their strong tides have frozen over. Of late, golf has been enjoyed almost year-round, and garden flowers often decorate the Thanksgiving table. (Cook)

THE SEVERE WINTER of 1902 trapped many fishing vessels in the ice of the harbor. (Cook)

A BLIZZARD accompanied the freeze of January 1902. It took the people of Provincetown several days to dig out. Meanwhile, all shops were closed. (Cook)

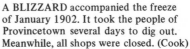

WHEN THE THAW CAME in early March of 1902, large chunks of ice broke up and washed ashore. Most of the beach and harbor were clear, and the lad standing in front of a mini-iceberg is about to brave the icy water and dig a mess of clams. (Cook)

THE INVENTOR of the wireless, Guglielmo Marconi, built in 1902 four steel towers on the sand bluffs of Wellfleet overlooking the great beach and sea. On January 18, 1903, the first telegraphic message was sent by radio across the Atlantic to Poldhu, in Cornwall on the southern tip of England. The message was a greeting from Pres. Theodore Roosevelt to King Edward VII saying, "Taking advantage of the wonderful triumph of scientific research and ingenuity. . . ." In the ten years that followed, communication by wireless was established around the world. Marconi's invention was the most significant contribution of the early 1900s. The station in Wellfleet was abandoned and the towers destroyed in 1920. Today only the concrete tower foundations mark the spot. The property is under the protection of the Cape Cod National Seashore Park. (Snow)

THE BUGGY AND THE WAGON were the Cape's prime means of transportation in the early 1900s. Mrs. C. W. Snow and her son, Horace, Jr., visited in 1904 the boy's uncle, Isaiah Snow (standing in the truck wagon), at his farm home seen on the hill in the background. (Snow)

COTUIT HARBOR in 1900. (CL)

CAPT. PHINNEY'S PARTY BOAT took out guests from the Hotel Pines in Cotuit. Orin Nickerson's boat had just left the pier. The fashionable hotel had its own pier in 1900 and was one of the first sumptuous summer places on the Cape. (CL)

COMMERCIAL STREET in Provincetown was called the "front street" by residents. The harbor is directly behind the buildings on the left. From this corner at Gosnold Street, the view is west on the narrow and busy thoroughfare, the main business section of town in 1900. Oil lamps lighted the streets at night.

HORSE-DRAWN "JIGGERS" were used for all types of hauling at the turn of the century. This one is parked in front of Nelson's Dry Goods Store in the exact center of Provincetown. Down Commercial Street, to the left or west, is Patrick's Newsstand and Sundry Store and the town's barber shop.

[48]

THE MAYO COTTAGE was an attractive
guest house on Commercial Street in the
east end of Provincetown.

TWO YOUNG BLADES of Provincetown
pose for a souvenir of a happy day in the
fall of 1904, when Labor Day, declared a
national holiday in 1894, was already the
end of the tourist season and the time for
Cape Codders to count profits and plan
entertainments for themselves. Trips to
Boston and ball games were memorable
occasions in September. (Paulman)

CODFISH DRYING on racks was a typical sight in Provincetown and almost all other settlements on the Cape in 1904 and many years to come, as codfish was an important and profitable food item. "Cape Cod turkey," a favorite dish, was boiled dried fish in cream sauce, garnished with strips of fried salt pork. (Cook)

CAPT. EDWARD PENNIMAN *(left)* was a whale-oil tycoon of the last century who made his fortune as the skipper of a fleet of Cape whaling vessels. He built this elegant mansion *(below)* as his residence. The mansard roof was red, in contrast to the yellow walls of the house which has long been considered a prime example of Victorian architecture. The captain kept a giant telescope in the cupola on the roof for peering out to sea when he was on shore. The Penniman house is now under the protection of the Cape Cod National Seashore Park, established by Congress in 1961. (NSP/Kelsey)

THE BATHING BEACH at Delight Cottage, a popular guest house in 1904 on the spot where the Pilgrims first landed: For fifty cents, swimmers who came just for the day could use the beach. Sailing parties and fishing trips from the Delight were part of the fun. (Seaman)

FALMOUTH CHAPEL, located on Falmouth Heights overlooking the sea but facing the town, dominated the residential section in 1900. It was a nonsectarian meeting place for all manner of community activities, from religious services to choral pageants. (Poisson)

BUSINESS WAS GOOD but conducted very placidly on Main Street in Hyannis in 1900, where customers came to shop from all over the Cape. The spire to the left (west) is of the Universalist Church, destroyed by fire in 1904, but rebuilt the next year.

BAKER'S GENERAL STORE and bicycle shop (H. H. Baker & Son) was a popular store on Main Street in the east end of Hyannis in 1900. It sold everything from fresh fish and groceries to fine fabrics at a time when most Cape women made their own clothes. Sewing accessories were sold in the annex at left, with the sign above the door, "Butterick Patterns." In those days bicycles were a prime means of transportation on the Cape, and Baker's sold, rented, and repaired them. The wagon in front is for deliveries. (Tales)

TOURISTS HEADED UP-CAPE from Provincetown in the early 1900s would have seen this prestigious hotel in Wellfleet extending out into Cape Cod Bay. It was built and opened by Capt. Lorenzo Baker in 1886 and catered to distinguished summer guests until 1940, when winter storms destroyed it. This picture is from the first decade of the twentieth century, when the inn was at its height of popularity. (Williams)

THE LONGEST AND DEEPEST INLAND WATERWAY on the Cape is the Bass River, which cuts into the town of Yarmouth. The bridge was built in 1902. The river was already noted for its abundant fish when the Indians were the only inhabitants of the Cape. When the bass were biting in spring and summer, it was not uncommon to see sports fishermen casting shoulder to shoulder along the bridge.

THE INNER HARBOR of Hyannis is a deep inlet running north into the town and south toward Nantucket Sound. When this picture was taken in 1904, a rich residential section was developing in the area. The new Normal School is in the background. (Williams)

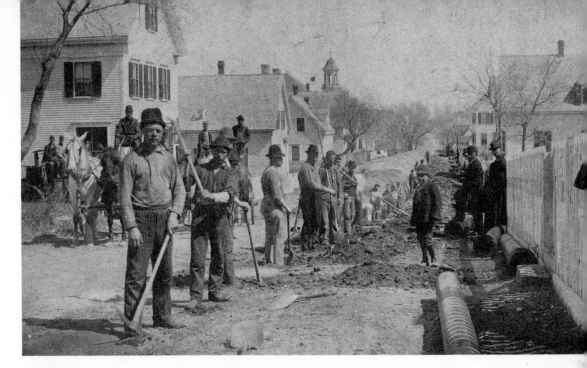

PRISONERS from the Barnstable House of Correction widened and repaired Bradford Street (what the town called the "back street") of Provincetown in the fall of 1905, before the weather turned cold *(above)*. The view here is to the west. Because they had done such a good job, the prisoners were put to work laying watermains there, for which they earned a dollar a day, to be paid upon release from prison. By the late spring of 1906, the more affluent homes in Provincetown had running water. (Cook)

THE NAME OF THE SHIP and its captain have been lost, but the date was 1907, and the harbor was Cotuit. It is said that this was the last of the sea-going sailing vessels to put into a Cape Cod port. (Williams)

SMALL CRAFT like this dory rigged with a sail were ideal for a boy's first training in seamanship, or for a visit to one of the neighboring towns, if the weather was fair. (Cook)

THE DISTINGUISHED Gifford House, still popular, has not changed since it was opened by James Gifford in Provincetown in 1868. At first it was the post stop for the Boston stage coach. President Roosevelt and his party were its guests in 1907, when it accommodated visitors who arrived on the three daily trains that ran to the Cape tip during the summer. Pres. William Taft and several generations of Vanderbilts also stayed here.

THE NORCROSS HOUSE was located on Monument Beach at the head of the Cape. It was the last word in luxurious accommodations for vacationers in 1905. (CL)

STERN'S CLUB and casino on Monument Beach was built in 1903, but in 1935 an annex was added for housing guests. The main building was used for gambling, dancing, and those who could afford the action and enjoyed it. (CL)

[57]

TAYLOR'S CAFE AND CREW: William "Bill" Taylor, standing in the background, opened the first sizable commercial restaurant at the head of Town Wharf on Commercial Street in Provincetown in 1908, the date of this picture. Steamer passengers passed it as they came off the ship, and often spent an hour of their time enjoying a shore dinner with this crew to serve them. (Howes)

THE SAME BILL TAYLOR, in the cap, invented and put into operation the first ice-cream plant in the area as an adjunct to his restaurant. Real cream was a must, and he introduced some exotic flavors unheard of in 1909. Mr. Taylor claimed he could estimate the season's economy by the daily volume of ice cream sold. (Howes)

FOURTH-OF-JULY PARADE, 1909: Townspeople of the Cape provided many diversions for their summer guests, and civic and social groups organized parades of local bands and decorative floats. Community picnics and clambakes, supervised by well-known bakemasters, often followed the Fourth-of-July parade in Provincetown. (Paulman)

CHURCH FESTIVALS with accompanying parades have always been a common sight in Provincetown. (Paulman)

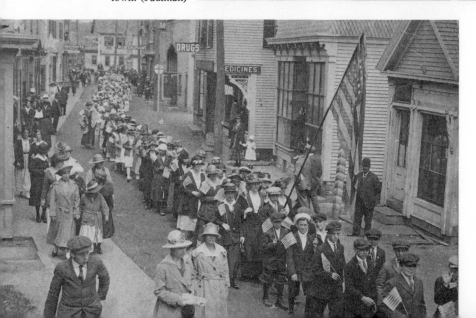

A LARGE NEW STEAMSHIP, the *Dorothy Bradford*, began to make the Boston-Provincetown excursion run in 1910. It cut the sailing time of the *Cape Cod* by almost an hour, giving travelers more time ashore, and offered better service. Passengers could enjoy a bar, a dance floor with a 1910 rag-time band, and staterooms were available. The steamship line provided a handy way for longer-staying vacationers to get themselves and their luggage to the Cape, and gave a boost to early tourism. (Seaman)

BOSTONIANS spending the day in Provincetown could buy a souvenir at the Advocate Shop in the center of town on Commercial Street. This post-card shop was owned by the Advocate Press, the town's weekly newspaper publisher. (Seaman)

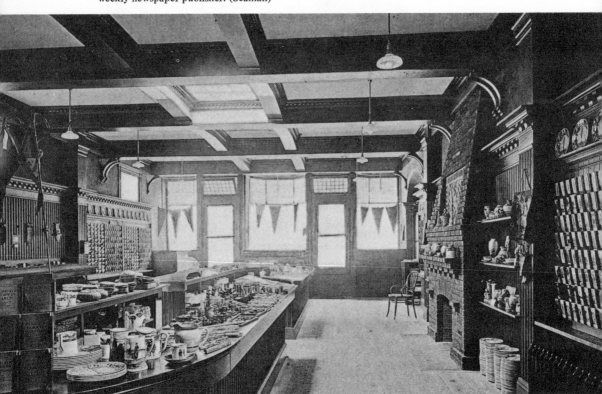

THE BARNSTABLE INN, built in 1799, was one of the most famous inns in New England, until it was torn down in 1972. It was located in the center of Barnstable village, the county seat, on historic route 6A (King's Highway). Before trains arrived, it was the mid-Cape post stop for the Boston stage coach. Famous judges and lawyers made the Barnstable Inn their headquarters when court was in session across the road. (Williams)

JOSEPH GODOY, until his recent death Peruvian consul at Boston, lived in the Octagon House in Hyannis since 1910. His wife Marian was Capt. Rodney Baxter's granddaughter. Dr. Susan Godoy, center,

is a music specialist in the Boston school system and today owns and occupies the interesting structure. (Godoy)

[61]

OCTOBER SHADOWS fall on another old Octagon House, this one in the west end of Provincetown. The eight-sided dwelling was built in 1850 by whaling captain Robert Soper who, like other seafarers, believed that this form of construction afforded better protection against the fury of storms, and was easier to heat. This cherished landmark has been a popular guest house for a hundred years; it is still in fine condition. (Paulman)

THE PILGRIM MEMORIAL MONUMENT located on Town Hill in Provincetown commemorates the landing of the Pilgrims in Provincetown harbor and the signing of the compact of government, the first charter to espouse a democratic form of government in the world's history, on November 11, 1620.

The cornerstone of the monument was laid on August 20, 1907, by the Grand Lodge of Masons in the presence of Pres. Theodore Roosevelt, who led the ceremonies.

The height of the structure is 252 feet 7½ inches, from the ground to the topmost battlement. Town Hill is 100 feet above tidewater, making the elevation of the monument 352 feet above sea level. It is built of Maine granite and is 28 feet square at its base.

Its Italian-Renaissance design, copied from the Torre del Mangia in Siena, Italy, is similar to the campanile of the Palazzo Vecchio in Florence. Plans of the tower were created by the office of the United States Corps of Engineers, with Lt. Col. Edward Burr in charge of the project.

The cost of the monument was $95,000, $40,000 of which was funded by an act of Congress. $25,000 came from the Commonwealth of Massachusetts, and Provincetown gave $5,000. The remaning funds came from individuals in all parts of the country, who contributed sums from a dollar to one thousand dollars. Maintenance of the landmark is met by visitor's fees. The government funds were granted under the condition that in case of war the monument could be used as an observation station—the view from the top extends many miles to sea.

Since the tower was completed and dedicated by Pres. William Howard Taft on August 5, 1810, untold thousands of visitors have climbed its gently ascending ramps to the top. It is Cape Cod's main tourist attraction, and also serves as a beacon for ships at sea who have sailed the turbulent waters of the North Atlantic. (PMA)

FALMOUTH HARBOR around 1911 was dominated by the Tower Hotel. Falmouth Heights, in the background, was the fashionable resort and residential area of the town. (Palmer)

THE RED INN, located on the harbor in the far west end of Provincetown, opened in 1905, but this picture was taken in 1915. At high tide, guests could dive into the water from the front porch. (MacLean)

THIS BACKSIDE VIEW of Provincetown was taken in 1913, three years after the monument was opened. The town's new normal school stands in the center of the picture. (Howes)

[63]

THE LIGHTHOUSE off Bourne at the head of the Cape warned against treacherous tides for many years before the Cape Cod Canal opened in 1914. The white tower seen here was built to accommodate the keeper's family which is receiving its monthly supplies.

[64]

HANDS ACROSS THE BIG DITCH: Financier August Belmont, on the right, stretches out his hand to congratulate on June 30, 1914, the engineers and crew who planned, constructed, and completed the Cape Cod Canal. One month after this picture was taken, the canal opened for traffic, and the shoals of Cape Cod were no longer a threat to world shipping.

The Cape Cod Canal

THE CAPE COD CANAL, opened in 1914, had been a long-cherished dream of financiers, shipping magnates, transportation-conscious Cape Codders, skippers of coastal craft, and local fishermen.

George Washington instigated the first survey for a proposed canal connecting Cape Cod Bay to the Atlantic Ocean to save the ships of the young Navy as well as commercial mariners from the rip tides off Race Point and the hazardous bars off Nauset.

From that time on, financiers and various teams of engineers tried to make the Cape Cod Canal a reality. The embryo project had brought five companies to the fringe of bankruptcy, including the Maryland Trust Company, one of Baltimore's most solid banks.

Some firms got so far as hiring crews for digging and dredging, but the funds required seemed as limitless as the sand and soil which continually refilled the excavation as it was worked, making the labor fruitless. Time after time nothing could be shown to disappointed stockholders but a ditch filled with mud and water.

In 1904, August Belmont, the imaginative multi-millionaire, became interested in the project, and ten years later, he made the three-hundred-year-old dream come true.

AFTER OCTOBER 1916, the United States Navy patrolled the waters surrounding Cape Cod with battleships, or battle cruisers like this one, because the German submarine U-53 had sunk nine British merchant vessels between Cape Cod and Nantucket without violating international law. For Cape Codders, the European war was getting too close for comfort. (Cook)

ST. PETER'S CHURCH on the canal was towed from the mainland when the congregation around Marion, Massachusetts, declined, and the people in Bourne needed an additional church. Since the canal is thirty-two feet deep at low tide, big vessels must wait for high tide to pass through. The suspension bridge was opened shortly after the opening of the canal.

THE MARINES LANDED in Provincetown a few weeks after President Wilson
announced the declaration of war against
Germany on April 6, 1917. The unit was
broken up to form recruiting stations in
various Cape towns. Many Cape men
could secure commissions in the Coast
Guard and Navy, and the Army and Marines had to work at recruiting volunteers.
The draft began the next month, on
May 18. (Seaman)

DURING WORLD WAR I, blimps were
used for reconnaissance over the Cape
Cod area. This picture was taken from an
Army airplane over Monomoy and Chat-
ham the September before the armistice.
(Kelsey)

THESE LITTLE PIGS went to market in 1918. During the war years, Cape farmers and fishermen did much to relieve the food shortage. Charles Alexander and his family were prosperous farmers and expert fishermen on the lower Cape. (Paulman)

THE LABOR DAY PARADE of 1918 was especially patriotic in theme, and anticipated the celebrations that would follow on November 11 when the armistice was declared. Here, red, white, and blue-colored floats, decorated with flags, inch down Commercial Street in Provincetown. (Paulman)

THIS FAMILY PORTRAIT was taken in
the early twenties when the Portuguese
who had come in the middle 1800s were
increasingly important to the social, economic, and cultural life of the lower
Cape. Warren Alexander heads this family, at right, followed by his wife Almer-
da Souza, Barbara, Warren, Jr., and John.
The three-year-old girl, Dorothy, became
the author's friend. (Paulman)

DR. FREDERICK HAMMET, seated in
his laboratory, established a cancer research center in Truro in 1923. Cancer
specialists from all over the world were
frequent guests of the doctor and his
wife who were beloved year-round residents. (Howes)

THESE SUMMER COTTAGES built by C. W. Snow on the Truro beach sold for fifteen hundred dollars
in 1894. By 1922, more cottages were added to the development, and sold for six thousand and more.
The home on the hill in the background was the Snow homestead. (Snow)

NAUSET—"A man may stand there and put all America behind him. . . ." Henry David Thoreau (Smith)

The Arts Take Root

IT WOULD SEEM that in the 1920s all of the nine Muses floated down from their Olympian home to set up shop on Cape Cod.

After his walking journeys covering the Cape in 1849, 1850, and 1855, David Henry Thoreau recalled in his book *Cape Cod* that "nothing remarkable was ever accomplished in a prosaic mood," observing that the Cape's ever-changing color and climate never sustain such a mood. This is perhaps one reason why Cape Cod has consistently inspired artists in all the creative fields.

Here, the tender tints of spring suddenly change to the languid shimmer of summer, which is then transformed into autumn's royal wardrobe. In winter, the Cape dresses itself in white—the satin-white of a wedding gown or the white-gray gauze of a shroud.

And each day on the Cape sees its changes. In fair weather, the morning fog lifts into an atmosphere of transparent clarity, and the day ends in fiercely divine sunsets, glowingly revealing the abode of the oldest gods, while the rhythm of the sea forever beats in time with nature.

Sometimes, with its brother, the wind, the sea's song is wild and ferocious with lyrics that say, "See, little man, we the great elements are still in charge of a world you think is yours!" But, in a matter of hours, the sea can laugh at its own ferocity and become a field of sapphires shot with gold.

Like the land itself, its people, too, seem set apart from the mundane world.

Thoreau, observing the assortment of fellow passengers in the stage coach during his first visit, said "I was struck by the pleasant equality which reigned among the stage company, and their broad and invulnerable good humor.

They were what is called free and easy, and met one another to advantage, as men who had at length learned how to live. They appeared to know each other when they were strangers, they were so simple and downright. They were well met, in an unusual sense, that is, they met as well as they could meet, and did not seem to be troubled by any impediment. They were not afraid nor ashamed of each other, but were content to make just such a company as the ingredients allowed. It was evident that the same foolish respect was not here claimed for mere wealth and station that is in many parts of New England; yet some of them were 'first people,' as they were called, of the various towns through which we passed. Retired sea captains, in easy circumstances, who talked of farming as sea captains are wont; an erect, respectable, and trustworthy-looking man, in his wrapper, some of the salt of the earth, who had formerly been salt of the sea; or a more courtly gentleman, who, perchance, had been a representative of the General Court in his day; or a broad, red-faced Cape Cod man, who had seen too many storms to be easily irritated. . . ."

And had not the Portuguese of the lower Cape created the social and civic atmosphere of Southern Europe's laissez-faire, so dear to ·the heart of the artist? Small wonder that artists in every branch of creative endeavor found Cape Cod an inspiring and congenial home.

By the early 1920s, the artists, writers, and dramatists who had come to sniff the Cape summers a decade before had now forsaken their urban habitats to make Cape Cod their homes for all seasons. It was in the twenties, too, that the galleries in the great art centers of the world began to exhibit canvases of Cape-based painters; publishers and literary agents haunted the area in search of next season's bestsellers; and Broadway looked to the Cape for another O'Neill, or at least talented young players who had been schooled on the stages of the Cape's summer playhouses.

In no way were the impresarios disappointed, for the names of those who made outstanding contributions to American culture while living on Cape Cod during this period are legion.

Facing page: THE DUNES OF NAUSET meet the beach: "There I got the Cape under me, as much as if I were riding it barebacked. It was not as on the map, or seen from the stage; but there I found it all out of doors, huge and real, Cape Cod!" Henry David Thoreau (Smith)

WITH THE ARTISTS CAME THE ART PATRONS: At the height of Col. George Blaney's army career, he moved his wife Edith and daughters Alice and Marguerite to the Cape where he began to buy paintings from local artists and to patronize the theatre. Something of a historian, he helped to establish "Tales of Cape Cod," a historical society which published an interesting magazine of Cape history. Mrs. Blaney was a popular Centerville hostess. (MacLean)

DRESSED FOR THE Artist's Ball, Mrs. Mayme Claxton (left) and Mrs. Norman Cook pose in Gay-Nineties garb in the Roaring Twenties for a gala party given on the lower Cape. (Cook)

COMMERCIAL ARTIST and night-club entertainer Morgan Denis poses with a model and a "pooch" for a promotional picture in the 1920s at the popular Beach Terrace in Provincetown. He created the well-known black-and-white Scotty drawings for a liquor firm, and performed a night-club act in which he pretended to be drawing a picture of a beautiful girl holding a dog. When finished, he would dramatically turn the picture to the audience to reveal a picture of just the dog.

[74]

SANDWICH GLASS had become precious by 1925, when this display was photographed in Mechanics Hall, Boston. Any glass manufactured before the furnaces died in Sandwich in 1888 became collectors items. Antique shops began to spring up on the Cape, often started with only a few pieces of "grandmother's old glass." (SGM)

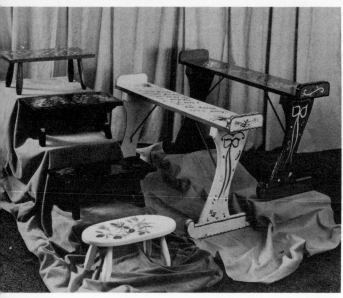

THE PINK GERANIUM Teahouse just outside of Hyannis was run by the Hastings
family when this type of roadside enterprise
was very common on the Cape. Clam chow-
der and other delicious native dishes were
served and an adjoining gift shop sold items
of local handcraft, including furniture decorated by one of the family. An artist is
sketching on the lawn to the right. (Hastings)

THE CAPE PLAYHOUSE in Dennis, 1927: This famous summer theatre first raised its curtain on July 4, 1927, starring Basil Rathbone and Violet Kemble Cooper in the *Guardsman*. Raymond Moore, a veteran of the Provincetown Players, established this professional enterprise featuring Broadway plays with famous stars. The building was an abandoned Quaker meeting house that he had found in Hyannis and moved to Dennis. (CP)

MORE POLISHED IN looks a few years later, the Cape Playhouse had added a box office, on the left, and an awning. Since producer-director Raymond Moore was also a landscape architect, it has always been a showplace and a prime summer attraction. One of the oldest professional theatres on the summer circuit, it looks the same today as it did forty-five years ago. (Cape Playhouse)

LOOKING VERY SLEEPY this was Barnstable harbor in the mid-1920s. By the end of the decade it had become the home of a prosperous fishing fleet. Capt. John Veterino had begun to modernize its fishing facilities when this picture was taken. (Veterino)

THE JENNY LIND TOWER in 1927 was placed in the Truro dunes by Henry Aldrich as a memorial to his father, a great admirer of the "Swedish nightingale." In 1905, when her managers had oversold a concert in Boston, the singer climbed this turret, then a part of the old Fitchburg depot, and sang to the angry crowd waiting for admission. When the depot was demolished, Aldrich bought the tower and had it erected, stone by stone, near his home in Truro. Old-timers say that on moon-lit nights the ghost of Jenny Lind can be heard singing over the dunes.

SCARGO TOWER, overlooking beautiful Scargo Lake, stands on Scargo Hill, the highest elevation on the Cape, and is associated with one of the Cape's oldest Indian legends. The story recalls that the lovely Princess Scargo caused her tribe to dig the lake for her two pet fish, gifts from her sweetheart. Built in 1902, the tower was given to the town of Dennis in 1929 by the family of Thomas Tobey, an early settler of Sandwich who came to Dennis in 1678.

THE ORIGINAL PROVINCETOWN PLAYERS made this sail loft, jutting out into the harbor, their home by courtesy of the owner, Mary Heaton Vorse. In June of 1916 the doors opened with Eugene O'Neill's first play, *Bound East for Cardiff*. This was the start of summer theatre on Cape Cod. By 1920, many members of the original company had become famous. The same group opened the first successful off-Broadway theatre in New York, in an old stable off McDougall Street. (Seaman)

THEY CALLEND THEMSELVES the "Sixes and Sevens" (some nights six performed, and some nights seven?) and entertained at a night club that took over the Vorse sail loft in the 1920s, a few years after the Provincetown Players. From left to right are Walter Hayn, Reeves (Eddie) Euler, Jerry Farnsworth, Pat Finley, Burr Rahn, and Courtney Allen—all from Washington, D. C., and all exhibiting artists by 1930. (Euler)

A MILLIONAIRES' RETREAT with the most exclusive private membership on the Cape, the Oyster Harbor Club, faced Cotuit Bay, between Hyannis and Falmouth. In this 1928 air view, the nine-hole golf course behind the club is not yet ready for play, but the members and their guests had sixty rooms and baths—and this elegant lounge. The landscaped villas of the upper Cape, like the Oyster Harbor Club, were in sharp contrast to the rural seaside atmosphere of the Cape tipe. (Williams)

Likker Ashore!

A BIZARRE INCIDENT opened the 1930s. It was a blustery day in March 1930, before the repeal of Prohibition in 1933, when a huge shipment of grade A uncut liquor was washed ashore in Provincetown. It was a sensational and profitable happening for the people of the town.

A colorful description of the event is chronicled by Mary Heaton Vorse in her charming book, *Time and the Town*. The story goes that some rumrunners had planned a landing on the Westend beaches of the town. They were interrupted by the alert Coast Guard before the landing was completed, or frightened off before contact could be made with the distribution trucks. In order to escape capture, the rumrunners abandoned their cargo in shallow water off the beach, and before the Coast Guard could retrieve the loot, the townspeople swung into action. Even the children engaged in the plunder.

This is how Mary Heaton Vorse described the scene:

"Rumors flew around. The Jasons had eight cases. The Deavilas had found three. Little Minnie Crummins had been out that morning in her canoe and bumped right into a case. She was towing it into shore when along came the Coast Guard. . . .

Something for nothing! Illicit gains. Liquore ashore!

The old red gods were riding through town. The old days of smuggling and buccaneering were back again. Everyone's blood ran quicker.

There was a full stop to the workaday routine. Everyone was dreaming of a good time, of free liquor. Our town in the old days was a great pirate town. The smugglers and wreckers of the old days have worthy descendants."

Mary Heaton Vorse's account of the incident was published in 1941. She was a celebrated novelist, journalist, and labor leader until her death in 1966. Although Provincetown was her home, she traveled the world over in pursuit of her assignments.

Her book *Labor's New Millions* was a best-selling testimony to her dedication to the early labor movement. Her concepts were far ahead of her time.

It was her wharf property which first housed the Provincetown Players, and she was one of the most famous and beloved residents of the Cape. The chapter in *Time and the Town* called "Likker Ashore" set the tone of the gala decade that was to follow.

The Depression did not bite deeply into the economy and social atmosphere of Cape Cod.

Cash was scarce, but limp purses were not new to Cape Codders and were of little consequence as long as the larder was well stocked. The tradespeople were already accustomed to extending credit for the nine off-season months. Fish was plentiful, and the fishermen were generous to their neighbors. Farms were still productive, and the produce was shared.

Despite the Depression, so acutely felt in other parts of the country, vacationers seemed to have money, and tourism grew and thrived. The opening of bars and package stores in 1933 gave the Cape economy a lift, and the opening of the beautiful bridge at Buzzards Bay in 1936 tripled tourism.

The 1930s also saw the development of the world-renowned oceanographic research center at Woods Hole, and the full recognition of the Cape as a haven for celebrated artists.

The Cape Playhouse, furthermore, under the leadership of producer Richard Aldrich and director Arthur Sircom, made the town of Dennis a prime center for dramatic art and started professional summer theatre on its way.

LIQUOR ASHORE! Townspeople of the lower Cape investigate a cargo of "booze" abandoned by rumrunners in Prohibition days. (Howes)

THE LOCATION of the ruins of the old Aptuxcet Trading Post has long been known, but it was not until 1930 that the Bourne Historical Society undertook the faithful reconstruction of this place where merchants met daily with homesteaders, adventurers, and Indians in the early decades of this century. (CC)

THE COTTAGE-LIKE FACADE on the Coffee House on Sea Street in Hyannis is deceiving. It used to be the smartest hotel in town, with a large structure extending many feet to the rear. It had the longest bar on the Cape, and a sizable ballroom. At the repeal of Prohibition in 1933, wealthy guests kept the place hopping, and big-name bands played nightly. It was built and operated by the Binda family in the 1930s.

A CENTER for young people and their activities through the 1930s, the Christian Scientist Church in Province-town offered the learning and good fellowship of choral groups and year-round theatre workshops to the whole community.

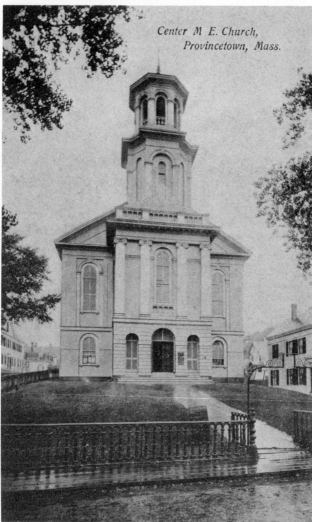

Center M E. Church, Provincetown, Mass.

THIS IMPOSING CHURCH, the Center Methodist Episcopal Church of Provincetown, enjoyed a large congregation in the 1930s, but its membership gradually diminished until it became too expensive to maintain. In the early 1950s, it was sold to Walter Chrysler, Jr., to become the Chrysler Museum of Art, one of the Cape's major latter-day attractions.

WINTER STORMS AND high tides on the ocean side of Race Point had their way with this shack that Eugene O'Neill had lived in while writing some of his early plays. While still used as the Peaked Hill Coast Guard Station, it started its slide down the bluff in 1931. The neighboring Coastguardsmen, who had abandoned the shack several years before, rescued O'Neill's books and personal effects.

FROM A MODEST START with the Provincetown Players, Eugene O'Neill had become America's foremost playwright during the 1930s. He was recognized as the dramatist who had crossed the barriers of traditional playwriting into realism, opening a fresh chapter in the performing arts and the American theatre.

WHEN EACH TOWN had its "character" in the 1930s, "Scarry Jack," who rode the streets of Provincetown selling fish, was one of the most beloved. Each spring he repainted his truck with flowers, and, when he made "house calls," very often a bouquet of flowers came with the fish—and conversation too. (Howes)

THE FALMOUTH AREA in the thirties offered the Tower Hotel as its most distinguished and popular. resort. It stood on Falmouth Heights overlooking the harbor.

THE OLD-FISHING-DORY BAR at the Flagship Restaurant on the waterfront at Provincetown would surely add a taste of salt to your beer. "Pat" Patrick opened the place in 1934, but, before then, Inez Hogan, an author-illustrator of children's books, ran a non-alcoholic nightspot there, serving depression sandwiches of bread, butter, and watercress for one nickel. The Beachcombers, a prestigious group of creative men, many of them well-known artists, have met there for years every Saturday night for fun and games.

EAST BAY LODGE, opened in 1934 in Osterville between Hyannis and Falmouth, offered luxurious accommodation to summer guests through the thirties. Today, the lodge houses one of the finest restaurants on the Cape. (CL)

THREE EXALTED RULERS of the Hyannis Elks Lodge 1549, established in 1929, pose as the leadership is formally passed on in 1935. From left to right are William A. Jones, State Representative; Arthur H. Hardy, head of the Registry of Motor Vehicles; and Elmer A. E. Richards, who for thirty years directed the Elks' youth programs and social functions, where prizes to the press and other civic groups were awarded. He also started programs for service men and women during World War II. (EL)

LOCAL GOVERNMENT and small businesses were in good hands during the 1930s on Cape Cod with men like the Snows. They were community leaders in Truro and Wellfleet for many generations. Standing left to right are Horace H. Snow, Sr., and David Snow. Charles, Norman, and Isaiah are seated. The Snows developed the land on the Truro shore. (Snow)

THE BUZZARDS BAY BRIDGE over the Cape Cod Canal opened with much fanfare in 1936 with marching bands and a cavalcade of dignitaries. Beatrice Gibbs, a handsome young woman of Sagamore, was named "Miss Bridges" and was featured in the ceremonies. A boom in the tourist trade soon followed. (NBST)

THE BIRTHPLACE OF TECHNICOLOR is the old Captain Phinney house in Centerville. Art and science met here in 1936 when Dr. Herbert T. Kalmus from the Massachusetts Institute of Technology established offices and a laboratory for the development of his invention, Technicolor, that gave color and depth to motion pictures. (MacLean)

JOSEPH SEAMAN, a celebrated authority on admiralty law in the 1930s, is shown in courtroom attire, resting—or pleading—his case. His offices in Boston and Provincetown specialized in representing shipping and fishing industries that operated on the Massachusetts seaboard. (Seaman)

[88]

THE OLD WOODS HOLE AQUARIUM was the
first one on Cape Cod and the headquarters for all
information pertaining to fish and wildlife. Built
and maintained by the United States Department
of the Interior in the 1930s, it was a popular tourist
attraction as the first institution devoted to marine
science. It was the forerunner of the Woods Hole
Oceanographic Institution. (Poissons)

THE *Atlantis (left)* was the institution's first research vessel, a sea-going ship with convenient living
quarters, equipped to carry on investigations at all
depths used in the various types of sea service.
Launched in Copenhagen, the *Atlantis* began its
duty at Woods Hole in 1931. She continued in
operation for thirty-five years, covering a half-
million miles of sea, until replaced by the *Atlantis
II* in 1966 *(below)*.

GALE WARNINGS! A big blow is expected and the Chatham Coast Guard Station hoists the alert for all ships to seek harbor. These flags denote the most critical of all signals: "A severe storm is on the way." (Kelsey)

SNUG HARBOR: The *Baltic*, one of the last of the whaling schooners, lies at rest in its Provincetown berth. The dawn of the 1940s marked the end of sea-going sailing ships, which for two centuries had shrouded the Cape with a mystique of adventure and glamour. (Cook)

CAPT. JOHN VETERINO *(right)* organized and led the Barnstable fishing fleet
into the 1940s, as fishing continued to be
the leading industry of Cape Cod. He began to improve the Barnstable docks and
fishing facilities *(below)* and continued
the rebuilding and updating all through the
1940s, only temporarily slowed down by
the war years. (Veterino)

Following page: BARNSTABLE
Harbor in an air view of the
1930s: By this time Captain
Veterino had made it a prosperous
fishing center. (Veterino)

[91]

JOSEPH SEAMAN DRESSED as Paul Revere showed the lighter side of the prominent Boston and Cape lawyer who deserted the courtroom for the annual Artists' Ball in Provincetown at the end of the summer season of 1937. Paul Revere's horse accounts for two more merrymakers. The ball, sponsored by the Beachcombers, raised funds during the thirties for never-spoken-of charities. Everybody went, and a Mardi-Gras atmosphere of "anything goes" prevailed. (Seaman)

[94]

THIS FIGUREHEAD POISED over the sign of an apartment house on Commercial Street in Provincetown was found in an old sail loft in 1935 and restored by local artists. The Figurehead House *(below)* was a beloved landmark because of the figurehead over its doorway and both were conversation pieces for tourists in days when the old sailing ships no longer graced the ports and figureheads had become scarce. (AA)

RICHARD ALDRICH, producer-manager of the Cape Playhouse at Dennis since 1938, has enjoyed giving demonstration lectures on the technical aspects of the theatre for many years. He begins in the rear of the playhouse near the barn-studio where the scenery is designed, constructed, and painted. Always making his summer home in Dennis, near the theatre, he continues using founder Raymond Moore's successful format—new Broadway plays featuring well-known actors. Arthur Sircom, a famous director first hired by Moore, remained twelve more years under the new management. Aldrich married one of his favorite stars in 1940, Gertrude Lawrence.

[95]

CATHARINE HUNTINGTON, the actress and directress, was the cofounder of the Provincetown Playhouse-on-the-Wharf.

THE PROVINCETOWN Playhouse-on-the-Wharf was the third summer theatre in that town. This is how it looked in 1940 when it was first taken over by Catharine Huntington and Virginia Thoms.

GERTRUDE LAWRENCE is holding her pet "Angus" on the lawn in front of the Falmouth Playhouse which her husband, Richard Aldrich, began to remodel in 1949 to make it the most beautiful summer theatre in America.

KITTY BAKER is a well-known Cape columnist who, since 1945, covered the social and entertainment scene in and around Falmouth. She also was one of the founders of the Falmouth Theater Guild.

[97]

MABEL MOODY of Chatham was an enthusiastic friend of Monomoy Theatre. She rarely missed a show put on by the Ohio University Players in the summer or by the Chatham Drama Guild in winter. She appeared on stage with both companies.

WHEN HELEN HAYES came to Dennis to star in *The Showoff* at the Cape Playhouse in 1947, she was accompanied by her two children, Mary and Jimmy McArthur.

HARVESTING THE SEA, a fisherman from Barnstable brings in tuna—or horse mackerel—caught in Cape Cod Bay. (Veterino)

THE INTERIOR of John Veterino's plant in Barnstable in the 1940s: After the fish were brought in, they were sorted, graded, and packaged for market. (Veterino)

CAPTAIN VETERINO (in center with peaked cap) and his crew (at right) entertain a group on a cruise of the bay off Barnstable. Cape fishermen were always very hospitable to summer visitors. (Veterino)

WHALES OCCASIONALLY still beach themselves along the Cape Cod shores. If they are alive, the fishermen tow them back to deep water. Dead whales now are only a chore for the sanitation department—quite a contrast to the Cape's early days, when a beached whale was an asset to be rendered for its valuable oil. (Veterino)

A PRIZE CATCH, this tuna was caught by Captain Veterino and his fishermen in Cape Cod Bay. This giant of the sea weighed 946 pounds and was 10 feet, 6 inches long, and 82 inches in girth. Captain John stands to the left with Harry Fogliano. Charles Morgan and Jack Veterino, the captain's son, are on the right. (Veterino)

NATIONAL DEFENSE took the spotlight in the Independence Day parade down Main Street in Hyannis the summer of 1941. (EL)

A REAL ELK'S HEAD made a figurehead for the prow of the Elks Lodge float in the Independence Day parade of 1941 in Hyannis, a few months before the attack on Pearl Harbor and the United States' entry to World War II. Defense was on everyone's mind. (EL)

[100]

The Crest of the Wave

A WAVE OF PLEASURE and opulence broke on Cape Cod's beaches as the 1940s dashed in, and the people of the Cape rode on the crest of the wave.

Fishing and its allied industries had never been more profitable, and since the summer of 1938, tourism had enriched the economy to an unprecedented degree. Lodging places, restaurants, bars, gift shops, craft studios selling hand-wrought jewelry and custom-made sandals, jelly houses, and flower and produce stands all flourished.

"No Vacancy" signs decorated the lawns of hotels and guest houses. Time and money for off-season leisure seemed to be assured.

These affluent conditions gave impetus to the development of the arts. The artists, members of the historic Provincetown Art Association, had time to consider their directions, and they divided into factions—academic painters versus modern artists. Art exhibitions were controversial and well-patronized.

Along with all this activity, symphonies and choral groups were planned, young Cape writers began to realize publication, and the winter amateur theatre companies became a force in the communities.

People of means, heretofore summer residents, began in 1940 to buy property and improved it for year-round living. Cape real estate boomed, and the cocktail hour, whether enjoyed in a home garden or a popular bistro, became a daily way of life.

Cape Codders were enjoying the fruits of their industry. They were on a binge and enjoying every minute of it.

In the summer of 1940, Mary Heaton Vorse returned from an assignment in Europe, where she had interviewed numerous major officials of the countries involved in the increasing hostilities. At a garden party, surrounded by young people, she was heard to say: "Make well of this happy time, for very soon the whole world will change, even Cape Cod, and we will never know this serenity again."

The Cape was deep in snow when the announcement of the Pearl Harbor holocaust blared over the radio. The night before, at the Cape tip, Dr. and Mrs. Carl Murchison had given a party in their castle-like home at the extreme end of the Cape. The guest list included almost everyone on the lower Cape. The event heralded the start of the Christmas parties, a Cape tradition. Cape Cod met Pearl Harbor with a hangover.

Perhaps no other area of the country felt the boot of Mars with the devastating, sudden impact as Cape Cod. Within a matter of hours, men of every town, schooled in seamanship since childhood, left their homes and stormed the off-Cape Naval and Coast Guard induction centers, with the hope of obtaining ratings. Almost all of them secured commissions instantly.

This left a gap in selective service, and the harassed draft boards were hard pressed to meet their quotas. The result was that older, established business men, some with families, were summarily inducted into the Army.

By New Year's Day of 1942, Cape Cod was left to women and children, aside from old men and a few 4-Fs.

In a few weeks, the younger women without children left the Cape to join the services or obtain highly-paid jobs in war-related industries, and many of the 4-Fs became civilian employees of the services.

By February, the shelves in the grocery stores were nearly ampty. During the winter months, Cape Cod had never been a large or profitable market for the chain stores. Now they had all they could do to supply the needs of their urban outlets. Fuel and truck parts, suddenly precious, could not be used for the regular long runs down the Cape, and thus deliveries were cut again and again.

In the package stores and bars all stock diminished rapidly. By February after Pearl Harbor, only cheap domestic wines and cordials were available. Tobacco and soft drinks were not to be had.

One of the ugliest phases of the early war years, however, was the spreading of frightening rumors. It was said that certain young Coast Guardsmen, third- and fourth-generation Americans of Portuguese descent, distrusted their elderly relatives who were now operating the fishing fleets. They were suspected of rendezvousing with the ubiquitous German submarines. The suspicions seemed justified when loaves of bread from the Portuguese bakery in Provincetown were allegedly found aboard a submarine captured off New Port. From then on the Coast Guard kept a sharp but unobtrusive eye on certain fishing vessels.

All neighbors with German names became suspect, especially if they had recently come to the Cape. The sighting of enemy submarines near shore was

A COMMUNICATION CENTER is being set up on Cape Edwards near Falmouth in late summer, 1941. World War II uniforms have not yet arrived and uniforms from World War I are being used. Construction began here two years before the war.

THE YOUNG MEN in this group leaving from the Hyannis railroad station are heading out for an induction center in Boston a few days after Pearl Harbor. Many others were able to secure Coast Guard and Navy commissions—just as in World War I—but these draftees are destined for the Army.

reported daily, and a landing party was said to have cleaned out a chicken ranch in Wellfleet. Oldsters shook their heads and hearkened back to earlier wars when the Cape had fallen into enemy hands.

Worse was yet to come. In the early months of 1943, a U-boat torpedoed a liner carrying freight and passengers, almost within sight of the Provincetown harbor. Only about half the crew and passengers survived the disaster. The town wharf was heaped with dead and wounded. Dr. Daniel Heibert was the hero of the hour. He led Civilian Defense units from all over the Cape which rushed to the scene. A contingent from the Red Cross arrived, but its limited knowledge of the Cape and its facilities made its help of little value. The Town Hall, meanwhile, became a hospital and mortuary.

Then a strange thing happened. The Cape found itself cut off from outside communications. Telephones and Western Union ceased to function. No newsmen arrived. The Naval Bureau in Washington did not want the nation to be informed of the disaster. Censorship! An unfamiliar and hateful word to Americans. But somehow, the news was leaked out to Bob Considine, the syndicated columnist in Boston, and it was he who alerted the authorities to the vulnerability of Cape Cod.

The Cape saw real hardship during the early years of World War II, especially with the men gone. But matters improved when service training centers were opened from Truro to Camp Edwards, near Falmouth, and sections of our own fleet began to cruise Cape waters.

Church groups and fraternal organizations took over the task of lifting the spirits of those who remained on the Cape as well as the service personnel stationed on nearby posts. The last year of the war turned out to be less grim.

As the war ended, the Cape quickly reverted to the prosperous peacetime atmosphere it had enjoyed before the hostilities. But Mary Heaton Vorse's observation made in the summer of 1940 proved to be prophetic, for even as peace lulled the country into a new and more sophisticated prosperity, the Cape's rural seaside charm was threatened by the "fast buck" and in danger of becoming a raffish and expensive resort area.

The end of the 1940s was reminiscent of the Roaring Twenties, but without the innocent and congenial family and social life Cape Codders had enjoyed when F. Scott Fitzgerald was writing his novels, and Eugene O'Neill his plays.

Everything took on a professional patina. Stately old hotels gave way to strings of cheap, modern cottages renting for sums unheard-of before the war, and while the summer visitors continued to flock to the Cape, they divided themselves into classes. The wealthy summer residents kept to themselves. Fun was the consideration of the two-week vacationers, and young people came in droves as the colleges closed, looking for and finding summer

THESE WAAC OFFICERS stationed at Camp Edwards attended a birthday party for their unit in the fall of 1942. The Women's Auxiliary Army Corps (WAAC) had been established by an act of Congress on May 14, 1942. By Christmas of that year, Cape Cod was a center for all branches of the armed forces.

THIS PRETTY WAVE is calling her folks in California. At Christmastime 1942, the Elks' Hyannis lodge presented all service people in the area with a free telephone call home.

jobs. The members of the post-war generation sought time off from their jobs to do "their thing." But their thing was the pursuit of a good time rather than the cultivation of the arts that had been the goal of the Cape's young visitors before the war.

Services had to be improved and updated in justification of the rising cost of vacations. Now, life guards patrolled the beaches, and twilight cookouts on the beach, along with casual night swimming, were enjoyments of the past.

By the end of the 1940s, it was busy hustle and bustle for the residents of Cape Cod, from Memorial Day to Labor Day, and the almighty dollar was king. Peter Hunt, the celebrated artist, observed in his charmingly illustrated cookbook that "winter is the best time."

And so it was, and is.

"HAIL! HAIL! THE gang's all here!"—or at least the Navy was. All service people stationed on the Cape or on ships off Cape Waters were invited to a festive Christmas party hosted by the Hyannis Elks Lodge in 1941. A short time later in 1943, the lodge opened its cocktail lounge so that enlisted men and non-commissioned officers could enjoy a reasonable drink in a pleasant atmosphere. Even more, they arranged a ballroom in their clubhouse that featured imported professional entertainment, and they held open-house all during the war. Cape girls acted as hostesses, and if the fleet was nearby, and the "old man" was generous with shore leave, a full house could be expected. (EL)

[107]

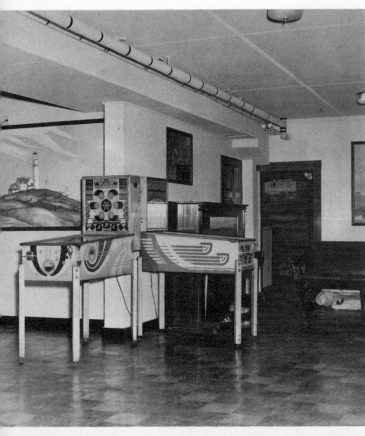

SHORE LEAVE FUN and games for
these World War II "gobs" included the
pool table, and sometimes the pin-ball
machines, at the Elks' clubhouse in
Hyannis. (Elks)

A PARTY WAS GIVEN by Navy Chiefs to honor Capt. Frederick Ridgeway, commanding officer of a British ship that was cruising Cape waters during the war. The captain (facing forward in the left background under the flag) said at dinner, "For the English, Yanks may be hard to get on with, but men from this part of the country make first-class sailors and fighting men." (Elks)

SAILORS were always popular with the girls of Cape Cod. During the war years attractive dates were plentiful. (Elks)

ALTHOUGH THE REST of the country was on strict rationing, there was no shortage of good food and drinks when the Elks entertained. The boys from this unit are from the Deep South. During the harsh winter months, Cape Codders were especially hospitable to the Southern men. (Elks)

LT. COMDR. RICHARD SULLIVAN, USN, receives a gift and citation from Elks member Elmer A. E. Richards before being transferred from his Cape post in 1945. Other Elks in attendance are Alfred Dumont, Harry Lawes, police chief of Barnstable, and attorney Joseph B. Loury. In the closing years of the war, Cape Codders had to say goodbye to their war-time friends. (Elks)

THE HYANNIS EMBLEM CLUB aided the Elks in all of their programs and activities through the years. On June 25, 1944, the ladies had their picture taken. Seated from left to right are Mrs. Charles V. Thayer, Mrs. John Barrows, Mrs. Harry W. Lawes, Jr., Mrs. Edward L. Bennett, Mrs. Elmer A. E. Richards. Standing: Mrs. Merton K. Goodall, Mrs. Joseph Dextadeur, Mrs. George Devine, Mrs. Enoch Sutcliffe, Mrs. Adrian Preble, Mrs. Edward B. Nelson, Mrs. John S. Bearse, Mrs. Hubert F. Hearn, Mrs. Henry Benjamin, Mrs. Jack Dranetz, Mrs. Christ Terpos, Mrs. Colin F. Woodbury.

GOV. MORRIS TOBIN (seated at center) and his lady attended a banquet in their honor at the Hyannis Elks Lodge in 1944. Standing here at the governor's left, Elks' master of ceremonies, Elmer A. E. Richards, is about to introduce state and local dignitaries. Alfred Dumont, seated next, is talking to the Rev. Carl Schultz, minister of the Federated Church. Harry Lawes, chief of police of Barnstable, stands by the window. (Elks)

THREE CIVIC-MINDED GENTLEMEN of fraternal organizations who, even during the disruptive and exciting war years, managed to lead fund-raising programs that aided veterans' hospitals on the mainland as well as their own, newly-built Cape Cod Hospital. From left to right are Joseph Lyons, Elmer A. E. Richards, and Anthony Foster.

FOR OVER TWENTY-FIVE YEARS, the Elks have honored local athletic achievements. These are the spring basketball trophies, standing, as always, at the head banquet table with flowers that denote the season. (Elks)

THIS TROOP of Girl Scouts was the first to receive the Elks' generosity and hospitality when they began to sponsor youth groups directly after World War II. (Elks)

KATHRINE NEHUBIAN, standing at the left, presents an award to the captain of the girls' basketball team at Barnstable High School. Miss Nehubian was the popular girls' athletic director and coach there from the middle 1940s through the early 1960s.

MEETING GUESTS from New York and Boston on Friday afternoons at the Hyannis railroad station was a weekly summer event in the 1940s. Fast and comfortable train service between the mainland urban areas and the Cape was available until mid-century.

CONVENIENT DAILY scheduled trips by air, connecting New York and Boston to the Cape, began around 1948. The late afternoon flight was known as the "Daddy plane" to many Cape youngsters.

A NORTHEAST AIRLINES DC-6 landed a group of political officials from Washington at the Hyannis Airport in 1949.

MARY HEATON VORSE in about 1949: This novelist, journalist, overseas war correspondent, leader of the early labor movement, and long-time resident of Cape Cod enjoyed a brilliant career. The Kibby Cook house in Provincetown was her home. (Vorse)

WHEN THIS BIG TOP, called the "Melody Tent," was set up in Hyannis in the 1950s, it wasn't the circus that had come to town. Actress Gertrude Lawrence believed the Cape ready for a fifteen-hundred-seat summertime music hall with Broadway musicals featuring Broadway stars. She persuaded her husband Richard Aldrich, the producer at the Cape Playhouse in Dennis, to foster the enterprise, and its first season began with a gala opening on her birthday, July 4, 1950. (Williams)

SOME OF THE CAST of the *Student Prince* are holding up their steins as if ready to sing the "Drinking Song" or to toast the success of the production. They played at the Melody Tent in Hyannis in its first summer in 1950. A few other players in the operetta (right background) know enough to get in the shade on a hot summer day. (Williams)

The New Professional Theatres
of 1949-50

DURING THE WINTER of 1949, negotiations got underway for the purchase of properties to establish three major summer theatres on the Cape. Producer Richard Aldrich, spurred by the success of the established Cape Playhouse in Dennis, looked to increase his holdings, and he fostered the two most significant deals.

Gordon and Betsy Argo, a young couple from Providence, Rhode Island, who were experienced in operating community theatres, also envisioned a summer playhouse.

It was Gertrude Lawrence (Mrs. Aldrich or "Mrs. A.," as she was affectionately called on the Cape) who became fascinated by the idea of a music tent, centrally located in Hyannis. She chose a location in the center of town and encouraged her husband to carry the project through. During the fall of 1949, ground work on the tent was started. The showplace (originally called the "Music Circus") opened with *New Moon* on July 4th, 1950, Miss Lawrence's birthday and the couple's tenth anniversary.

Richard Aldrich also had his eyes on a scenically located lakeside structure in Falmouth that had been a veterans' rehabilitation center, and was up for sale.

He pictured a theatre which would accommodate Broadway productions led by stars—the formula which had proved so successful at the Cape Playhouse. It would include a cocktail lounge, bar, and restaurant. Several lakeside cottages where visiting stars could be housed were already on the property. In the winter of 1949 financial negotiations were completed, and the Falmouth Playhouse was born, to become the most beautiful theatre on the East Coast.

At the same time the Argos found exactly the property they had been looking for in the town of Orleans. It was a fine old building which had served as the Orleans Town Hall. It was set on a terraced knoll in the center of town, surrounded by spacious lawns and fine old trees. Cottages for the Argo family and the players were included in the purchase price.

The auditorium, formerly used for town meetings, provided a platform which could be used as a basis for a thrust stage, and was still large enough to accommodate a central playing area.

The imaginative Argos opened the Orleans Arena Theatre in the early summer of 1950. This playhouse and the new tent brought theater-in-the-round to Cape Cod.

These three new enterprises, added to the venerable Cape Playhouse and the Provincetown group, offspring of the original Provincetown Players, established Cape Cod as the principal center of professional summer theatre in the United States.

LEE REMICK is on top of the heap in this rehearsal in the Melody Tent during its first season in 1950. Unlike many under-canvas enterprises, the theatre offered arm-chair comfort to its audiences.

BEFORE THE MELODY TENT opened on her birthday, July 4, 1950, Gertrude Lawrence tried out the new "in-the-round" stage for size and sound. (Williams)

DAVID HOLTZMAN, a famous theatrical attorney, met Liza Minelli and her mother, Judy Garland, when Miss Minelli was not quite sixteen. Soon after the Melody Tent was established, Mr. Holtzman, a long-time summer resident of the Cape, bought the enterprise which today is owned and operated by Mr. Holtzman's widow, Sondra Holtzman.

THE FALMOUTH PLAYHOUSE property looked handsome even when Richard Aldrich bought it in 1949, although it had formerly been a rehabilitation center for World War II veterans. Many improvements were required, however, including the tearing down of the shed on the left and replacing with a tiled dining area. On that side of the building, the rolling lawn ends at a silvery lake. A year after the theatre opened, Aldrich sold it to Mrs. Sidney Gordon of New York and Boston, who has been owner-producer of the Falmouth Playhouse ever since.

WHEN GORDON and Betsy Argo of Providence bought the old Orleans town hall in 1949, they turned it into a charming playhouse-in-the-round called the "Orleans Arena Theatre," and opened it the following summer. Like the Falmouth Playhouse, extensive repairs were required to transform the old hall into a workable theatre.

BETSY ARGO, actress producer of the Orleans Arena Theatre, has headed the project for the last twenty-six years. When the Argos bought the project, she was already an established actress and director, having been associated with many professional theatrical companies in Providence, Rhode Island, before coming to the Cape.

MRS. CAROLYN ST. JOHN of Dennis (left) and Mrs. Ransom Somers of Brewster, two early patrons of the Cape Playhouse, join director Charles Mooney for the traditional party to celebrate an opening night in the 1950s at a local spot called "La Coquille." Mr. Mooney joined the staff of the theatre in 1947 as assistant producer, and a few years later became managing director when Richard Aldrich deserted Broadway and Dennis to become the cultural attache to Spain.

AT AN OPENING-NIGHT PARTY at the Cape Playhouse in Dennis in the early 1950s are Mrs. Gene Rayburn (at right), Kitty Carlisle, and managing director Charles Mooney (who also manages the Ahmanson Theater and a third one in the Los Angeles Center on the West Coast). Miss Carlisle has, through the years, appeared in countless productions at the Cape Playhouse and the Falmouth Playhouse.

[121]

SCENIC DESIGNERS Herbert Senn and Helen Pond joined the Cape Playhouse staff as a team in 1950. Important assets to the company, both designers are the most sought-after in New England. In winter they design sets for the Boston Opera Company, and their credits frequently appear in the programs of Broadway productions.

AMATEUR THEATRE had its devoted artists, too, including this cast for *The Little Foxes*, a production of the Barnstable Comedy Club that played the fall and winter of 1949-50. Doris St. Coeur directed this play and many others offered by this group. The cast here (but not in order) included Myra and Bruce Jerald, founders of the club in 1922, Marianne McCarty (now radio commentator for station WLPM in Plymouth), Simon Gesin, Joe Bismore, Jessica MacSwan, Elliott McSwan, Gordon Davis, Ellen Turner, and Edward Souza.

THE BARNSTABLE COMEDY CLUB'S Christmas pageant of 1950 had nearly all the children in town participating. It told the story of the "Willow Tree Plate," and a young choral group added to the entertainment. The young man in the center is John Veterino, Jr., age twelve, playing the role of the Chinese emperor. Today, Mr. Veterino is the lighting expert for the club.

THE BARNSTABLE COMEDY CLUB was formed in 1922 by a group of dedicated theatre buffs who were year-round mid-Cape residents. They first met in the old Barnstable Inn opposite the Court House on route 6A in Barnstable Village. By 1950, the club's membership approximated two hundred and was well established in its present home, across the road from the inn in the Barnstable Village Hall, which was no longer used for town meetings.

Just before mid-century, the club's membership swelled to include many who had been associated with the performing arts. Some had retired from the stage; others had come to make Cape Cod their base of operations between engagements. From that time on the quality of the Comedy Club's productions became a cut above community theatre. Their shows often equalled and sometimes surpassed the fare offered by the star-studded playhouses during the summer season.

1974 marked the fifty-second anniversary of the Barnstable Comedy Club, making it the oldest and most consistently successful amateur theatre group in the country. Its regular fall, winter, and spring productions are very good answers to the question so often asked by summer visitors: "What do you do up here in the winter?"

SUZANNE HOWES looked like this in 1945 when she began to play starring roles for the Barnstable Comedy Club, and she has consistently appeared in its productions ever since. Mrs. Howes is a versatile actress who adds a professional polish to the work of this amateur theatre group.

WELLFLEET is one of the most picturesque towns on the Cape. It has always been completely sea-oriented, for as the Cape narrows toward its tip, Wellfleet is tightly embraced by the ocean and the bay. The Congregational Church in the center is an authentic Christopher Wren design, and the clock in its spire the only exposed, land-based time piece in the world that chimes ship time. In the background is the square-towered Methodist Church. (Kelsey)

HIGHLAND LIGHT in Truro became a tourist attraction in the 1950s—perhaps because the first nude bather was spotted by the Coast Guard in 1950? In any event, bathing in the buff has been permitted ever since on the beach just below the bluff on which the light stands. (Kelsey)

THE AUTHOR'S CAT LEO, a distinguished ginger tom, taste-
fully trimmed in white: During his time before World War II, he
was the acknowledged sovereign of the neighborhood. (Jakobsky)

AN ALL-AMERICAN Cape Cod cat—at least one of his parents was a wild, native bobcat. (Gilli)

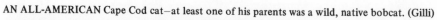

Cape Cats

CAPE CODDERS love cats, and no home is complete without at least one. On the lower Cape, from Orleans down, households often support whole families of felines.

Perhaps the tradition springs from the old sailing days when no ship would leave port without its complement of mousers; or is the witch's great regard for her cat familiar remembered? Whatever the reason, Cape cats can boast of *Mayflower* ancestry.

Dr. Sam Fuller, the genial physician who accompanied the Pilgrims, brought his pet cat Abbie to New England. The day the *Mayflower* passengers put ashore in Plymouth, Abbie was given shore leave. In exactly nine weeks to the day, she bore four healthy kittens. To the amazement of Dr. Sam and the colony, Abbie's little kittens had no tails—proof positive that the English cat's spouse had been a native-born American!

Many Cape cats have knobs for tails, and many more are born with double paws on their forefeet, which makes fishing along the waterfront easier—a sport Cape cats enjoy.

While hunting dogs, especially retrievers, are the most popular canines, and several of this breed were *Mayflower* passengers, too, the house cat is nevertheless queen on Cape Cod.

A VIEW OF THE INNER HARBOR of Hyannis in the 1950s.

THE KENNEDY COMPOUND on the shore of Hyannisport: Joseph Kennedy, father of the late president of the United States, bought this property as a summer home for his growing family. John F. Kennedy along with his brothers and sisters spent their summers and holidays here. In 1950, while still a senator, Kennedy added new dwellings to the compound to accommodate the next generation. The picture shows the road leading into Hyannis and the beach where the Kennedy children played.

A Poet's Dream Came True

THE IDEA of reproducing a full-size *Mayflower* replica of 92 feet, 180 tons was conceived by a Londoner, Warwick Charlton, during the North American campaigns in World War II. His dream was to memorialize the common heritage of English-speaking peoples, and to express his country's gratitude for American aid in times of great stress.

Mayflower II was constructed of English oak and Oregon pine at an ancient shipyard in Bixham, Devon, from plans drawn up after five years of research by William A. Baker, shipyard executive with the Bethlehem Steel Corporation. More than a quarter-million English people contributed shillings and pence to the "Project-Mayflower" fund.

As it slowly got under way, a well-known Provincetown poet, Harry Kemp, learned of the enterprise. He thought that a champion on this side of the Atlantic was needed, and so the "Poet of the Dunes" took up the romantic and noble cause. American interest and help was inspired by Harry Kemp's facile pen as the cost of the project approached the million-dollar mark. He saw to it, furthermore, that Provincetown Harbor on Cape Cod would not be overlooked nor lose its rightful place in history as the exact spot where the Pilgrims first landed.

After many delays and much correspondence, *Mayflower II* was ready to make its perilous way under sail across the Atlantic. Rough weather was encountered, and the trip proved almost as hazardous as the original voyage.

At last the great day came in 1958, and the people of Provincetown, led by their beloved poet, Harry Kemp, were ready to re-enact the historic moment. A long-dreamed dream had come true.

THREE "TOWN FATHERS" march to the waterfront in 1958 to board an escort boat that will welcome the *Mayflower II* to Provincetown. They are John Snow, town counsel, Harry Kemp, the "Poet of the Dunes," and Dr. Daniel Hiebert, the community's beloved physician. (Gunther)

THE WELCOMING BOAT that greeted the *Mayflower II* in Provincetown Harbor in 1958 was filled with latter-day Pilgrims. Walter Chrysler, Jr. stands in the center foreground; the portly gentleman on the left is John Snow; between the two is the white-haired poet Harry Kemp; and a bevy of town beauties was included also, as the enactment of the historic event got under way. (Gunther)

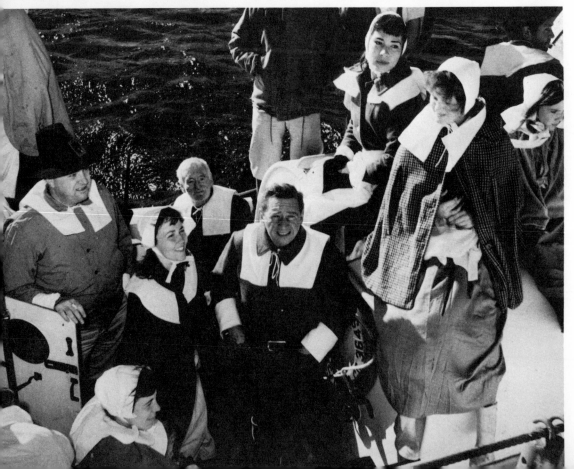

A TOUCHING PROCLAMATION was read by Dr. Daniel Hiebert when he opened the ceremonies in honor of passengers of *Mayflower II,* which had just duplicated the voyage of the original *Mayflower.* Harry Kemp and John Snow are seen kneeling on the far right; the other men in the foreground are from the ship. Although it happened almost twenty years ago, this day is vividly remembered by the history-conscious people of Cape Cod. (Gunther)

Writing rhymes turns to nothing all other delight:
I started with daylight: I've written all night:
The stars stand all pale in the change-waiting sky;
The world's still asleep; one bird wakes with a cry—
Another bird answers in drowsy reply;
The power of the Muse for a while has foregone me.
Like laughter in Heaven the dawn breaks upon me!

Harry Kemp
The Poet of the Dunes

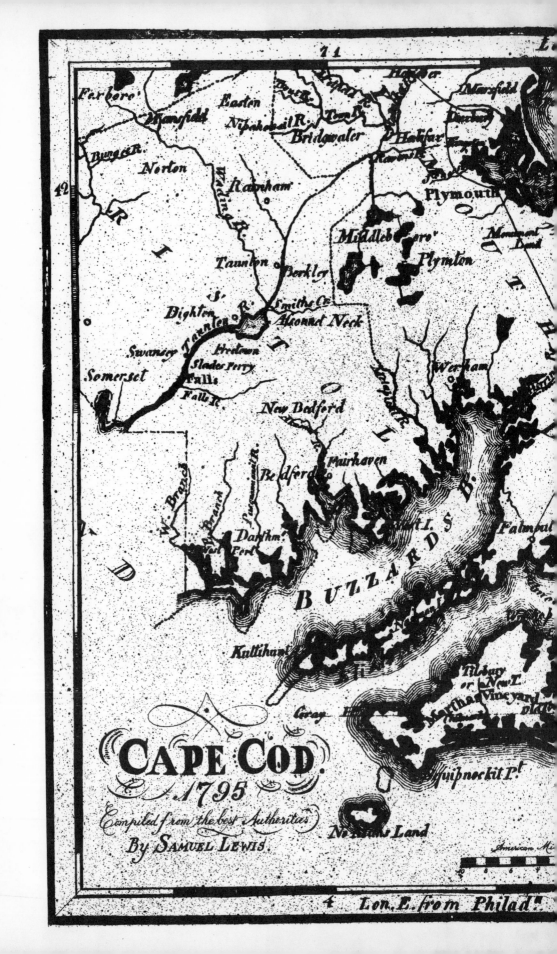

CAPE COD

1795

Compiled from the best Authorities
By SAMUEL LEWIS.

Barcod

SO-BJG-455

FASHION: CRITICAL AND PRIMARY SOURCES

VOLUME 4

FASHION: CRITICAL AND PRIMARY SOURCES

THE TWENTIETH CENTURY TO TODAY

Edited by Peter McNeil

Oxford • New York

Stockholm
University

English edition
First published in 2009 by
Berg

Editorial offices:
First Floor, Angel Court, 81 St Clements Street, Oxford OX4 1AW, UK
175 Fifth Avenue, New York, NY 10010, USA

Berg is the imprint of Oxford International Publishers Ltd.

Library of Congress Cataloging-in-Publication Data

A catalogue recored for this book is available from the Library Congress.

British Library Cataloguing-in-Publication Data

A catalogue record for this book is available from the British Library.

ISBN 978 1 84788 509 8 (volume 4)
     978 1 84788 292 9 (set)

Typeset by SAGE India.

Printed in the United Kingdom by the MPG Books Group.

www.bergpublishers.com

CONTENTS

VOLUME 4
THE TWENTIETH CENTURY TO TODAY

PREFACE

If humankind eats what it is, it often thinks what it wears.

S.A.M. Adshead
Material Culture in Europe and China, 1400–1800

It is a common refrain at academic conferences that fashion's connection to ancient critiques of luxury, Judeo-Christian doctrinal concerns about the display of the body, immorality and wantonness, and contemporary critiques of some of the fashion industry's unethical and unsustainable practices, place particular strains on those who choose to study it (researchers), conceive and produce it (designers and manufacturers), and exhibit it (curators and dealers). There is a longstanding tradition within antiquarian, ethnographic and historical scholarship of studying fashion, and sometimes the historical and the contemporary are seen as antithetical. That fashion studies and fashion design are increasingly popular as an academic programme and a vocation, reflected in increasing enrolments, new university programmes and media attention, prompts some to assume that the field of fashion research is new. This anthology rebuts that proposition by presenting more than 100 pieces of writing dating back to 1860 – mainly scholarship, some essays and prose-journalism – on the topic of fashion. The volume of work indicates that the study of fashion constitutes an already large and sophisticated field of academic research, with contributions from both trained scholars and amateur writers. It also shows that the wide-ranging geographical and historical parameters present particular challenges as well as opportunities for students and researchers wishing to engage with the field. Early writings on fashion, even if they appear somewhat 'old fashioned' in their determinist bent, provide an enormous and frequently elegant resource for the study of both historical and contemporary fashion.

FASHION: A FLUX OF FORMS AND MATERIALITIES

Historians have proposed different dates for the birth of fashion and placed it in both the East and the West. The conventional view of fashion is that it developed in the West; the discourse of fashion is inalienably Eurocentric. The readings assembled here retell parts of that widely held narrative, which may endure as it is reinforced by too many facts of power and cultural belief. The *Annales* School historian Marc Bloch once noted that two types of comparative history can be mobilized, one in which the examples are fundamentally alike – such as France and the Low Countries – and one in which each example is fundamentally unlike the other – France and Japan, for example. The inclusion of texts on Asia at certain points in these volumes is deliberate. They are included as internal challenges or retorts to the largely Eurocentric tale. In the combination of parts, and in the dissonance of views, a new narrative overview of fashion that has not yet been written might emerge.

It is striking how much reference there is to Asia even within those texts that demand that Europe be seen as the birthplace of fashion. Asia is presented as a source of raw materials and technologies for producing fashion, a network of concepts and imaginary forms, and also as a fascinating Cathay, or an immobile luxury monolith, certainly the vision propagated historically by many Westerners viewing the East. Was fashion formed by and in the modernizing West, or should the relationship between Europe and Asia be seen as the place in which fashion emerged? What role did the image play in supplementing older oral traditions about dress? How was fashion represented as opposed to dress or 'costume' and how did such imagery contribute to the development of Western fashion? Can we see fashion (as a concept and a material manifestation) as the result of a historical process? If scholars as different as Fernand Braudel and S.A.M. Adshead argue that there was no fashion system in Asia during this period, only luxury, what is the effect of this construction on readings of Asian dress?

COSTUME TO FASHION

The notion of 'costume history' has largely disappeared as a designation in recent years, replaced by the study of dress and culture, or clothing and appearance. This was in part a function of the effect of 1970s literary theory and the New Historicism that questioned the universal subject and objectivity. 'Costume' also carries within it the notion of a formal and structured system, rather than the element of more personal expression associated with fashion. Sometimes these 'costumes' are opposed to fashion in the sense of rapidly changing styles. Costume also suggests types of dress that were regional and recognizable, as indeed they were to any early-modern traveller. The falling away of this term, which encompassed 'fashion', 'dress' and 'clothing', frequently including the anthropological, places certain new demands on the definition of fashion. The latter cannot be simply a matter of adorning and extending the body. Many of the scholars featured in this volume debate precisely this problem. What is fashion, what type of intensity must it hold, does it concern a more abstract notion of form rather than privilege its materiality, who may access it, and how variable need it be? As the economic historian Negley Harte has remarked, one could also distinguish between the incidence of fashion and the rate of fashion. Can Western fashion from the Renaissance to the Age of Empire be seen as being produced through an East–West dialog of artistic and craft exchange, trade and product development? What role did travellers who lacked diachronic understanding have on the outcome of this process? As Michelle Maskiell notes in Volume 3 of this anthology, the notion of the unchanging East had major ramifications in terms of imposed consumption: in the 1860s, some British manufacturers claimed that they had a good opportunity to market their cloth in India because there were no changes in material and style there, that patterns had been the same for centuries, and that 'fashion did not have to be contended with'.

COMPILING FASHION

The history of fashion touches on and inflects the history of ideas, technology, social life and *mentalités*. Is fashion a code, a message, a type of luxury or a protocol? What is the difference between costume and fashion? Writers have speculated on dress since the Ancient world. The Roman writer Tacitus, writing about first-century Germany in *The Agricola and Germania*, for example, suggested that the aboriginal tribes used tight-fitting costume to distinguish the wealthy. But it would be foolhardy to suggest that Tacitus's focus as a writer was fashion. Costume books have existed since the Renaissance. The *Encyclopédie* included 100 entries that attempted to explain the derivation of dress, and other Enlightenment writers published numerous texts that attempted to explain the etymology of costume in every field from wigs to cod-pieces; the title of G.F.R. Molé's *Histoire des Modes Françaises, ou Révolutions du costume en France, depuis l'établissement de la Monarchie jusqu'à nos jours, contenant tout ce qui concerne la tête des Français, avec des recherches sur l'usage des Chevelures artificielles chez les Anciens*, (Amsterdam and Paris: Costard, 1773) is a representative example. The nineteenth century produced ambitious compendia of costume, notably J. Quicherat's *Histoire du Costume en France depuis les temps les plus reculés jusqu'à la fin du XVIIIe siècle* (Paris: Hachette, 1875) and Auguste Racinet's six-volume *Le costume historique* (Paris: Firmin-Didot et Cie, 1888). Such texts tended to focus on individual explanations for wildly various items of clothing and they were not systematic attempts to synthesize dress and costume scholarship with broader understandings of historical time.

Late nineteenth-century and early twentieth-century historians, sociologists and economic historians such as Jacob Burckhardt, Werner Sombart and Georg Simmel incorporated their research into fashion within their wider investigations of social forms. Members of the Prague Linguistic Circle, such as Petr Bogatyrěv and the German scholar Matilda Hain, who had worked with the linguist J. Schwietering, criticized existing costume studies and interrogated the existing body of ethnographic research in order to develop abstractions. The emphasis on functions – decoration, modesty and adornment – which to Bogatyrěv included the definition of the social and the exhibition of the aesthetic, is highly significant, as until post-structuralism the matter of function and differential relations would dominate speculation and research into fashion. The study of fashion flourished before post-modernism and the focus on embodiment and subcultural style that characterizes recent publishing in the field. It may be that 'fashion studies' is rooted in that particular conjunction of historical and theoretical interests that followed on from British cultural studies of the late 1960s. Much of the important scholarship published in the 1970s and 1980s regarding fashion was positioned within the fields of women's and gender studies, labour history, media and film theory and cultural studies.

The contents of these volumes point to the considerable difficulty that has faced scholars in capturing the significance and meaning of fashion. Sometimes there is real prevarication on their part as to what constitutes fashion and how it might differ from dress or costume, or what some scholars rather coyly call 'vestimentary novelty'. Certain questions recur. When and where does fashion begin? What elements must be present? Is a mentality – the fundamental value and assumption underlying a society – sufficient, or must there be a 'system'? Should fashion be defined as a Western phenomenon or must this view be dismantled? Does the dominance of tradition point to the absence of fashion? How does fashion itself become a type of ritualized tradition in the twentieth century? Here one of the ironies of fashion is exposed, for fashion is marketed and swiftly adopted by large segments of the contemporary population. As the authors in these volumes point out, not everyone can be fashionable and the role of the 'stylist' in all periods is to reveal those who make 'mistakes'.

Finally, these volumes are offered as a critique of the 'triumphal' mode of dress history, which creates a type of Darwinian lineage of rapidly changing modes, lines and silhouettes. There is a commonsensical notion of fashion that one thing leads to another, that just as today, some are more 'trendy' than others, and that people rid themselves of fashions because they are bored with them. The study of history reveals this convenient triumphalism to be very partial. Concepts such as 'emulation', 'conspicuous consumption' and 'pecuniary expenditure', promulgated by sociology 100 years ago, were once very useful ideas that are challenged by much of the writing collected here. They have taken on the guise of an orthodoxy that drives contemporary fashion journalism and populist understandings of the motives for fashion.

The theorist will find here studies useful for comparative purposes, including sociological analysis of fashion dating back to the 1890s. The researcher, student and designer will also find much to inform their sense of the cadence and changing form of fashionable clothes. By using this collection as a starting point, researchers from other domains who wish to access fashion scholarship, and students who wish to pursue an understanding of fashion, may expand their horizons. The volumes aim for a balance between some object-based studies informed by material-culture methodologies, alongside historical, art historical, economic and sociological as well as hybrid contemporary approaches drawn from post-structural, feminist and queer theories of identity. In juxtaposing the approaches, it is hoped that the psycho-analytically inclined might engage more with history, or an art historian with economics. As the volumes indicate, writers and thinkers have engaged with fashion since the Renaissance, frequently charting their own musings on the quixotic nature of fashionable change with their wider intellectual enquiry on topics ranging from etiquette to the economy. One would wish that those scholars, students and designers who do not 'identify' with a limited notion of fashion continue their contribution to the field.

A Note on Image Reproduction

For reasons of copyright, none of the illustrations or images used in the original texts has been reproduced here. Where appropriate, mentions of the omitted figures or illustrations have been removed from the text. However, please note that, in some instances, references to the omitted figures remain.

In certain cases, the notes have been removed, in some cases following the example of the first edition: Fernand Braudel, for example, noted in later editions of his work that he had retrieved his notes imperfectly. Similarly the notes comprising lengthy texts in the original language have generally been omitted. Bibliographies have been added to those texts where further explication is essential, including several essays on Renaissance Italy, Japan and China.

ACKNOWLEDGMENTS

The editor both owes a huge debt and pays respect in these volumes to his teachers, Associate Professor Emeritus Margaret Maynard, University of Queensland; Dr Michael Carter, Honorary Research Fellow, University of Sydney; and Professor John Clarke, Director, Australian Centre for Asian Art and Archaeology, University of Sydney. They will see in these volumes reference to their imaginative scholarship and innovative teaching programmes in the area of fashion, as well as the findings of their doctoral candidates, notably Dr Toby Slade, University of Tokyo. I also wish to thank Professor Caroline Evans, London College of Fashion; Professor Christopher Breward, Victoria & Albert Museum; Professor Antonia Finnane, University of Beijing; Dr Giorgio Riello, University of Warwick; Professor Ulrich Lehmann, Kent Institute of Art, Rochester, UK; Professor Beverly Lemire, Henry

Marshall Tory Chair, University of Alberta; Dr Negley Harte, University College London; Professor Aileen Ribeiro, Courtauld Institute of Art; Professor Margaretha Rossholm Lagerlöf, Art History, Stockholm University; Professor Astrid Söderbergh Widding, Cinema Studies, Stockholm University; Dr Louise Wallenberg, Dr Patrik Stoern and Philip Warkander, The Centre for Fashion Studies, Stockholm University; Martin Kamer, London and Zug; Anthony O'Brien and Simon Lee, Sydney; Professor Desley Luscombe, Bronwyn Clark-Coollee, Biz Heyman, Emily Howes and Despina Thiakos of the Faculty of Design, Architecture and Building, University of Technology, Sydney, for their intellectual and practical support for the project. Especial thanks go to the Research Assistants on this project, Emma Lindblad (Stockholm) and Kevin Su (Sydney). Finally, I thank Ken Bruce of Berg and the team at SAGE India who copy edited and typeset the volumes with such care; and my commissioning editors, Julia Hall and Tristan Palmer. The latter managed the project from its conception with his usual deftness and intelligence.

These volumes are dedicated to Dr Ian Henderson, King's College London, for academic engagement and friendship since 1994.

Twentieth-Century Fashion

Peter McNeil

If all change is painful, it is as necessary as the air we breathe.

Cecil Beaton
The Glass of Fashion (1954)

Many explanations are presented for the social role of fashion in modern life. The structure and form of Western European clothes are not simply a matter of adornment, or social interaction, nor are they vessels for pre-existing social attributes. Rather, they actively shape and make possible shifts in the lives of men and women at times of dynamic social change. Echoing some of the ideas proposed by the nineteenth-century critic Charles Baudelaire for the role of fashion in urban life, in 1969 the sociologist Herbert Blumer wrote that 'fashion operates as an orderly preparation for the immediate future' and that 'fashion is a very adept mechanism for enabling people to adjust in an orderly and unified way to a moving and changing world which is potentially full of anarchic possibilities'. Like many of the sociologists, anthropologists and ethnologists who wrote about dress in the twentieth century, the author was trying to make sense of the rapid changes in the appearance of men, but especially women, in modern life. Perhaps reflecting the turbulent decade, the 1960s, in which it was written, Blumer also noted that: 'Not all prestigeful persons are innovators – and innovators are not necessarily persons with the highest prestige.' The decade of flower power, retro dressing and ethnic borrowings posed challenges to the 'century of fashion', the period 1860–1960, which had been dominated by the rise of *haute couture* and the 'dictator-designer' system, mainly men who determined hem lengths and silhouettes for women. This is perhaps the biggest shift affecting issues of fashionable style in recent times: highness of birth and access to money no longer determine the outcomes or the uptake of fashion.

This volume includes 'primary' sources that contributed to the academic study of fashion in the twentieth century, developed from fields including anthropology, art, sociology, marketing, psychology and psycho-analysis. Certain contemporary scholars are included when their examination of a topic also provides a methodological innovation, or when their enquiry enabled a significant new perspective on an established subject. If one studies the bibliography of a recent and highly sophisticated text such as Christopher Breward's *Fashioning London*, it is striking how little costume history was at use at all to the author (Breward, 2004). Sources instead are derived mainly from urban geography, material culture, theories of memory, and some labour history.

Although the notion of celebrity designers dominates the popular media and contemporary branding strategies, the scholarly study of twentieth-century fashion is not the study of designers *per se*. It is more useful to consider how scholars and innovative designers see fashion as a possibility that either structures and reinscribes gender and other social categories, or disrupts and dis-orders the notion of generally 'woman', but sometimes also 'man'. The challenge of the fashion scholar is to make judicious use of the vast amount of material now available about fashion of all periods, including our own.

Exemplary articles on designers and stylists, such as Nancy Troy on Paul Poiret, Rebecca Arnold on Madeleine Vionnet, Richard Martin on Andy Warhol, and Caroline Evans on Martin Margiela, are included. Underlying much contemporary scholarship about fashion is feminist theory and spectator theory (film theory) and psycho-analytic perspectives, whose efficacy is indicated in the research of Caroline Evans and Rebecca Arnold amongst others. The volume also includes a cross-section of the feminist re-writing of fashion studies, from the connection of film theory to fashion by Maureen Turim, to the study of sub-cultural politics by Angela McRobbie. To this end, the main themes that characterize twentieth-century fashion are mirrored by an exercise in historiography; we see the way in which major parts of the field were 'fashioned'.

Parts of the volume refer to early centuries, as great thinkers on fashion theory drew their references widely. They come from a wide range of backgrounds, from art to economics to sociology. The discourse about fashion before the 1960s was also frequently an artistic, literary and an amateur one and it included figures ranging from the wealthy patron Anne-Marie de Noailles to Cecil Beaton. The distinction between high and low forms was very marked, signalled in Beaton's revelatory fashion exhibition at the Victoria and Albert Museum (1971), which featured only *couture*. The sense of thinking through clothes about wider social change is frequently apparent in these texts. Speculations from sociologists on the ritualistic nature of the Paris couture in the 1950s present a new perspective on the anthropology of elite fashions. The counterculture of the 1960s posed challenges to these mainly men speculating on fashion, as well as the models that quantitative sociology had established to study change, the variations in the shape of skirt, for example. How the world changed, and how right Barthes was, in his slightly shocked prose: 'We will see in clothes, the further attenuation of the difference between the sexes. Men will wear perfume. Women will have tattoos.'

That some of these writings come from 'outside' the field of fashion studies and even from 'outside' scholarship is deliberate. The only way in which the field developed new conceptual frameworks was through an encounter between different ways of thinking and writing about fashion. The parallels between thinking through fashion, and theorizing social change as evidenced in fashion, are strongest in this volume on the twentieth century. Radical thinkers and thoughtful intellectuals who were appalled at what many saw as the ugliness, discomfort and inconvenience of late-Victorian dress attempted to find theoretical lessons by studying the feudal dress of the past. Many of them pondered the history of dress for what it might reveal about the apparently entrenched nature of early twentieth-century fashion, particularly men's fashion, which appeared to have become intractable and antiquated.

Part 1, *Fashion's Structures*, commences with the extract 'Dress as an Expression of the Pecuniary Culture' from Thorstein Veblen's *The Theory of the Leisure Class. An Economic Study of Institutions* (1899). Veblen treated status-driven consumption as a sociological question; in this model, fashions maintain class difference. Veblen built on the research of Max Weber's study of luxury, in which he argued that over-consumption was not superfluous but a matter of social self-assertion. Commencing his analysis of how economic principles 'apply to everyday facts', Veblen observes the plutocrats and *nouveau riche* society of pre-war America and argues: 'no line of consumption affords a more apt illustration than expenditure on dress'. Veblen refutes the explanation of dress as a matter of protection, citing respectability instead: 'our apparel is always in evidence and affords an indication of our pecuniary standing to all observers at first glance'. Veblen does not simply see vulgar waste: 'But dress has subtler and more far-reaching possibilities than this crude, first-hand evidence of wasteful consumption only'. Dress makes plain that the wearer is not involved in any productive labour. The 'need of dress is eminently a "higher" or spiritual need'. Elegant dress must show 'the insignia of leisure', particularly the garments of women, her corsetry, but also the cane and top hat of the gentleman.

Veblen then attempts to find an understanding for the operation of regular fashion change. It cannot be a matter of adornment, or else fashion would have moved progressively towards 'a permanently tenable artistic ideal'. New styles in cities are ugly, Veblen claims, as they must also adhere to the 'requirement of reputable wastefulness and futility'. A natural sense of beauty will escape the parvenus; the codes of the former elites will fall into abeyance as the 'canon of pecuniary reputability' expands, and the 'more grotesque and intolerable will be the varying styles that successively come into vogue'. Finally, women's super-elaborate clothing is famously described by Veblen in terms of a patriarchal structure in which the woman is the chief ornament; the wife's clothes must be more elaborate than the husband's as 'the lady of the house is the chief menial of the household'.

Unlike Veblen, Georg Simmel did not entertain the possibility that fashion might advance towards an ideal. Born in 1858, Simmel witnessed the development of modern culture. His sociology studied interpersonal relations rather than quantitative measures in order to conclude how objects attain value. Observing the historicism of the design culture around him, Simmel theorized how 'the individual constructs his environment of variously stylized objects; by his doing the objects receive a new centre, which is not located in any of them alone'.[1] In another essay, *The Problem of Style* (1908), Simmel argued that objects and surroundings must be stylized in order to make a 'person the main thing'.[2] In this focus on endless differentiation of objects and details, the debt that later theorists of everyday life, including Roland Barthes, owed to Simmel is clear. Simmel felt that the middle class and the metropolis had become synonymous with fashion, as the rich and the poor occupied a different cadence of life. Even the rise of travel and the cutting up of the year into segments of time to mark the concept of vacations was, to Simmel, sign of the heightened neurasthenia of the modern. Simmel studied the fashion paradox of the opposing urge of wishing to belong or conform and to simultaneously express individuality. He noted that 'the peculiarly piquant and stimulating attraction of fashion lies in the contrast between its extensive, all-embracing distribution and its rapid and complete transitoriness...'

This anthology reproduces *The Philosophy of Fashion* and *Adornment* (1905). In the original German, the latter was printed in smaller type as 'Exkurs über den Schmuck', a difficult expression that has been translated as adornment or jewellery. To Simmel there can be no fashion in a pre-industrial society. Simmel argues that fashions are always 'class fashions' and have the 'double function of holding a given social circle together and at the same time closing it off from others'. In a fragmented modern life, 'the pace, tempo and rhythm of gestures is fundamentally determined by clothing'. Like many of the theorists in this volume, Simmel sees in his contemporary world evidence for his theoretical speculation. Thus the woman of the modern age, with her 'indifference' to fashion (presumably the transitional clothing of the pre-war years which included masculine walking, riding and driving outfits), seeks to 'approach towards the whole differentiation of personality and activity of the male sex'. The section on jewellery or adornment provides some beautiful word-pictures, far more elegant than many subsequent speculations on the modification of the body. As a connection with Roland Barthes, in a passage reminiscent of Barthes' essay on modern jewellery, reproduced in this anthology, Simmel notes that 'Adornment intensifies or enlarges the impression of the personality by operating as a sort of radiation emanating from it ... an inextricable mixture of physiological and psychic elements.'

Pierre Clerget, Director of the Ecole supérieure de commerce in Lyon, France, published papers from a very early date – 1908 – that linked psychiatry and advertising. He was in search of rational answers for the mechanism of fashion, which he described in his 'The Economic and Social Role of Fashion' (*Annual Report of the Smithsonian*

Institution, 1913) as 'a social custom, transmitted by imitation or by tradition. It is a form of luxury, luxury in ornamentation.' Clerget continued aspects of the *geistesgeschichte* model employed by Jacob Burckhardt in which clothes embody the human spirit expressed by an age. Fashion is taken to infer everything from mood to a taste in paintings. Changes in modes mean real changes in people, as custom is powerful and not easily over-turned. Clerget argues for and lists what he sees as the universal following of fashion. Prefiguring Gilles Lipovetsky, he notes that although a taste for luxury and finery extend to the Mycenaean period, this 'democracy of fashion' is quite recent. Clerget argues that modern life has transformed the creation of fashion as well as its economic organization, 'this instability, the changing at every season, which helps Paris in great measure to maintain its leading influence on fashion'. Although fashion is judged to destroy local customs and to lead to abuses of expenditure, fashion is also seen as a positive force in which 'Human fancy thus asserts its supremacy over animals'. Fashion in this model is thus natural and irreversible.

Gerald Heard was a historian, science writer and theologian who contributed to the development of the consciousness-development movement, leading among others things, to Alcoholics Anonymous. He was also concerned with clothes in modern society. In 'The Cerementing of the Gentleman', a chapter from his *Narcissus. An Anatomy of Clothes* (1924), Heard describes an evolution towards a contemporary fear of squalor and a reification of hygiene in clothes. His argument shifts the focus away from clothes to the human face, 'perhaps now the centre of attraction, since it is the greatest part of the body uncovered by civilized man'. Heard considers various hygienic and aesthetic explanations for the development of the modern male face, noting that the contemporary American face 'is the smoothest and least hairy in the world, outside of China'. Heard notes the rise of dentistry, 'polished teeth, varnished nails, depilation, and finally wigs', which he argues will be defended through arguments of modernity and hygiene. The perfect modern American tooth he compares to 'the only living architecture in the world, the smooth, steel-evident, columnar invention of the skyscraper'. America as an ideal and as a new source of bodily aesthetics constantly recurs in early-twentieth-century writing on dress.

J.C. Flügel is perhaps the most-cited and the least understood commentator on male fashion. Coining the famous term 'the great masculine renunciation' and developing a theory of why men ceased to be beautiful, the ideas for his influential *The Psychology of Clothes* (1930) were developed from his earlier papers. His essay 'The Predominance of Male Homosociality' was first published in *The British Journal of Medical Psychology* in 1927. Flügel saw all motive for fashion as resting in competition. He sets out in a rational and considered manner the marked homosociality of young men before marriage from primitive societies to the clubs of the nineteenth century. He then sought psychological and sociological explanation for why this situation would be more marked for men than for young women. Using the theories of Thorstein Veblen, that fashion indicated a sociological power in which mutability between the orders was key, Flügel wondered whether, in a 'class-less' modern society in which women also worked, there would be any need for fashion. Nudity conducted within the new central heating was preferable to him as all dressing was a disguised aphrodisiac.

Flügel's argument revolved around his claim that men had repressed narcissism in the last 100 years or so – a topic he explicitly examined in *Men and Their Motives* (1934):

> Modern clothing, for instance, allows few outlets for personal vanity among men; to be dressed "correctly" or "in good taste" is the utmost that a modern man can hope for; all originality or beauty in clothing (to say nothing of the even more direct gratification of Narcissism in actual bodily exposure) being reserved for women.

In a direct critique of the muscular Christianity movement associated with sports and scouting, Flügel noted that 'some of the male substitutes for female Narcissism (e.g. pride in muscular development) may lead to forms of rivalry which are as disrupting to social bonds as is the more passive love of the female for her own bodily beauty'. Flügel then introduced into the rhetoric of men's fashion the famous notion of loss, that men had suddenly and finally relinquished something special in the eighteenth century: 'men may be said to have suffered a great defeat in the sudden reduction of male sartorial decorativeness which took place at the end of the eighteenth century ... Man abandoned his claim to be considered beautiful'. Flügel argued that the renunciation worked to inhibit the narcissistic and exhibitionistic desires that were so flamboyantly expressed through aristocratic sumptuousness in preceding centuries. He stated that twentieth-century men seek out alternative routes of gratification; sublimation into showing off (sport) and a reversal into scopophilia, i.e. a male identification of woman as spectacle. According to Flügel, the latter results in the desire to be associated with a beautifully dressed woman, or is expressed as a 'deviance', such as adopting female mannerisms and dress. Flügel associated the change with the late 1780s and the French Revolution, claiming that 'democracy had no use for the gorgeous and complicated trappings which had flourished in a preceding age of absolutism and of highly accentuated class distinctions'.

Around the same time that Flügel was publishing his scientific research, the artist and type-designer Eric Gill published *Clothes. An Essay upon the Nature and Significance of the Natural and Artificial Integuments Worn by Men and Women* (1931), whose 'Epilogue on Trousers' is included in this anthology. Gill, like Flügel, also wishes to consider the 'violent contrast, both in form and workmanship, between men's clothes and women's'. His activist aim is that 'proper reform' should work 'towards an obliteration of these contrasts'. Although he advances dress reform for the genders, Gill recognized that European society will simply not accept men wearing women's clothes. He then playfully turns this duality around by writing that 'if trousers are abominable for women they are abominable for men'. The beard, natural and gracefully cultivated, Gill argues, is sufficient to serve as a gender-marker, the 'all-sufficing garment of differentiation'. His point makes an interesting parallel with Will Fisher's study of the Renaissance beard, included in Volume 1.

To Gill, revolution is in the air nonetheless: 'As the puritan and industrial bases of our civilization crumble beneath us, and signs of instability are not wanting, a change of clothes becomes inevitable, and the direction of such a change must be towards the skirt.' This change will also result in a new respect for the dressmaker and their materials rather than those of the taylor. 'Men are as beautiful as women already, but the fact is hidden by their clothes', remarks Gill. The homoerotic tenor of much of this writing, reinforced by Gill's artfully naïve woodcuts, is striking. The Viennese émigré architect and author Bernard Rudofsky, who directed and designed the exhibition entitled *Are Clothes Modern?* at the Museum of Modern Art in New York in 1944–5, must have derived many of his ideas from Gill. Rudofsky points to the derivation of the 'pantalone' in the male figure of the *Commedia dell'Arte*, noting that this was an ironic twist of fate for modern man.

Dress reformers and modernist artists saw in peasant and regional dress a solution for the contemporary clothing impasse. The study of peasant dress was investigated between the wars by theorists who also examined the dichotomy of draped and sewn clothing. Those linguists and structuralist thinkers focussing upon costume acknowledged the role of urban fashion and military uniforms in re-shaping supposedly static peasant dress. Petr Bogatyrěv's *The Functions of Folk Costume in Moravian Slovakia* was first published as Volume I of *Publications of the Ethnographic Section of Matica Slovenska* in 1937. The Russian scholar, a participant in the Prague Linguistic Group, refused any binary distinction between the dress of the folk and what he called the fashions of the town, noting instead that they existed in relationship to each other. The one-page introduction included here is significant for its long explanatory end note. Bogatyrěv defines folk costume as 'in many respects the antithesis of clothing which is subject to fashion changes'. However, in a move which indicates a nuance lost in many subsequent debates, Bogatyrěv refuses an opposition of folk dress versus 'town dress', and notes that 'even folk dress does not remain unchanged, that it does take on features of current fashion'. Bogatyrěv argued that clothes expressed the will of the people, a dynamic formulation for understanding fashion. 'Urban dress is subject to the discretion of the tailors who create it.'

In post-war America, commentators such as Jessica Mitford criticized the 'American way of death' and the funeral industry as a type of commodified obscenity and conspicuous consumption forced on American consumers. A general questioning of the rigidity of social codes, snobbery, decorum and propriety around dress was inevitable in post-war life. Unlike the early twentieth century, this questioning did not necessarily result in 'dress reform'; rather it resulted in a questioning of whole systems. Economic theorists attempted to reshape the fashion agenda by moving the emphasis from the individual, to the study of the capacity to produce and stimulate the desires of consumers. In 1947 Paul M. Gregory published 'An Economic Interpretation of Women's Fashions' in the context of that rationalizing era, post-war life. His series of commonsense views about the function and role of fashion in contemporary life rehearse the popular interpretation that still dominates media discourse today. To Gregory, fashion is a pure monopoly element and the big losers from the fashion business are the consumers. 'Fashion is intimately related to waste in production and consumption, to seasonality in production and excess plant production and excess plant capacity, to the business cycle, to advertising and the maturity of industry, and through all of these, fashion changes impinge directly on consumer welfare'. Manufacturers are paid rewards for risk taking in this volatile sector. As Cecil Beaton famously wrote at much the same time (1954), those who work in the fashion 'breathe the air of instability; they are like the Mexican farmer who several years ago discovered a volcano growing in his cornfield' (Beaton 1954: 330). Gregory notes that the garment industry works against sensible consumers, and that the former opposed the 'Truth in Fabrics Bill' (USA, 1938) that worked towards sensible labelling, as this industry feared the rational buyer. In Gregory's model, new fashions are not added to older ones; they displace them. So his study is also one of clothing depreciation and obsolesence. Gregory sees in fashion an example of a much more distorted consumer good: 'Fashion and advertising are a gigantic burlesque show at which millions gape.' If people lack the purchasing power to indulge, this 'sets up tensions which cumulate' and this desire 'probably contributes to the neurotic personality of our time'. Fashion 'limits the genuine variety available to consumers' and 'fashion encourages wasteful buying'. In Gregory's model, men suffer less from fashion than women, the middle class suffer more than the rich and than the poor. Businesses 'build a folklore of fashion; they invest goods with subjective qualities which they cannot possess, and prescribe their wares as a panacea, a sedative, an elixir'. Gregory's negative characterization removes all agency from the act of purchasing clothes and describes a consumer landscape of constraint, stupidity and false consciousness: 'Consumers are ignorant, gullible, and full of vanity.'

Part 2, *Fashion and Fantasy*, moves the emphasis from fairly negative scenarios in which consumers are either dupes or *parvenus* to studies that see fashion as a type of participation in modern democracy. Murray Wax's 'Themes in Cosmetics and Grooming', published in *The American Journal of Sociology* in 1957, is an essay by a market researcher that draws on mainly German intellectual thought (Simmel on sociability; Gustav Ichheiser on beauty). It summarizes moral and theological objections to cosmetics and body modification, and then speculates on contemporary attitudes towards practices ranging from the denial of body odour to permanent waving for the older woman; two-thirds of white women in the USA had their hair permanent waved in 1956, the author notes. The practice of modification is analysed in terms of the dialetic of plasticity and control. The author argues that grooming is to be understood from the perspective of sociablity, not of sexuality, and he argues that women dress and groom themselves 'in anticipation of a social situation'. At a time when more women were entering the workforce in professional roles, Wax identifies a divide between the career woman and the housewife, who need not 'dress', as there is no 'audience' for her.

The functionalist seeks an understanding of fashion in terms of its social role rather than origins and causes. Dwight E. Robinson's 'The Economics of Fashion

Demand', published in *The Quarterly Journal of Economics* in 1961, argues that fashion possessed cycles which did not relate to external events. Robinson, who also published a cyclical study of the male beard, was interested in the symbolic nature of fashion that exceeded the content of clothing. He analyses writers stretching back to Hazlitt and Carlyle who have 'discovered a great deal of order in the seeming chaos'. Acknowledging a debt to Quentin Bell, Robinson singled out Cecil Beaton's study *The Glass of Fashion* (1954) as 'a marvelously sophisticated review of fashion origination in the twentieth century'. Perhaps recalling Beaton's metaphor of the Mexican farmer cited previously in this Introduction, Robinson notes that 'fashion preserves us from what would otherwise be the Midas-like curse of durability. It permits us to live in a world of freshly cut blooms where without it we would suffer from an oversupply of artificial flowers.'

Numerous scholars at the beginning of the twentieth century were edging towards a theory of fashion; Ulrich Lehmann notes a precursor to Roland Barthes in Charles Bally, a follower of Ferdinand de Saussure and a number of psychoanalytic writers such as Stephan Hollos.[3] From work commenced in the 1950s, Roland Barthes identified fashion as a linguistic system of signification. The related 'vestimentary' system functions through the signifying operation of clothing in the real world. Barthes removes dress from any discussion of makers (originators), *facture*, production and distribution. Barthes's keen interest in nineteenth-century aesthetics and his debt to the fashion writing of Mallarmé, included in Volume 3 of this anthology, is clear in the delightful essay entitled *From Gemstones to Jewellery* (1961). Barthes describes the passage from the precious jewel as commodity to democratic copy that might be rendered in plastic or wood: 'Jewellery is no longer routinely given the job of showing off a prize'. His essay would have been extra compelling, being written at a time when the 'idea' of the object was challenging the commercial value of the materials. So jewellery, like fashion clothing, might now be made from plastic or paper rather than gold, silver or stones. According to Barthes, fashion is a language, and 'the copy is no longer a hypocritical way of being rich on the cheap'. What Barthes really addresses is the rise of design, which developed in the Belle Epoque among jewellers such as Lalique, working with enamel, glass and non-precious stones – even pebbles. Fashion was becoming democratized though the ability of post-war design to cast creativity as the new bullion of the era.

To Baudrillard, writing around the same time in the late 1960s, this new contemporary life of mass society and advertising represents a complete rupture with older world ideas and cultural patterns. He argued that modern consumption is not heavy with connotation, such as at a feudal feast or within nineteenth-century bourgeois extravagance, but is about a sign relationship and the idea of that relationship. Objects are arbitrary and lack the symbolic value of a nineteenth-century description, as might be found in the literature of Honoré de Balzac, for example. Consumption is about neither emulation nor psychology; consumption is founded on a lack that proliferates endlessly. Baudrillard's account, for which readers should consult *The System of Objects* (1968), in part explains the eclectism of fashion and interior design in the post-war period as well as highlighting the notion of rapidly changing 'lifestyle' as separate from older models of 'taste'.

Part 3, *Fashion and Fantasy*, compels this anthology into the youthquake of the 1960s, feminism, black power and gay liberation. Herbert Blumer, in 'Fashion: From Class Differentiation to Collective Selection' (*The Sociological Quarterly*, 1969), produced a fascinating study of the operation of fashion. Perhaps reflecting the turbulent decade in which it was written, the author notes that: 'Not all prestigeful persons are innovators – and innovators are not necessarily persons with the highest prestige'. Blumer reviews the role of sociologists such as Simmel (1904), Edward Sapir (1931)[4] and Kurt and Gladys Langs (1961) as failing to 'observe and appreciate the wide range of operation of fashion'. He critiques Simmel's view that fashion's primary function is the 'oscillating differentiation and unification of social classes' (Blumer, p. 290). He reviews the psychological turn in fashion writing. He notes the failure of the academy to engage with fashion, as the topic is perceived to lie 'in the area of the abnormal and irrational', as well as fundamental failures from scholars to engage with the real 'nature' of fashion. Echoing the later argument of Gilles Lipovetsky, fashion is sensed by Blumer in all fields from medicine to mortuary practices. His case study of the Paris couture buyers is particularly amusing and illuminating. Reminiscent of some of the ideas proposed by nineteenth-century journalism such as Baudelaire, Blumer concludes that 'fashion operates as an orderly preparation for the immediate future' ... 'fashion is a very adept mechanism for enabling people to adjust in an orderly and unified way to a moving and changing world which is potentially full of anarchic possibilities'. This idea has been taken up recently in a study of the art-fashion nexus. As Peter Gross notes, 'Fashions and trends compensate for the loss of certainties and offer spaces and times for operation, since there is consolation in being part of a community.'[5]

In 'Why the Midi Failed' (*Journal of Advertising Research*, 1972), Fred D. Reynolds and William R. Darden examine 'the rejection of new clothing styles'. This is a question that challenges much costume history, which rarely documents failures of innovations and of new fashion goods. It is a useful counter to the rather triumphal air of successive styles frequently found in fashion history. The article attempts to understand the 'structure and function of information sources' that lead to new consumer behaviour regarding fashion. Different types of information sources are analysed and consumers divided into fashion 'opinion leaders' and 'non-leaders'. The article concludes that no amount of marketing can sell a product if the new style is 'incongruent with the characteristics desired by the market'.

The theorist Pierre Bourdieu rejected all commonsense notions of privilege and power. To Bourdieu, the dominant class benefits from power, and has its power reproduced through social institutions and practices. An extract entitled *Time and Money* has been selected from Bourdieu's *The Production of Belief: Contribution to an Economy of Symbolic Goods* (1977). His examination of the field of 'cultural production' permits connections to be made between the operations of what on face value appear to be very different fields. All short-cycle production, Bourdieu suggests, is like *haute couture* fashion production, i.e. 'heavily dependent on a whole set of agents and institutions specializing in "promotion" ... which must be constantly maintained and periodically mobilized' (with the annual literary prizes performing a function analogous to that of fashion 'collections'). In its examination of poles of the French publishing industry, Bourdieu considers best-sellers and classics, which in turn create 'two completely different ways of organizing production and marketing'. In a note, Bourdieu argues that the devaluation entailed in 'mass appeal' of any product is most clearly visible in fashion, 'where the consecrated establishments are able to keep going for several generations' through exclusive concessions (Caron, Chanel) and the ageing hence vulgarized brands (Coty, Worth) 'have a second career, down-market'.

One of the most fruitful turns for the study of fashion has been spectator theory derived from psycho-analysis and media studies. In 'Fashion Shapes: Film, the Fashion Industry and the Image of Woman' (*Socialist Review*, 1983), Maureen Turim argues that fashion 'molds human beings into visual designs' and that film plays an unparalleled role in this process. Turim argues that there is an overall conservatism to fashion which 'learned to profit from the fantasies and desires of all classes of women'. Her conclusion is more ambiguous: 'we express and choose ourselves through fashion even while the film and fashion industries seek to efface our subjectivity and render us as segments of a consumer profile'. Thus Turim opens up a particular turn of fashion studies.

Karen Tranberg Hansen's *Other People's Clothes? The International Secondhand Clothing Trade and Dress Practices in Zambia* considers the used-clothing export trade to sub-Saharan Africa. By the late nineteenth century, the mass-produced clothing described in Volumes 2 and 3 of this anthology had reduced the possibility of selling second-hand on European markets. Countries such as France turned to the colonies. In the late twentieth century some countries attend very closely to the trade, countries such as Nigeria and Kenya at times banning such imports. Transen examines the enormous world market in second-hand clothes and using ethnographic methods analyses what this clothing means to those who both market it and purchase it. Dress practices in contemporary Zambia, Transen notes, are primarily 'visual and sensual'. Certain combinations of colours and textures are preferred over others. In relation to the comments on fashion and form in my introduction to Volume 1, Transen's interviewees note that the overall shape or form of their clothing composition is much more important than other elements; it must be neat with smooth lines and careful colour mixing. Economics and poverty are inadequate, she notes, to explain the popularity of the *salaula* (second-hand clothes in Zambia). Many women wear a different combination of skirt and dress every day and such uniqueness is highly desired. In a spatial metaphor useful for some general points examined in these volumes, western fashion is rarely used as a category. Rather fashion from the 'outside' is referred to, which includes neighbouring countries. The West, Hansen argues, is an imagined place from which conventional fashion and subcultural elements alike might appear in a market stall. The men selling in the markets become, rather like the figures of the eighteenth-century French appearance industry, walking advertisements for their wares. These men might wear red nail polish and slip second-hand priests' robes and *peignoirs* over their male clothes, not, Transen contends, to play with cross-gender or queer stylistics, but to stand out and to make a sale. Such clothing purchases enable social change, and dressing is undertaken to escape a sense of 'economic powerlessness, momentarily and vicariously'.

Although production and distribution is central to how Hansen argues, the domain of aesthetics is therefore also present in her analysis of fashion. Part 4, *Fashion and Aesthetics*, connects visual regimes with some of the important shifts in making and marketing twentieth-century fashion.

Pointing to new modes of representing the world in 1920s cinema, painting, photography and design, in 'To Cut is to Think' (1997), Germano Celant draws a parallel between the 'cut' in modernist art and the act of cutting cloth, in order to argue that the first modern design springs 'in a practical as well as a linguistic sense, from Cubism and its cuttings'. Here Celant uses an argument from the history of art and aesthetics, that the cubist cut-out and collage did not simply represent or interpret an object; but rather 'constructed and produced it'. Thus new clothes can be seen as dynamic forces that helped produce the 'modern woman', not the other way around, that is to say the women becoming modern and demanding fresh clothes.

Richard Martin, one of the most imaginative curators of fashion at the end of the twentieth century, combined a keen sense of the materiality of dress with its intellectual history. His writing, in its sharp and sometimes arcane observation, recalled some of the great fashion journalism of nineteenth-century Paris. He frequently referred to the relationship between art and fashion, without ever collapsing the two in a crude measure. An example of Martin's writing, 'Illuminations – Warhol in the 1950s' on Warhol's drawings for advertisements of shoes, brings together art and design history in his typically artful manner. Warhol, whose personal taste was frequently snobbish, first worked for the post-war clothing sector that brought together industry and fashion. These elegant blotted drawings made by the son of a poor immigrant joined many of the ideas of post-war life, in which class aesthetics were replaced by youth aesthetics. New marketing strategies overturned the older link of mass production with poor quality, transforming the nature of branding. Cultural intermediaries in trades from window dressing to styling were able to imbue Seventh Avenue with the allure of a magic that suggested Paris, but was thoroughly contemporary and American.

Caroline Evans's critical evaluation of the work of designer Martin Margiela, 'The Golden Dustman: A Critical Evaluation of the Work of Martin Margiela and a Review of *Martin Margiela: Exhibition (9/4/1615)*' connects many of the themes that are found in the contents of the four volumes of this anthology. There is the matter of the fresh and the second-hand clothing, the ability of earlier eras to remake, recast and reformulate fashions. There is the matter of the proliferation of clothes

as but one of immunerable commodities in nineteenth-century life, the types of objects which once used, were picked over by the rag-pickers of Paris, a figure who, like
the prostitute, lived on the margins of society, but to Baudelaire was a modern poet.
There is the matter of abjection, of the way in which clothes take on the stains of the
body that can never be erased. There is the matter of the spaces of the city, so clearly
set out by Elizabeth Wilson, and owing its formulation to the writings of Walter
Benjamin and later the situationist *dérive*. And there is the matter of the new type of
creator described by Roland Barthes and Gilles Lipovetsky, who takes advantage
of and becomes one of the installation or performance artists of contemporary
society. Margiela, Evans concludes, survives commercially and experimentally at the
same time. In converting second-hand garments and clothes he performs a number
of reversals in which new life is given to second-hand clothes and things abject recast
as the top of a new hierarchy of prestige. In showing his fashions in the liminal and
abject spaces of the city, from old theatres to warehouse corridors, Margiela doubly
emphasizes the 'grain' or patina 'that cannot be simulated' by a mere industry. 'It is
their forgotten history that he brings back to life,' Evans writes. His fashion design
connects modernist *bricoleurs* with postmodern *pasticheurs*, who find new meanings in the refuse of the late-capitalist city. Finally, in a point connecting this review
to Evans's other work on fashion and death, she emphasizes the views of Walter
Benajmin that fashion is a type of newness 'in a struggle against natural decay'. The
frenetic pace of fashion change in this model, Evans concludes, is 'anattempt to ward
off the ageing process and stay the passage of time'.

Rebecca Arnold's 'Vionnet & Classicism' (2001) accompanied an innovative installation from the private collection of Martin Kamer at the Judith Clark Costume
Gallery, London. Arnold offers a thoughtful reading of Vionnet's fashion design in
which its classicism is explored as an emblem both timeless and subversive. Madeleine
Vionnet, called the 'Euclid of Fashion', as the rectangle and platonic forms dominated her thinking, based her innovative design on motion and cut. Vionnet thought
of the woman's body as a moving sculpture and deployed an original tailoring
method in which she cut on the bias. These techniques were not new, but had been
used in fields such as expensive underwear and nightgowns. Her working process
was to drape specially woven double-width fabric onto a dressmakers' mannequin
that was 80 centimetres (about 31.5 inches) tall. As Arnold notes, this permitted
a three-dimensional view of the body, not a 'fractured vision of back, front, top,
bottom'. Vionnet delighted in the play of white, nude and transparent black chiffon,
as well as making fabric appear 'alive' in different types of light by cutting into it
diamond-shapes, for example, in which the pile runs in opposite directions in each
row of diamonds. There is a paradox, Arnold writes, within this modern clothing
'liberation' and the rise of transparent and nude dresses, which were also linked to a
vision of racial whiteness. Vionnet is proof that it is not just male designers who have
a particular vision of how their female customer should appear in their fashions. In a
famous interview of 1973, Vionnet praised the height, full hips, 'undulating buttocks'

and bosoms of Argentinian and Cuban women, and declared: 'They always said I loved women too much' (cited in Chatwin, 1989: 90–1).

Elite fashion from the late nineteenth century was created by designers who pretended that commerce was not their business and instead cultivated the aura of the artist or patron. Nancy Troy, in 'Paul Poiret's Minaret Style: Originality, Reproduction and Art in Fashion', builds in significant ways on many of the ideas contained in Elizabeth Wilson's *Adorned in Dreams*, that fashion in early twentieth-century society was a type of performance art, and also a source of tension between the original and the copy. The research is exemplary in showing how information about designers can be used to underscore a wider theoretical point. Troy sees both Poiret and Coco Chanel (1883–1971) as embracing modern ideas of the ready-made, which sat somewhere between the original and the mechanical reproduction. Thus Poiret licensed 'genuine copies' of his clothes in the USA and *Vogue* compared Chanel's little black dress to the Model T Ford. Poiret, the master marketing expert, promoted his minaret fashion line through a range of devices from plays to department-store promotions, then faced the diffusion, copying and piracy of his self-construction as artist and innovator. Troy notes the irony that, in his North American tours, Poiret embraced a model of vulgar theatre – the fashion show- that attempted to stave off the vulgarized copying of his own already theatrical designs. Going beyond the language of fine art, Poiret turned to the law, threatening to prosecute all but the 'genuine copies' of his clothes. His trademark might be protected, but copyright law did not protect clothing and textile designs, which had to resort to design patents, much more difficult to obtain and to pursue. American copyright law failed to recognize his garments as works of art; patent law failed to identify the originality in his designs. In North America, Troy concludes, Poiret was neither artist nor inventor, simply the owner of a trademark and an entrepreneur, the very label he had struggled to flee. As with Arnold's research, Troy finds Poiret's use of orientalizing and classicizing motifs to be contradictory and paradoxical; they could be expressions of conventional luxury or transgressive at the same time. In his successor, Chanel, Troy finds a figure who unlike Poiret, found in the notion of reproduction and standardization 'a means of representing the contradictory forces at work in modern culture'.

Although there are numerous authors who are chroniclers of subcultural style, notably Ted Polhemus, McRobbie manages to be both sympathetic (not impartial) to the subject of her study and also scholarly. Her writing is among the most important to connect dress, music and urban space. At the same time, she does not apply a type of unreconstructed anthropological 'eye' that pervades the recent writing of some sociologists, whose encounters with subculturalists seem almost to be like white encounters with Papua New Guineans at the turn of the twentieth century. Her 'Art, Fashion and Music in the Culture Society' (1999) is a provocative piece on the status of the contemporary fashion designer.

McRobbie argues that the 'DIY' (do it yourself) ethos and the subcultural field of second-hand, retro and street markets, in which British fashion flourished in the 1980s, indicate that a history of designers or *haute couture* cannot narrate the story of fashion. Instead, 1980s fashion design can be seen as a form of popular culture with links to music, clubbing and alternative lifestyles. She argues that the British art and design school sector produced in the 1980s a new type of graduate who was an *auteur* (author) of a type of fine art practice. This differs from the French-derived model, where although the language of art is often used to describe creative practice, designers are strongly associated with the craft of making or the artisanal aspects of the *haute couture*. Her approach also differs from the post-structuralist interest in the connection between fashion, signification and lifestyle in which the liberation from the signifier is either associated with constraint, automation and repetition (Lefebvre) or appropriation and the diffusion of the empirical world (Baudrillard).[6]

McRobbie provides a trenchant critique of the state of fashion criticism and the lack of research into the culture industries. Art, fashion and music are a part of both commerce and tourism but art has long traditions to fall back on. Unlike British artists and musicians, British fashion designers, she notes, have never displayed a high political involvement nor engagement with any substantial theoretical trad- ition to underwrite their practice. McRobbie suggests that this cuts designers off from a source of their power. There is 'no developed language of art criticism which would introduce and comment upon the work of young British fashion designers'. Fashion, she argues, is hampered by its 'gendered, dressmaking history' and, instead of challenging this divide, it has merely sought to emulate a fine or high art mode 'as a kind of second best'. The only radical scholarship in the field is feminist and subcultural but designers shy away from this, McRobbie notes. 'It pays its respect to the street but needs the fine art tag to justify its presence.' This results, she con- cludes at the time of writing, in journalists being the principle cultural intermediaries who decide 'a vocabulary of approval' for contemporary fashion, a situation quite unlike art, architecture or music. The rise of on-line blogging might provide some of the independent voices that McRobbie so missed in 1999, although its quality is so partial that it cannot be a panacea.

In 'Hollywood Glamour and Mass Consumption in Postwar Italy' (2002), Stephen Gundle argues that, in a country such as Italy, the idea of American glamour 'has never been matched or superseded, only reworked, repositioned, and reelaborated'. Glamour, 'a structure of enchantment deployed by culture industries' is an English term dating to 1830, 'a delusive or alluring charm'. In post-war Western Europe, the Marshall Plan, the impact of Hollywood and the star system created a new notion of glamour. Glamour, Gundle argues, helped capitalism 'to bypass arguments about exploitation, imperialism, inequality, and alienation'. Through glamour, Italian society – which was not yet noted for a highly developed fashion design sector – was able to absorb and create 'an enchantment of its own'. The European Recovery Programme (ERP) was not just a matter of resources. It was also designed to stimulate European societies to 'develop their own mythologies of capitalism that would cut across, and ultimately displace, political ideologies'. These materialized both dreams and imagery that boosted exports and created a newly confident fashion sector.

Elizabeth Wilson, who has described herself rather modestly as the last fashion amateur, provides these four volumes with its conclusion. Her 'Magic Fashion' (2004) creates an important and accessible account of both the uncanny nature of fashion, and of the links between fashion, art and commerce in the inter-war period. In a wide-ranging piece of cultural comment, Wilson notes the Surrealist interest in the animate and the inanimate, the natural and the artifical, that created the power of Surrealist fashion. As she notes, 'the naked body *is* complete, but the garment is certainly a mere shadow of itself until it is inhabited'. Clothes 'make the body culturally visible, and, conversely, the clothes themselves are only complete when animated by a body'. Citing examples from the field of sport, Wilson notes that 'For many, perhaps most of us, articles of clothing not only affect our mood and self-perception, but not infrequently acquire quasi-magical properties and meanings'. In suggesting that fashion is a type of 'secular fetish', Wilson brings together at the conclusion at these volumes ideas from anthropology, Marx's theories of commodity fetish, nebulous desires and power, the whole 'the machinery of capitalism'. Wilson's plays with the paradox of the ongoing trivialization of dress in contemporary media and institutions despite its role as 'the vehicle for deeply significant ideas, aspirations, and feelings.' Her case-study of inter-war fashion and Surrealism, Wilson writes, 'gives us hope, suggesting that there are still gaps in the apparent seamlessness of consumer culture through which we can escape into re-enchanted worlds'.

NOTES

1. See Georg Simmel, 'The Problem of Style', in Frisby and Featherstone (1997: 215–16).
2. 'The Problem of Style' [published as 'Das Problem des Stiles' in *Dekorative Kunst*, 16 (1908); trans. Mark Ritter, in *Theory, Culture and Society. Explorations in Critical Social Science*, 8(3) (August 1991): 63–71.
3. See Lehmann (2000: 483).
4. Sapir was an anthropologist who read fashion in terms of display, and who saw fashion as 'functional irrelevance as contrasted with symbolic significance for the expression of the ego' (Robinson, 1961: 380).
5. See Peter Gross, 'What is Missing when Nothing is Missing. Modernity and Fashion', in Doswald (2006: 42–7).
6. On this important matter of fashion and the everyday, see Sheringham (2006: 176–88).

BIBLIOGRAPHY

Beaton, Cecil. 1954. *The Glass of Fashion*. London: Doubleday.
Breward, Christopher. 2004. *Fashion London: Clothing and the Modern Metropolis*. Oxford: Berg.
Chatwin, Bruce, *What am I doing Here?*, Picador, 1989
Doswald, Christoph (ed.). 2006. *Double-Face. The Story about Fashion and Art. From Mohammed to Warhol*. Zurich: Ringier-JRP.

Frisby, David and Featherstone, Mike (eds). 1997. *Simmel on Culture*. London: Sage.

Lehmann, Ulrich. 2000. 'Language of the PurSuit: Cary Grant's Clothes in Alfred Hitchcock's "North by Northwest"', *Fashion Theory*, 4(4): 467–85.

Robinson, Dwight E. 1961. 'The Economics of Fashion Demand', *The Quarterly Journal of Economics*, 75(3) August.

Sheringham, Michael. 2006. *Everyday Life: Theories and Practices from Surrealism to the Present*. Oxford and New York: Oxford University Press.

Part 1:
Fashion's Structures

CHAPTER ONE

Dress as an Expression of the Pecuniary Culture

THORSTEIN VEBLEN

It will be in place, by way of illustration, to show in some detail how the economic principles so far set forth apply to everyday facts in some one direction of the life process. For this purpose no line of consumption affords a more apt illustration than expenditure on dress. It is especially the rule of the conspicuous waste of goods that finds expression in dress, although the other, related principles of pecuniary repute are also exemplified in the same contrivances. Other methods of putting one's pecuniary standing in evidence serve their end effectually, and other methods are in vogue always and everywhere; but expenditure on dress has this advantage over most other methods, that our apparel is always in evidence and affords an indication of our pecuniary standing to all observers at the first glance. It is also true that admitted expenditure for display is more obviously present, and is, perhaps, more universally practised in the matter of dress than in any other line of consumption. No one finds difficulty in assenting to the commonplace that the greater part of the expenditure incurred by all classes for apparel is incurred for the sake of a respectable appearance rather than for the protection of the person. And probably at no other point is the sense of shabbiness so keenly felt as it is if we fall short of the standard set by social usage in this matter of dress. It is true of dress in even a higher degree than of most other items of consumption, that people will undergo a very considerable degree of privation in the comforts or the necessaries of life in order to afford what is considered a decent amount of wasteful consumption; so that it is by no means an uncommon occurrence, in an inclement climate, for people to go ill clad in order to appear well dressed. And the commercial value of the goods used for clothing in any modern community is made up to a much larger extent of the fashionableness, the reputability of the goods than of the mechanical service which they render in clothing the person of the wearer. The need of dress is eminently a "higher" or spiritual need.

This spiritual need of dress is not wholly, nor even chiefly, a naïve propensity for display of expenditure. The law of conspicuous waste guides consumption in apparel, as in other things, chiefly at the second remove, by shaping the canons of taste and decency. In the common run of cases the conscious motive of the wearer or purchaser of conspicuously wasteful apparel is the need of conforming to established usage, and of living up to the accredited standard of taste and reputability. It is not only that one must be guided by the code of proprieties in dress in order to avoid the mortification that comes of unfavourable notice and comment, though that motive in itself counts for a great deal; but besides that, the requirement of expensiveness is so ingrained into our habits of thought in matters of dress that any other than expensive apparel is instinctively odious to us. Without reflection or analysis, we feel that what is inexpensive is unworthy. "A cheap coat makes a cheap man." "Cheap and nasty" is recognised to hold true in dress with even less mitigation than in other lines of consumption. On the ground both of taste and of serviceability, an inexpensive article of apparel is held to be inferior, under the maxim "cheap and nasty." We find things beautiful, as well as serviceable, somewhat in proportion as they are costly. With few and inconsequential exceptions, we all find a costly hand-wrought article of apparel much preferable, in point of beauty and of serviceability, to a less expensive imitation of it, however cleverly the spurious article may imitate the costly original; and what offends our sensibilities in the spurious article is not that it falls short in form or colour, or, indeed, in visual effect in any way. The offensive object may be so close an imitation as to defy any but the closest scrutiny; and yet so soon as the counterfeit is detected, its æsthetic value, and its commercial value as well, declines precipitately. Not only that, but it may be asserted with but small risk of contradiction that the aesthetic value of a detected counterfeit in dress declines somewhat in the same proportion as the counterfeit is cheaper than its original. It loses caste aesthetically because it falls to a lower pecuniary grade.

But the function of dress as an evidence of ability to pay does not end with simply showing that the wearer consumes valuable goods in excess of what is required for physical comfort. Simple conspicuous waste of goods is effective and gratifying as far as it goes; it is good *prima facie* evidence of pecuniary success, and consequently *prima facie* evidence of social worth. But dress has subtler and more far-reaching possibilities than this crude, first-hand evidence of wasteful consumption only. If, in addition to showing that the wearer can afford to consume freely and uneconomically, it can also be shown in the same stroke that he or she is not under the necessity of earning a livelihood, the evidence of social worth is enhanced in a very considerable degree. Our dress, therefore, in order to serve its purpose effectually, should not only be expensive, but it should also make plain to all observers that the wearer is not engaged in any kind of productive labour. In the evolutionary process by which our system of dress has been elaborated into its present admirably perfect adaptation to its purpose, this subsidiary line of evidence has received due attention. A detailed examination of what passes in popular apprehension for elegant apparel will show that it is contrived at every point to convey the impression that the wearer does not habitually put forth any useful effort. It goes without saying that no apparel can be considered elegant, or even decent, if it shows the effect of manual labour on the part of the wearer, in the way of soil or wear. The pleasing effect of neat and spotless garments is chiefly if not altogether, due to their carrying the suggestion of leisure – exemption from personal contact with industrial processes of any kind. Much of the charm that invests the patent-leather shoe, the stainless linen, the lustrous cylindrical hat, and the walking-stick, which so greatly enhance the native dignity of a gentleman, comes of their pointedly suggesting that the wearer cannot when so attired bear a hand in any employment that is directly and immediately of any human use. Elegant dress serves its purpose of elegance not only in that it is expensive, but also because it is the insignia of leisure. It not only shows that the wearer is able to consume a relatively large value, but it argues at the same time that he consumes without producing.

The dress of women goes even farther than that of men in the way of demonstrating the wearer's abstinence from productive employment. It needs no argument to enforce the generalisation that the more elegant styles of feminine bonnets go even farther towards making work impossible than does the man's high hat. The woman's shoe adds the so-called French heel to the evidence of enforced leisure afforded by its polish; because this high heel obviously makes any, even the simplest and most necessary manual work extremely difficult. The like is true even in a higher degree of the skirt and the rest of the drapery which characterises woman's dress. The substantial reason for out tenacious attachment to the skirt is just this: it is expensive and it hampers the wearer at every turn and incapacitates her for all useful exertion. The like is true of the feminine custom of wearing the hair excessively long.

But the woman's apparel not only goes beyond that of the modern man in the degree in which it argues exemption from labour; it also adds a peculiar and highly characteristic feature which differs in kind from anything habitually practised by the men. This feature is the class of contrivances of which the corset is the typical example. The corset is, in economic theory, substantially a mutilation, undergone for the purpose of lowering the subject's vitality and rendering her permanently and obviously unfit for work. It is true, the corset impairs the personal attractions of the wearer, but the loss suffered on that score is offset by the gain in reputability which comes of her visibly increased expensiveness and infirmity. It may broadly be set down that the womanliness of woman's apparel resolves itself, in point of substantial fact, into the more effective hindrance to useful exertion offered by the garments peculiar to women. This difference between masculine and feminine apparel is here simply pointed out as a characteristic feature. The ground of its occurrence will be discussed presently.

So far, then, we have, as the great and dominant norm of dress, the broad principle of conspicuous waste. Subsidiary to this principle, and as a corollary under it, we get as a second norm the principle of conspicuous leisure. In dress construction this norm works out in the shape of divers contrivances going to show that the wearer does not and, as far as it may conveniently be shown, can not engage in productive labour. Beyond these two principles there is a third of scarcely less constraining force, which will occur to any one who reflects at all on the subject. Dress must not only be conspicuously expensive and inconvenient; it must at the same time be up to date. No explanation at all satisfactory has hitherto been offered of the pheno-menon of changing fashions. The imperative requirement of dressing in the latest accredited manner, as well as the fact that this accredited fashion constantly changes from season to season, is sufficiently familiar to every one, but the theory of this flux and change has not been worked out. We may of course say, with perfect consistency and truthfulness, that this principle of novelty is another corollary under the law of conspicuous waste. Obviously, if each garment is permitted to serve for but a brief term, and if none of last season's apparel is carried over and made further use of during the present season, the wasteful expenditure on dress is greatly increased. This is good as far as it goes, but it is negative only. Pretty much all that this consideration war-rants us in saying is that the norm of conspicuous waste exercises a controlling sur-veillance in all matters of dress, so that any change in the fashions must conform to the requirement of wastefulness; it leaves unanswered the question as to the motive for making and accepting a change in the prevailing styles, and it also fails to explain why conformity to a given style at a given time is so imperatively necessary as we know it to be.

For a creative principle, capable of serving as motive to invention and innovation in fashions, we shall have to go back to the primitive, non-economic motive with which apparel originated, – the motive of adornment. Without going into an extended dis-cussion of how and why this motive asserts itself under the guidance of the law of ex-pensiveness, it may be stated broadly that each successive innovation in the fashions is an effort to reach some form of display which shall be more acceptable to our sense of form and colour or of effectiveness, than that which it displaces. The changing styles are the expression of a restless search for something which shall commend itself to our æsthetic sense; but as each innovation is subject to the selective action of the norm of conspicuous waste, the range within which innovation can take place is somewhat restricted. The innovation must not only be more beautiful, or perhaps oftener less offensive, than that which it displaces, but it must also come up to the accepted standard of expensiveness.

It would seem at first sight that the result of such an unremitting struggle to attain the beautiful in dress should be a gradual approach to artistic perfection. We might naturally expect that the fashions should show a well-marked trend in the direction of some one or more types of apparel eminently becoming to the human form; and we might even feel that we have substantial ground for the hope that to-day, after all the ingenuity and effort which have been spent on dress these many years, the fashions should have achieved a relative perfection and a relative stability, closely approximating to a permanently tenable artistic ideal. But such is not the case. It would be very hazardous indeed to assert that the styles of to-day are intrinsically more becoming than those of ten years ago, or than those of twenty, or fifty, or one hundred years ago. On the other hand, the assertion freely goes uncontradicted that styles in Vogue two thousand years ago are more becoming than the most elaborate and painstaking constructions of to-day.

The explanation of the fashions just offered, then, does not fully explain, and we shall have to look farther. It is well known that certain relatively stable styles and types of costume have been worked out in various parts of the world; as, for instance, among the Japanese, Chinese, and other Oriental nations; likewise among the Greeks, Romans, and other Eastern peoples of antiquity; so also, in later times, among the peasants of nearly every country of Europe. These national or popular costumes are in most cases adjudged by competent critics to be more becoming, more artistic, than the fluctuating styles of modern civilised apparel. At the same time they are also, at least usually, less obviously wasteful; that is to say, other elements than that of a display of expense are more readily detected in their structure.

These relatively stable costumes are, commonly, pretty strictly and narrowly localised, and they vary by slight and systematic gradations from place to place. They have in every case been worked out by peoples or classes which are poorer than we, and especially they belong in countries and localities and times where the population, or at least the class to which the costume in question belongs, is relatively homogeneous, stable, and immobile. That is to say, stable costumes which will bear the test of time and perspective are worked out under circumstances where the norm of conspicuous waste asserts itself less imperatively than it does in the large modern civilised cities, whose relatively mobile, wealthy population to-day sets the pace in matters of fashion. The countries and classes which have in this way worked out stable and artistic costumes have been so placed that the pecuniary emulation among them has taken the direction of a competition in conspicuous leisure rather than in conspicuous consumption of goods. So that it will hold true in a general way that fashions are least stable and least becoming in those communities where the principle of a conspicuous waste of goods asserts itself most imperatively, as among ourselves. All this points to an antagonism between expensiveness and artistic apparel. In point of practical fact, the norm of conspicuous waste is incompatible with the requirement that dress should be beautiful or becoming. And this antagonism offers an explanation of that restless change in fashion which neither the canon of expensiveness nor that of beauty alone can account for.

The standard of reputability requires that dress should show wasteful expenditure; but all wastefulness is offensive to native taste. The psychological law has already been pointed out that all men – and women perhaps even in a higher degree – abhor futility, whether of effort or of expenditure, – much as Nature was once said to abhor a vacuum. But the principle of conspicuous waste requires an obviously futile expenditure; and the resulting conspicuous expensiveness of dress is therefore intrinsically ugly. Hence we find that in all innovations in dress, each added or altered detail strives to avoid instant condemnation by showing some ostensible purpose, at the same time that the requirement of conspicuous waste prevents the purposefulness of these innovations from becoming anything more than a somewhat transparent pretense. Even in its freest flights, fashion rarely if ever gets away from a simulation of some ostensible use. The ostensible usefulness of the fashionable details of dress, however, is always so transparent a make-believe, and their substantial futility presently forces itself so baldly upon our attention as to become unbearable, and then we take refuge in a new style. But the new style must conform to the requirement of reputable wastefulness and futility. Its futility presently becomes as odious as that of its predecessor; and the only remedy which the law of waste allows us is to seek relief in some new construction, equally futile and equally untenable. Hence the essential ugliness and the unceasing change of fashionable attire.

Having so explained the phenomenon of shifting fashions, the next thing is to make the explanation tally with everyday facts. Among these everyday facts is the well-known liking which all men have for the styles that are in vogue at any given time. A new style comes into vogue and remains in favour for a season, and, at least so long as it is a novelty, people very generally find the new style attractive. The prevailing fashion is felt to be beautiful. This is due partly to the relief it affords in being different from what went before it, partly to its being reputable. As indicated in the last chapter, the canon of reputability to some extent shapes our tastes, so that under its guidance anything will be accepted as becoming until its novelty wears off, or until the warrant of reputability is transferred to a new and novel structure serving the same general purpose. That the alleged beauty, or "loveliness," of the styles in vogue at any given time is transient and spurious only is attested by the fact that none of the many shifting fashions will bear the test of time. When seen in the perspective of half-a-dozen years or more, the best of our fashions strike us as grotesque, if not unsightly. Our transient attachment to whatever happens to be the latest rests on other than æsthetic grounds, and lasts only until our abiding æsthetic sense has had time to assert itself and reject this latest indigestible contrivance.

The process of developing an æsthetic nausea takes more or less time; the length of time required in any given case being inversely as the degree of intrinsic odiousness of the style in question. This time relation between odiousness and instability in fashions affords ground for the inference that the more rapidly the styles succeed and displace one another, the more offensive they are to sound taste. The presumption, therefore, is that the farther the community, especially the wealthy classes of the community, develop in wealth and mobility and in the range of their human contact, the more imperatively will the law of conspicuous waste assert itself in matters of dress, the more will the sense of beauty tend to fall into abeyance or be overborne by the canon of pecuniary reputability, the more rapidly will fashions shift and change, and the more grotesque and intolerable will be the varying styles that successively come into vogue.

There remains at least one point in this theory of dress yet to be discussed. Most of what has been said applies to men's attire as well as to that of women; although in modern times it applies at nearly all points with greater force to that of women. But at one point the dress of women differs substantially from that of men. In woman's dress there is an obviously greater insistence on such features as testify to the wearer's exemption from or incapacity for all vulgarly productive employment. This characteristic of woman's apparel is of interest, not only as completing the theory of dress, but also as confirming what has already been said of the economic status of women, both in the past and in the present.

As has been seen in the discussion of woman's status under the heads of Vicarious Leisure and Vicarious Consumption, it has in the course of economic development become the office of the woman to consume vicariously for the head of the household; and her apparel is contrived with this object in view. It has come about that obviously productive labour is in a peculiar degree derogatory to respectable women, and therefore special pains should be taken in the construction of women's dress, to impress upon the beholder the fact (often indeed a fiction) that the wearer does not and can not habitually engage in useful work. Propriety requires respectable women to abstain more consistently from useful effort and to make more of a show of leisure than the men of the same social classes. It grates painfully on our nerves to contemplate the necessity of any well-bred woman's earning a livelihood by useful work. It is not "woman's sphere." Her sphere is within the household, which she should "beautify," and of which she should be the "chief ornament." The male head of the household is not currently spoken of as its ornament. This feature taken in conjunction with the other fact that propriety requires more unremitting attention to expensive display in the dress and other paraphernalia of women, goes to enforce the view already implied in what has gone before. By virtue of its descent from a patriarchal past, our social system makes it the woman's function in an especial degree to put in evidence her household's ability to pay. According to the modern civilised scheme of life, the good name of the household to which she belongs should be the special care of the woman; and the system of honorific expenditure and conspicuous leisure by which this good name is chiefly sustained is therefore the woman's sphere. In the ideal scheme, as it tends to realise itself in the life of the higher pecuniary classes, this attention to conspicuous waste of substance and effort should normally be the sole economic function of the woman.

At the stage of economic development at which the women were still in the full sense the property of the men, the performance of conspicuous leisure and consumption came to be part of the services required of them. The women being not their own masters, obvious expenditure and leisure on their part would redound to the credit of their master rather than to their own credit; and therefore the more expensive and the more obviously unproductive the women of the household are, the more creditable and more effective for the purpose of the reputability of the household or its head will their life be. So much so that the women have been required not only to afford evidence of a life of leisure, but even to disable themselves for useful activity.

It is at this point that the dress of men falls short of that of women, and for a sufficient reason. Conspicuous waste and conspicuous leisure are reputable because they are evidence of pecuniary strength; pecuniary strength is reputable or honorific because, in the last analysis, it argues success and superior force; therefore the evidence of waste and leisure put forth by any individual in his own behalf cannot consistently take such a form or be carried to such a pitch as to argue incapacity or marked discomfort on his part; as the exhibition would in that case show not superior force, but inferiority, and so defeat its own purpose. So, then, wherever wasteful expenditure and the show of abstention from effort is normally, or on an average, carried to the extent of showing obvious discomfort or voluntarily induced physical disability, there the immediate inference is that the individual in question does not perform this wasteful expenditure and undergo this disability for her own personal gain in pecuniary repute, but in behalf of some one else to whom she stands in a relation of economic dependence; a relation which in the last analysis must, in economic theory, reduce itself to a relation of servitude.

To apply this generalisation to women's dress, and put the matter in concrete terms: the high heel, the skirt, the impracticable bonnet, the corset, and the general disregard of the wearer's comfort which is an obvious feature of all civilised women's apparel, are so many items of evidence to the effect that in the modern civilised scheme of life the woman is still, in theory, the economic dependent of the man, – that, perhaps in a highly idealised sense, she still is the man's chattel. The homely reason for all this conspicuous leisure and attire on the part of women lies in the fact that they are servants to whom, in the differentiation of economic functions, has been delegated the office of putting in evidence their master's ability to pay.

There is a marked similarity in these respects between the apparel of women and that of domestic servants, especially liveried servants. In both there is a very elaborate show of unnecessary expensiveness, and in both cases there is also a notable disregard of the physical comfort of the wearer. But the attire of the lady goes farther in its elaborate insistence on the idleness, if not on the physical infirmity of the wearer, than does that of the domestic. And this is as it should be; for in theory, according to the ideal scheme of the pecuniary culture, the lady of the house is the chief menial of the household.

Besides servants, currently recognised as such, there is at least one other class of persons whose garb assimilates them to the class of servants and shows many of the features that go to make up the womanliness of woman's dress. This is the priestly class. Priestly vestments show, in accentuated form, all the features that have been shown to be evidence of a servile status and a vicarious life. Even more strikingly than the everyday habit of the priest, the vestments, properly so called, are ornate, grotesque, inconvenient, and, at least ostensibly, comfortless to the point of distress. The priest is at the same time expected to refrain from useful effort and, when before the public eye, to present an impassively disconsolate countenance, very much after the manner of a well-trained domestic servant. The shaven face of the priest is a further item to the same effect. This assimilation of the priestly class to the class of body servants, in demeanour and apparel, is due to the similarity of the two classes as regards economic function. In economic theory, the priest is a body servant, constructively in attendance upon the person of the divinity whose livery he wears. His livery is of a very expensive character, as it should be in order to set forth in a beseeming manner the dignity of his exalted master; but it is contrived to show that, the wearing of it contributes little or nothing to the physical comfort of the wearer, for it is an item of vicarious consumption, and the repute which accrues from its consumption is to be imputed to the absent master, not to the servant.

The line of demarcation between the dress of women, priests, and servants, on the one hand, and of men, on the other hand, is not always consistently observed in practice, but it will scarcely be disputed that it is always present in a more or less definite way in the popular habits of thought. There are of course also free men, and not a few of them, who, in their blind zeal for faultlessly reputable attire, transgress the theoretical line between man's and woman's dress, to the extent of arraying themselves in apparel that is obviously designed to vex the mortal frame; but every one recognises without hesitation that such apparel for men is a departure from the normal. We are in the habit of saying that such dress is "effeminate"; and one sometimes hears the remark that such or such an exquisitely attired gentleman is as well dressed as a footman.

Certain apparent discrepancies under this theory of dress merit a more detailed examination, especially as they mark a more or less evident trend in the later and maturer development of dress. The vogue of the corset offers an apparent exception from the rule of which it has here been cited as an illustration. A closer examination, however, will show that this apparent exception is really a verification of the rule that the vogue of any given element or feature in dress rests on its utility as an evidence of pecuniary standing. It is well known that in the industrially more advanced communities the corset is employed only within certain fairly well defined social strata. The women of the poorer classes, especially of the rural population, do not habitually use it, except as a holiday luxury. Among these classes the women have to work hard, and it avails them little in the way of a pretense of leisure to so crucify the flesh in everyday life. The holiday use of the contrivance is due to imitation of a higher-class canon of decency. Upwards from this low level of indigence and manual labour, the corset was until within a generation or two nearly indispensable to a socially blameless standing for all women, including the wealthiest and most reputable. This rule held so long as there still was no large class of people wealthy enough to be above the imputation of any necessity for manual labour and at the same time large enough to form a self-sufficient, isolated social body whose mass would afford a foundation for special rules of conduct within the class, enforced by the current opinion of the class alone. But now there has grown up a large enough leisure class possessed of such wealth that any aspersion on the score of enforced manual employment would be idle and harmless calumny; and the corset has therefore in large measure fallen into disuse within this class.

The exceptions under this rule of exemption from the corset are more apparent than real. They are the wealthy classes of countries with a lower industrial structure – nearer the archaic, quasi-industrial type – together with the later accessions of the wealthy classes in the more advanced industrial communities. The latter have not yet had time to divest themselves of the plebeian canons of taste and of reputability carried over from their former, lower pecuniary grade. Such survival of the corset is not infrequent among the higher social classes of those American cities, for instance, which have recently and rapidly risen into opulence. If the word be used as a technical term, without any odious implication, it may be said that the corset persists in great measure through the period of snobbery – the interval of uncertainty and of transition from a lower to the upper levels of pecuniary culture. That is to say, in all countries which have inherited the corset it continues in use wherever and so long as it serves its purpose as an evidence of honorific leisure by arguing physical disability in the wearer. The same rule of course applies to other mutilations and contrivances for decreasing the visible efficiency of the individual.

Something similar should hold true with respect to divers items of conspicuous consumption, and indeed something of the kind does seem to hold to a slight degree of sundry features of dress, especially if such features involve a marked discomfort or appearance of discomfort to the wearer. During the past one hundred years there is a tendency perceptible, in the development of men's dress especially, to discontinue methods of expenditure and the use of symbols of leisure which must have been irksome, which may have served a good purpose in their time, but the continuation of which among the upper classes to-day would be a work of supererogation; as, for instance, the use of powdered wigs and of gold lace, and the practice of constantly shaving the face. There has of late years been some slight recrudescence of the shaven face in polite society, but this is probably a transient and unadvised mimicry of the fashion imposed upon body servants, and it may fairly be expected to go the way of the powdered wig of our grandfathers.

These indices, and others which resemble them in point of the boldness with which they point out to all observers the habitual uselessness of those persons who employ them, have been replaced by other, more delicate methods of expressing the same fact; methods which are no less evident to the trained eyes of that smaller, select circle whose good opinion is chiefly sought. The earlier and cruder method of advertisement held its ground so long as the public to which the exhibitor had to appeal comprised large portions of the community who were not trained to detect delicate variations in the evidences of wealth and leisure. The method of advertisement undergoes a refinement when a sufficiently large wealthy class has developed, who have the leisure for acquiring skill in interpreting the subtler signs of expenditure. "Loud" dress becomes offensive to people of taste, as evincing an undue desire to reach and impress the untrained sensibilities of the vulgar. To the individual of high breeding it is only the more honorific esteem accorded by the cultivated sense of the members of his own high class that is of material consequence. Since the wealthy leisure class has grown so large, or the contact of the leisure-class individual with members of his own class has grown so wide, as to constitute a human environment sufficient for the honorific purpose, there arises a tendency to exclude the baser elements of the population from the scheme even as spectators whose applause or mortification should be sought. The result of all this is a refinement of methods, a resort to subtler contrivances, and a spiritualisation of the scheme of symbolism in dress. And as this upper leisure class sets the pace in all matters of decency, the result for the rest of society also is a gradual amelioration of the scheme of dress. As the community advances in wealth and culture, the ability to pay is put in evidence by means which require a progressively nicer discrimination in the beholder. This nicer discrimination between advertising media is in fact a very large element of the higher pecuniary culture.

NOTE

Source: *The Theory of the Leisure Class: An Economic Study of Institutions* (George Allen and Unwin, 1925), 167–87.

CHAPTER TWO

The Philosophy of Fashion

GEORG SIMMEL

Our manner of apprehending the phenomena of life causes us to feel a number of forces at every point of our existence, and in such a way that each of these forces actually strives beyond the real phenomenon, suffusing its infinity with the others and being transformed into mere tension and longing. For the human being is a dualistic creature from the very beginning, but this does not affect the unit of his or her actions; in fact, they only prove to be powerful as the result of a multiplicity of elements. A phenomenon which lacked this branching of its root forces would be impoverished and empty to us. Only if every inner energy pushes outwards beyond the measure of its visible expression does life gain that wealth of inexhaustible possibilities which enhances its fragmentary reality. Only in this manner do its phenomena give a hint of deeper forces, more unresolved tensions, struggle and peace of a more comprehensive kind than those betrayed by its immediate facticity.

This dualism cannot be described directly, but only in the individual antagonisms that are typical of our existence, and are felt to be its ultimate, structuring form. The first hint is provided by the physiological foundation of our nature: the latter requires motion as well as rest, productivity as well as receptivity. Continuing this analysis into the life of the mind, we are directed, on the one hand, by the striving for the general, as well as by the need to grasp the particular; the general provides our mind with rest, while the particular causes it to *move* from case to case. And it is no different in emotional life: we seek calm devotion to people and things just as much as energetic self-assertion against them both.

The whole history of society is reflected in the conflict, the compromise, the reconciliations, slowly won and quickly lost, that appear between adaptation to our social group and individual elevation from it. Whether the oscillation of our inner life between these two poles is expressed philosophically in the antagonism between cosmotheism and the doctrine of the inherent differentiation and separate existence of every cosmic element, or whether it is grounded in practical conflict as the partisan antagonisms between socialism and individualism, it is always one and the same fundamental form of duality which is finally manifested biologically in the contrast between heredity and variation. The former of these represents the idea of generality, of uniformity, of inactive similarity of the forms and contents of life; the latter stands for motion, for the differentiation of separate elements producing the restless development of one individual aspect of life into another. Within its own sphere, every essential form of life in the history of our species represents a unique way of unifying the interest in duration, unity and equality, and similarity with that in change, particularity and uniqueness.

Within the social embodiment of these oppositions, one side is usually maintained by the psychological tendency towards *imitation*. Imitation could be characterized as a psychological inheritance, as the transition of group life into individual life. Its attraction is first of all that it also permits purposive and meaningful action even where nothing personal or creative is in evidence. We might define it as the child of thought and thoughtlessness. Imitation gives the individual the assurance of not standing alone in his or her actions. Instead, it elevates itself over the previous practice of that activity as if on a solid foundation, which now relieves the present practice of it from the difficulty of maintaining itself. Whenever we imitate, we transfer not only the demand for creative activity, but also the responsibility for the action from ourselves to another. Thus the individual is freed from choosing and appears simply as a creature of the group, as a vessel of social contents. The drive to imitate as a principle characterizes a level of development upon which the wish for purposive personal activity is alive, but the ability to gain individual contents from it is not yet present. The progress we have made beyond this level is that thinking, action and feeling are no longer determined only by what exists, by the past and by tradition, but also by the *future*: the teleological human being is the opposite of the imitative one.

Thus we see that imitation in all the instances where it is a constitutive factor, represents *one* of the fundamental directions of our nature, namely, that which contents itself with the absorption of the individual into the general, and emphasizes the permanent element in change. Conversely, wherever change is sought in permanence, wherever individual differentiation and self-elevation above generality are sought, imitation is here the negating and restraining principle. And precisely because the longing to abide by that which is given, to act and be like others, is the irreconcilable enemy of those striving to advance to new and individual forms of life, social life appears to be the battleground upon which every inch is stubbornly contested by both sides, and social institutions may be seen as the – never permanent – reconciliations, in which the continuing antagonism of both principles has taken on the external form of cooperation.

The vital life conditions of fashion as a universal phenomenon in the history of our species are circumscribed by these factors. Fashion is the imitation of a given pattern and thus satisfies the need for social adaptation; it leads the individual onto the path that everyone travels, it furnishes a general condition that resolves the conduct of every individual into a mere example. At the same time, and to no less a degree, it satisfies the need for distinction, the tendency towards differentiation, change and individual contrast. It accomplishes the latter, on the one hand, by the change in contents – which gives to the fashions of today an individual stamp compared with those of yesterday and of tomorrow – and even more energetically, on the other hand, by the fact that fashions are always class fashions, by the fact that the fashions of the higher strata of society distinguish themselves from those of the lower strata, and are abandoned by the former at the moment when the latter begin to appropriate them. Hence fashion is nothing more than a particular instance among the many forms of life by the aid of which we seek to combine in a unified act the tendency towards social equalization with the desire for individual differentiation and variation. If we were to study the history of fashions – which hitherto have been examined only from the viewpoint of the development of their *contents* – with regard to their significance for the form of the social process, then we would find that it is the history of attempts to adjust the satisfaction of these two opposing tendencies more and more perfectly to the conditions of the prevailing individual and social culture. The individual psychological traits that we observe in fashion all conform to this basic essence of fashion.

Fashion is, as I have said, a product of class division and operates – like a number of other forms, honour especially – the double function of holding a given social circle together and at the same time closing it off from others. Just as the frame of a picture characterizes the work of art inwardly as a coherent, homogeneous, independent entity and, at the same time, outwardly severs all direct relations with the surrounding space; just as the uniform energy of such forms cannot be expressed unless we analyse the double effect, both inwards and outwards, so honour owes its character and above all its moral rights for us – rights, however, that are frequently considered to be unjust from the standpoint of those standing outside a social class – to the fact that the individual, in his or her personal honour, at the same time represents and maintains that of their social circle and their class. Thus, on the one hand, fashion signifies a union with those of the same status, the uniformity of a social circle characterized by it, and, in so doing, the closure of this group against those standing in a lower position which the higher group characterizes as not belonging to it.

Connection and differentiation are the two fundamental functions which are here inseparably united, of which one of the two, although or because it forms a logical contrast to the other, becomes the condition of its realization. That fashion is such a product of social needs is perhaps demonstrated by nothing stronger than the fact that, in countless instances, not the slightest reason can be found for its creations from the standpoint of an objective, aesthetic or other expediency. Whereas in general our clothing, for instance, is objectively adapted to our needs, there is not a trace of expediency in the method by which fashion dictates, for example, whether wide or narrow skirts, short or long hair styles, or coloured or black ties should be worn. Judging from the ugly and repugnant things that are sometimes modern, it would seem as though fashion were desirous of exhibiting its power by getting us to adopt the most atrocious things for its sake alone. The complete indifference of fashion to the material standards of life is illustrated by the arbitrary manner in which it recommends something appropriate in one instance, something abstruse in another, and something materially and aesthetically quite indifferent in a third. This indicates that fashion is concerned with other motivations, namely solely with formal social ones. Of course, it may occasionally adopt objectively justified elements but, as fashion, it is only effective when its independence from any other motivation becomes positively palpable, just as our dutiful action is only considered completely moral when we are not motivated by its external content and goal, but solely by the fact that it simply is our duty. This is the reason why the domination of fashion is most unbearable in those areas which ought to be subject only to objective decisions: religiosity, scientific interests, and even socialism and individualism have all been the subject of fashions. But the motives which alone should lead to the adoption of these contents of life stand in absolute opposition to the complete lack of objectivity in the developments of fashion.

If the social forms, the clothes, the aesthetic judgements, the whole style in which human beings express themselves are conceived in the constant transformation through fashion, so fashion – that is, the latest fashion – in all these things affects only the upper strata. Just as soon as the lower strata begin to appropriate their style – and thereby overstep the demarcation line which the upper strata have drawn and destroy the uniformity of their coherence symbolized in this fashion – so the upper strata turn away from this fashion and adopt a new one, which in its turn differentiates them from the broad masses. And thus the game goes merrily on. Naturally, the lower strata look and strive towards the upper, and they encounter the least resistance in those fields which are subject to the whims of fashion, because it is here that mere external imitation is most readily accessible. The same process is at work – although not always as visible here as it is, for example, between mistress and maid – between the different strata within the upper classes. Indeed, we may often observe that the more closely one stratum has approached the other, the more frantic becomes the hunt for imitation from below and the flight towards novelty above. The prevalence of the money economy is bound to hasten this process considerably and render it visible, because the objects of fashion, embracing as they do the externalities of life, are particularly accessible to the mere possession of money, and therefore through these externalities conformity to the higher stratum is more easily acquired here than in fields which demand an individual proof of worthiness that money cannot secure.

The extent to which this element of demarcation – alongside the element of imitation – forms the essence of fashion is especially apparent wherever the social structure does not possess any layered hierarchy of social strata, in which case fashion asserts itself in neighbouring strata. Among some primitive peoples it is reported that closely connected groups living under exactly similar conditions sometimes develop sharply differentiated fashions, by means of which each group establishes uniformity within itself, as well as differentiation from outsiders. On the other hand, there exists a widespread predilection for importing fashions from outside, and such foreign fashions assume a greater value within a particular social circle, simply because they did not originate there. Even the prophet Zephaniah expressed his indignation at the aristocrats in foreign clothing. As a matter of fact, the exotic advantage of fashions seems to favour especially strongly the exclusiveness of the groups which adopt them. Precisely because of their external origin, these imported fashions create a special and significant form of socialization, which arises through the mutual relationship to a point located outside the circle. It sometimes appears as though social elements, just like the axes of vision, converge best at a point that is not too near. Thus, among primitive peoples, money – and thus economic value itself – is the object of the most intense general interest, and often consists of objects that are brought in from outside. In some areas (on the Solomon Islands, and in Ibo on the Niger, for example) there exists a kind of industry for the production of shells, or other monetary symbols that are not employed as a medium of exchange in the place of production itself, but in neighbouring districts, to which they are exported – just as the fashions in Paris are frequently created with the sole intention of them becoming a fashion elsewhere. In Paris itself, fashion displays the greatest tension and reconciliation of its dualistic elements. Individualism, the adaptation to what is personally flattering stylewise, is much deeper than in Germany, but at the same time a certain very broad framework of general style – the current fashion – is strictly observed, so that the individual appearance never *clashes* with the general style, but always *stands out* from it.

If one of the two social tendencies essential to the establishment of fashion, namely, the need for integration on the one hand and the need for separation on the other, should be absent, then the formation of fashions will not occur and its realm will end. Consequently, the lower strata possess very few fashions and those they have are seldom specific; for this reason the fashions of primitive peoples are much more stable than ours. By virtue of their social structure, they lack that danger of mixing and blurring which spurs on the classes of civilized peoples to their differentiations of clothing, manners, taste, etc. Through these very differentiations, the sections of groups interested in separation are held together internally: the pace, tempo and rhythm of gestures is fundamentally determined by clothing and similarly dressed people behave in relatively similar ways. For modern life, with its individualist fragmentation, this is particularly valuable. And this is why fashions among primitive peoples will also be less numerous, that is more stable, because the need for the newness of impressions and forms of life – quite apart from its social effects – is much less acute among them. Changes in fashion reflect the extent of dullness of nervous impulses: the more nervous the age, the more rapidly its fashions change, simply because the need for the appeal of differentiating oneself, one of the most important elements of all fashion, goes hand in hand with the weakening of nervous energy. This fact in itself is one of the reasons why the real seat of fashion is found among the upper strata.

With regard to the purely social motives of fashion, two neighbouring primitive peoples provide very telling examples of its goals of integration and differentiation. The Kaffirs have a very rich structured and stratified social order, and although clothing and jewelry are subject to certain legal restrictions, one finds a quite rapid change of fashions among them. The bushmen, on the other hand, among whom no class formation whatsoever has occurred, have not developed any fashions at all, that is no interest has been noted among them with regard to changes in clothing and jewelry.

The same negative reasons have occasionally also prevented the formation of fashions at the heights of culture, but in a completely conscious manner. It is said that around the year 1390 in Florence there was no prevailing fashion in men's clothing because each one wished to present himself in his own special way. Thus, in this instance, one of the elements of fashion – the desire for integration – was absent, and without it there can be no fashion. On the other hand, it is reported that the Venetian *nobili* had no fashion since they were all required by a specific law to wear black, so as not to make their small numbers all too obvious to the lower strata. Here there was no fashion since the other constitutive element was missing, because differentiation from their social inferiors was to be deliberately avoided.

The essence of fashion consists in the fact that it should always be exercised by only a part of a given group, the great majority of whom are merely on the road to adopting it. As soon as a fashion has been universally adopted, that is, as soon as anything that was originally done only by a few has really come to be practised by all – as is the case in certain elements of clothing and in various forms of social conduct – we no longer characterize it as fashion. Every growth of a fashion drives it to its doom, because it thereby cancels out its distinctiveness. By reason of this play between the tendency towards universal acceptance and the destruction of its significance, to which this general adoption leads, fashion possesses the peculiar attraction of limitation, the attraction of a simultaneous beginning and end, the charm of newness and simultaneously of transitoriness. Fashion's question is not that of being, but rather it is simultaneously being and non-being; it always stands on the watershed of the past and the future and, as a result, conveys to us, at least while it is at its height, a stronger sense of the present than do most other phenomena.

If the momentary concentration of social consciousness upon the point which fashion signifies is also the one in which the seeds of its own death and its determined fate to be superceded already lie, so this transitoriness does not degrade it totally, but actually adds a new attraction to its existing ones. At all events, an object does not suffer degradation by being called 'fashionable', unless we reject it with disgust or wish to debase it for other material reasons; in which case, of course, fashion becomes a concept of value. In the practice of life, anything else that is similarly new and suddenly disseminated in the same manner will not be characterized as fashion, if we believe in its continuance and its *objective* justification. If, on the other hand, we are convinced that the phenomenon will vanish just as rapidly as it came into existence, then we call it fashion. Hence, among the reasons why now-a-days fashion exercises such a powerful influence on our consciousness there is also the fact that the major, permanent, unquestionable convictions are more and more losing their force. Consequently, the fleeting and fluctuating elements of life gain that much more free space. The break with the past which, for more than a century, civilized human kind has been labouring unceasingly to bring about, concentrates consciousness more and more upon the present. This accentuation of the present is evidently, at the same time, an emphasis upon change and to the extent to which a particular strata is the agent of this cultural tendency, so to that degree will it turn to fashion in all fields, and by no means merely with regard to clothing. Indeed, it is almost a sign of the *increased* power of fashion that it has overstepped the bounds of its original domain, which comprised only externals of dress, and has acquired an increasing influence over taste, theoretical convictions, and even the moral foundations of life in their changing forms.

From the fact that fashion as such can never be generally in vogue, the individual derives the satisfaction of knowing that, as adopted by him or her, it still represents something special and striking; while at the same time the individual feels inwardly supported by a broad group of persons who are striving for the same thing, and not, as is the case for other social satisfactions, by a group that is doing the same thing. Therefore the feelings which the fashionable person confronts are an apparently agreeable mixture of approval and envy. We envy the fashionable person as an individual, but approve of them as a member of a group. Yet even this envy here has a peculiar nuance. There is a nuance of envy which includes a sort of ideal participation in the envied objects. An instructive example of this is furnished by the conduct of the worker who is able to get a glimpse of the feasts of the rich. In so far as we envy an object or a person, we are no longer absolutely excluded from them, and between both there now exists some relation or other, and between both the same psychological content now exists, even though in entirely different categories and forms of sensation. This quiet personal usurpation of the envied property – which is also the pleasure of unrequited love – contains a kind of antidote, which occasionally counteracts the worst degenerations of the feeling of envy. The elements of fashion afford an especially good chance for the development of this more conciliatory shade of envy, which also gives to the envied person a better conscience because of his or her satisfaction with regard to their good fortune. This is due to the fact that, unlike many other psychological contents, these contents of fashion are not denied *absolutely* to anyone, because a change of fortune, which is never entirely out of the question, may play them into the hands of an individual who had previously been confined to the state of envy.

From all this we see that fashion is the genuine playground for individuals with dependent natures, but whose self-consciousness, however, at the same time requires a certain amount of prominence, attention, and singularity. Fashion elevates even the unimportant individual by making them the representative of a totality, the embodiment of a joint spirit. It is particularly characteristic of fashion – because, by its very essence, it can be a norm which is never satisfied by everyone – that it renders possible a social obedience that is at the same time a form of individual differentiation. In slaves to fashion (*Modenarren*) the social demands of fashion appear exaggerated to such a high degree that they completely acquire a semblance of individuality and particularity. It is characteristic of the slave to fashion that he carries the tendency of a particular fashion beyond the otherwise self-contained limits. If pointed shoes are in style, then he wears shoes that resemble spear tips; if pointed collars are all the rage, he wears collars that reach up to his ears; if it is fashionable to attend scholarly lectures, then he is never seen anywhere else, and so on. Thus he represents something totally individual, which consists in the quantitative intensification of such elements as are qualitatively common property of the given social circle. He leads the way, but all travel the same road. Representing as he does the most recently conquered heights of public taste, he seems to be marching at the head of the general process. In reality, however, what is so frequently true of the relation between individuals and groups also applies to him: that actually, the leader is the one who is led.

Democratic times obviously favour such a condition to a remarkable degree, so much so that even Bismarck and other very prominent party leaders of constitutional governments have emphasized the fact that, in as much as they are leaders of a group, they are bound to follow it. Such times cause persons to seek dignity and the sensation of command in this manner; they favour a confusion and ambiguity of sensations, which fail to distinguish between ruling the mass and being ruled by it. The conceit of the slave to fashion is thus the caricature of a democratically fostered constellation of the relations between the individual and the totality. Undeniably, however, the hero of fashion, through the conspicuousness gained in a purely quantitative way, but clothed in a difference of quality, represents a genuinely original state of equilibrium between the social and the individualizing impulses. This enables us to understand the outwardly so abstruse devotion to fashion of otherwise quite intelligent and broad-minded persons. It furnishes them with a combination of relations to things and human beings that, under ordinary circumstances, tend to appear separately. What is at work here is not only the mixture of individual distinctiveness and social equality, but more practically, as it were, it is the mingling of the sensation of domination and subordination. Or, formulated differently, we have here the mixing of a male and a female principle. The very fact that this mixing process only occurs in the sphere of fashion as in an ideal dilution that, as it were, only realizes the form of both elements in a content that is in itself indifferent, may lend a special attraction to fashion, especially for sensitive natures that do not care to concern themselves with robust reality. From an objective standpoint, life according to fashion consists of a mixture of destruction and construction; its content acquires its characteristics by destruction of an earlier form; it possesses a peculiar uniformity, in which the satisfaction of the destructive impulse and the drive for positive elements can no longer be separated from each other.

Because we are dealing here not with the significance of a single content or a single satisfaction, but rather with the play between both contents and their mutual distinction, it becomes evident that the same combination which extreme obedience to fashion acquires can also be won by opposition to it. Whoever consciously clothes or deports themselves in an unmodern manner does not attain the consequent sensation of individualization through any real individual qualification of his or her own, but rather through the mere negation of the social example. If modernity is the imitation of this social example, then the deliberate lack of modernity represents a similar imitation, yet under an inverted sign, but nonetheless one which offers no less a testimony of the power of the social tendency, which makes us dependent upon it in some positive or negative manner. The deliberately unmodern person accepts its forms just as much as does the slave to fashion, except that the unmodern person embodies it in another category: in that of negation, rather than in exaggeration.

Indeed, it occasionally becomes decidedly fashionable in whole circles of a large-scale society to clothes oneself in an unmodern manner. This constitutes one of the most curious social–psychological complications, in which the drive for individual conspicuousness primarily remains content, first, with a mere inversion of social imitation and, secondly, for its part draws its strength again from approximation to a similarly characterized narrow circle. If a club or association of club-haters were founded, then it would not be logically more impossible and psychologically more possible than the above phenomenon. Just as atheism has been made into a religion, embodying the same fanaticism, the same intolerance, the same satisfaction of emotional needs that are embraced in religion proper; and just as freedom too, by means of which a tyranny has been broken, often becomes no less tyrannical and violent; so this phenomenon of tendentious lack of modernity illustrates how ready the fundamental forms of human nature are to accept the total antithesis of contents in themselves and to show their strength and their attraction in the negation of the very thing to whose acceptance they still seemed a moment earlier to be irrevocably committed. Thus, it is often absolutely impossible to tell whether the elements of personal strength or of personal weakness have the upper hand in the complex of causes of such lack of modernity. It may result from the need not to make common cause with the crowd, a need that has as its basis, of course, not in independence from the crowd, but rather in an inner sovereign stance with respect to the latter. However, it may also be due to a weak sensibility, which causes individuals to fear that they will be unable to maintain their little piece of individuality if they adopt the forms, tastes and customs of the general public. Such opposition to the latter is by no means always a sign of personal strength. On the contrary, personal strength will be so conscious of its unique value, which is immune to any external connivance, that it will be able to submit without any unease to general forms up to and including fashion. Rather, it is precisely in this obedience that it will become conscious of the *voluntariness* of its obedience and of that which transcends obedience.

If fashion both gives expression to the impulse towards equalization and individualization, as well as to the allure of imitation and conspicuousness, this perhaps explains why it is that women, broadly speaking, adhere especially strongly to fashion.

Out of the weakness of the social position to which women were condemned throughout the greatest part of history there arises their close relationship to all that is 'custom',
to that which is 'right and proper', to the generally valid and approved form of existence. For those who are weak steer clear of individualization; they avoid dependence
upon the self, with its responsibilties and the necessity of defending oneself unaided.
Those in a weak position find protection only in the typical form of life, which prevents the strong person from exercising his exceptional powers. But resting on the firm
foundation of custom, of the average, of the general level, women strive strongly for
all the relative individualization and general conspicuousness that thus remains possible. Fashion offers them this very combination to the most favourable extent, for we
have here, on the one hand, a sphere of general imitation, the individual floating in
the broadest social current, relieved of responsibility for their tastes and their actions,
and yet, on the other hand, we have a certain conspicuousness, an individual emphasis, an individual ornamentation of the personality.

It seems that there exists for each class of human beings, indeed probably for each
individual, a definite quantitative relationship between the impulse towards individualization and the drive for immersion in the collectivity, so that if the satisfaction
of one of these drives is denied in a certain field of life, it seeks another, in which it
then fulfils the amount that it requires. Thus, it seems as though fashion were the
valve, as it were, through which women's need for some measure of conspicuousness
and individual prominence finds vent, when its satisfaction is more often denied in
other spheres.

During the fourteenth and fifteenth centuries, Germany displayed an extraordinarily
strong development of individuality. To a great extent, the collectivistic regulations of
the Middle Ages were breached by the freedom of the individual person. Within this
individualistic development, however, women still found no place and the freedom of
personal movement and self-improvement was still denied them. They compensated for
this by adopting the most extravagant and exaggerated fashions in dress. Conversely,
we see that in Italy during the same epoch, women were given free play for individual
development. The women of the Renaissance possessed extensive opportunities for culture, external activity, and personal differentiation such as were not offered to them
again for many centuries. In the upper classes of society, especially, education and freedom of expression were almost identical for both sexes. Yet it is also reported that
no particularly extravagant Italian female fashions emerged from that period. The
need to exercise individuality and gain a kind of distinction in this sphere was absent,
because the impulse embodied therein found sufficient satisfaction in other spheres.
In general, the history of women in their outer as well as their inner life, in the individual aspect as well as in their collectivity, exhibits such a comparatively great
uniformity, levelling and similarity, that they require a more lively activity at least in
the sphere of fashions, which is nothing more nor less than variety, in order to add an
attraction to themselves and their lives – for their own feeling as well as for others.

   Just as in the case of individualism and collectivism, so there exists between the
uniformity and the variety of the contents of life a definite proportion of needs, which
is tossed to and fro in the different spheres and seeks to balance the refusal in the one
by consent, however acquired, in the other. On the whole, we may say that the woman,
compared to the man, is a more faithful creature. Now fidelity, expressing the uniformity and regularity of one's nature only according to the side of one's feelings, demands
a more lively change in the outward surrounding spheres in order to establish the
balance in the tendencies of life. The man, on the other hand, who in his essence is
less faithful and who does not ordinarily maintain an emotional relationship that
he has entered into with the same absoluteness and concentration of all his vital
interests, is consequently in less need of external variation. Indeed, the lack of acceptance of changes in external fields, the indifference towards fashions in outward appearance are specifically a male quality, not because a man is more uniform, but
because he is the more many-sided creature, and for that reason, can exist without external changes. Therefore the emancipated woman of the present, who seeks to approach towards the whole differentiation, personality and activity of the male sex, lays
particular stress on her indifference to fashion. In a certain sense, fashion also gives
women a compensation for their lack of social position in a professional group. The
man who has become absorbed in a vocation has thereby entered into a relatively uniform social circle, in which he resembles many others within this stratum, and is thus
often only an exemplar of the concept of this stratum or occupation. On the other
hand, and as if to compensate him for this absorption, he is invested with the full
importance and the objective as well as the social power of this stratum. To his individual importance is added that of his stratum, which often can cover over the defects
and deficiencies of purely personal existence.
   Fashion accomplishes this identical process by other means. Fashion too supple-
ments a person's lack of importance, their inability to individualize their existence
purely by their own unaided efforts, by enabling them to join a group characterized
and singled out in the public consciousness by fashion alone. Here too, to be sure,
the personality as such is adapted to a general formula, yet this formula itself, from a
social standpoint, possesses an individual colouring, and this makes up by a socially
roundabout way for precisely what is denied to the personality in a purely individual
way. The fact that the *demi-monde* is so frequently the pioneer of new fashion is due
to its distinctively uprooted form of life. The pariah existence to which society condemns the *demi-monde* produces an open or latent hatred against everything that has
the sanction of law, against every permanent institution, a hatred that still finds its
relatively most innocent expression in the striving for ever new forms of appearance.
In this continual striving for new, previously unheard-of fashions, in the ruthlessness
with which the one that is most opposed to the existing one is passionately adopted,
there lies an aesthetic form of the destructive urge that seems to be an element
peculiar to all who lead this pariah-like existence, so long as they are not inwardly
completely enslaved.

And if we seek to gaze into the final and most subtle movements of the soul, which are difficult to express in words, so we find that they too exhibit this antagonistic play of the fundamental human tendencies, which seek to regain their continually lost balance by means of ever new proportions. It is in fact fundamental to fashion that it makes no distinction at all between all individualities alike, and yet it is always done in such a way that it never affects the whole human being; indeed it always remains somewhat external to the individual – even in those spheres outside mere clothing fashions. For the form of mutability in which it is presented to the individual is under all circumstances a contrast to the stability of the sense of self, and indeed the latter must become conscious of its relative duration precisely through this contrast. The changeableness of the elements of fashion can express itself as mutability and develop its attraction only through this enduring element of the sense of self. But for this very reason fashion always stands, as I have pointed out, at the very periphery of the personality, which regards itself as a *pièce de résistance* to fashion, or at least can be experienced as such in an emergency.

It is this significant aspect of fashion that is adopted by refined and special persons, in so far as they use it as a kind of mask. They consider blind obedience to the standards of the public in all externals as the conscious and desired means of reserving their personal feelings and their taste, which they are eager to keep to themselves alone; indeed, so much to themselves that they do not care to allow their feelings and tastes to be seen in a form that is visible to all. It is therefore precisely a refined feeling of modesty and reserve which, seeking not to resort to a peculiarity in externals for fear perhaps of betraying a peculiarity of their innermost soul, causes many a delicate nature to seek refuge in the masking levelling of fashion. Thereby a triumph of the soul over the given nature of existence is achieved which, at least as far as form is concerned, must be considered one of the highest and finest victories: namely, that the enemy himself is transformed into a servant, that precisely that which seemed to violate the personality is seized voluntarily, because the levelling violation is here transferred to the external strata of life in such a way that it furnishes a veil and a protection for everything that is innermost and now all the more free. The struggle between the social and the individual is resolved here in so far as the strata for both are separated. This corresponds exactly to the triviality of expression and conversation through which very sensitive and retiring people, especially women, often deceive one about the depth of the individual soul behind these expressions.

All feeling of shame rests upon the conspicuousness of the individual. It arises whenever a stress is laid upon the self, whenever the attention of a social circle is drawn to an individual, which at the same time is felt to be in some way inappropriate. For this reason retiring and weak natures are particularly inclined to feelings of shame. The moment they step into the centre of general attention, the moment they make themselves conspicuous in any way, a painful oscillation between emphasis upon and withdrawal of the sense of the self manifests itself. In so far as this individual conspicuousness, as the source of the feeling of shame, is quite independent of the particular content on the basis of which it occurs, so one is actually frequently ashamed of good and noble things. If in society, in the narrower sense of the term, banality constitutes good form, then this is due not only to a mutual regard, which causes it to be considered bad taste to stand out through some individual, singular expression that not everyone can imitate, but also to the fear of that feeling of shame which forms a self-inflicted punishment for those departing from the form and activity that is similar for, and equally accessible to, everyone.

By reason of its distinctive inner structure, fashion furnishes a conspicuousness of the individual which is always looked upon as proper, no matter how extravagant its form of appearance or manner of expression may be; as long as it is fashionable it is protected against those unpleasant reflections which the individual otherwise experiences when he or she becomes the object of attention. All mass actions are characterized by the loss of the feeling of shame. As a member of a mass, the individual will do many things which would have aroused uncontrollable repugnance in their soul had they been suggested to them alone. It is one of the most remarkable social–psychological phenomena, in which this characteristic of mass action is well exemplified, that many fashions tolerate breaches of modesty which, if suggested to the individual alone, would be angrily repudiated. But as dictates of fashion they find a ready acceptance. The feeling of shame is eradicated in matters of fashion, because it represents a mass action, in the same way that the feeling of responsibility is extinguished in participants in mass criminality, who if left to themselves as individuals would shrink from such deeds. As soon as the individual aspects of the situation begin to predominate over its social and fashionable aspects, the sense of shame immediately commences its effectiveness: many women would be embarrassed to confront a single male stranger alone in their living room with the kind of low necklines that they wear in society, according to the dictates of fashion, in front of thirty or a hundred men.

Fashion is also only one of the forms through which human beings seek to save their inner freedom all the more completely by sacrificing externals to enslavement by the general public. Freedom and dependency also belong to those pairs of opposites, whose ever-renewed struggle and endless mobility give to life much more piquancy, and permit a much greater breadth and development than could a permanent, unchangeable balance of the two. Just as, according to Schopenhauer, to each person a certain amount of joy and sorrow is given, whose measure can neither remain empty nor be filled to overflowing, but in all the diversity and vacillations of internal and external circumstances only changes its form, so – much less mystically – we may observe in each period, in each class, and in each individual either a really permanent proportion of dependency and freedom, or at least the longing for it, whereas we can only change the fields over which they are distributed. And it is the task of the higher life, to be sure, to arrange this distribution in such a way that the other values of existence thereby acquire the most favourable development. The same quantity of dependency and freedom may help, at one time, to increase moral, intellectual and aesthetic values to the highest point and, at another time, without any change in quantity but merely in distribution, it may bring about the exact opposite result. As a whole, one could say that the most favourable result for the total value of life will be obtained when all unavoidable dependency is transferred more and more to the periphery of life, to its externalities. Perhaps Goethe, in his later period, is the most eloquent example of a wholly great life, for by means of his adaptability in all externals, his strict regard for form, his willing obedience to the conventions of society, he attained a maximum of inner freedom, a complete saving of the centres of life from the unavoidable quantity of dependency. In this respect, fashion is also a social form of marvellous expediency, because, like the law, it affects only the externals of life, and hence only those sides of life which are turned towards society. It provides human beings with a formula by means of which we can unequivocally attest our dependency upon what is generally adopted, our obedience to standards established by our time, our class, and our narrower circle, and enables us to withdraw the freedom given us in life and concentrate it more and more in our innermost and fundamental elements.

Within the individual soul these relations of equalizing unification and individual demarcation are, to a certain extent, actually repeated. The antagonism of the tendencies which produce fashion is transferred, as far as form is concerned and in an entirely similar manner, even to those inner relations of some individuals who have nothing whatever to do with social obligations. The phenomenon to which I am referring exhibits the often emphasized parallelism with which the relations between individuals are repeated in the correlation between the psychological elements of individuals themselves. More or less intentionally, the individual often establishes a mode of conduct or a style for him or herself which, by the rhythm of its rise, its sway and decline, becomes characterized as fashion. Young people especially often display a sudden singularity in their behaviour; an unexpected, objectively unfounded interest arises that governs their whole sphere of consciousness, only to disappear in the same irrational manner. We might characterize this as a personal fashion, which forms a limiting case of social fashion. The former is supported, on the one hand, by the individual demand for differentiation and thereby attests to the same impulse that is active in the formation of social fashion. The needs for imitation, similarity, and for the blending of the individual into the mass, are here satisfied purely within the individuals themselves: namely through the concentration of the personal consciousness upon this one form or content, through the uniform shading his or her nature receives from that concentration, through the imitation, as it were, of their own self, where here replaces the imitation of others.

A certain intermediate stage is often realized within close social circles between individual style and personal fashion. Ordinary persons frequently adopt some expression, which they apply at every opportunity – in common with as many others as possible in the same social circle – to all manner of suitable and unsuitable objects. In one respect this is a group fashion, yet in another it is really individual, for its express purpose consists in having the *individual* make the *totality* of his or her circle of ideas subject to this formula. Brutal violence is hereby committed against the individuality of things – all nuances are blurred by the curious supremacy of this one category of expression, for example, when we designate all things that we like for any reason whatever as 'chic', or 'smart' – even though the objects in question may bear no relation whatsoever to the fields to which these expressions belong. In this manner, the inner world of the individual is made subject to fashion, and thus repeats the form of the group dominated by fashion. And this also occurs chiefly by reason of the objective absurdity of such individual manners, which illustrate the power of the formal, unifying element over the objective, rational element. In the same way, many persons and social circles only ask that they be uniformly governed, and the question as to how qualified or valuable is this domination plays a merely secondary role. It cannot be denied that, by doing violence to objects treated in this way, and by clothing them all uniformly in a category that we apply to them, the individual exercises an authority over them, and gains an individual feeling of power, an emphasis of the self over against these objects.

The phenomenon that appears here in the form of a caricature is noticeable to lesser degrees everywhere in the relationship of people to objects. It is only the most noble human beings who find the greatest depth and power of their ego precisely in the fact that they respect the individuality inherent in things. The hostility which the soul bears to the supremacy, independence and indifference of the universe continuously gives rise, as it were – beside the loftiest and most valuable strivings of humanity – to attempts to oppress things externally. The self prevails against them not by absorbing and moulding their powers, not by recognizing their individuality in order to make them serviceable, but by forcing them outwardly to subjugate themselves to some subjective formula. To be sure, in reality the self has not gained control of the things themselves, but only of its own falsified fantasy image of them. However, the feeling of power, which originates from this, reveals its lack of foundation and its illusory nature by the rapidity with which such expressions of fashions pass away. It is just as illusory as the feeling of the uniformity of being, that springs for the moment out of this schematization of all expressions.

We have seen that in fashion, as it were, the different dimensions of life acquire a peculiar convergence, that fashion is a complex structure in which all the leading antithetical tendencies of the soul in one way or another are represented. This makes it abundantly clear that the total rhythm in which individuals and groups move will also exert an important influence upon their relationships to fashion; that the various strata of a group, quite aside from their different contents of life and external possibilities, will exhibit different relationships to fashion simply because their contents of life are evolved either in a conservative or in a rapidly varying form. On the one hand, the lower masses are difficult to set in motion and are slow to develop. On the other hand, it is the highest strata, as everyone knows, who are the most conservative, and who are frequently enough quite archaic. They frequently dread every movement and transformation, not because they have an antipathy to the contents or because the

latter are injurious to them, but simply because it is transformation as such and because they regard every modification of the whole, which after all provides them with
the highest position, as suspicious and dangerous. No change can bring to them any additional power; at most they have something to fear from each change, but nothing
more to hope for from any transformation.

The real variability of historical life is therefore vested in the middle classes and, for
this reason, the history of social and cultural movements has taken on an entirely different pace since the *tiers état* assumed power. This is why fashion, itself the changing
and contrasting form of life, has since then become much broader and more animated.
This is also because of the transformations in immediate political life, for people
require an ephemeral tyrant the moment they have rid themselves of an absolute and
permanent one. The frequent changes in fashion constitute a tremendous subjugation
of the individual and in that respect form one of the necessary complements to increased social and political freedom. A class which is inherently so much more variable, so much more restless in its rhythms than the lowest classes with their silently
unconscious conservatism, and the highest classes with their consciously desired conservatism, is the totally appropriate location for a form of life in which the moment
of an element's triumph marks the beginning of its decline. Classes and individuals
who demand constant change – because precisely the rapidity of their development
secures them an advantage over others – find in fashion something that keeps pace
with their own inner impulses. And social advancement must be directly favourable to
the rapid advance of fashion, because it equips the lower strata so much more quickly
to imitate the upper strata and thus the process characterized above – according to
which every higher stratum throws aside a fashion the moment a lower one adopts it –
acquires a breadth and vitality never dreamed of before.

This fact has an important bearing upon the content of fashion. Above all, it creates
a situation in which fashions can no longer be so expensive and, therefore, obviously
can no longer be so extravagant as they were in earlier times, where there was a compensation in the form of the longer duration of their domination for the costliness of the
first acquisition or the difficulties in transforming conduct and taste. The more an article
becomes subject to rapid changes of fashion, the greater the demand for *cheap* products
of its kind. This is not only because the larger and therefore poorer classes nevertheless
have enough purchasing power to regulate industry and demand objects which at
least bear the outward and precarious semblance of modernity, but rather also because even the higher strata of society could not afford to adopt the rapid changes in
fashion forced upon them by the pressure of the lower classes if its objects were not
relatively cheap. The speed of development is of such importance in genuine articles of
fashions that it even withdraws them from certain economic advances that have been
won gradually in other fields. It has been noticed, especially in the older branches of
production in modern industry, that the speculative element gradually ceases to play
an influential role. The movements of the market can be better observed, requirements
can be better foreseen and production can be more accurately regulated than before,

so that the rationalization of production makes greater and greater inroads upon the fortuitousness of market opportunities and upon the unplanned fluctuations of supply and demand. Only pure articles of fashion seem to be excluded from this. The polar fluctuations, which in many cases the modern economy knows how to avoid and from which it is visibly striving towards entirely new economic orders and formations, still predominate in the fields immediately subject to fashion. The form of feverish change is so essential here that fashion stands, as it were, in a logical contradiction to the developmental tendencies of modern societies.

In contrast to this characteristic, however, fashion possesses the quite remarkable quality that each individual fashion to a certain extent makes its appearance as though it wished to live forever. Whoever purchases furniture today that should last a quarter of a century, countless times purchases according to the newest fashion and no longer considers articles that were in vogue even two years earlier. Yet is evident that, after a couple of years, the attraction of fashion will desert the present article in precisely the same way as it left the earlier one, and satisfaction or dissatisfaction with both forms will then be determined by other, objective criteria. A distinctive psychological process seems to be at work here, in addition to the mere bias of the moment. A fashion always exists and it is therefore, as a general concept, as a fact of fashion as such, indeed immortal; and this seems to reflect in some manner or other upon each of its manifestations, although the essence of each individual fashion is precisely that of *not* being immortal. In this instance, the fact that change itself does not change endows each of the objects which it affects with a psychological shimmer of permanency.

This permanency within change is actually realized in the individual contents of fashion in the following distinctive manner. Fashion, to be sure, is concerned only with change, yet like all phenomena it has the tendency to conserve energy; it endeavours to attain its objects as completely as possible, but nevertheless with the relatively most economical means. For this very reason, fashion repeatedly returns to old forms – as is illustrated particularly in the fashion for clothes – so that the course of fashion has been likened to that of a cyclical course. As soon as an earlier fashion has been partially expunged from memory there is no reason why it should not be allowed to return to favour and why the charm of difference, which constitutes its very essence, should not be exercised against that very fashion which derived its attraction when it came onto the scene from its contrast to the style now being revived.

In all events, the power of the form of motion from which fashion lives is not strong enough to dominate every content uniformly. Even in the spheres governed by fashion, all forms are not equally suited to become fashion, for the peculiar character of many of them furnishes a certain resistance. This may be compared with the unequal relation that the objects of external perception bear to the possibility of their being transformed into works of art. It is a very tempting, but hardly a profound or tenable view, that every object of reality is equally suited to become the object of a work of art. The forms of art, as they have developed historically – determined by a thousand fortuitous events, frequently one-sided and affected by technical perfections and imperfections – are by no means equally elevated above all the contents of reality. On the contrary, the forms of art possess a closer relationship to some of these contents than they do to others. Some of these contents assume artistic form without apparent effort, as though nature had created them for that very purpose, while others, as though wilful and created differently by nature, avoid all transformation into the given forms of art. The sovereignty of art over reality by no means implies, as naturalism and many theories of idealism so steadfastly maintain, the ability to draw all the contents of existence uniformly into its sphere. None of the formations with which the human mind masters the material of existence and adapts it to its purpose is so general and neutral that all objects, indifferent to their own structure, should uniformly conform to it.

Thus fashion can absorb to all appearances and *in abstracto* any chosen content: any given form of clothing, art, conduct, or opinion can become fashionable. And yet there lies within the inner essence of some forms a special disposition to live themselves out as fashion, just as others put up an inward resistance. Thus, for example, everything that may be termed 'classic' is comparatively far removed from fashion and alien to it, although occasionally, of course, the classic also falls under the sway of fashion. For the essence of the classical is a concentration of appearance around a sublime middle point; the classical possesses something collective, which does not offer so many points of attack, as it were, from which modification, disturbance and destruction of the balance might emanate. What is characteristic of classical sculpture is the total concentration of the limbs: the whole is absolutely governed from within the spirit and the feeling of life governing the whole uniformly embraces every part, because of the visible unity of the object. That is the reason why we speak of the 'classical repose' of Greek art. It is due exclusively to the concentration of the object, which permits no part to bear any relation to any extraneous powers and fortunes, and thereby incites the feeling that this formation is exempt from the changing influences of general life. In contrast to this, everything eccentric, immoderate and extreme will be drawn to fashion from within: fashion does not take hold of things characterized in this way as an external fate, but rather, as it were, as the historical expression of their objective peculiarities. The widely projecting limbs of the Baroque statue are, as it were, always in perpetual danger of being broken off, since the inner life of the figure does not exercise complete control over them, but lays them open to the fortuitous elements of external life. Baroque forms already possess within themselves the unrest, the character of fortuitousness, the subjugation to the momentary impulse which fashion realizes as a form of social life. An additional factor confronts us here: namely, that we soon grow tired of eccentric, bizarre or fanciful forms and thus, from a purely psychological standpoint, long for the change that fashion outlines for us. Here too lies one of the deep relationships between the classical and the 'natural' composition of things that people have claimed to discover. No matter how weakly delimited and erroneous in general the concept of the 'natural' may often be, one can at least make the negative statement that certain forms, tendencies and viewpoints have *no* claim to this title, and that these are the very ones that succumb especially quickly to the change of fashions, precisely because they lack a relation to the abiding centre of things and life which would justify their claim to a lasting existence. Thus, Elizabeth Charlotte of the Palatinate, a sister-in-law of Louis XIV, who was an exceedingly masculine personality, inspired the fashion at the French court of women deporting themselves like men and being addressed as such, while men conducted themselves as women. It is self-evident that such behaviour can only become a fashion, because it is so far removed from the inalienable substance of human relations to which the form of life will eventually and, in some way or other have to return. Just as little as we can say that all fashion is somewhat unnatural – not least because fashion as a form of life is itself natural to the human being as a social being – so conversely one can indeed say of the absolutely unnatural that it can at least exist in the form of *fashion*.

To sum up the whole issue, the peculiarly piquant and stimulating attraction of fashion lies in the contrast between its extensive, all-embracing distribution and its rapid and complete transitoriness, in the right to be unfaithful to it. Furthermore, the charm of fashion lies no less in the tightness with which it draws a given social circle together – the intimate connection of which it expresses as both cause and effect – than it does upon the decisiveness with which it separates the given social circle from others. Finally, the appeal of fashion also lies in its being supported by a social circle, which demands mutual imitation from its members and thereby releases the individual from all responsibility – both ethical and aesthetic – as well as in the possibility of producing within these original nuances, whether it be through exaggeration or even through rejection, the elements of fashion. Thus fashion reveals itself to be only a single, particularly characteristic example among those manifold structures in which social expediency has objectivized the antagonistic tendencies of life on equal terms.

NOTE

Source: *Simmel on Culture* David Frisby and Mike Featherstone (eds) (SAGE Publications, 1997), 187–206.

Adornment

Man's desire to please his social environment contains two contradictory tendencies, in whose play and counterplay in general, the relations among individuals take their course. On the one hand, it contains kindness, a desire of the individual to give the other joy; but on the other hand, there is the wish for this joy and these 'favours' to flow back to him, in the form of recognition and esteem, so that they be attributed to his personality as values. Indeed, this second need is so intensified that it militates against the altruism of wishing to please: by means of this pleasing, the individual desires to *distinguish* himself before others, and to be the object of an attention that others do not receive. This may even lead him to the point of wanting to be envied. Pleasing may thus become a means of the will to power: some individuals exhibit the strange contradiction that they need those above whom they elevate themselves by life and deed, for they build their own self-feeling upon the subordinates' realization that they *are* subordinate.

The meaning of adornment finds expression in peculiar elaborations of these motives, in which the external and internal aspects of their forms are interwoven. This meaning is to single the personality out, to emphasize it as outstanding in some sense – but not by means of power manifestations, not by anything that externally compels the other, but only through the pleasure which is engendered in him and which, therefore, still has some voluntary element in it. One adorns oneself for oneself, but can do so only by adornment for others. It is one of the strangest sociological combinations that an act, which exclusively serves the emphasis and increased significance of the actor, nevertheless attains this goal just as exclusively in the pleasure, in the visual delight it offers to others, and in their gratitude. For, even the envy of adornment only indicates the desire of the envious person to win like recognition and admiration for himself; his envy proves how much he believes these values to be connected with the adornment. Adornment is the egoistic element as such: it singles out its wearer, whose self-feeling it embodies and increases at the cost of others (for, the same adornment of all would no longer adorn the individual). But, at the same time, adornment is altruistic: its pleasure is designed for the others, since its owner can enjoy it only in so far as he mirrors himself in them; he renders the adornment valuable only through the reflection of this gift of his. Everywhere, aesthetic formation reveals that life orientations, which reality juxtaposes as mutually alien, or even pits against one another as hostile, are, in fact, intimately interrelated. In the same way, the aesthetic phenomenon of adornment indicates a point within sociological interaction – the arena of man's being-for-himself and being-for-the-other – where these two opposite directions are mutually dependent as ends and means.

Adornment intensifies or enlarges the impression of the personality by operating as a sort of radiation emanating from it. For this reason, its materials have always been shining metals and precious stones. They are 'adornment' in a narrower sense than dress and coiffure, although these, too, 'adorn'. One may speak of human radioactivity in the sense that every individual is surrounded by a larger or smaller sphere of significance radiating from him; and everybody else, who deals with him, is immersed in this sphere. It is an inextricable mixture of physiological and psychic elements: the sensuously observable influences which issue from an individual in the direction of his environment also are, in some fashion, the vehicles of a spiritual fulguration. They operate as the symbols of such a fulguration even where, in actuality, they are only external, where no suggestive power or significance of the personality flows through them. The radiations of adornment, the sensuous attention it provokes, supply the personality with such an enlargement or intensification of its sphere: the personality, so to speak, *is* more when it is adorned.

Inasmuch as adornment usually is also an object of considerable value, it is a synthesis of the individual's having and being; it thus transforms mere possession into the sensuous and emphatic perceivability of the individual himself. This is not true of ordinary dress which, neither in respect of having nor of being, strikes one as an individual particularity; only the fancy dress, and above all, jewels, which gather the personality's value and significance of radiation as if in a focal point, allow the mere *having* of the person to become a visible quality of its *being*. And this is so, not *although* adornment is something 'superfluous', but precisely *because* it is. The necessary is much more closely connected with the individual; it surrounds his existence with a narrower periphery. The superfluous 'flows over', that is, it flows to points which are far removed from its origin but to which it still remains tied: around the precinct of mere necessity, it lays a vaster precinct which, in principle, is limitless. According to its very idea, the superfluous contains no measure. The free and princely character of our being increases in the measure in which we add superfluousness to our having, since no extant structure, such as is laid down by necessity, imposes any limiting norm upon it.

This very accentuation of the personality, however, is achieved by means of an impersonal trait. Everything that 'adorns' man can be ordered along a scale in terms of its closeness to the physical body. The 'closest' adornment is typical of primitive peoples: tattooing. The opposite extreme is represented by metal and stone adornments, which are entirely unindividual and can be put on by everybody. Between these two stands dress, which is not so inexchangeable and personal as tattooing, but neither so unindividual and separable as jewelry, whose very elegance lies in its impersonality. That this nature of stone and metal – solidly closed within itself, in no way alluding to any individuality; hard, unmodifiable – is yet forced to serve the person, this is its subtlest fascination. What is really elegant avoids pointing to the specifically individual; it always lays a more general, stylized, almost abstract sphere around man – which, of course, prevents no finesse from connecting the general with the personality. That new clothes are particularly elegant is due to their being still 'stiff'; they have not yet adjusted to the modifications of the individual body as fully as older clothes have, which have been worn, and are pulled and pinched by the peculiar movements of their wearer – thus completely revealing his particularity. This 'newness', this lack of modification by individuality, is typical in the highest measure of metal jewelry: it is always new; in untouchable coolness, it stands above the singularity and destiny of its wearer. This is not true of dress. A long-worn piece of clothing almost grows to the body; it has an intimacy that militates against the very nature of elegance, which is something for the 'others', a social notion deriving its value from general respect.

If jewelry thus is designed to enlarge the individual by adding something supraindividual which goes out to all and is noted and appreciated by all, it must, beyond any effect that its material itself may have, possess *style*. Style is always something general. It brings the contents of personal life and activity into a form shared by many and accessible to many. In the case of a work of art, we are the less interested in its style, the greater the personal uniqueness and the subjective life expressed in it. For, it is with these that it appeals to the spectator's personal core, too – of the spectator who, so to speak, is alone in the whole world with this work of art. But of what we call handicraft – which because of its utilitarian purpose appeals to a diversity of men – we request a more general and typical articulation. We expect not only that an individuality with its uniqueness be voiced in it, but a broad, historical or social orientation and temper, which make it possible for handicraft to be incorporated into the life systems of a great many different individuals. It is the greatest mistake to think that, because it always functions as the adornment of an individual, adornment must be an individual work of art. Quite the contrary: *because* it is to serve the individual, it may not itself be of an individual nature – as little as the piece of furniture on which we sit, or the eating utensil which we manipulate, may be individual works of art. The work of art cannot, in principle, be incorporated into another life – it is a self-sufficient world. By contrast, all that occupies the larger sphere around the life of the individual, must surround it as if in ever wider concentric spheres that lead back to the individual or originate from him. The essence of stylization is precisely this dilution of individual poignancy, this generalization beyond the uniqueness of the personality – which, nevertheless, in its capacity of base or circle of radiation, carries or absorbs the individuality as if in a broadly flowing river. For this reason, adornment has always instinctively been shaped in a relatively severe style.

Besides its formal stylization, the *material* means of its social purpose is its *brilliance*. By virtue of this brilliance, its wearer appears as the centre of a circle of radiation in which every close-by person, every seeing eye, is caught. As the flash of the precious stone seems to be directed at the other – like the lightning of the glance the eye addresses to him – it carries the social meaning of jewels, the being-for-the-other, which returns to the subject as the enlargement of his own sphere of significance. The radii of this sphere mark the distance which jewelry creates between men – 'I have something which you do not have'. But, on the other hand, these radii not only let the other participate: they shine in *his* direction; in fact, they exist only for his sake. By virtue of their material, jewels signify, in one and the same act, an increase in distance and a favour.

For this reason, they are of such particular service to vanity – which needs others in order to despise them. This suggests the profound difference which exists between vanity and haughty pride: pride, whose self-consciousness really rests only upon itself, ordinarily disdains 'adornment' in every sense of the word. A word must also be added here, to the same effect, on the significance of 'genuine' material. The attraction of the 'genuine', in all contexts, consists in its being more than its immediate appearance, which it shares with its imitation. Unlike its falsification, it is not something isolated; it has its roots in a soil that lies beyond its mere appearance, while the unauthentic is only what it can be taken for at the moment. The 'genuine' individual, thus, is the person on whom one can rely even when he is out of one's sight. In the case of jewelry, this more-than-appearance is its *value*, which cannot be guessed by being looked at, but is something that, in contrast to skilled forgery, is *added* to the appearance. By virtue of the fact that this value can always be realized, that it is recognized by all, that it possesses a relative timelessness, jewelry becomes part of a supra-contingent, supra-personal value structure. Talmi-gold and similar trinkets are identical with what they momentarily *do* for their wearer; genuine jewels are a value that goes beyond this; they have their roots in the value ideas of the whole social circle and are ramified through all of it. Thus, the charm and the accent they give the individual who wears them, feed on this supra-individual soil. Their genuineness makes their aesthetic value – which, too, is here a value 'for the others' – a symbol of general esteem, and of membership in the total social value system.

There once existed a decree in medieval France which prohibited all persons below a certain rank to wear gold ornaments. The combination which characterizes the whole nature of adornment unmistakably lives in this decree: in adornment, the sociological and aesthetic emphasis upon the personality fuses as if in a focus; being-for-oneself and being-for-others become reciprocal cause and effect in it. Aesthetic excellence and the right to charm and please, are allowed, in this decree, to go only to a point fixed by the individual's social sphere of significance. It is precisely in this fashion that one adds, to the charm which adornment gives one's whole appearance, the *sociological* charm of being, by virtue of adornment, a representative of one's group, with whose whole significance one is 'adorned'. It is as if the significance of his status, symbolized by jewels, returned to the individual on the very beams which originate in him and enlarge his sphere of impact. Adornment, thus, appears as the means by which his social power or dignity is transformed into visible, personal excellence.

Centripetal and centrifugal tendencies, finally, appear to be fused in adornment in a specific form, in the following information. Among primitive peoples, it is reported, women's private property generally develops later than that of men and, originally, and often exclusively, refers to adornment. By contrast, the personal property of the male usually begins with weapons. This reveals his active and more aggressive nature: the male enlarges his personality sphere without waiting for the will of others. In the case of the more passive female nature this result – although formally the same in spite of all external differences – depends more on the others' good will. Every property is an extension of personality; property is that which obeys our wills, that in which our egos express, and externally realize, themselves. This expression occurs, earliest and most completely, in regard to our body, which thus is our first and most unconditional possession. In the *adorned* body, we possess *more*; if we have the adorned body at our disposal, we are masters over more and nobler things, so to speak. It is, therefore, deeply significant that bodily adornment becomes private property above all: it expands the ego and enlarges the sphere around us which is filled with our personality and which consists in the pleasure and the attention of our environment. This environment looks with much less attention at the unadorned (and thus as if less 'expanded') individual, and passes by without including him. The fundamental principle of adornment is once more revealed in the fact that, under primitive conditions, the most outstanding possession of women became that which, according to its very idea, exists only for others, and which can intensify the value and significance of its wearer only through the recognition that flows back to her from these others. In an aesthetic form, adornment creates a highly specific synthesis of the great convergent and divergent forces of the individual and society, namely, the elevation of the ego through existing for others, and the elevation of existing for others through the emphasis and extension of the ego. This aesthetic form itself stands above the contrasts between individual human strivings. They find, in adornment, not only the possibility of a reciprocal organization that, as anticipation and pledge of their deeper metaphysical unity, transcends the disharmony of their appearance.

NOTE

Source: *The Sociology of Georg Simmel* Translated and edited by Kurt H. Wolff (The Free Press, 1950), 338–44.

CHAPTER THREE

The Economic and Social Rôle of Fashion[1]

PIERRE CLERGET

Fashion is a social custom, transmitted by imitation or by tradition. It is a form of luxury, luxury in ornamentation. Voltaire says:

> There is a fickle, teasing goddess
> Fantastic in her tastes, playful in adornment,
> Who at every season seems to flee, return, and rise again.
> Proteus was her father, her name is Fashion.

Many writers have sounded the caprices of fashion, its frequent coming, its suddennness. It is changeable,[2] unreliable, frivolous; the most careful calculations are often brushed aside for the most trifling causes. Another characteristic is its universal following. Domineering, it reigns supreme over all classes of society. While this "democracy of fashion" is quite recent, yet the taste for finery is as old as the world.

An English archeologist, Mr. Evans, found in the Mycenaean palace of Knossos in Crete some frescoes painted 1,400 years before our era, showing ladies of the court clothed in resplendent garments, with enormous leg-of-mutton sleeves held to the neck by a narrow ribbon; their flounced skirts, ornamented with embroidered bands, are expanded behind by enormous bustles.

Writings and monuments tell us that under the Empire changes of fashion and peculiarity in costumes were customary at Rome. During the Middle Ages, an author of the twelfth century wrote: "France, whose humor varies continuously, ought to have some garments which would proclaim her instability." In the fifteenth century, Robert Gaguin reproached Parisians "for always being eager for novelties and unable to retain the same style of clothing for 10 successive years."[3]

Until the thirteenth century, women's costumes were chiefly tunics or robes, marked by plain and natural simplicity. It was only toward the fourteenth and fifteenth centuries, under Francis I and Henry II, that dresses were designed following the lines of the body. Women then appeared with fitted doublets, skirts, and wraps with collars. The sleeves were leg-of-mutton and balloon shaped, filled with plaits, or very tight, and these shapes often have been imitated in our day. This was the starting point of fashion which will sleep only for perpetual reawakening, making evolutions in irregular cycles at the will of its creators. Under Henry III we find the pointed waist, held in place by a stiff corset, the puffed sleeves; the dress already had the hoop-petticoat which fashion revived again in 1830.

The reign of Henry IV brought us the great bell skirt, built on springs, which we find later with the crinoline. This tendency toward fullness in the skirt kept increasing until 1605, bringing some dresses to enormous proportions, with ruffles adding to their size. Then, toward the end of the seventeenth century the fullness diminished, giving way to padded dresses, concealed under mantle wraps, and in 1880 they reappeared again. Reduction in the size of the skirt continued until about 1750 when fullness again came into fashion, and by 1785 the skirts were ridiculously full, expanded with great hoops. There was another reaction and the hoop-skirt gave way first to the bustle, then in 1793 came the one-piece dress, with a running string and without ornamentation. Greek robes were seen at fêtes and on the stage. The directoire dress, very close-fitting, exaggerated the plaited style and resembled the trousers skirt of recent date. The empire costume, with the waist high under the bosom, was only another transformation of the directoire dress, showing at that time a tendency to fullness in the form.

After 1805 the cycles began to shorten, the wheel turned faster, and without stopping, until we find a general style used by all classes of society. Skirts were worn very full again toward 1810 and, passing through all sorts of gradations, with a partial return of fullness in the back, ended in 1860 to 1865 in the culminating point of the crinoline. This marks the departure from Orientalism and brings us toward the epoch when very simple and straight robes were worn until we reach the other extreme, the clinging gown, not forgetting the harem skirt, an exaggerated revised edition of the eccentricities of the period from 1805 to 1815. We must pause to resume slowly but surely the march toward the puffed or padded styles.[4]

How is fashion created? Since the days of Worth in 1846, it has been the well-known modiste who has been the creating artist. His popularity is such that it has become a regular habit to visit his establishment, and as Pierre Mille[5] says, "he knows how to make the worldly minded dress and how to prattle," as shown by Gervex's painting "chez Paquin à cinq heures." The modiste seeks out the designs, fits the forms, harmonizes the lines and styles. Each establishment decides upon a model and then selection is made from public opinion expressed at the great gatherings at Auteuil and Longchamp. Each modiste has a representative there and in broad daylight they make comparisons, listen to criticisms, make after-touches, and the "complete results of the races" told in the Paris evening papers omit the most striking act of the day: Fashion was born and a humble seamstress may have had the chance to invent it.[6]

The fashion created, there is haste to make it known, to launch it. Under the monarchical régimes and under the first and second empires, the court fulfilled that duty and gave fashion some distinction. It is only since the first Republic, or particularly since the third Republic, that the prevailing style has been anything more than the reflection of the will of the sovereign whose ideas and customs had the force of law. Under the first empire, Josephine abhorred a stiff style of garment; she preferred the low-neck gown with high waist and flexible skirt; her hair arranged with the bandeau. Roman art then ruled, brought about by Josephine. Empress Eugénie had like influence under the second empire, and to her we owe the taste for a comfortable style, and stuffed, silk-covered furniture.[7]

To-day the style is made public by mannequins at the race course, on the street, at the theater, by actors on the stage, and by such social functions as a wedding or a ball. The fashion at the theater seems to be playing an increasing rôle. Fashionable modistes have recently announced their intention of having their mannequins replaced by actresses, who on the stage, by their grace, their elegance, their beauty, their prestige, would tend to a more ready acceptance of fashion's extravagant innovations. Madame Jane Hading, in the play of L'Attentat, introduced the dress known as the "aile de cabeau" or winged pannier. And Madame Martha Brandès created the style of sleeves since known by her name. When La Walkyrie was first presented at the opera, white wings like those attached to Brunehilde's helmet were worn on hats, and the armor of the warlike maiden gave to dressmakers the idea of spangled robes, much resembling the breastplate. The use of pheasant plumage became more general after the presentation of Chanteclair. We already had the "Dame Blanche" fichus, and the Lutheran bonnet was popular after Les Huguenots was played.

Any striking idea may inspire a fashion. Under Louis-Philippe "all the fashionable young men of the capital wanted their trousers plaited at the hips like those of the African chasseurs; they had their turbans and their Arab checias (skull caps) at their homes."[8] Trocadero ribbons became the rage as a souvenir of the voyage of the Duke of Angoulême to Spain, and the Russo-Japanese War gave us the kimono. It is to the passion for sports that we owe the English styles, the success of the tailor-made costume, the fashion for furs and leather garments, and also that "war hat" attempted by some Americans.

Literature also has been a great inspiration, as shown by the curious and interesting book of Louis Maigron on "Romantisme et la Mode." The essential characteristic of the romantist revolution was the return to national tradition, the style of the Middle Ages, which forced itself quickly and in every direction, taking the place of the empire style. According to Mons. Maigron, "romanticism creeps from books into the daily life through social diversions." The masquerade thus makes some pretensions, often justified, of reconstructing history; old engravings are appealed to for aid in costuming.

The works of Victor Hugo, especially Hernani, have had an influence on fashion as great as pre-Raphaelism has to-day on gowns and hairdressing. The use of white muslins was the inspiration of Taglioni, as were the "waves of the Danube" taffetas. The "Atala" collars and the "Marie Stuart" hats were successively worn. The "battlement" hat was designed in part from a headdress looked upon as that of Jeanne d'Arc, and likewise the "leg-of-mutton" sleeve recalls the costume of the sixteenth century.

There is a complete revolution in the work of gold- and silver-smiths. Jewelry is made in the shape of pointed arches with knights in steel armor, pages with plumed toques, helmets, grey hounds, coats of arms, escutcheons. A complete feudal arsenal is designed in chased work and enamels. In architecture the Gothic comes into full vogue, and it is constantly the romance styles which are most fashionable.

The red waistcoat of Theophile Gautier had its imitators; the waistcoat was at one time the chief thought of young Frenchmen. It is all a program that one cultivates and lives up to. Men's fashions extend to lace facings, braids, furs, Merovingian style of hair, and whiskers of an Assyrian king; the cravat is of a gloomy black.[9]

It is this individualism directing the present style, this instability, the changing at every season, which helps Paris in great measure to maintain its leading influence on fashion, and this is not of recent origin. Isabel of Bavaria, in 1391, and Anne of Brittany, in 1496, sent to the queens of England and Spain dolls dressed in the latest style. During the war of the succession in Spain the courts of Versailles and St. James accorded safe conduct to the alabaster doll which accredited the newest fashions from the other side of the Channel.[10] It is Paris that "decrees the sumptuary law of nations," it is she that sells the models, and the best advertisement of a foreign modiste is to announce her "return from Paris." One can understand that this advantage would be envied outside of France, and they have tried, especially in the United States, to wrest it from her. These attempts have not ceased. It can readily be seen that there is involved in this the question of a convenient center which is not found elsewhere. Copying styles is so very easy that a committee of defense of Parisian fashions has been formed, which has brought about a closer connection between the release of models and the opening of the season, and there has been adopted a stamp of origin, furnished by the syndics of needlework.

While we have spoken up to this point simply of clothing and hairdressing, we should not think that this is the limit of fashion's domain. It controls conversation, the manner of walking, how to shake hands. Such a word as "épatant" (stunning) owes to fashion its recent admittance to the "Dictionary of the Academy." The general use of such a drink as tea, the abandonment of wine in certain circles, vegetarianism, may all be regarded as fashions, likewise the adoption of some state of the mind which takes the lead at times, as sensitiveness or calmness. We have already spoken of architecture and furniture. The passion for traveling and for sports becomes widespread; there is less taste for home; there is less desire for books and interior ornaments.

The influence of fashion is reflected also on the sales of works of art. The great sales recently held in Paris have shown that there is a revival in favor of productions of the eighteenth century. In June, 1912, at a Doucet sale a pastel of "Quentin de la Tour," the portrait of "Duval de l'Epinoy," purchased in 1903 for 5,210 francs ($1,042), brought 660,000 francs ($132,000); the "Jardin de la ville d'Este," by Fragonard, which sold for 700 francs ($140) in 1880, brought 21,300 francs ($4,226); and the "Sacrifice au Minotaure," by the same painter, for which 5,300 francs ($1,060) was paid in 1880, was held at 396,000 francs ($79,200). Such fluctuations, of which we could give many examples, are attributed by M. Paul Leroy-Beaulieu to certain notions, among which fashion forms a large part; the personal satisfaction of connoisseurs, the desire for distinction, snobbishness, which is a grand master in fashionable life, the spontaneous adaptation of art of the eighteenth century to conditions of contemporary life and the development of large fortunes.[11] In the statistics of foreign commerce works of art show the greatest change; in the fiscal year 1911–12 the importation of that class into the United States rose to more than $36,000,000, an increase of 60 per cent over 1910–11.

Other industries are also answerable to fashion – the fur trade, ornamental plumes, jewelry, toys, and artificial flowers. The style in furs changes every year, from the tippets to the stoles and scarfs of to-day, and the consumption of skins increases in enormous proportions. In 1848 there were sold in London at public auction 225,000 muskrat skins, at a maximum price of 2 cents each; while in 1910 sales reached 4,000,000 pieces, at a maximum price of 14 cents. Russian ermine, which in 1888 were valued at 15 copecks (11 cents), sold in 1910 for 4.30 roubles ($3.25); beautiful sable skins, which sold for 5 roubles ($3.75) in 1880, brought up to 800 roubles ($600) in 1910.[12]

Artificial flowers, originating in China, now used more for hats and similar purposes than in decorating rooms, give employment in Paris alone to 10,000 women and 3,000 men, receiving $2,200,000 in wages, for a production valued at $6,700,000. The manufacture of toys is regulated almost exclusively by the current demand; it is enough to say that a toy is fashionable. The industrial arts peculiar to the colonies seem again to have come into favor after having been for a long time out of style. And it is to fashion that is due the present prosperity in false hair and perfumery trades. Each year 130,000 kilograms of hair are utilized in France, and the importations from China and Japan vary from year to year with change in style, from 8,000 to 16,000 kilograms. The fashion for rouge is as old as the desire of women to look beautiful; in very general use in Roman times, it revived with the Renaissance, when the habit spread even to the nuns. Madame de Sévigné wrote: "Rouge may be regarded as the law and the prophets; it is all christianity." Rice powder and "crème Simon" have no less success to-day than has the tinting of the hair. Finally, fashion is advantageous in the constantly increasing love for sports and travel and in the development of industries connected with these, particularly the hotel business.

What are the economical results of fashion? In the industrial world, first of all, it seems to be a stimulant to production; but it is solely in objects to which it offers itself, for the estimates are not elastic – an increase in one article leads to retrenchment in another, and the demand is merely changed from one industry to another. Thus enormous fluctuations are shown each year in the silk industries, on which the uncertainties of fashion are most particularly centered.[13] Ribbon is most affected, being much used, both on hats and clothes. It loses first one fashion, then another, and the evolution is tending rapidly toward the cheapest grades used so much for ornaments and in the thousand little gewgaws of women. The situation in dress goods is hardly any brighter, following the alnage law, showing from this that the close-fitting costume continues to be the style. "Praised by some, condemned by others," as the Figaro says, this fashion will leave in the history of textile industries the souvenir of an ill-omened influence. The quantity of material needed to make a costume has been reduced one-half or two-thirds, and, besides, it does away with undergarments and linings, which for many years represented a very heavy employment of tissues of plain silk. The inspector of silks at Lyons showed a registration of 7,590,445 kilograms of silk in 1911, as compared with 8,344,566 in 1910, a difference of 9.03 per cent. The two inspectors at Milan show still greater decreases of 15.60 and 9.68 per cent, respectively. An analogous reduction took place in the woolen goods industries. The French Chamber of Commerce of Montevideo complained last year of the effect of measurement inspection on the exportation of woolens. All the related industries of spinners and weavers were affected in the same degree, and the dyers, dressers, and stampers.

As Mons. Maurice Deslandres has ingeniously expressed it, fashion not only displaces the products of one industry by those of another, but also impedes the latter industry by demanding quick changes in machinery; retards it until the last moment by some extensive changes in the work, and the trend is steadily toward low prices and inferior qualities which are not durable. The result is to raise the net cost by requiring the manufacturer to make earlier settlement for apparatus, and necessitating expenses for the setting up of new models.[14]

From the commercial standpoint there is a tendency to an increase in prices because of manufacturers stocks unsold, and the hesitation of jobbers to lay up large supplies. The relations with customers are no longer easy, the latter delay their orders, are undecided about their choice, require more urging, and all the orders begin to accumulate during the last days preceding the opening of the season.

In the agricultural world, fashion has produced transformations no less serious, some of them unfortunate. The abuse of ornamental feathers has brought about the destruction of all sorts of birds which had protected the crops against the ravages of various insects. It is to the democracy of fashion, as well as to its instability, that we must attribute the conditions in textile manufactures, where we find a reduction in the use of flax, an enormous increase in cotton, and the displacement of vegetable dyes by the more brilliant though less serviceable dyestuffs derived from coal tar. In the animal world certain species of fur animals are on the verge of extinction, and there should be either attempts at domestication, as in the case of the blue fox and the opossum, or hunting regulations by the creation of open districts with complete prohibition during a certain period. In Siberia a recent law suspends the hunting of the sable from the 1st of February, 1913, to the 15th of October, 1916. Likewise an international agreement between England, Canada, Russia, Japan, and the United States prohibited May 11, 1911, the hunting of fur seals in the open sea of the North Pacific.[15]

The present democracy of fashion is the great social factor to be emphasized. It has encouraged a great consumption of products; a depreciation in quality and prices; it has induced a very great instability, which disconcerts both producers and buyers; manufacturers must make the same classes of products for all markets; fashion is followed at the same time by all classes of society. The wheel turns quickly and ceaselessly. On the other hand, these rapid changes do not take place without a slack season for the workman, without quick fluctuations in salaries, or without change of specialization.

"To follow the fashion" becomes not only a pastime, but even a duty; "intellects are made frivolous thereby; those who pride themselves in appearing elegant are obliged to make the clothing of themselves a veritable occupation and a study, which assuredly does not tend to elevate the mind, nor does it render them capable of great things."[16]

To this moral and social evil an economic difficulty is also added. Fashion is a waste; "it has the privilege of casting things aside before they have lost their freshness; it multiplies consumption and condemns that which is still good, comfortable, and pretty for something that is no better. Besides, it robs a State of that which it consumes and that which it does not consume."[17] Mons. Pierre Mille told recently in this Revue of patrons who spent as much as $60,000 each year, others up to $16,000, and a still greater number up to $5,000. But it is mostly among the middle and laboring classes, whose means are more limited, that unreasonable expenditure in following fashions is most harmful.

These abuses, this tyranny of uniformity in nearly all outer manifestations of life, leads notably to the banishment of provincial costumes, the representatives of climate, products of local art, so full of interest from an historical standpoint, picturesque, stable, durable, which are handed down from generation to generation. Among these costumes of historic interest are the Caux cap recalling the steeple headdress of ladies of the fourteenth century; the little Nicæan hat reproducing the coiffure called "Thessalanian" by the Greeks, and the antique Phrygian hat, still worn by the Arlesians. Although formerly there was variation according to place and uniformity as to the season, we now tend more and more toward a uniformity as to place and variation as to season.

The abuses denounced, it would be useless to demand, on the contrary, an immutability in complete opposition with the transformations of all sorts which surround us. Tertullian in his treatise "De pallio," says that nothing is more natural than changing the costume and that nature sets us an example in assuming varied forms. Human fancy thus asserts its supremacy over animals, obliged always to wear the same livery. Austere philosophers have understood perfectly the esthetic and social significance of fashion. Renan, writing on Marcus Aurelius, admits that "woman in dressing herself well fulfills a duty; she practices an art, an exquisite art, in a sense the most charming of arts. * * * A woman's toilet, with its refinements, is a great art in its way. Ages and countries which know how to carry it out well are great ages, great countries."

The appearance of a new style of garment is the visible sign that a transformation is taking place in the intellect, customs, and business of a people. The rise of the Chinese Republic, for instance, led to doing away with plaited hair and to the adoption of the European costume. Taine wrote this profound sally: "My decided opinion is that the greatest change in history was the advent of trousers. * * * It marked the passage of Greek and Roman civilization to the modern. * * * Nothing is more difficult to alter than a universal and daily custom. In order to take away man's clothes and dress him up again you must demolish and remodel him."[18] It is also an equally philosophical conclusion which Mons. Louis Bourdeau gives in his interesting "Histoire de l'habillement et de la parure": "There where the same style of clothing is used for centuries, as among barbarous peoples, one has the right to say that civilization remains stationary. There, on the other hand, where, as in Europe, garments are subject to continual modifications, one may see evidence of great comfort and rapid progress. * * * Far from being a custom of incurable frivolity the changes of fashions mark a high civilization, subject to change because it is growing and because it has wide latitude to refine its ideal in proportion as its productions are varied."[19] Again, it is necessary that that versatility and refinement be not turned to extravagance or to impropriety, compromising the reputation for good taste, elegance, and distinction which the fashions of Paris enjoy throughout the entire world.

What can we do for or against fashion? Can we direct it or can we prevent its abuse? Let us find out first the power of the law, religious or civil. Very early popes and councils strove in vain against the low-neck gown and the dresses "terminating in the serpent's tail." Kings imitated them, Charlemagne setting the example, but sumptuary decrees have had no more effect than ordinances against dueling. Mons. Victor du Bled reports that Philippe le Bel was urged to promulgate some sumptuary laws by his wife, who, making her formal entrance at Bruges in 1301, saw a crowd of common people so richly clothed that she cried out with vexation, "I thought myself the queen, and I see hundreds of them." Charles IX proscribed hip pads of more than 5 feet, gold chains, pieces of jewelry with or without enamel. In 1567 he regulated the garments of each class, permitting silk only to princesses and duchesses, forbidding velvet. But these laws were intended very much more to limit foreign importation and to encourage home industry than to regulate fashion.[20] Seventy-two decrees prohibiting the use of India cloth were rendered from 1700 to 1760 and proved to be powerless against the rulings of fashion. In 1706 a certain French chamber of commerce voted "that officers may have the power to arrest on the streets persons who are found clothed in this kind of goods, and they should be condemned to pay a large fine." In 1912 another chamber of commerce voted for ministerial intervention against some noted dressmakers to check the use of clinging dresses, against which the American clergy and some members of the German medical corps preached without success.

The intervention of manufacturers injured in their interests by reduction to the metric system or the abandoning of such and such an ornament is of no effect. A committee of propaganda, formed at Saint-Etienne with a view to reviving the fashion for fine qualities of ribbon, has produced no appreciable result. Those only have influence upon fashion who make it and promote it, those who offer it and those who can refuse it – the tailor and the customer. The first is too much concerned in the changes of fashion to expect him to make any effort to restrain them; the second is quiet, provided that he be included. If fashion responds to an innate tendency of our nature, the fondness for change, the actual rapidity of this change is neither disastrous nor necessary, as the long use of the tailor-made costume shows. The last word shall be given to the social leagues of buyers and the leagues of consumers, because of the very interesting initiative taken by the former in favor of handmade lace with a view to reviving that valuable rural industry. After having brought about the assembling at Paris of an exposition of women's work, they asked their members simply to require mention of the origin "handmade" or "machine-made" on the laces put on sale.

NOTES

Source: *Annual Report Smithsonian Institution* (Smithsonian Institution Scholarly Press, 1913), 756–65.

1. Translated by permission from the Revue Économique Internationale, Brussels, vol. 2, No. 1, Apr. 15–20, 1913.
2. "One fashion has hardly brushed aside another when it is abolished by a new one and this in turn gives way to one which follows, but this one will not be the last." – La Brugère. "The new style of dressing makes the older fashion out of date, so forcefully and with such general agreement that it might be called a kind of mania which turns the senses round." – Montaigne.
3. Cited by L. Bourdeau, Histoire de l'habillement et de la parure. 8° F. Alcan, 1904, p. 197.
4. Bulletin des Soies et des Soieries, Aug. 18, 1911.
5. Pierre Mille: Une des industries intellectuelles de Paris, la grand couture. Revue économique internationale, May, 1912.
6. Bulletin des Soies et des Soieries, Nov. 10, 1900.

7. E. Mazille: Comment se crée la mode dans l'industrie de la soierie. Bulletin trimestriel de l'Association des anciens élèves de l'Ecole supérieure de Commerce de Lyon, March, 1908.

8. Louis Maigron: Le Romantisme et la mode. Champion, 1911. Cf. also O. Uzanne: Un siècle de modes féminines, et la française du siècle. H. Bouchot: Le luxe français: Challamel: Histoire de la mode.

9. L. Maigron, op. cit., passim.

10. V. du Bled. Les évolutions du luxe dans la Société polie. Revue Économique Internationale, September, 1906.

11. Économiste français, June 22, 1912.

12. Les Échos de l'Exportation, Jan. 1, 1913.

13. It is interesting to compare the fluctuations of the silk industry (as capricious as those of agricultural productions) with the regularity of other industrial products influenced only by periodical crises, cf. the chart in our "Manuel d'économie commerciale." A. Colin, Paris.

14. Maurice Deslandres. La mode, ses conséquences économiques et sociales. Bulletin des ligues sociales d'acheteurs, vol. 1, 1912, pp. 25–37.

15. On this subject see our work, L'exploitation rationelle du globe, 1 vol., Doin & Son, 1912.

16. E. de Laveleye, quoted by E. Picard. Le luxe et les grandes fortunes. Revue Économique Internationale, July, 1905.

17. J. B. Say, quoted by E. Picard, op. cit.

18. H. Taine. L'Italie et la vie italienne. Revue des Deux-Mondes, 1865.

19. L. Bourdeau, op. cit., p. 195.

20. V. du Bled, op. cit. Cf. Dr. A. Velleman, Der Luxus in seinen Beziehungen zur Sozial-Oekonomie. Halle, 1898.

CHAPTER FOUR

The Cerementing of the Gentleman

Gerald Heard

The characteristic of this ultimate style is naturally finish. Man's power of taking notice seems steadily to have increased. Of course it must vary among different races, but on the whole (cf. Myers, *Psychology*, where natives' power of picking a trail is said to be if anything below that of a civilised man trained to look for the indications), it seems to develop *pari passu* with civilisation. The Chinese have wrought up their sense for the surface of glazes to an unsurpassed delicacy. In the line of our own descent the Roman seems the first generally to appreciate textures for their own sake,[1] though perhaps the cultured Egyptians acquired such a taste. Certainly they had time to do so[2]. The Greeks in this, as in much other detail, coarser than their masters, or perhaps one should say their fellow-slaves, liked paint, and with what an obliterating thickness they laid it on the plaster-surfaced marble shafts of their best work suggests. The Romans, with their love for fine-grained and highly polished woods, their use of glass, crystalline mosaics and "split-marble" sheets, show a capacity for seeing into material which perhaps can be developed only amid long-civilised peoples. We know they used the tweezer where the razor failed. Up to our own sixteenth century it has been noted, however, a man seems to have been considered clean shaven so long as the outline of his chin was visible. Earlier, a priest's brass has nearly always the chin well stippled, as though it were a seemly thing to be bristling. Then notice begins to be taken, and soon powder is in demand. But still Queen Elizabeth's dresses have not a little of the rich squalor of savagery about them when the Irish Viceroy has to report that he cannot dispose of casts-offs, as was purposed as presents to a chieftainess, because they "are so slobbered." The second part of the seventeenth century is the period of Refinement's birth. The Long Parliament abolishes torture and the sudden shrinking from a nauseous spectacle is rationalised as a step to abandon an ineffective way of obtaining truth. Washing comes back and Pepys, who could stand his cellar being a cesspool – till he discovered that the sewage was another household's – is put off his food by his Aunt Fenner's dirty hands when she dishes a dinner. Stained velvets will no longer be treasured by people who ceasing to eat with their fingers, no longer wipe them on the table-cloth. By the end of the eighteenth century the *School for Scandal* shows that society had begun to notice teeth as well. By the nineteenth, the bath, the tooth-brush, and the nail-scissors are everywhere taken for granted, so that politeness winces from the detailed pride with which the gallant of the end of the sixteenth has himself painted toying with a pocket combination of tooth-pick and ear-scoop, while that Byzantine princess, who, coming as Dogaressa to early Venice, brought her little gold fork, and, on dying, probably of the insanitation of the mud-banks, was chronicled as destroyed by God for her indecent pride, becomes one of the martyr-patronesses of refinement. The hollow-ground razor gives an ever smoother shave, though the exacting eye keeps pace[3] until it would seem for the swarthy that, unless electrolysis can do something for them, the canonical seven times a day will hardly surpass their razings. The surface involved also spreads. The heavy moustache of the last generation has not survived, though a nostril patch may be worn. The Boston cut sweeps the clean shave round the neck almost to the ears, and above, so sleeked as to make smooth the passage from the nature of hair to the artificiality of a silk skull cap,[4] the crest of man is again changing into a wig. As with the extended cut, so throughout in this intensified sense of surface America leads the way. It may be due to the influence on a highly suggestible people of the only living architecture in the world, the smooth, steel-evident, columnar invention of the sky-scraper.[5] In any case American teeth are advanced beyond the state of English, as these are above the Irish. American nails are being brought up to the same unprecedented standard. Polished teeth, varnished nails, depilation, and finally wigs will all be defended against conservatism's cry of decadence by the counterclaim, hygiene. True enough no doubt, but nevertheless as much a rationalisation as was the defence of the abolition of torture in the interests of truth. The twentieth century fears to be called effeminate – so did the seventeenth. Today men powder after shaving their faces, tomorrow, after shaving their heads as well, they may be powdering their wigs. Already American skin is the smoothest and least hairy in the world, outside China. The intensification of focus, which accounts for all the above, is naturally hardest on the face, and what in the end manipulative surgery may not do with the tired elastic, which after a few years of expression gives out in so depressing a manner, none can say. Suffice it that there is no change that woman and man will not undergo provided it is convincing. That is the whole issue, and this fact, this curious manner in which we look at each other's faces, when considered, brings a curious problem to light. Though the face is studied more narrowly than anything else in nature, so that a change sometimes of less than of an hundredth of an inch allows us to recognise one person from another, we really see it still with an wholly unanalytic observation. We search there for meanings and motives, for evidence of age, expenditure and temperament, but actually not for appearance. We can tell exactly the impression that a face has given, but how it gave it, what details composed the sum, and how it was added, we cannot reckon. If, therefore, a make-up is successful we feel how well the maker looks. If it fails, we experience a little of the disgust of decay. A wig begins to fall, false teeth slip, and we wince, for racially (which is actually as we are at the moment experiencing) we do not expect healthy, if unrelieved, baldness, clear hard gums, but something all the worse for being undefined. It is the supreme horror of life, corruption. We feel that we were in some way nearly trapped by a mask, and we start back, cruel fear vestigial in our contempt. This clear but quite conventional glance is largely akin to the animal's. We see features vividly enough, provided they fit into certain assumptions, as though we could set type provided that it made up comprehensible words but were unable to find it, should it not. The face is the focus of attention, and perhaps now the centre of attraction, since it is the greatest part of the body uncovered by civilised man. We therefore see it with an immediate, a prepossessing emotion. It makes or mars whatever may come after, and no mutilation is so terrific as serious facial damage. It is irrational that we should be so moved, but we may recall for our comfort that the great Greeks could hardly conceive of a man being good who was even ugly (cf. Plato on Socrates as the one exception). We may, however, hope to modify the conventional mask into which, with subconscious violence, we would force all features. There may in the end be something approaching facial fashions, and even cross-eyes may for a season have a look in. It is even less excusable when some of that vague, homogeneous judgment passes into our estimate of clothes. Women will often say that a man was well dressed when they could not recall anything he had on. It was right – that was all they knew. But such a standard, once the convention has ceased to move of itself and become dependent for its progress on individual enterprise, is sterilising. It only knows that personal departure is wrong. It waits for a class-movement that will never again come.

Some such unreflective judgment once ruled architecture too. The mass was aware only that a building they had made for them was seemly. Whether before the Renaissance the builders themselves understood the exact contribution of the parts to the whole, could analyse and hold apart, resolve and compose, may be doubted. Perhaps analysis is the end of Art, as the world has so far understood it. No doubt you can take apart once and again, and the pieces like dislocations will slip back, only a little strained. But once too often the organism may be deranged, something alien may slip in, the whole may fall irretrievably to pieces. We may lose the power of seeing the thing as a whole, lose our conductivity that allows that immediate shock of pleasure or disgust, whereby we "stand moved."

Will the complexion and the hair, then, follow where clothes are going and architecture has gone? Shall we attain a perfect make-up and then change it at will? At present, teeth are so sound as shams, and the position they occupy so defensible that they seem inclined to stabilise the taste for a mouth full of white lumps, and, though the United States is trying to popularise a chryselephantine parti-colour,

English good taste, as ever, is set against anything, even in the mouth, that is loud. Hair, however, is having a hard time, and perhaps, as in Egypt, people will come to prefer the smooth smear of a cosmetic eye-brow, gold for tea, purple for dinner, than the bristling home-grown ridge.

Such a development would be haled as decadence, but in its definite departure, its conscious artificiality, it would be evidence of a new vigour. [...]

NOTES

Source: *Narcissus: An Anatomy of Clothes* (E.P. Dutton & Co., 1924), 122–31.

1. Seneca was mocked, for though calling himself a stoic, he had many hundred tables inlaid with lemon wood.
2. The sham lapis they make of gold-flaked glass suggests this.
3. This is another example of the alternating poles of evolution whereby progress is obtained by competition of defence and attack, supply and demand: e.g. armour plate and artillery, and spindle and loom.
4. Women have had some success with silk wigs. Certainly the silk-worm spins a thread the glossiness of which we can imitate only on ours with oil, and antimacassars are out of fashion.
5. I seem to notice where American fashions can escape the British authority, in the middle west tailors' advertisements a tendency to the perpendicular, especially in the wide revival for boys of the long "Norfolk" with parallel bands running from shoulder to thigh.

CHAPTER FIVE

The Predominance of Male Homosociality

J. C. Flügel

Hitherto we have treated homosociality in general and have refrained from dealing – except quite incidentally – with any differences between the homosociality of the two sexes. There can be little doubt, however, that such differences exist and are important. So far as I am aware, all the authors who have approached this subject have been impressed with the greater sociality of men as compared with that of women. Among anthropological writers Schurtz in particular[1] has maintained that among many primitive peoples such male homosocial institutions as the Men's House and the Age Classes are the real carriers of culture. It is they which foster social feeling and co-operation and which provide the possibilities of social advance. In such societies, as in ours, marriage is an institution that is in many ways antagonistic to social life, this latter depending largely on the activities of young unmarried men. The sexual life of these societies of young men living together is usually free and promiscuous, contrasting strongly with the much more stable sexual connections formed later on in marriage – thus again exhibiting the fact that sexual relations of a superficial and fleeting character are in certain important respects less antagonistic to social life than those of a more permanent nature. Dealing with modern civilized conditions and approaching the matter from the psychological point of view, Blüher[2] has studied some typical forms of association between boys and young men, more or less clearly based on an undercurrent of homosexuality, and he has shown the high degree of social co-operation and social feeling developed in such associations.

The club-life developed in our own country during the last century illustrates clearly both the antagonism between sexual and social sentiments and the greater development of social life among men. Until quite recently at any rate, nearly all successful clubs were confined to one sex, the other sex being for the most part rigorously excluded. Men's clubs, however, vastly predominated, both in number and in social importance, and usually exhibited a distinctly antifeminine bias, manifesting at once a fear and a contempt of women. The fear component of this attitude is pretty clearly due for the most part to the dread of the socially disturbing and disrupting influence of sex attraction, though it is possible that psycho-analysis might reveal the existence of more subtle and complicated motives also. The element of contempt is almost certainly dependent ultimately upon deep-seated factors, such as those based on the castration complex (contempt for women as not possessing the penis) and what might be termed the "prostitute complex" (dissociation of the elements of tenderness and sensuality, with contempt for the object that excites this latter).[3]

Among primitive peoples secret societies are undoubtedly also in many cases an important element in social life. These too are nearly always confined to one sex and generally confined to men. The same statement holds good of the analogues of these societies among civilized nations, from the very large, widespread and permanent groups, such as that of the Freemasons, to the smallest secret group in a college or a school. Such secret societies, in whatsoever stage of culture they be found, usually have as an interesting feature some form of initiation test or initiation ceremony, through which novices have to pass before being admitted to the full privileges of membership. Reik, in his penetrating psycho-analytic study of these initiation ceremonies,[4] has shown that their main purpose (for their total psychological significance is markedly complex and ambivalent) is an attempt to cement the social bonds between men (especially between the elders and the youths) by a reconciliation based on mutual sacrifice of heterosexual desires and privileges – a conclusion that is in full accord with our present point of view.

THE CAUSE OF THIS PREDOMINANCE

This fact (assuming it to be a fact) of the much more widespread occurrence and much greater cultural influence of associations between men as compared with those between women is obviously a matter of much interest both to the psychologist and the sociologist and we may well devote a little consideration here to its probable causes. These causes are themselves, in all likelihood, both psychological and sociological in nature. Dealing first with those in which the psychological influences appear to predominate, we may note the following:

(1) The greater Narcissism of women probably affects their social relations, as it does their directly sexual relations, by making them in certain ways more self-centred and less actively influential in their dealings with others. As in love, so also in social relations, they seek to attract others, so as to make others do things to them or for them, rather than themselves to do things to others. In a society composed exclusively of women this would tend to a less active intercourse and a consequent lesser formation of social bonds as compared with the state of affairs in a society

of men, the individual members of which would exercise a more direct and active influence upon one another.

We should, however, be on guard against an overemphasis of this factor, since some of the male substitutes for female Narcissism (*e.g.* pride in muscular development) may[5] lead to forms of rivalry which are as disrupting to social bonds as is the more passive love of the female for her own bodily beauty. Moreover it seems quite probable that the difference between the sexes that is here in question is not so strongly marked in primitive cultures as in civilized and sophisticated conditions, where women have more leisure, and also that it was not so great formerly as it is today. Certain changes that have taken place during the last hundred years or so point to a remarkable repression of Narcissism among men – a repression that has at any rate not taken place to a corresponding extent among women. Modern clothing, for instance, allows few outlets for personal vanity among men; to be dressed "correctly" or in "good taste" is the utmost that a modern man can hope for; all originality or beauty in clothing (to say nothing of the even more direct gratification of Narcissism in actual bodily exposure) being reserved for women. Up till recently in human history, men were dressed as gaudily and were allowed as much individuality in clothing as were women, and among primitive peoples it seems to be the men rather than the women who have leisure and opportunity for personal adornment. Such adornment, moreover, is not infrequently connected with the activities of exclusively male (secret) societies; a fact which should warn us again not to attribute too great importance to this factor of Narcissism at all times and places.[6] [...]

NOTES

Source: *Men and their Motives: Psycho-Analytical Studies, with Two Essays by Ingeborg Flügel* (Kegan Paul, Trench, Trubner & Co., 1934), 61–65.

1. *Altersklassen und Männerbünde.*
2. *Vom Gemeinschaftsleben der Jugend.*
3. Cf. Freud, *Collected Papers*, iv, p. 203.
4. *Probleme der Religionspsychologie*, pp. 59 ff.
5. But need not necessarily.
6. For a fuller study of the social influence of clothing, see the present author's *Psychology of Clothes.*

CHAPTER SIX

Epilogue on Trousers

Eric Gill

Several times in the course of this book we have drawn attention to the violent contrast, both in form and in workmanship, between men's clothes and women's, and, in one place at least, have hinted that the direction in which a proper reform should go was towards an obliteration of those contrasts. We may now deal with this question with more particularity.

The first thing to be said is that men, that is to say Englishmen, European men and all so-called civilized men, have got to rid themselves of the preposterous notions that trousers are specially a male garment, and that skirts are specially for women. Looking at the matter without any reference to the goodness either of trousers or of skirts in themselves, without considering whether such garments are or are not a rational covering for human limbs and without considering whether tailoring is a better way of making clothes than dressmaking, or dressmaking than tailoring, it is clear that, to get the thing right, two courses are possible: either men can wear the same clothes as women, or women can wear the same clothes as men; either men can take to the skirt, or women can take to trousers.

But in saying this, and we are quite aware that many otherwise sane people will go almost mad at the suggestion, we do not of course suggest that men should wear exactly the same clothes as women wear now, or that women should take to braces and pants – we ourselves are maddened by such a notion. Moreover, such a procedure would be ridiculous physically. However similar in general arrangement men's bodies are to women's, there is sufficient difference, as, for example, in proportionate width of hips and shoulders and circumference of waist, between men and women to make mere fitting impossible. But apart from questions of physical fit there is no reason why women should not wear coats and trousers and waistcoats, or, better still, simply trousers and shirts as 'land girls' did during the war. Even now, though war-time enthusiasms have faded, many women who are engaged in occupations similar to men's wear a feminine version of men's clothes. A feminine version! And this does not mean that it has fundamental differences, but simply that the slight physical differences between women's bodies and men's have been allowed for and the traditional grace which centuries of dress-making (as opposed to tailoring) has made customary in women's clothes has given to such feminine versions of male attire an elegance of cut absent in men's clothes of the same sort. Thus girls' motor-cycling or aviation suits are exactly like men's but for trifling differences in physical shape, and that difference of grace. And, in the same way, there is no good reason why girl clerks and girl factory-hands – are not these now almost the majority of women? – should not wear exactly the same sort of clothes as the men engaged in identical occupations. If coat and trousers are suitable for men clerks, why not for women clerks? If men working in cotton-mills are clothed in dungaree overalls cut trouser-wise, why should not mill girls doing similar work wear a similar garment? The notion that the skirt is essentially female, and that there is something abominable in women in trousers, will not stand criticism for two minutes. If trousers are abominable for women they are abominable for men, and this may or may not be so – we shall come to that question later. Nor is there any necessity of confusion between the sexes in a world in which men and women dress in similar clothes. There is no such confusion in countries where they already do so, or have always done so. The Scotsman is not mistakeable for the Scotswoman, nor the Arab man for the Arab woman. The Swiss mountain girl who wears trousers is still a woman and she is still recognizable as such.

Moreover, and here we transcend the mere geographical business, the monk is not to be mistaken for the nun even when he covers his face with a cowl or a hood. There is plenty of scope for differentiation between male and female, even when there is no fundamental difference in dress. Some bishops, in cassocks and lace albs, do indeed look remarkably like old ladies, but this is no more derogatory to bishops than it is to old ladies, and even in such cases there is not really any possibility of mistake; for the episcopal dress is a uniform which everybody can recognize and in a reasonable society no women are bishops.

Then there is the bathing costume! Apart from the fanciful fashions of Brighton and Ostend, the only difference between the swimming suit worn by men and that worn by women is simply a matter of inches. Why should there be? And those charming garments called dressing-gowns and bath-wraps – the flowery fashions favoured by women are equally favoured by men, and excellent they look in them, and not in the least female. All these things go to show that sexual difference does not impose fundamental difference in clothes. We might do better to observe how the business is contrived in those suits of skin and hair with which we are born and in which we grow up. And here we notice at once how, by a most simple contrivance, the whole difficulty of differentiation is overcome. It is natural to dress up; it is natural to wear clothes. Both men and women have bodies and two arms and two legs. Both walk and both run. Both work and both play. But universally, apart from special circumstances wherein hiding seems desirable, all men and all women expose the face, and the face of woman remains hairless, but man grows a beard – and the beard grows at the very moment when differentiation becomes imperative. How simple, how excellent, how supremely intelligent!

What more need be said? Even if men and women wear identical clothes – and that is neither likely nor necessary, for their bodies are slightly different and their temperaments quite noticeably dissimilar – even if women wear braces and collars and ties and 'top' hats and short hair, even if they pad out their waists and flatten their bosoms, they cannot grow beards!

We might write a treatise on beards. We might show how shaving is primarily, and in its origins, a sign of penitence and voluntary celibacy – how the fashion of shaving among men who are neither penitent nor celibate derives from puritan notions of the vanity of male display (hence its universality in our puritan-industrial civilization) – how shaving is naturally approved of by women; for women, as Chaucer's Wife of Bath was at great pains to show, desire nothing more than power over their husbands – how the word 'barber' means cultivator of beards and not him who cuts them off – but we refrain. It is sufficient if we simply point out that the beard is the proper clothing of the male chin, and the all-sufficing garment of differentiation.

It is clear then, that in suggesting that the present divorce between men and women, so graphically displayed in the violent contrast between their clothes, might be healed as well by women adopting men's clothes as by men adopting women's, we are not suggesting anything which has not already plenty of good precedent. Even that garment which, in the industrial world, has come to be regarded as the male garment by definition (so that we say of a woman who has usurped her husband's position in the household that she 'wears the trousers') is seen to be not really more male than female. Drawers and knickers after all are a kind of trousers and are worn almost universally (it is no longer a secret), and an elongated and tailored version of them is not only already worn by women for farming and motor-cycling and similar purposes but a loose full sort of trousers has been worn by women of various races for many centuries. Moreover, regarded anatomically, trousers are even more convenient for women than for men.

And, this is a more important point than is ever publicly stated, the tucking away, and all sideways, of what is admittedly 'man's most precious ornament' is the sign and seal of the male degradation which Puritan-Industrialism spells. The thing has become a curious appendage – half-comic, half-dangerous and wholly indecent – no longer 'the middle of Dame Fortune's favours'. In the kilt or the cod-piece there is no such indignity and, though few women would admit it and few men to-day have thought of it, the whole business of birth-control is symbolized in this reduction of what is the primary sign of manhood into a mere organ of drainage.

But a case just as good or, as we think, better, can be made for the alternative remedy. Let men take to the skirt, with or without a leg-enclosing undergarment, rather than women to the coat and trousers.

At this suggestion the otherwise sane person to whom we referred in an earlier paragraph will be even more maddened. It is, he thinks, sufficiently abominable to suggest that women should take to the clothes of men, but that men should so far demean themselves (ha! 'demean' – that is the idea!) as to go about in 'petticoats' is simply an affair for the police – or, as the retired military officer in the club declared, he would simply 'shoot the blighters'. Never mind, we will proceed.

We have already pointed out that in all cases where dignity is desired it is the universal custom of mankind to dress in skirts, and this fact is in itself a complete answer to objectors. Even in England, the clergy in their churches, civil dignitaries in their courts and halls, men of religion in their monasteries, and all these people in public processions, are dressed in skirted robes; and this is not called 'wearing the petticoat'. We are aware that the appearance of habited monks and friars in the streets was, until recently, forbidden by Protestant legislation on the excuse that men should not dress as women – but this was obviously and admittedly merely to prevent Catholic exhibition. They liked to think that there were no Catholics because they could not see any. Then there is the Highland kilt; and here again there is no suggestion of effeminacy. And all over the world countless varieties of skirted male garments are worn. It is clear that the notion that there is anything abominable in men wearing skirts will not stand criticism for one minute.

But even if it be not actually abominable, what is there to be said for it? It is essentially the garment of dignity, and dignity is the essential object of clothes – that is the answer. That is the reason why reform in dress must take the direction of man's adoption of the dress of women rather than woman's adoption of the dress of men.

Now it must be made clear, though all intelligent people will take it for granted, that there is no suggestion here that all trades and both sexes should dress in the same or even similar clothes on all occasions. We have shown in a previous chapter that we make no such suggestion. As we have declared, our friend the 'boy in buttons' receives our whole-hearted admiration, and we have more than a sneaking admiration for a well-tailored Bond Street young man. But these clothes, like many others, are, as we pointed out, the clothes of special trades or for special sorts of people – let them be retained as such and if all men and most women are clerks, let all men and most women wear coats and trousers. That is a reform which can be made without destroying either our dejected Puritanism or our beloved Industrialism. Those who object to women showing their legs should be glad to see women dressed in trousers, and those who desire to retain our counting-house civilization should be glad to see the garb of the counting-house worn by all engaged in counting.

On the other hand, as the puritan and industrial bases of our civilization crumble beneath us, and signs of instability are not wanting, a change of clothes becomes inevitable, and the direction of such a change must be towards the skirt. Towards the skirt means towards the dressmaker and away from the tailor; it means also a renewed respect for materials (respect for material – another anti-puritan note!), and this will accelerate the return to full garments and strengthen the natural disinclination to cut up good stuffs. Trousers and even 'shorts' will be discarded, though both men and women will wear loose-fitting knickers or drawers when occasions, such as horse-riding, call for them. The clothes of the nursery will be retained by both boys and girls; and the skirts of both will lengthen as age and dignity increase. The tunic with the girdle will be the normal garment, with full cloaks and mantles embroidered according to fancy and lined with fur or wool according to season. In very cold climates full-length hose will be worn, and the tunic, otherwise short in the arm or with no arms at all, will be worn with long sleeves. We shall still have our 'boys in buttons' – little imps in red or black tights; we shall still have our bishops and mayors full robed in their present gorgeousness. We shall still have our jockeys, and fine ladies as fine as the ladies of Spain. We may even retain an army of clerks dressed as their service demands, in strait-waistcoats and trousers and, I hope, in chimney-pot hats.

And one thing more we shall have, and that is men looking and being as beautiful as women – marvellous thought! Men are as beautiful as women already, but the fact is hidden by their clothes. The difference between men and women is not chiefly a difference of beauty, as we make out at present, nor chiefly a difference of body, as the theory of trousers for men and skirts for women implies. The chief difference between men and women is the difference of character caused by the difference of sex; and though this difference of sex is primarily the difference between fatherhood and motherhood, and though fatherhood leaves man physically freer than motherhood leaves women, it does not destroy their essential unity of mind.

LAVS DEO

NOTE

Source: *Clothes: An Essay upon the Nature and Significance of the Natural and Artificial Integuments Worn by Men and Women* (Jonathon Cape, 1931), 186–97.

CHAPTER SEVEN

The Functions of Folk Costume in Moravian Slovakia: Introduction

Petr Bogatyrěv

In the present work I shall endeavor to analyze the functions served today and in recent times by folk costume in Moravian Slovakia. I have confined myself to the Moravian Slovak material for a number of reasons. First of all, considerable field material from the area has been collected recently (in the works of Húsek and A. Václavík) which, together with earlier studies (Josef Klvaňa and others), makes it possible for me to illustrate more thoroughly my findings on the nature and interrelationship of the various functions of costume. Secondly, the geographic and political position of the area itself has made it easier to demonstrate the functions of costume there. I wish to stress that it will not be my aim to exhaust the available data on Moravian Slovak costume. Rather, I shall simply try to shed some light on the general theoretical problems involved in the functionalism of costume in the above-mentioned region as well as a number of other places.

Much of what we learn in analyzing the functions of costume will be applicable to all clothing in general; however, folk costume has many features of its own which have nothing in common with urban dress, the latter being subject to rapidly-changing fashion.[1]

NOTES

Source: *The Functions of Folk Costume in Moravian Slovakia* (Walter de Gruyter, 1971), 33.

1. Folk costume is in many respects the antithesis of clothing which is subject to fashion changes. One of the chief tendencies of the latter is the ease with which it changes – the

new fashion must not resemble the one it replaces. The tendency of folk costume is NOT to change – grandchildren must wear the costume of their grandfathers. (I am speaking here of the TENDENCIES of urban fashions and of folk costume. Actually we know that even folk costume does not remain unchanged, that it does take on features of current fashion). Another basic distinction between folk costume and urban dress is that folk costume is subject to the sanction of the collective; the collective dictates what may or may not be changed in the costume. Urban dress is subject to the discretion of the tailors who create it. (Again, I am speaking only of tendencies. In point of actual fact, folk costume changes under the influence of urban fashion and therefore under the influence of the latter's creators; on the other hand, urban fashion itself is not immune to the sanction of the collective: there are cases where tailors, disregarding the sanction of the collective, produce items of apparel which are not accepted by urban clientele.) [. . .]

CHAPTER EIGHT

An Economic Interpretation of Women's Fashions

PAUL M. GREGORY

I

"The pretty babes that mourn'd for fashion, ignorant what to fear," are with us now in far greater numbers than in Shakespeare's year. The "mystery" of fashion changes has fascinated not only economists and sociologists, social historians and cultural anthropologists, but also philosophers and moralists, poets, playwrights, and novelists. Many of the latter have either poked fun at the lugubriousness of fashion and the foibles of its slaves, or have denounced it as an evil force in the world. To Shakespeare, fashion was a "deformed thief"; to Robert Burns it was an "idiot painter." The literary allusions to fashion are legion, and the subject has attained the dignity of Biblical mention.

Many theories of fashion have been expounded. This essay does not attempt to cover the whole subject in its myriad ramifications but simply examines some economic aspects of fashion; it takes the phenomenon of fashion changes and holds it up to the light of economic theory, in order to see its multihued facets. Such an analysis is desirable for two reasons: as a *partial* attempt to explain fashion itself, and as an exploration in applied economic theory.[1]

To begin with, fashion and style are not synonymous, although most writers use these words interchangeably. With reference to clothing, style is any distinctive mode of tailoring, while fashion is the style prevailing at any given time. A style evolves slowly, and reflects the people's way of life; fashion is a chameleon, ever changing, never in vogue long enough to reflect basic tastes and habits. Frequent fashion changes artificially shorten the period during which a style prevails; thus fashion is a parasite on style. As Elizabeth Hawes puts it:

Style is that thing which, being looked back upon after a century, gives you the fundamental feeling of a certain period in history. Style in Greece in 2000 B.C. was delicate
outdoor architecture and the clothes which went with it. Style in the Renaissance was
an elaborately carved stone cathedral and rich velvet, gold-trimmed robes. Style doesn't
change every month or every year. It only changes as often as there is a real change in the
point of view and lives of the people for whom it is produced.

   Style in 1937 may give you a functional house and comfortable clothes to wear in it.
Style doesn't give a whoop whether your comfortable clothes are red or yellow or blue,
or whether your bag matches your shoes. Style gives you shorts for tennis because they
are practical. Style takes away the wasp-waisted corset when women get free and active.[2]

Hoop skirts, togas, hourglass figures are not in fashion now, but they remain distinctive styles and – like Hattie Carnegie's bustles – they sometimes come back into
fashion through the process of adapting or reviving old styles with modern touches of
detail. Clothing styles give the social historian some insight into the life of the people
who wore them, as Anatole France realized. Two centuries hence historians may look
back upon the mid-twentieth century and infer from the functional design of bathing
suits, sports clothes, and the tailored severity of women's business suits, that ours was
an age in which women won for themselves greater physical freedom and economic
opportunity than our grandmothers had in the nineteenth century. This is a *style*. But
the long waistline of one season compared with that of another season, the raising or
lowering of skirts by two inches, will tell nothing of the life of the people. This is
fashion. As Elizabeth Hawes says, style changes every seven years or so, and "any
dress which isn't in style for at least three years isn't any good to begin with." It is our
purpose to examine fashion and fashion cycles or changes, not style itself.

   How, and why, do fashions begin? The ultimate causes of fashion are the subject
of much speculation, some of it fantastic, some of it plausible. One must beware of
monistic explanations. Veblen and others emphasized the role of conspicuous consumption and the desire for distinction through dress. Others attribute fashion
changes to the desire for decorative dress to enhance sex appeal. "No fashion is
ever successful unless it can be used as an instrument of seduction," according to
James Laver, costume authority of the Victoria and Albert Museum in England.[3]
This may explain decorative dress, but not the incessant *changes*. Then there is the
restless and unending search for perfect beauty. Curiosity leads to experimentation
with new costumes. In temperate zones, seasonal changes may accentuate the desire
for fashion changes. Finally, there is the social and economic class structure. The
rich, the bored, and those lacking in outside interests seek to distinguish themselves
from the masses by dress, and succeed in doing so temporarily. The imitativeness of the
lower-income groups, and the desire of the garment industry to capitalize on a novelty,
lead to imitations (and vulgarizations) of original designs, and deprive the "elite" of
their distinction. Thus the *haute couture* must constantly evolve "new" fashions in
order to continue to supply "exclusive" apparel for its clients. Incessant change taxes
the originality of designers, who must then resort to adaptions of old styles.

II

Profits from producing or selling fashion goods may be profits of monopoly, of in-novation, or of risk-taking. Producers or sellers who can control or influence the trend of fashion – sometimes through fashion magazines which "predict" what they have already decided to sell – and whose "creations" are not imitated, are largely relieved of risk and they receive monopoly profits, for their "exclusive" apparel sells at monopoly prices.[4] Even with imitations, sellers obtain profits of innovation as long as a new fashion remains exclusive. Eventually the "creations" of Hattie Carnegie, Valentina, *et al.*, are copied by the garment manufacturers on Seventh Avenue, New York, and these profits of innovation disappear. But by that time, still other "creations" are developed, and the profits of innovation may be permanent so long as the stream of new ideas does not run dry. Finally, those who can neither influence the fashion trend nor be among the first to introduce new designs, must anticipate the future demand. The manufacturer or seller who guesses correctly will gain profits which might properly be classified as a "reward for risk-taking," while those who guess wrong may take losses on unsold inventory, markdowns, etc., and may also suffer from the wastes which result from hand-to-mouth buying, seasonal production, and small-lot production.

Simply because some manufacturers and sellers lose from fashion's gyrations, it cannot be said that business in general suffers from fashion changes.[5] Large-scale producers take added risks, and some lose, but some gain enormous profits. The imi-tativeness of the lower-income groups, fostered by fashion and advertising, creates a steady market for replacement sales of clothing long before the clothing being worn is used up. If some producers lose from fashion, their loss is not the result of fashion itself, but the result of an incorrect anticipation of future fashion trends. In this re-spect, manufacturers' losses from fashion are analogous to producers' losses from other economic risks. If manufacturers always lost, they would oppose fashion changes! It is true that if fashion gyrations were eliminated, one of the risks of business would be gone and there would be less loss, but there would also be less profit from heavy repeat sales of clothing and accessories. Ultimately, the real losers from fashion are consumers. Some businessmen lose; others gain. And fashion editors, designers, fashion magazines that sell patterns, and the large and growing clan of publicity organizations whose business it is to make toeless shoes smart this summer and iridescent hosiery next winter, all stand to gain from the fashion merry-go-round.

Frequent fashion changes are stimulated by producers and sellers in order to make people dissatisfied with their present garments and buy new ones long before the old ones are worn out. Sales volume is based largely on repeat sales. If a garment is durable and well made and will last five years, a fashion change which makes con-sumers discard it in one year destroys four-fifths of its utility (assuming that its utility is the same each year; but see Section III, below). This puts a strain on the consumer's pocket-book, it reduces our scale of living, and it encourages a tremendous waste of economic resources. But fashion may have an even more insidious effect:

> If the emphasis is to be upon fashion, and fashions must change rapidly, why then make a garment durable, well made, or of any intrinsic value? Why not work for an *effect* at a low cost, sell the garments quickly, and trust to their passing style phase to bring the customer back to the retailer for more "new" fashions before she has a chance to discover or a disposition to complain about the basic worthlessness of the purchase?[6]

Fashion gyrations may encourage some unscrupulous manufacturers to adulterate their product. They feel safe in making shoddy goods; in cutting costs by not allowing enough material for shrinkage or alterations; in saving a few yards of material per hundred dresses by skimping on yardage, causing seams to split; by using fugitive dyes, composition buttons which melt, and similar methods. Producers who suffer from cutthroat competition use fashion changes as a means to distinguish their product. They also try to beat the price of their rivals, not by more efficient production, but by diluting quality and durability, and they may succeed in this practice because the public has been taught to pay attention to fashion but not to inquire too closely about the technical composition of the materials. Indeed, part of the garment industry opposed the "Truth in Fabrics" bill (in 1938) because they feared that honest labelling would take women's attention from fashion and would make them buy more rationally.[7] When fashion does not lead to adulteration and reduced durability, it fosters premature replacement of apparel in order to stimulate sales volume. Elsewhere I have analyzed this business practice which causes obsolescence of clothing before it is worn out.[8] Perfectly good clothes are worn only a short time and then are discarded or left to hang unused in closets. Truly, "the fashion wears out more apparel than the man," as Shakespeare put it.

III

Durable and semidurable goods such as clothing yield services of diminishing marginal utility, because of depreciation and obsolescence. An exception is the rental of clothing, i.e., the purchase of a single service, for a single occasion. As the good's services decline in utility, the consumer must decide when to discard and replace it. Now the utility gained by replacing a not yet worn-out article is not the total utility of the new article, but the *difference* between the total utility of the new article and the utility (or potential services) remaining in the discarded article.

Elasticity of demand for, and the rate of replacement of, consumer goods is influenced by the price of the goods, the consumer's income, and the rate of depreciation and obsolescence. If the commodity is priced low, a consumer (with any given income) is warranted in replacing it earlier than if the price is high, for at a low price the marginal utility of the anticipated added services exceeds the marginal utility of money (i.e., exceeds the marginal utility anticipated from alternative purchases). The cheaper the good, the earlier it will be discarded and replaced, and the more elastic will be the demand for it, *over a period of time*. The richer the consumer, the lower is the marginal utility of money to him, and the earlier he is likely to discard goods and replace them. But since a dollar is worth more to a poor man, he should (rationally) use his existing goods longer before replacing them. Finally, wear and tear cause depreciation, while monotony, conspicuous waste, and, of course, fashion, all cause obsolescence. Even in the absence of wear and tear, it is usually claimed that long use of the same article is sometimes monotonous, and its utility will decline because people like change and novelty for its own sake. (This claim is evaluated in Section VI.) Also, in a pecuniary culture which stresses conspicuous display of wealth, people may lose prestige if they utilize the same good for a long time. These factors – largely outside the control of any individual or business firm – hasten the decline of marginal utility for durable consumers goods over a period of time.

But this discussion refers to goods discarded because of wear and tear (depreciation) and monotony and prestige factors (inevitable or "normal" obsolescence), and replaced by an *identical* good. Since fashion changes are influenced by business, they create deliberate or *purposeful* obsolescence of goods,[9] and induce premature replacement and much waste, even in the absence of wear and tear and such monotony and conspicuous consumption as is normal to most people.

Anything which arouses a want or desire without actually satisfying it seems to create *disutility* rather than utility. (Some goods, such as foods, arouse an appetite and at the same time satisfy it.) Psychologists tell us that, for normal people, tension is undesirable; satisfaction consists in the relief from tension. Fashion – and suggestive advertising, with which it is allied – makes people dissatisfied with their existing clothing, arouses desires and, if people lack the purchasing power to indulge their newly-created wants, sets up tensions which cumulate. Fashion and advertising are a gigantic burlesque show at which millions gape. Seeing new fashions temptingly and teasingly advertised – goods they can never hope to own, changes they cannot afford to keep up with – must set up a tremendous store of insatiety in the poor and the modest-income groups, an insatiety which probably contributes to the neurotic personality of our time. And fashion may destroy utility, not only for one, but for many. Just as becoming apparel is satisfying to all who behold the wearer, so a fashion change makes last year's apparel distasteful not only to the wearer, but also to her friends, who may be ashamed to be seen with her.

If fashion changes reflected changing tastes and habits, then each season's fashions might be an improvement over the last and might possess more utility by being a closer approximation to our basic needs. But this would be so only if styles changed gradually and were not forced. Unlike an oil painting or a piece of sculpture, the new fashion is not preserved but is soon scrapped for another "creation." New fashions are not added to older ones; they displace them. If fashions changed in order to attain beauty in dress, the result should be a gradual approach to artistic perfection. But this is not the case. As Veblen pointed out in the *Theory of the Leisure Class*, the alleged beauty of the prevailing fashions is spurious, since none of them will bear the test of time. Among the Chinese and Japanese, among the ancient Greeks and Romans, and among the peasants of many European countries there have evolved fairly stable styles which many critics consider more artistic and more satisfying than the fluctuating fashions of modern industrial communities. Indeed, in copying or adapting them, modern designers either admit their intrinsic superiority, or else attest their own poverty of creative imagination. (The same criticism can be made of revival architecture.)

Under any definition of utility, frequent rotation of fashions destroys utility. If the utility is physical, then the changed fashion forces consumers to discard still useful garments. For people who are concerned with wearing the "right" things, utility based on social approval is immediately destroyed when the old garment loses social caste. And if the true function of apparel is to attract attention to the wearer, if utility is based on novelty, then every change in fashion destroys the attention-arresting features of the displaced garment. In the absence of frequent fashion changes, all people would wear the same clothes longer, and more people than today would feel appropriately dressed. Industry ought to provide a wide range of styles at any given time, in order to complement the great variety of ages, physical types, and personalities. But it is not necessary to change fashions every season in order to achieve variety. Stability of styles is not the same thing as standardization.

IV

Although there is intense rivalry in the production and sale of clothing, fashion itself is a pure monopoly element. Fashion and fashion changes result in monopolistic competition by differentiating the goods of rival sellers, and they create further market imperfections by playing upon and reinforcing consumer ignorance.[10] Let us first examine fashion and differentiation.

Frequent fashion changes imply differentiation over time (temporal differentiation), as well as at a given time. Producers differentiate their goods from all rival brands at any one time, and each producer differentiates his own brand from the model he was selling last season. Sellers use distinctive styles in order to sell more goods than their rivals, or to sell at a higher price; they use fashion changes in order to sell more frequently than their rivals. (In the long run, more frequent sales mean greater sales volume, but the two policies have different implications, as explained below.) In the first sense, a distinctive or "exclusive" fashion has the same economic effect as a brand or trademark: it distinguishes a particular product in the minds of buyers and creates loyalty to a particular producer or seller; it lifts the product out of the market for more standardized goods and creates a specialty which is relatively free from comparative judgment of price, quality, or durability. In this sense fashion is a pure monopoly element. In the second sense (temporal differentiation) the incessant emphasis on "newness" makes people dissatisfied with their existing clothing and leads them to buy more. Their dissatisfaction begot of obsolescence, they do not necessarily forsake their original buying source. In fact, a producer or seller who can point to the "latest" fashions has a selling advantage over his more conservative rivals, once people are induced to think of utility in terms of novelty and get into the habit of frequently replacing their clothes. The garment industry, the millinery, shoe, glove, and other industries which depend on fashion for sales volume recognize the importance of temporal differentiation. They employ "adapters," who are not true creators or designers but whose function is to evolve dresses, hats, or other articles of apparel that are "new." These fashions must be definitely earmarked for the current season and must have at least one talking point – if only a new name for an old color – easily recognizable as different from last season's fashions.

Since some of the moribund fashions are still displayed and purchased, current fashions may increase the range of differentiation, thereby confusing purchasers and impeding rational choice because the new and the old models are likely to differ only in petty details or in color. But in the long run, free consumer choice is more seriously restricted by fashion than by ordinary brand differentiation, because merchants do not generally carry what are considered "unfashionable" goods, even though people may want them. Many women who buy and wear the clothing in vogue rather than the clothing they want explain it by saying: "It's what everybody is wearing. The stores don't even show anything else." Thus fashion limits the genuine variety available to consumers; and by taking women's minds off price, quality of materials, and workmanship, fashion encourages wasteful buying. In the case of ordinary brand differentiation, moreover, a consumer will insist on his favorite brand – though better or less expensive ones are available – but he can at least buy several units at a time (e.g., a carton of "Chesterfield" cigarettes instead of one pack). But in the case of temporal differentiation, the high rate of obsolescence of fashion goods makes people reluctant to buy ahead. If styles were more stable, and fashion changes nonexistent, a prudent buyer could purchase several identical items at once (at a "sale," or out of season), thus saving money and the time and energy of shopping, as well as being able to use one while letting the others "rest" or be repaired or renovated. In some markets, for example that of automobiles, the loss from annual model changes is to some extent the gain of the used-car buyer, for heavy trade-in sales swell the stock of used cars and facilitate automobile ownership by lower income groups. But unfashionable clothes do not so readily find their way to poorer people, either through charity or through secondhand clothing markets. The latter are not so highly organized as the used-car market, and, besides, there is some social stigma attached to wearing secondhand clothes. Last season's clothes are often discarded, or left to hang in closets. Thus fashion in clothing may create greater waste than style changes in automobiles, socially as well as personally.

In women's dresses, in 1939–40 the New York market produced 125,000 models; in dresses above $4.75 wholesale, less than 300 dresses per model; below $4.75, less than 1,000 dresses per model.[11] Some of these models are from earlier seasons; some are "new." Fashion as a brand or trademark (ordinary differentiation) accounts for some of the designs; but fashion, as a device to stimulate obsolescence and premature replacement (temporal differentiation) must account for the larger part of this multiplicity of models, for there could be great variety at any given time without so many models, if a "new" set were not "created" every season.

Many writers attribute the excessive number of models to design piracy, and urge the passage of legislation similar to that in France, to prevent and punish the copying of designs. This point is debatable. The two American attempts at legal design protection – the NRA garment industry codes and the Fashion Originators Guild of America (FOGA) – were both thrown out by the Supreme Court. Since standardized models have often led to cutthroat competition, producers and sellers rely on constantly shifting fashions in order to have a specialty which is removed from comparative judgment. Legal design protection would encourage further product differentiation and would make the market less competitive; for imitations, copies, and adaptions of "original creations" blur the sharp differences which are the essence of monopoly power in the area of fashion goods.

Nor does the entire fashion industry object to design piracy. Fabric manufacturers know that copying goes on all the time, and they realize that imitations boost the sale of their fabrics to garment factories and large department stores. The Paris couturiers are the display windows for the great French fabric manufacturers and are heavily subsidized by them. The manufacturer sells the material not only through the original designer, but also through the other firms which copy the model. In fact, fashion could not exist without imitations of high styles in lower price ranges.

Design piracy, like trademark infringement, would increase competition if the copy were a perfect one, for it would prevent monopoly profit from an "exclusive" design and would rapidly dilute the profits of innovation.[12] But in the garment industry the copy is seldom perfect; it is usually a vulgarization of the original, often frankly called a "copy" or "adaption" and sold to a different income group. The *haute couture* prepares originals for the rich, while the garment industry capitalizes on the imitative tendency of the lower income groups and taps a different segment of the demand curve by emphasizing price appeal as well as (an often superficial) "style appeal." This is not the same as attempted trademark duplication, through which a new firm tries to tap the same market in the same price range and to huddle under the umbrella of "goodwill" built up by the original firm through sustained advertising.

Where the customer is a poor judge of quality (for example, where rational buying requires technical knowledge or a highly developed esthetic sense), producers – by sheer propaganda – can sell inferior goods at high prices. The public is told that each season's fashions are new, different. But they are not genuine innovations; if they were, there would be some sense in the public's reliance on the tastes of "fashion leaders." The ignorance of consumers in the area of fashion is fostered by businessmen and copywriters who insist that fashion is a "mystery" which only the elect can understand.

Now there is nothing mysterious or esoteric in designing clothes that are truly attractive, functional and useful. If businessmen were interested in genuine style and quality the public would not be so bewildered and misled; they would not confuse novelty with utility. In the area of fashion, as in many other industries, businessmen are generally lacking in imagination, social vision, and daring. They rarely create an entirely new style; they simply vary an existing one. They seldom experiment with very low prices; they simply cut prices a little, or not at all, and trust to the forced obsolescence of goods to stimulate repeat sales in a stable price range. Most sellers would rather not cut prices, would rather not compete in price or quality; instead they use all the tricks of fashion to gain customers.

Fashion is intimately related to waste in production and consumption, to seasonality in production and excess plant capacity, to the business cycle, to advertising and the maturity of industry, and through all of these, fashion changes impinge directly on consumer welfare. By requiring highly specialized equipment, changes in dies and patterns, etc., fashion obstructs diversified production and reduces the mobility of investment. A sudden fashion change may make valuable equipment such as dress patterns or shoe lasts worthless. By requiring hand-to-mouth buying of materials, small-lot production, excessive inventories, niarkdowns of unfashionable goods, and by causing a host of other production wastes, fashion keeps prices too high in most cases, and wages and profits too low in many cases. Lack of space prevents further discussion of the wastefulness of fashion, which I have treated more extensively elsewhere.[13]

Frequent fashion changes imply the absence of genuine or workable competition. If clothing styles were stable, sellers' rivalry would take the form of price cuts or improved quality, or both. Producers would charge less for the same product or would sell a better or more durable product for the same price, and all selling rivalry would be reducible to price competition. Most so-called "quality competition" in the area of fashion goods is really an attempt to stimulate sales without reducing prices and without improving the product. "New" fashions seldom change the product; they change the mind of the buyer, they make her dissatisfied with her existing clothes, which therefore become prematurely obsolete. Emphasis on shifting fashions is an attempt to remove the product from comparative judgment of price, quality, and durability, and to create a specialty which will not have a host of imitators to share in the profits of monopoly or the profits of innovation. (When sellers are few – as in the automobile industry – they fear that their rivals' retaliation will cause a price war; hence annual style changes replace price-cutting.) In general, fashion gyrations are relied on to maintain sales volume by frequent replacements in the same income groups instead of by price reductions to stimulate sales to lower income groups. Thus fashion is employed to avoid price competition; it is a variant of monopolistic competition and (in some industries) of oligopoly. Finally, by playing upon and reinforcing consumer ignorance; by providing the shadow instead of the substance of variety and consumer choice; by taking the buyer's mind off price, materials, workmanship, and durability; by encouraging waste in production; by preventing the independent development of the public taste; by getting the public in the habit of following self-appointed fashion arbiters instead of relying on their own esthetic values or those of disinterested artists or designers; by substituting *ars gratia pecuniae* for *ars gratia artis* or *ars gratia populii* fashion intensifies imperfect competition.

V

Unequal distribution of income is one of the recognized *causes* of fashion gyrations, for markets would not become saturated so soon, and there would be less incentive for forced fashion, if the poor had greater purchasing power. But in this section we are interested in the effects of fashion on people of various income levels. Who suffers most from fashion changes? Some writers maintain that the poor, especially the working classes, do not lose as much from fashion as the middle classes do, because working clothes are functional and the poor do not need to keep up with the latest fashions. This may be true of overalls, uniforms, and special attire designed for particular types of work, such as factory employment, farming, or domestic service. But the very spirit of most fashions makes functional design difficult, for most fashions are designed in relation to women who lead lives of leisure; few of them are conceived in relation to the everyday lives of the masses. Very little advertising space is devoted to showing clothes designed especially for working girls, and the clothes which are available to them are poorly adapted to office work or most other employments.

The great in-between classes of American women, neither rich nor poor, with some money to spend but none to waste, are said to suffer most from fashion.[14] If this is true, it may be because middle class women attach more importance to social approval through dress than do poor women. Or, if poor women would also like to wear the latest fashions, they simply cannot afford to. Thus the poor may not waste as much money as the middle classes, through fashion changes, but if their desire is unrequited, they may lose more from fashion psychologically, as a result of frustration. It is true that some people lead a bohemian existence and pay no attention to fashion. This may be because they are poor, or it may result from a desire to husband their time and energy for more important activities of a creative nature. It is impossible to prove what class suffers most, but the following generalizations are probably valid. Except for some kinds of working clothes, which are fairly functional, the poor, who can afford it least, may suffer most from fashion changes, especially since emphasis on novelty is often at the expense of quality and durability; the rich, who can afford to discard unfashionable clothes and can have their clothes made to order, certainly suffer least; while the middle-income groups probably suffer in proportion to their desire to emulate the rich and to distinguish themselves from the masses. This may be one index of their middle-class status. In countless advertisements business teasingly dangles "new" fashions before the eyes of people who lack any kind of serviceable clothes. The poor, like Moses, see the Promised Land but do not enter.

Men suffer less from fashion than women do, and poor men, working men, suffer less than working women. Women in all walks of life seem to attach more importance to fashion than men do. As Elizabeth Hawes says:

> It is the prerogative of the working man, the lower class guy, to wear no collar and no tie. He may go without a hat if he likes. He can wear loose, unpleated blue jeans. He can show his suspenders if he wants. He can go shirtless in the hot summer, the straps of his overalls barely covering his hairy chest. . . . He is not admitted to the best clubs, nor even allowed to ride up in the elevator of the Squibb Building without a coat. . . . But he has nothing to risk by being comfortable.
>
> His boss will not look askance if he turns up in sandals in the summer. He will not be fired for choosing to wear no collar to work.[15]

Whereas women of all classes seek variety and incessant change, men's clothes are more standardized and stable. (They may also be less comfortable, but here we are interested in fashion changes, not in intrinsic suitability of clothes.) The only difference between the evening suit of a millionaire and that of an office boy is in the quality of materials used. Some people believe that men's clothes are less variable than women's because men are largely engaged in earning a living and have so little time to indulge in conspicuous consumption that they put the burden on women, who have more leisure. But this theory may be questioned, for working women take at least as much pride in clothes as nonworking women do. It is interesting to note that, in men's clothes, changes toward greater comfort generally come from the working men and slowly – oh, so slowly – influence the middle and upper classes; while in the case of women, the changes come (more rapidly) from the top of the economic and social hierarchy.

We must also consider the age distribution of the population. The American population is aging. From 1930 to 1940 the average age increased 2 1/2 years, and the trend continues. Will this encourage or discourage the desire for novelty? Are older (wiser?) people less likely to be influenced by fashion and more likely to insist on stability? Certainly, tastes become more settled with age, older persons tend to have a larger percentage of their income taken up with commitments, and after years of experiment one finds the styles which are most satisfying to him. Young people may welcome frequent fashion changes, which give them a chance to experiment and still be like everybody else. Ruby Turner Norris says:

> As persons grow older, it is often said that they become 'fixed in their ways.' This means that more of their total income has been satisfactorily allocated in habitual ways, leaving less for the experimental new developments which change taste patterns. Also the mental effort of choice and the physical effort of shopping become more onerous with advancing years. Very aged persons seldom add or substitute a single new good or brand during a year, unless forced to do so by changing incomes. For the aged, often, income is in the period of contraction and this in itself tends to cut out the experimental residue. Because of the possession of typically increasing income, lack of

experience, and the mental and physical vigor necessary for choice, . . . the younger income recipients make more deliberate choice between alternative consumption goods than older income recipients.[16]

To a large extent, fashion advertising is addressed to the young, but this is not always the case; some fashions are promoted for middle-aged people who seek a more youthful appearance. Moreover, as one grows older, one gets in the habit of expecting and following changing fashions. And some young people, such as college girls, are, temporarily, able to ignore fashion changes because they can achieve a feeling of security within their group simply by wearing comfortable sweaters, skirts, and moccasins, or other clothes approved by their peers, and therefore partaking of the nature of a campus uniform. Their independence of fashion is similar to that of the nun, or member of an order, but it is only a group independence, for it imposes on the individual a uniformity as tyrannical as that of fashion.

Fashion changes more rapidly in a democracy than in a caste society where the masses are restricted in purchasing power and in social position. And fashions change most frequently in time of great social upheaval, such as war or revolution. For instance, in the two years from 1784 to 1786 French fashions in women's hats changed 17 times.[17] Gina Lombroso states the matter admirably:

> Woman's clothes acquire stability when times are such that social conditions are fast and rigid, when it is not possible to pass abruptly from one class to another. When woman's position is stable her costume becomes almost invariable, as in religious or charitable orders, where her position is not affected by her appearance and where she can assert herself by other means than by her clothes and jewels.
>
> But when society is more or less in upheaval (as was the case during the French Revolution) her clothes change perpetually, no matter how poor she may be or how trying are political conditions. When woman's position is unstable and there is a possibility for her to pass easily from one class to another, her costumes vary incessantly, as she changes banner and coat of arms.[18]

The influence of war on fashion is two-sided. War, with its insatiable demand for men and materials, creates a condition of universal scarcity and at the same time swells the purchasing power of large groups in society. Moreover, the heavy backlog of deferred demand tends to exceed the supply of clothes in the immediate postwar period. The resulting sellers' market, with no need to stimulate sales volume, ought to minimize the influence of fashion during war and postwar years. In wartime, social pressure and scarcities tend to reduce conspicuous consumption by the wealthy and emulation by the poor and middle classes. Durability, comfort, and simplicity are emphasized, and distinction is sought in direct or indirect social service, or its appearance; in a wartime economy, the pecuniary canons of taste are temporarily weakened.

But in another sense, war strengthens the hand of fashion, which adapts itself to the wartime psychology. Civilian apparel and accessories use the wartime motif and, except for government restrictions on materials, such as CPA's Order L-85, fashion is stimulated by war. For war brings new ideas, breaks down old customs, and is an ally of rapid change. Even during a war, postwar style changes are planned and are hinted at in advertisements. Wartime restrictions cause the public to overemphasize novelty and change when these restrictions are finally lifted. Once the custom has been established, each firm considers frequent fashion changes necessary as an advertising device to maintain its market position. And the wartime development of new fabrics of great durability, to be put on the market after the war, increases the reliance on fashion to stimulate replacement sales. Moreover, by getting people in the habit of prematurely discarding clothes, fashion intensifies wartime shortages, thereby delaying conversion of plants to war production, and later, by inducing a buying spree, it fans the flames of postwar inflation.

VI

From an economic – and probably from a social and psychological – viewpoint, there is little to be said in favor of fashion. Nevertheless, we can appreciate the wisdom which Gina Lombroso expressed when she said that the enormous stress which women lay on everything pertaining to clothes and the art of personal adornment is connected with the tendency to crystallize sentiment into an object.

> Clothes constitute part of a woman's personality as determined by tradition and sanctified by religion. Woman symbolizes every important event in her life, every important feast in her religion, by a special dress. The temptation of dress is the last step in the ceremony to which the novice has to submit before entering the cloister. The memory of the gown which she, too, might have worn, was the strongest temptation that assailed St. Catherine before she took her solemn vows – a gown embroidered with gold and stars like those her sisters had worn, which her grandchildren would have gazed at with eyes filled with wonder and admiration.

> * * * * *

> A jewel, a beautiful gown mean to a woman what an official decoration means to a man.
> If woman's clothes cost the family and society a little time, money and activity, they allow woman, independently of lies and calumnies, to triumph and come to the fore outside of man's world and competition. They allow woman to satisfy her desire to be the first in the most varied fields by giving her the illusion that she is first, and at the same time enabling her rival to have the same illusion. Clothes absorb some of woman's activity which might otherwise be diverted to more or less worthwhile ends; they give woman real satisfaction, a satisfaction complete in itself and independent of others, and I think that under present conditions at least, they constitute a safety valve which saves society from much greater and more dangerous evils than those which they cause.[19]

The truth of these observations lies in their emphasis on clothes which are really beautiful and distinctive. But fashion is not primarily concerned with beauty; and fashion connotes uniformity, not the individuality so cherished in our society and so artfully suggested by the copywriters. Many people who follow fashions rigorously believe they are following their own inclinations; they are unaware of the primitive tribal compulsion, and this is true of fashions in manners, morals, and literature, as well as clothes.

Most writers – even stern critics of fashion – assume that the desire for novelty and change in clothes inheres in human nature. If this is so, then businessmen can truly claim that they are simply meeting a deep-seated public need. But this explanation assumes too much. There is a general desire for novelty and change, but it need not express itself in our apparel. Dress is simply an easy way for otherwise undistinguished people to distinguish themselves, or to have the illusion of distinction. We do not seem to tire of living in the same house, listening to the same great music, enjoying social intercourse with the same old friends. In fact, we grow more attached to certain possessions through long use, for example, houses, pipes, and even some articles of clothing. The so-called monotony of wearing the same styles a long time does not really flow from inadequacies in the clothes themselves. The constant desire for novelty in clothes (never to be confused with beauty or variety) flows from boredom and lack of more genuine goals in life than merely impressing people or courting social approval through externals such as dress. It may also stem from absence of an integrated personality, from monotony of ideas, and from personal and social frustrations. Fashion changes are thus a symptom of intellectual, emotional and cultural immaturity. The subtle insinuations of the fashion industries lead people to believe that newer fashions in clothes will solve their problems. But they do not, will not, cannot solve our problems. Whence, change is incessant. Canny businessmen know that people seek an easy escape from personal inadequacies or from the slings and arrows of outrageous fortune. So they build a folklore of fashion; they invest goods with subjective qualities which they cannot possess, and prescribe their wares as a panacea, a sedative, an elixir. Failure in the economic arena, love unrequited, confusion in a chaotic world – all these lead people to fashion's balm. Come unto me all ye that are heavy laden, and I will give you – something "new."

In the absence of fashion changes, people would grow accustomed to using their clothes a longer time, and their desire for change and novelty would express itself in other fields – perhaps in other goods, perhaps in absorbing activities, perhaps (I hope) in the world of ideas, which offers an amazing variety to tempt the most jaded palate. As our culture is now constituted, monotony does appear to lie behind most fashion changes, but this monotony is not natural. Business has a vested interest in promoting new fashions and in thereby intensifying the monotony of existing styles. Consumers are ignorant, gullible, and full of vanity, but when we hear businessmen say they must adapt their production and advertising to irrational consumer behavior, we seem to hear Aesop's wolf complaining of the lamb.

The social disadvantages of fashion are many, and, like other social institutions, there is room for reform without going to utopian extremes. It seems to me that he who would look upon the face of Fashion and keep his balance must have a saving grace of humor. Only our laughter at Charlie Chaplin's antics saved us from tears over his all-too-human predicaments. Lacking this ingredient, reform becomes a demand for repression, the true moralist is silenced, and the shrill small voice of Mrs. Grundy is heard in the land.

NOTES

Source: *Southern Economic Journal,* 14(2) (Southern Economic Association, 1947), 148–62.

1. P. H. Nystrom's *Economics of Fashion* was written before the rigorous concepts of monopoly and competition were developed. This book is a valuable and interesting study of fashion from the eclectic viewpoint of cultural anthropology, psychology, and social history, and it brings out many facts about the business organization of fashion, but it contains little economic analysis and makes no attempt to explain fashion in the light of modern economic theory.
2. Elizabeth Hawes, *Fashion is Spinach*, p. 5.
3. *Life*, March 24, 1947, p. 65.
4. For example, cotton house dresses, originally $3.95, were sold for $19.50 after Mary Lewis, then of Best & Company, promoted them as fashionable frocks. Roy Sheldon and E. Arens, *Consumer Engineering*, pp. 118–119. See also the case of ostrich feathers (p. 61), and seal skins (pp. 146–149).
5. In an otherwise admirable discussion, Leland J. Gordon insists that "the only possible gainers from the artificial stimulation of fashion are a few specialists producing fashion goods. Large-scale producers manufacturing in anticipation of demand stand to lose as a result of capricious changes in fashion. . . ." *Economics for Consumers*, p. 131. This is not always so.
6. Margaret Dana, *Behind the Label*, a guide to intelligent buying, p. 104.
7. "Nothing should be done that would take the woman's attention from fashion and direct it toward the technical composition of materials," said an industry witness before a congressional committee. *New York Herald Tribune*, May 12, 1938.
8. P. M. Gregory, "A Theory of Purposeful Obsolescence," *Southern Economic Journal*, July 1947.
9. *Ibid.*
10. For a more thorough treatment of the material in this section, see P. M. Gregory, 'Fashion and Monopolistic Competition," *Journal of Political Economy*, Oct. 1947.
11. M. D. C. Crawford, *The Ways of Fashion*, p. 16.
12. *Cf.* Edward Chamberlin, *The Theory of Monopolistic Competition*, Appendix E, "Some Arguments in Favor of Trade Mark Infringement and 'Unfair Trading,'" pp. 218–222.
13. Gregory, "A Theory of Purposeful Obsolescence," *loc. cit.*
14. For example, Dana, *op. cit.*, pp. 108–9.
15. Hawes, *op. cit.*, pp. 324–5.
16. Ruby Turner Norris, *The Theory of Consumers' Demand* p. 113.
17. Frank A. Parsons, *The Psychology of Dress*, p. 211.
18. Gina Lombroso, *L'Anima della Donna* (translated as *The Soul of Woman: Reflections on Life*), pp. 83–84.
19. *Ibid.*, pp. 82, 83, 85.

Part 2:
Fashion and Fantasy

CHAPTER NINE

Themes in Cosmetics and Grooming

Murray Wax

ABSTRACT

Cosmetic and grooming practices are universal among human societies. These practices may be analyzed according to casualness and control, exposure and concealment, and plasticity and fixity. The modern brassière illustrates the dialectic of exposure and concealment as well as the plastic manipulation of the body. Permanent waving illustrates the dialectic of casualness and control (manageability): the young girl exemplifies casualness in grooming; the older woman, control. Grooming is employed not merely in the service of sexuality but primarily to denote the status and role of the person in relationship to some audience.

This paper deals with some practices concerning highly conscious, social aspects of physical appearance, in particular the appearance of women.[1] These go under the names of "grooming" and "cosmetics," and they involve the manipulation of one's superficial physical structure so as to make a desired impression upon others.[2] The manipulations include bathing, anointing, and coloring the skin; cutting, shaving, plucking, braiding, waving, and setting the hair; deodorizing and scenting the body; coloring or marking the lips, hands, nails, eyes, face, or other exposed regions; cleansing, coloring, and filing the teeth; molding, restraining, and concealing various parts of the body; and so on.

As a class, these activities are universal among human beings. Some of the oldest artifacts discovered indicate the usage of cosmetics, for example, the presence of red ocher in Cro-Magnon graves and the elaborate toilette sets of the Egyptians. The Bible relates varied instances of the use of cosmetics: Esther and the other maids being prepared for King Ahasuerus and the anointing of Jesus in Bethany.

The cosmetic and grooming practices of other peoples sometimes appear to us as peculiar or outrageous (e.g., lip-stretching, foot-binding, tattooing, head-shaping, scarification), but in every case the custom can be understood as an attempt to modify or mold the superficial physical structure of the body into patterns considered attractive and appropriate to the status of the individual.

Apparently, there has been little analysis of the meaning of cosmetics by those in the sociological-anthropological profession.[3] Ethnographers have reported the tremendous variety of forms that personal ornamentation and grooming may take. More important, they have observed – and characterized as such – the association of patterns of dress and grooming with social status, noting how changes in dress and grooming are universally employed to denote the movement from one social status to another (infancy, childhood, sexual maturity, marriage, maternity, anility, death) or the assumption of special office (chief, priest, medicine man, Doctor's degree).

One of the main sources of literature on cosmetics and grooming is that of the moral critics. Throughout the recorded history of the West there have been repeated denunciations of the use of cosmetics. Isaiah's stern eschatology supplies the reader with both his attitude and a fair picture of how the sophisticated women of his time appeared:

> In that day the Lord will take away the bravery of their tinkling ornaments about their feet, and their cauls, and their round tires like the moon,
> The chains, and the bracelets, and the mufflers,
> The bonnets, and the ornaments of the legs, and the headbands, and the tablets, and the earrings,
> The rings, and the nose jewels,
> The changeable suits of apparel, and the mantles, and the wimples, and the crisping pins,
> The glasses, and the fine linen, and the hoods, and the veils.
> And it shall come to pass, that instead of a sweet smell there shall be stink; and instead of a girdle a rent; and instead of well set hair baldness; and instead of a stomacher a girding of sackcloth; and burning instead of beauty.[4]

(The prophet grants that the effect was "beauty.")

A more or less continuous line of critical commentary runs from the Old Testament through the medieval moralists to Shakespeare[5] ("The harlot's cheek beautied with plastering art")[6] and on to modern times. Evidently those who employed cosmetics were less vocal and less literary than their critics but equally persistent.

The themes of this criticism are, first, that women should be interested in more spiritual matters than the vanity of beautifying their physical appearance; second, that cosmetics make women more attractive to men and thus lead both parties from the path of virtue; third, that cosmetics are deceitful, inasmuch as they give women a better appearance than they natively have; and, fourth, a modern criticism,[7] that cosmetics are an instrument of the ubiquitous modern drive for conformity, in which all persons must look alike and act alike.

THE MODERN USE OF COSMETICS

Some insight into the meanings of adornment, cosmetics, and grooming may be gained from three themes, expressed by opposing pairs of concepts: *casualness* and *control, exposure* and *concealment*, and *plasticity* and *fixity*. While these notions are not so clearly separable as might be required in a polished conceptual scheme – and, indeed, they may be but different aspects of the same theme – nonetheless, they will assist this preliminary study.

The brassière is a pointed illustration of the theme of exposure and concealment. On the one hand, the brassière is the principal one of several articles of clothing that serve to conceal the bosom from view. On the other hand, the brassière makes the bosom more conspicuous, so that, even beneath several layers of clothing, the on-looker can appreciate the feminine form. Many brassières are designed with the purposes of exposing and emphasizing certain portions of the body and skin while concealing others.

The brassière also illustrates the theme of plasticity: it molds the bosom into forms that are considered attractive and elegant but that are found naturally, if ever, only among a few. Women differ in their emphasis on one or another of the opposing terms that compose a theme; for example, in discussing how they judged whether a brassière fitted, some said that they wished to feel a firm and definite, yet comfortable, lift, while others said that they made sure the garment fitted smoothly so that there would be no underarm exposure when they wore a sleeveless dress or blouse. Inci-dentally, the recent fashion in bosoms has called forth critical comment from social analysts in such terms as "infantilism" and "momism." On the other hand, the cur-rent ideal of the full yet high bosom is more mature and more sane than past emphases upon the flat chest and virginal torso.

The themes of concealment and control are pungently illustrated by the current emphasis on eliminating the odors of the body and its products. Bathing and even sterilizing the skin, reducing the rate of and absorbing perspiration, and personal and household sanitary techniques have spread widely throughout our society as devices for reducing human odor. Happily, the more old-fashioned *plastic* theme (which aims at the positive enhancement of body odor) has not been affected; the consumption of perfumes and scents seems to be increasing.

The demand for control of body odor seems to be experienced in several kinds of situations, primary among which is the enforced intimacy of heterosexual office work. In the office, people live with one another in close physical proximity for more of their waking hours than they do with their families. This minimizing of human odors may be interpreted as part of the attempt to minimize the physical being and to emphasize the social role and office. Office workers must strive to interact with each other in official roles, with a restrained personal interest, rather than as phys-ical intimates. While physical intimacy between office personnel may occur, it is exceptional and contrary to the folkways. This does not deny to business its share

of the sexual wickedness of the world but simply notes the restraints that seem automatically to be imposed when a small group of people must work hard together in
the public eye.

THE PERMANENT WAVE AS AN ILLUSTRATION

The way in which the motives for control and plasticity interlock and the efforts that
women make to achieve the proper appearance are illustrated by modern "permanent"-
waving customs. About two-thirds of the white women in the United States had
their hair permanent-waved last year. For most of these women it was more or less
habitual; they had had the operation performed several times during the year. Most
permanent waves are given at home, using kits that cost only a few dollars. The
successful merchandising of the home wave kit has put the waving process within
the economic reach of the large majority of American women, and most of them
have accepted the invitation.

On the face of it, the situation is peculiar. The cold-waving process, employing
thioglycolate salts, is simple in principle, but, in practice, much depends on the skill
and care with which the operations are performed and on the condition of the hair.
Most women have experienced or seen cases of overprocessing that gave frizzy hair
or of misprocessing that left no wave but dried the hair. Also, the waving process is
unpleasant: while the odor of the waving lotion has been improved, the scent remains
far from agreeable; the lotion is not kind to the skin; and the process is usually messy.
Added to this is the uncertainty of the outcome.

When asked to describe what they seek, most women will answer, or accept the
phrase, "A soft, natural wave." Since a majority of women have to go through the process just described in order to achieve this wave, it is difficult to agree that it is natural.
But it has been a rather consistent cultural ideal of the West for some centuries that
this type of wave is the natural and ideal kind of hair for women, while straight hair
is natural and ideal to men. As a cultural ideal, it is as reasonable as many another,
but it has little relation to sex-linked genes.

"Softness" of wave is likewise a loaded term. The student discovers painfully
that a *soft wave* is by definition the kind of wave a woman wants, whether this be
in fact the slightest of twists to the hair fibers or the most extreme rotation short of
breakage. The soft wave is not an end in itself but only a proximate goal. Women
wave their hair not merely for the wave per se but also because it gives them plastic
control over their hair. Hair that is artificially or naturally curly has what women call
"body" and may be arranged in an almost indefinite variety of coiffures. That curly
hair thus becomes a plastic yet consciously controllable aspect of a woman's appearance is indicated by such expressions as "It will take a set" or "You can do something
with it."[8]

Although they sound contradictory, plasticity and control actually require each
other. Control is not possible unless there is some way to make a plastic arrangement

or modification of the portion of the body, bringing it from a less to a more controlled state, and plasticity would be meaningless unless the rearrangement accomplished through plasticity could be fixed for some period of time.[9]

In permanent waving, women differ in their emphasis on sides of the plastic-fixed, casual-control themes. Some wish just enough wave to achieve some body and manageability and are fearful that too much curl will appear unnatural, that is, not casual. Others wish a wave that will enable them to keep their hair always neat and ordered; they do not want their hair to fly casually about. The firmer the wave, the easier it is to *manage* the hair and to keep it under control. Younger women constitute the largest market for loose, casual waves; older women, for tight, curly waves. Loose waves appear softer and more "feminine" but are more difficult to manage and can best be adapted to informal casual styles of grooming. Most women seek a compromise between the wave that is too soft to manage well and the wave that is so tight (controlled) that it appears unnatural or unfeminine, and many pursue the elusive goal of the soft wave and completely manageable hair.

WOMAN MAKES HERSELF

Among some peoples the costume proper to the socially and sexually mature man or woman is relatively fixed. It may be a tattoo or a style of dress or of coiffure; but, whatever it is, it changes only slightly, if at all, unless the person moves into a distinctly different status. In the United States fixed dress and grooming are peculiarly distinctive of religious orders and some religious sects that cling to a stylized version of what was common and decent at the time that the sect or order was instituted.

Such fixity or rigidity of grooming practices is not characteristic of all peoples, and, particularly, it is not characteristic of the typical American woman, who, following the plastic theme, tends to view her body as a craftsman or artist views his raw material. This is the matter which she can shape, color, and arrange to produce an object which, hopefully, will be at once attractive, fashionable, and expressive of her own individuality. Devices which increase her ability to mold her body (e.g., permanent waving) are received much as the *avant-garde* artist receives new techniques and modalities for his work.

The clearest expression of the (casual) plastic motif is afforded by the ideal of a girl in late adolescence. Continually experimenting with new styles of dress and grooming, she is in effect trying on this or that role or personality to see what response it will bring to her. She is most aware of new products and new styles, and she uses them to manipulate her appearance this way and that.

To some social observers, however, the teen-ager appears as the slave to fad and fashion and not as the experimenter. A more accurate formulation would be that the teen-ager follows fad and fashion – to the extent that she does, and not all do – because she is experimenting with herself and has not yet developed a self-image with which she can be comfortable. An older, more stable woman, who knows herself and her roles and how she wishes to appear, can ignore fad and follow fashion at a distance.

A clear expression of the conceal and control theme is given by the woman who is striving to eliminate her feminity and reduce herself to an *office*. She tries to minimize her natural shape, smell, color, texture, and movement and to replace these by impersonal, neutral surfaces. She is not opposed to cosmetics or grooming aids – indeed, she employs them vigorously for purposes of restraint and control – but she is critical of grooming aids when they are employed in the service of casual, exposed femininity. It is understandable that these types sometimes go with petty, bureaucratic authority, sitting as guardians of the organizational structure against the subversive influence of the less restrained of their own sex. It is interesting to compare these controlled women, who have reached the zenith of their careers, with the attractive girl who manipulates, rather than restrains, her appearance and employs it as an instrument for her upward mobility.

A different expression of plastic control, this time accompanied by a higher ratio of exposure, is afforded by those mature women who are engaged in the valiant battle against being classed as old. Our culture classifies old age as retirement from sexual, vocational, and even sociable activity, and the woman who is battling age is trying to prevent too early a retirement. She employs the techniques of grooming to conceal the signs of aging and to accentuate (and expose) the body areas where her appearance is still youthful. Some search hopefully for new techniques that will reverse the aging process in particular areas (e.g., "miracle" skin cream), others are shining examples of self-restraint and self-discipline (e.g., diet and exercise), and still others become virtuosos in the use of plastic devices of grooming (e.g., hair color rinses).

Interestingly, plastic control of grooming involves not only creativity but the application of the capitalistic ethic: beauty becomes the product of diligence rather than an inexplicable gift from the supernatural.[10] Thus, those with an interest in the elaboration of the grooming ritual (e.g., charm schools, cosmetic manufacturers, cosmeticians, beauty shops) issue advice that has a hortatory, even a moral, character. The woman is informed of the many steps she must take to maintain a "beautiful," that is, socially proper, appearance. She is praised when she fulfils every requirement and condemned for backsliding. It is ironic to compare this moral voice of modern society, with its insistence on perfect grooming, with the moral voice of the past as represented by Isaiah.

THE SOCIAL FUNCTION OF GROOMING

There is also the social function of grooming, reported by the ethnographer: cosmetics and dress are often used to denote differences in status. So, in our society, cosmetics help to identify a person as a female of our culture and, generally speaking, as a female who views herself and should be treated as socially and sexually mature. The girl who wears cosmetics is insisting on her right to be treated as a woman rather than a child; likewise, the elderly woman wearing cosmetics is insisting that she not be consigned to the neutral sex of old age.

To some critics modern grooming practices represent cultural demands for a high degree of conformity, but this is a view based on a limited study of the case and a limited knowledge of other cultures. Most societies have rather restricted notions of what are acceptable costumes for those who are socially and sexually mature. In this respect our society is less severe than most, and it is very unusual in the emphasis that it gives to individual expression in the designing of appearance. The woman who has the patience, the skill, and, most important, the eager and self-disciplined attitude toward her body can – even with limited natural resources – make of her appearance something aesthetically interesting and sexually exciting.

The question is sometimes raised, usually in the feature sections of newspapers: For whom does a woman dress – does she dress for men or women? We have observed that one indispensable kind of answer includes a reference to culture, or, more concretely, to the social situation. A woman dresses and grooms herself in anticipation of a *social situation*. The situations that require the most careful grooming are those in which her peers or social superiors will be present and which are not defined as informal (casual). The woman who is isolated from men who are her peers, for example, the suburban housewife, can "neglect her appearance." Her dress and grooming tend to be casual. When questioned, she replies defensively that she is "too busy" to worry about her appearance; but the career woman has far more demands on her time, newspaper feature editors notwithstanding. The point is that the career woman always has an audience of male and female peers alert to her appearance, while the housewife seldom has one.

It may seem as though the function of cosmetics and grooming in heightening the sexual attractiveness of one sex to the other has been neglected. This de-emphasis reflects the facts of the case, particularly as it is in modern society. Certainly, cosmetics and grooming practices are influential in courtship, and, moreover, novel practices seem to emerge within this relationship and spread to less sexualized areas of existence. (Thus it has happened that the grooming practices of courtesans have been adopted by respectable women.) But, while sexuality is thus basic to grooming, it cannot serve to explain grooming as a social activity any more than it can the American dating complex.

The function of grooming in our society is understandable from the perspective of *sociability*, not of *sexuality*.[11] A woman grooms herself to appear as a desirable sexual object, not necessarily as an attainable one. In grooming herself, she is preparing to play the part of the *beauty*, not the part of the erotically passionate woman. In this sense, cosmetics and grooming serve to transmute the attraction between the sexes from a raw physical relationship into a civilized *game*.

Some may carp at the game, feeling that activity should be functional and that beauty should therefore denote the superior female, the ideal sex partner and mother. Here the question becomes evaluative: Should cosmetics and grooming be judged as a form of *play*, engaging and entertaining its participants, or should they serve a nobler purpose? We leave Isaiah to confront the sculptor of the Cnidian Aphrodite.

NOTES

Source: *The American Journal of Sociology,* 62(6) (The University of Chicago Press, 1957), 588–93.

1. For the past several years I have been intensively occupied in market research and am currently employed by a company that produces cosmetic and other items of personal care for women. The notions presented in this paper are derived from my research experience but, since the data and findings are the property of the client, cannot be offered in support of my arguments; the reader must judge validity by his own experience.

2. Excluded from this paper but involved in the phenomena here discussed are certain other significant phenomena: gesture, facial expression, and demeanor as elements in the process of communication (*see* several articles by Erving Goffman) and physique, carriage, gait, and the development and tonus of the major muscles.

3. There is a literature, particularly in German, on the nature of physical beauty (see, e.g., Gustav Ichheiser, "The Significance of the Physical Beauty of the Individual in Socio-psychological and Sociological Explanation," *Zeitschrift für Völkerpsychologie und Soziologie,* 1928, a translation of which by Everett C. Hughes appears in Carl A. Dawson and Warner E. Gettys, *An Introduction to Sociology* [rev. ed.; New York: Ronald Press Co., 1935], pp. 749–53). This literature becomes relevant to the present problem to the extent that the analyst moves from considering "natural" beauty to considering the "artificial" creation or supplementation of physical beauty via cosmetics and grooming.

4. Isa. 3:18–24.

5. Gwyn Williams, "The Pale Cast of Thought," *Modern Language Review,* XLV (1950), 216–18.

6. *Hamlet*, Act III, scene 1.

7. Note on "Nails," *New Statesman and Nation,* XIV (1937), 245–46.

8. In contrast, straight hair can be controlled but not so plastically. It can be imprisoned in a braid or a bun or cut so short that it is often considered unattractive or unfeminine ("the boyish bob"). Allowed to hang free, straight hair of any length is somewhat of a problem for its possessor and her intimates, although it can be beautiful.

9. Hair sprays, which are a technique for applying a fixative, usually a lacquer – which is, incidentally, flammable – to hair which has been set, may change habits of hair care, but they do not substantially alter the present analysis.

10. Ichheiser notes that beauty may be "cultivated" or "denatured" and, further, that the socioeconomic position of the woman is important in facilitating or curtailing her access to the implements of cultivation (see Ichheiser's article cited above, n. 3). The mass-production society has reduced the differential due to socioeconomic position as far as access to cosmetic and personal care items is concerned. There remain significant differentials associated with ethnicity and income and perhaps most apparent in areas of aesthetic judgment (taste) and health so far as the present inquiry is concerned.

11. Georg Simmel, "The Sociology of Sociability," translated from the German by Everett C. Hughes, *American Journal of Sociology,* LV (November, 1940), 254–61.

CHAPTER TEN

The Economics of Fashion Demand

DWIGHT E. ROBINSON

I. INTRODUCTION: FASHION AND ECONOMICS

Fashion, as the subtlest and most volatile form of luxury, is also the most difficult to understand. It is to fashion, therefore, that the economist must turn if he is ever to win an acute perception of non-necessitous expenditure and to transcend thereby the rather heavy-handed and somewhat prejudicial projections of Veblen, which, whatever their faults, represent the most serious probing of this momentous subject presently available. Economists have, however, paid remarkably little attention to luxury and next to none to fashion, defined most simply as change in the design of things for decorative purposes.[1] This seems the more regrettable since the ascendancy of either over demand has never been more pronounced than in contemporary Western culture. While to the casual observer the mention of fashion immediately conjures up visions of desiccated mannequins displaying the latest Paris modes, no one can survey the modern market in consumer goods without realizing that very few indeed are exempt from the same relentless pressure for style change which characterizes dresses and millinery. If fashion students themselves have concentrated most of their attention on costume, the explanation is not to be sought in force of habit alone, but also in their realization that no other form of decoration provides quite so lively and suggestive a field for observation of the general tendency. Quentin Bell put the matter very deftly when he likened fashion in dress as a subject of social study to "the role allotted to *Drosophila*, the fruit fly, in the science of genetics."[2]

Admittedly, exact quantification of the proportions of the values of goods that are fashion-induced is visionary. It is no surprise, of course, that people in the garment industry with one voice tell us that everything that matters, everything that spells success or failure, everything that gives their trade its nature and place in the world

must be ascribed to fashion.[3] Even wear and tear can be dismissed as of little importance, for its permissible limits are determined far more by concern for appearances
than by serviceability. True, the further we depart from personal adornment the less
obvious the impact of fashion becomes. Yet anyone at all familiar with the workings of
the automobile industry, for example, is fully cognizant of the unremitting attention
and staggering expense which the manufacturers lavish on the yearly introduction of
new body styles. He also knows that the popular impression of momentous mechanical advances is far more an achievement of the advertiser than of the engineer. The
"styling sections" with their own highly paid vice-presidents employ many hundreds
if not thousands of people and are advised by regiments of market researchers.
After the stylists are done, the real expense begins: that of translating their design
concoctions into steel. Almost all the annual "retooling" investment which Detroit
publicizes so fully is for styling. Economist readers familiar with national statistics
will surely recognize that it is only necessary to review in this manner a few more
appropriate industries – residential construction, decoration and home furnishings
spring readily to mind, but even household appliances are heavily saturated with
stylishness – in order to establish style change as one of the nation's most pervasive
and omnivorous costs of production. How often are we reminded that even the
most vital need-serving industries, including food processing and distribution and
those supplying the medical profession, are by no means free of a rich admixture of
fashion predicated elements? Nor should we forget that fashion's empire encroaches
upon other seemingly exempt industries wherever these produce consumer goods and
services which *support* the requirements of fashion, such as packaging, cleaning
and repair services for delicate fabrics, toiletries and cosmetics, consumer credit and
many others. It is really difficult to know where to stop. Shall we treat as economically important the shopping time expended by women? And then there is that final
bewilderment to the practical-minded that even functional changes may be introduced
for fashion appeal!

   Despite the importance of fashion's role (which is really not new development
so much as an increasingly widespread one), it is scarcely surprising that the study
of the subject has had a rather checkered career; after all, it bespeaks a side of life
which rationally disposed men of learning have been almost bound to dismiss as sheer
feminine caprice.[4] Nevertheless, a highly diverse assortment of writers has built up
a modestly presented but quite impressive book of analysis on the subject. Happily
for those of us who are analytically inclined, they have discovered a good deal of
order in the seething chaos.[5] Even as long ago as 1833, Thomas Carlyle, remembered
by economists primarily as the arch-foe of the utilitarian philosophy, voiced a
misapprehension which has persisted down to the present day when he lamented that
"little or nothing of a fundamenal character, whether in the way of philosophy or
history, has been written on the subject of clothes,"[6] fashion's aboriginal guise. To cite
but one of many "philosophical" examples, the pre-eminent English critical essayist
of the Romantic movement, William Hazlitt, had contributed a penetrating essay

"On Fashion" to *The Edinburgh Magazine* as far back as September, 1818.[7] Hazlitt's prescient interpretation deserves quoting at some length because of its striking proximity to the central tendencies of the contemporary theory of fashion.

> Fashion is an odd jumble of contradictions, of sympathies and antipathies. It exists only by its being participated among a certain number of persons, and its essence is destroyed by being communicated to a greater number. It is a continual struggle between "the great vulgar and the small" to get the start of or keep up with each other in the race of appearances, by an adoption on the part of the one of such external and fantastic symbols as strike the attention and excite the envy or admiration of the beholder, and which are no sooner made known and exposed to public view for this purpose, than they are successfully copied by the multitude, the slavish herd of imitators, who do not wish to be behind-hand with their betters in outward show and pretension, and which then sink, without any farther notice, into disrepute and contempt. Thus fashion lives only in a perpetual round of giddy innovation and restless vanity. To be old-fashioned is the greatest crime a coat or a hat can be guilty of. To look like nobody else is a sufficiently mortifying reflection; to be in danger of being mistaken for one of the rabble is worse. Fashion constantly begins and ends in the two things it abhors most, singularity and vulgarity . . . It is a sublimated essence of levity, caprice, vanity, extravagance, idleness, and selfishness. It thinks of nothing but rot being contaminated by vulgar use, and winds and doubles like a hare, and betakes itself to the most paltry shifts to avoid being overtaken by the common hunt that are always in full chase after it. It contrives to keep up its fastidious pretensions, not by the difficulty of the attainment, but by the rapidity and evanescent nature of the changes.[8]

Considering that fashion analysts themselves have always fought rather shy of insisting on the strategic importance of fashion's role in the modern society and its economy, it is entirely understandable that the economist has at best left fashion and the "changing tastes" associated with it among those "other things" which if not equal are, at any rate, indeterminate and, hopefully, of not too great theoretical consequence.[9] As might be expected, any loss which this inattention has entailed for economic theory is matched by a corresponding weakness and lack of development in the explication of the economic components of fashion behavior. The only remedy for either of these deficiencies seems to lie in careful examination of fashion aims in the light of economic concepts.

II. THE STATE OF FASHION THEORY

Hazlitt's observation that fashion is "a race of appearances" or, in the terminology of the sociologist, a mode of symbolic expression, has met with no disagreement among contemporary students of behavior. Seen in this light, the choice of an eminent cultural anthropologist whose own work centered on language studies, the late Edward Sapir, to prepare the article on "Fashion" for the *Encyclopedia of the Social Sciences*,[10] becomes intelligible and significant.

Sapir finds egoistic assertion powerfully at work in the motivation which shapes and alters its symbolic content. He puts forward as a basic hypothesis of fashion theory: "Functional irrelevance as contrasted with symbolic significance for the expression of the ego is implicit in all fashion."[11] Specifically, it serves "as an outward emblem of personal distinction or of membership in some group to which distinction is ascribed."[12] Moreover, Sapir is as far as possible from the position that fashion is a casual or superficial aspect of social and individual development. Taking us beyond questions of immediate economic concern, he writes:

> Fashion concerns itself closely and intimately with the ego. Hence its proper field is dress and adornment. There are other symbols of the ego, however, which are not as close to the body as these but which are almost equally subject to the psychological laws of fashion. Among them are objects of utility, amusements, furniture . . . Many speak of fashions in thought, art, habits of living and morals. It is superficial to dismiss such locutions as metaphorical and unimportant. There is nothing to prevent a thought, a type of morality or an art form from being the psychological equivalent of a costuming of the ego.[13]

In asserting the egoistic impulsion behind fashion, Sapir is, of course, in company with the overwhelming majority of his fellow anthropologists – or, for that matter, of psychologists and sociologists. In the matter of clothes, anthropologist after anthropologist assures us that its key motivation is display, with protection a poor second and modesty trailing far behind. Representative of their findings is R. H. Lowie's observation:

> Man is a peacock. He likes to flirt, to smile, to wallow in riches, but he will play ascetic or spendthrift if it gives him a chance to strut. Mere power and material profit are not enough, they do not make life worthwhile without the tinsel of prestige.[14]

One of the few books dealing with the psychology of fashion which happens at the same time to be written by a professional psychologist is a competent work by J. C. Flugel.[15] It is revealing that Dr. Flugel, though a member of the psychoanalytic school and, therefore, hardly to be suspected of slighting the impact of the libido in favor of the ego, is in close accord with writers on fashion representing other disciplines. While his book contains many scattered references to erotic drives and symbolic derivatives therefrom, the main burden of his theoretical explanation rests squarely upon the ego. He concludes:

> There can be little doubt that the ultimate and essential cause of fashion lies in competition; competition of a social and sexual kind, in which the social elements are more obvious and manifest and the sexual elements more indirect, concealed and unavowed, hiding themselves, as it were behind the social ones.[16]

From the economist's standpoint, for that matter, it is not of compelling interest whether people dress up and indulge in other forms of fashionable display to impress each other from amiable or antagonistic motives. So long as the aim is to create an effect relative to the performance of others, be the emotional drive erotic or aggressive as you will, the consequences for economic theory will not be altered.[17]

The emulative motivation of fashionable behavior works itself out through a conflict of aims arising between two theoretically distinguishable groups within the social structure. On the one hand, it is the aim of the majority as a group to approximate as nearly as practicable the design choices of those to whom it looks up in terms of social status and, on the other hand, it is the aim of the minority as a group inhabiting the highest levels or prestige or affluence to preserve the distinctive character of its design choices in the face of the efforts of the majority to nullify them through imitation. Both aims (or sets of aims) are subject to a high degree of ambivalence, a behavioral pattern which is emerging as one of the central concepts in psychology. The minority is at one and the same time repelled *and* flattered by majority imitation, while the latter simultaneously shows empathy in seeking self-identification with the former *and* antipathy in trying to nullify its distinctiveness.

To this direct conflict of aims, the most intricate workings of the fashion process can ultimately be traced as they take form under the molding influences of any particular social structure and set of circumstances. Of course, this is to present the model in its extremely simplified form. The possibilities for the refinement of fashion study are as endless as the social fabric is richly complex. If at some points the theory of fashion seems to do violence to our established habits of thought, it is useful to reflect that in a field of behavior which is emulative in aim and symbolic in reference, it is only to be expected that the competitive stratagems of individuals and groups will necessarily give rise to all sorts of illusory devices and consequent misleading impressions. More often than not, the fashion-minded will be unconscious of the real purposes underlying the tactical ruses to which they resort. Consequently, it is the familiar experience of the patient observer that time after time a seemingly hopeless paradox will present itself only to be resolved into the simplest of explanations after a little examination.

Obviously, as in all other human affairs, individual behavior is conditioned by and predicated upon a multitude of variously related and often overlapping sub-cultural groups. Assuming organization in the society, as by definition we must, then it follows that whether they are viewed horizontally or vertically the contiguity of such groups will be to some extent sequential or systematic: they cannot logically all be equally contiguous. Accordingly, any given group (or cluster of groups forming a class) will tend to take its cues from those contiguous with it. Horizontally fashions will spread outward from central loci; and vertically – the more important consideration – any given group will tend to adopt as its mentor not the highest distinguishable group but, rather, those immediately above it. In consequence of the vertical contiguity of class groupings, new fashions tend to filter down by stages through the levels of affluence. The process of discarding any fashion will be a mere reflex of its proliferation. For an object of fashion to lose its meaning for the topmost class it is only necessary for it to be taken up by the secondmost and so on down the line.[18]

In the course of modern history, the sway of fashion and the extent of social mobility have grown side by side. Indeed, the sumptuary laws culminating in the sixteenth century may be regarded equally well as attempts to resist either development. Social mobility introduces interclass competition in consumption standards to a degree unknown in rigidly stratified societies.

It is nothing but a logical consequence of the opposition of aims set forth above that only the emulated minority has anything to gain from the exercise of originality in choice of design. So far as the members of the majority are concerned (whether these be taken in groups or as individuals) they can only advance their own standings *inter se* through conformity with the standards established by the minority's leadership. From the standpoint of fashion theory, the various forms of nonconformity or eccentricity which are bound to be present in any society are simply imperfections. If we are concerned with the fashion interest *in abstracto*, then everyone outside of those who exercise style leadership must be regarded as essentially conformist. Taking dress again as an illustration of similar tendencies in other forms of consumption, girls in choosing clothes will give expression to peculiarities of their own personalities and physiques and above all to their specific locations in the social structure. Yet the taboo that everybody must be "different" as well as the same is merely a kind of counter, implementing the rules of competition, in the manner of the distinguishing colors worn by opposing teams.[19] Experienced observers of the garment industry seldom bother to distinguish between the effects of the desire for individuality and the desire to be up to the minute, but lump both indifferently under the head of fashion.

Confronted with this social universe of conformity and consequent imitation, the distinction-seeking sector is at continual pains to seek out such things as are currently difficult to come by and to reject and avoid those which are becoming commonplace. This is why the world of luxury, *le bel monde*, displays a continual interweaving of threads of continuity with accents of change. So long as the fashion mentor is confident of the rarity of anything under consideration for acquisition or retention, the question of its novelty or familiarity is incidental. Something new, like bird-of-paradise feathers when they were first discovered, or something long-prized, like costly furs, are alike worthy of approval. Indeed, it is the highly developed capacity to eschew the ordinary and to espy the rare with due regard for the resources of tradition as well as of novelty that is of the essence in the definition of "discerning" or "exquisite" taste. It has too long been overlooked in consumer studies that the exercise of taste is a very positive, energy-demanding undertaking: it is an unending quest. Horace Walpole was close to the heart of the matter when in 1754 he coined the expression *serendipity* to denote the faculty of those who are "always making discoveries, by accidents and sagacity, of things they were not in quest of."[20] It is precisely in this compulsive pursuit of the rare that we find our bridge between the social psychology and the economics of fashion.

III. THE ECONOMIC FOUNDATIONS OF FASHION

The Pursuit of Rarity

As a preliminary to applying the pursuit of rarity as a key to the understanding of fashion demand, a brief review of definitions is in order. For *rarity* as understood by those who are concerned with the market for luxury has a significantly different meaning from its closely-allied synonym *scarcity*, so consequential in economic reasoning.

In general or everyday usage, of course, both words designate merely limitation with respect to quantitative comparison, although "rare" may suggest more extreme limitation. A species of birds is rare because its numbers make up only a small fraction relative to the populations of many other species; a resource is economically defined as scarce when its quantity – however great – is small relative to the quantity of wants attaching to it. But, as is true of the economic definition of scarcity, when rarity is employed in a social context it presupposes a dependency on, or relationship with, human desires – essentially a normative signification. It is in their normative significations that an analytically important distinction arises. That distinction may be expressed in this way: in speaking of the rare we have in mind something which is not only in limited supply but which is also recognized by those interested in it as "highly distinguished" or "unusually excellent,"[21] whereas in speaking of scarcity we mean anything of which there is an insufficient amount to satisfy all possible wants for it. To put the matter slightly differently: when we say that something is rare (an art object, a collector's stamp or a vintage wine) we do so in recognition that much, at any rate, of the interest attaching to it actually *rests* on the difficulty of its acquisition; when, as economists, we say that a good is scarce we imply that it possesses *inherently* desirable or satisfying properties, but that there happens not to be enough of it readily available so that no sacrifice need be forthcoming to enjoy it. Pressing the difference a little farther, the attribution of rarity to a necessitous good would be nothing but a contradiction in terms unless there were the added intent to suggest something unusual or special about it – as in the case of a rare sort of food such as caviar. But many necessitous goods are, of course, scarce.

Such definitional niceties, for reasons which will soon become apparent, are quite imperative in the interests of clear understanding in matters of luxurious values. This is particularly true because writers, including economists, have not always been as careful as they might have been to avoid confusion by guarding firmly against the hidden value judgments which can so easily creep into these terms. For one thing, the interest in rarity which, as we have just seen, bears its own unique denotation of obvious operational significance to the analysis of demand, has often been loosely thrown into the general category of scarcity as if it made no difference. Actually, we would be better off to employ the two terms rarity and scarcity only in the most colorless quantitative sense unless we make what we are doing quite explicit when we intend the richer meanings. In the following discussion, I shall take the liberty of employing "scarcity" in this noncommittal sense of limited quantity, for no ulterior purpose beyond convenience of exposition.

The Factor of Demonstrability

In seeking to measure the effects on demand of conditions of scarcity, we immediately encounter the difficulty that the only basis of measurement we have, that of physical quantity, is meaningless per se. The difficulty is that everything is scarce in the sense that its supply is limited because nothing is universally or infinitely abundant. Is gold, for example, "scarcer" than iron? Certainly, in terms of weight and volume. But if the supply of either has effective limits why is one any better suited than the other for the emulative display of command over forms of scarcity? The problem is reminiscent of the conundrum concerning the pound of feathers and the pound of lead.

In a theory of economic choice based solely on emulative assumptions, the capacity to demonstrate possession over a given fraction of the known supply of any distinctive and not readily duplicated material must be regarded as operationally the same as demonstrating possession of the same fraction of any other. Except for accidental influences or cultural predilections stemming from the past, it is difficult to see why as between two natural substances whose sensory appeals seem negligibly different (gold and platinum, for example), there should be any difference in the value of their total supplies. Unless we can find some reason or relationship to explain why differences in sheer physical volume affect the emulative interest in things there can under our assumption be no basis for preference between them.

Yet the weight of empirical evidence seems to suggest that degree of scarcity in terms of bulk does tend to augment the value in exchange of any substance. Precious stones are physically scarcer than semiprecious and we find that the portion of annual national income expended on them for ornamental purposes is, as census figures invariably show, by far the greater. The inference may be drawn that the elasticity of demand for natural ornamental substances is actually less than unity or perhaps inversely proportional to their physical volume in supply. When hitherto naturally scarce substances like oriental pearls, sapphires or mink pelts begin to be perfectly simulated at greatly reduced cost and in far greater bulk, at first the total money sales volume may increase as larger segments of the public are able to afford them but this is presumably because the illusion of former scarcity lingers on. In due course the comparative sales volume of the entire trade generally declines indicating a long-run elasticity of demand less than unity.[22] The market-control policies of the diamond syndicate seems to accord with these indications as, indeed, although less evidently, do those of the women's dress and apparently all luxury goods trades.

In order to find an explanation for this high inelasticity of demand for scarce substances we need to return to the consideration that their values in the first place are dependent upon the aims of symbolic emulation. In order to subserve such aims, a substance must lend itself with some reasonable degree of convenience to display. Let us call this the factor of *demonstrability*. Given the properties of the human organism operating under whatever social conditions, the display of certain materials is bound to prove comparatively awkward or otherwise inconvenient. To illustrate, bodily adornment will always loom large in human motivation: in this very central sphere of symbolic emulation, iron obviously will be less prized than gold or platinum since (as was not always the case) the value of a bearable weight of iron is very slight.[23] It is also quite conceivable that the physical supply of something may be too slight for purposes of effective display. This would be the case if even the wealthiest people could only afford quantities so minute as to be barely visible. Presumably, the physical quantities of some substances tend – like the temperature of Goldilocks' porridge – to be "just right" for demonstrability.[24] Moreover, natural limitation of supply (scarcity in the uncolored sense) cannot be socially meaningful unless it is discerned and it is this need of discernment, determined in turn by the psychocultural context in any case, that creates rarity.[25]

If the pursuit of the rare is, as it appears to be, essential to an intelligible explanation of the world of luxury as perceived from the vantage point of fashion behavior, then we must conclude that while sensory gratification *may* be an attribute of any luxury good rarity is a *necessary* condition. If we were to study luxuries only in a static sense, this important proposition might not assert itself so clearly for we would always have difficulty balancing rarity appeal against putative degrees of sensory gratification since the latter are so notoriously uncertain and indecipherable. But, fortunately, it is just as notorious that, sensorily, the fashion article of one style period is no whit preferable to that of another: the fur of an animal that *is* modish provides no greater sensory gratification than did that which *was* modish. Since the sensory gratification of fashion articles is, except fortuitously, a constant, we can only conclude that rarity is the determinant of attractiveness in one great mode of luxurious behavior. That being the case, it is difficult to suppose that consumers are likely to ignore this criterion in other directions of luxurious choice.

Our theoretical conclusion is, then, that insofar as the luxury market is concerned, degrees of demonstrability will tend to determine the relative values of things, especially in the realm of immediate personal adornment. In the main, the smaller the physical supply of any natural substance the greater the value of its total stock (as marginally indicated) is likely to be. In less direct media of personal embellishment – housing, transportation and the like – the correlation will be more complex but essentially the same.

An interesting consequence of this hypothesis is that the rate and direction of technological advances in the production of scarce substances or materials must, as it were automatically, alter their relative desirabilities as luxuries. In advanced industrial economies the erosion of luxury values takes place continually in consequence of the innovation of new goods, synthetic materials, improved efficiencies in production and the like. When a rarity is deprived of its previous exclusiveness (as determined by the supply: demonstrability relationship) by industrial ingenuity, it will sooner or later lose favor first in the eyes of fashion leaders and then, as if by reflex action, in the regard of the multitude. Technological advances, then, introduce a dynamic element into the standards of luxury.

Since fashion epitomizes dynamism in luxurious consumption it is tempting to regard this process of reaction to ongoing production efficiencies as part of fashion. This, however, would be to depart from our strict definition of the latter as change in the design of things for purposes of decoration. As our definition indicates, people who are closest to fashion behavior (including those who live by it) think of the consumer's appetite for design change as purposeful. Decorative modifications are pursued as ends in themselves and are by no means mere passively accepted readjustments to supply changes. In short, there is the consumer's taste innovation as well as the producer's technical innovation, and, the two, although they interact, are separate and distinct. Economically, as we shall see in a moment, highly interesting consequences are to be derived from this neglected distinction.

Fashion as Demonstrated Command over Current Factors of Production

A predilection for fashion, the majority of my readers will doubtless agree, is the next thing to synonymous with extravagance. To the buyer, its costliness is manifested in the way novelties have of not remaining novel very long; to the purveyor (and especially the purveyor of ready-made articles) it takes the form of the expensive readjustment which shifting from the production of one design to another necessarily entails. It is through tracing the connections between the cost of fashion as seen from these two vantage points and the pursuit of rarity as already defined that we can arrive at an understanding of the distinctive economic role of fashion. Economically, the gist of the matter is that the consumer willingly pays the producer for the latter's trouble and outlay in affixing the stamp of impermanence on the commodities he offers for sale.

As is not the case with the stable elements in luxury, time is an essential condition of the value of an article of fashion. Fashion serves not only as evidence that labor (to speak of no other resources) has been expended at some time or other, but it is also testimony that labor has been expended recently. In other words, an article of fashion demonstrates command over a given portion of *current* labor as distinguished from any amount that may have been expended in the past.[26] Any physically durable artifact represents the expenditure of labor; but it is only when we see a commodity whose design reflects the fancy of the moment that we are assured that it is of recent manufacture.

The economic importance of this distinction which fashion confers on the durable goods of its choosing rests upon the force and effect of the factor of demonstrability. We must remember that if all the durable consumer goods ever manufactured had been retained, the surface of the earth would groan with an insupportable weight of elaborate and unmanageable junk. If we were totally indifferent to demonstrated recency of production, the task of displaying command over resources through the medium of durable artifacts would be hopelessly awkward. The fruits of past labor if preserved would in time simply bulk too large to permit in any practicable way their enlistment in the cause of demonstrable rarity. For this reason, the distinction between current labor and past labor as forms of rarity appeal is one of the great fault lines in all the economic evaluation that takes place within the area of luxury. Command over the former is practically demonstrable; command over the latter is not.

Only in the case of those old artifacts which have a ceremonial or institutionally exclusive significance or which, as in the case of antiques, have achieved rarity by virtue of the decimation of other relics of the same ilk, is the quantity small enough to be of conceivable interest to a luxury-minded humanity. Museums themselves have their problems of storage and display space: indeed, the provision of such space is their primary economic service. Nor is it economically inconsequential that even the excavation of precious minerals as a means of displaying command over productive resources suffers from the ambiguity that there is nothing in the mineral to show whether the necessary effort was expended currently or not. Consequently, even the most precious of gems are not proof against the visitation of fashion in the form of constant recutting to novel patterns. Fashion preserves us from what would otherwise be the Midas-like curse of durability. It permits us to live in a world of freshly cut blooms where without it we would suffer from an oversupply of artificial flowers. Just as surely as petals must fall from fresh blossoms so the fashion connotations of durable goods ineluctably vanish. From the esthetic viewpoint designs in the latest manner may be more or less pleasing: from the economic viewpoint they are in effect just so much current labor.

To understand the full uniqueness of fashion's economic effects we must go beyond its comparability with perishable goods to consider the cost to the supplier of continual modification of design. The economic distinction which fashion (defined, let us remind ourselves, as demand for design modification) shares with no other form of demand is its *exploitation of the versatility or partial fluidity of the factors of production in order to demonstrate command over currently disposable factors of production.* Labor, and to a lesser degree, capital, is mobile enough to be set to a variety of alternative purposes. It can be put to mining obsidian as well as gold or to designing baroque-type furniture as well as the most severely functional. If, on the one hand, the factors were inflexible or entirely immobile, the emulative display of command over them would have to take the form of unceasing accumulation of the same things, after the manner of pyramid-building or the ritualistic potlatch. If, on the other hand, the factors were perfectly mobile or fluid, fashion would also lose much of its meaning, for then design change would involve no cost. Fashion would serve no purpose that could not be served as well by such uses of labor as the direct display of the domestic services of retainers or the production of perishable commodities. But as things are, change of design is costly. Producers of distinctive articles of décor of high quality must employ talented and highly trained designers and must bear, as well, the uncertainties of innovation. But even manufacturers who customarily copy or "pirate" designs cannot avoid time-consuming and often frustrating complications in preparing for new production runs. It is precisely the imperfect mobility of the factors of production – their viscosity as it were – that provides fashion with means to achieve its economic *raison d'être*. One is reminded of A. N. Whitehead's oft-quoted observation: "Every scheme for the analysis of nature has to face these two facts, *change and endurance.*"[27]

While the greatest economic effect of fashion is, no doubt, its reduction of the staying power of physically durable goods (together with its power of hastening the depreciation of semidurables), this additional prepotency to occasion expense in the shifting of imperfectly mobile factors from one form of design to another is the very characteristic which enables fashion to invade any field of expenditure, even including that of perishable goods. It would naturally be cheaper for a perishable goods industry simply to go on turning out the same varieties. Unfortunately for production costs, however, fashion does not permit this, but rather involves the producers of perishable necessities and luxuries alike in the uncertain business of providing appealing novelties. The processor of foods must experiment with new recipes to whet jaded appetites and the horticulturalist with cross-pollination in the quest for intriguing new varieties. If there has been a stepping up as well as spread of fashion interest in the modern world it must be because change in design is particularly proof against latter-day developments which have tended to nullify other forms of rarity. Naturally scarce substances are more and more readily synthesized; ingenious mechanical devices have robbed elaborate goods, such as lace, of their distinctiveness; egalitarian ideals and measures have nearly eliminated the domestic servant as a form of command over current labor. But entrepreneurial ingenuity in satisfying wants is still and irremediably challenged by the alteration of those wants through the modification of tastes.

IV. SOME IMPLICATIONS FOR ECONOMIC FIELDS

Value and Welfare

Few thinkers have taken the curse of Adam with greater seriousness than economic philosophers. Reasoning from assumptions entirely appropriate to the bare necessities of life but more and more dubious as attention draws closer to its indulgences and fripperies, scarcity has come to be regarded in economic writings as entirely a negating obstacle to human welfare, a grim exigency like death or disease thrust upon an innocent humanity by an implacable external universe. The strong likelihood that such a position is ill-taken with respect to luxury has not been squarely faced. Surely it should be, for whether or not we approve of luxury we cannot wish it away from our data.

After all, what is really so surprising or implausible in the supposition that scarcity has been freely adopted by humanity as pretext for the exercise of emulative propensities? Emulation takes many forms of expression: physical combat, legal disputation, occupational competition, games and so on. The securing of command over scarce resources for purposes of display is simply one great order of many outlets for competitive energies. What is really much more surprising is that the intrusion of emulation into consumption has been glossed over so persistently. Instead of thinking of consumption as a kind of final reward or state of rest where all passion is spent, it seems imperative (once we look beyond vital needs and the far more conditional question of sensory gratification) to recognize consumption for what it largely is, another arena of rivalry and competition. We deliberately devise medals and ribbons and restrict their number so that their award will be regarded as recognition for rare excellence of performance; we purposely place sand traps and other hazards on golf courses so as to render the achievement of low scores difficult. Yet simply because another agency than ourselves has disposed that gold and caviar be scarce and securing them laborious, it seems largely to have escaped us that the interest we display in them is really little different from the coveting of symbolic rewards of our own contriving. Actually, the weight of historical and anthropological evidence suggests that our ancestors initially sought out rare materials for display rather than for any other use.

In consequence of the disturbing leitmotif of Keynes's *General Theory*, namely that consumption needed reappraisal, the conceptual possibility that economic wants may be socially interdependent over wide ranges of satisfaction began to attract serious attention. It was given impressive empirical support by Duesenberry and Modigliani, whose inquiries suggested that the saving: consumption ratio is far more closely correlated with income rank in the community than with the absolute level of real income. And yet in the American Economic Association's *A Survey of Contemporary Economics*,[28] the two contributors most directly concerned expressed serious critical reservations concerning the merit of the case. Ruth Mack admitted that she found "the theory in its extreme form . . . unconvincing," although she did not specify why.[29] Moses Abramovitz believed that "other explanations are possible, and some independent test of the importance of emulative drives is still necessary."[30] If our hypothesis that emulation is essential to a theory that fits the facts of fashion is correct, then, with all due allowance for the effects of necessitous and sensuous wants and satisfactions, such an independent test seems to have been provided.

These observations need not mean that our culturally sanctioned aim of expanding productivity is no more than a form of idiot's delight or the welfare counterpart of chasing our tails in unprogressive circles. As surely as all cultures have developed their characteristic modes of affording expression for humanity's impulses toward activity, ours has found its own in the great purpose of improving the standard of living (including luxury) through technical and scientific advance. To this it has added the unending refreshment of novelty in design. Removal or suppression of such avenues of expression would surely give rise to very serious forms of social imbalance.

Economic Competition and Organization

If the women's garment industry may be taken as the purest form of fashion purveying, it is equally certain that no more classic example of monopolistic competition can possibly be found. Indeed, it is not stretching things too far to say that the product or output of this industry *is* product differentiation. Just as the consideration of selling costs (as initially demonstrated by Chamberlin) exposes the disabilities of traditional cost and demand curve analysis, so, in almost a purer sense, does an examination of the dependence of dress manufacturers on furnishing designs which are fashionably attractive. When we speak of selling costs we can still talk as if it were possible to distinguish the effects of advertising and other marketing devices from the products, such as cigarettes, packaged foods, gasoline and so on. But in the pure fashion market the commodity itself – conceived as separate from the design it carries and, therefore, independently of its design costs – is utterly incidental. The cost of making the physical dress is a dependency of the cost centering on design. Even the cost of material and workmanship is in large part a design cost because, among other things, if the design will not sell, then both material and workmanship are almost pure loss.

The central function of the entrepreneur in a fashion industry is far less the efficient organization of the production of a given commodity and much more the shrewd anticipation of the changing preferences of his numerically restricted clientele – his own small niche in "the great neighborhood of women." In essence, what the entrepreneur offers for sale is his experienced judgment and willingness to assume risks in the matter of design. The extraordinarily high rate of failure in such an industry is far more often due to erroneous style decisions and anticipations than to production inefficiencies. And not only is the entrepreneur's reward dependent on his stylistic and, therefore, qualitative determinations, but even his quantitative decisions relating to the number of copies of a given design that should be produced are themselves rendered *qualitative*, for the simple reason that the number he can dispose of profitably will in every case be uniquely determined by the nature of the design! He is virtually stopped from testing the elasticity of demand for any of his products, since, owing to unceasing modification in tastes, he must catch his buyers when he can. To do this he must usually commit himself to a production schedule, one that may never be repeated, well in advance of the sales period. It is as if, either in the qualitative or quantitative case, his inelastic demand curve were to shift upwards and to the right whenever he became shrewder (or luckier) and downwards and to the left whenever his diviner's rod faltered. Just as his demand curve shifts so his acumen varies in its value as a factor of production.

In applying assumptions about demand consistent with the theory of fashion to the analysis of industrial organization, extreme inelasticity of product demand would seem, once again, to be the master key. For that matter, it is a familiar enough reflection among economists that businessmen in their group behavior everywhere do in fact act as if they regarded product demand as almost catastrophically inelastic. Moreover, the same key obviously promises to fit many puzzles in industrial organization, especially that of the determination of firm size. For a notable example, the assumption of extreme inelasticity should help to resolve the question that has puzzled theorists since Marshall concerning the establishment of equilibrium for an industry and its firms with increasing (real) returns.[31]

Economic Development and Cycles

The economist's unfortunate tendency to treat the consumer in terms of passivity may very well have retarded deepening insights into the course of the economic growth of advanced economies, a condition which promises to be corrected through the study of stylistic innovation and propagation. Indeed, almost all of Schumpeter's elaborations of how producer innovation transforms an otherwise stable economy may be applied *pari passu* to the demand side. It is proverbial wisdom that satisfactions can be changed through modifying wants as well as through providing means of satisfaction: the quotient of an act of measurement is just as much affected by a change in the scale of the measuring unit as by the object measured. In particular, we must bring into focus of analysis the great style leaders, properly deserving the title of "entrepreneurs of taste," who by converting the world of fashion to new wants have exercised potent and immediate influence on the course of economic development. The social activity we call consumption *is* active: it is for the most part hard work, it is filled with risks and uncertainties and it molds behavior. Goods and services are not satisfying – hence they are not wealth – until they have been recognized as having utility in a process of living.

Change in the design of commodities and in consumer tastes is an interlocking and reciprocating affair. Although any class of product – the dress, the automobile, the chair – will always to some extent have its own design history, ultimately taste in all its ramifications is powerfully integrated around one central point of reference: the style of life characteristic of a society in a particular era. "The lady of the house" is seldom disposed to adopt fashions in one compartment of her life which are of a different taste vantage or vintage from those in another. There is always a master stylistic code. It may be complex and rich, frequently permitting or even encouraging contrasts and variances: antiques from different periods may be thrown together, restraint and exuberance may be played off one against the other. But, fundamentally, there is an integrating order constantly asserting itself and constantly denying the outmoded.

Experience shows very clearly that the reconstruction of design in conformity with a new schematism in tastes transpires in bursts of activity followed by lulls, rather than pursues a smooth, unhurried course. To speak of fashion waves is immediately to think of those other waves of behavior – business cycles – with which they cannot fail but be significantly related. The building cycle, for example, must be in part a function of desires to give body to the ideas of a new school of architecture. It is quite conceivable that our statistical search for lead indicators of cyclical movements might be more successful if attention were paid to the proportion of buildings (or other goods) being constructed at any time in accordance with novel or radical as opposed to long-established architectural standards. At the beginning of a style wave, for example, we might find that the number of residential houses being built was small and unpromising but that the ratio of *new* designs to old was high and increasing. The latter factor might well foreshadow a strong demand for new housing where sheer number-counting would not. In short, the correlation of waves of fashion activity with business cycles offers means of effectively enriching that presently vacuous and stagnant vein of cycle theory known as "psychological factors."

V. CONCLUSION

The analysis of fashion behavior points to the conclusion that the pursuit of demonstrable rarity for its own sake is a principal key to the motivation underlying the demand for luxuries. Rarities, in turn, are to be understood as conditions of physically limited supply which have excited the interest of the fashionably inclined. It seems to follow, therefore, that scarcity (defined as nothing more than supply limitation) is a positive consideration in consumer motivation over the entire range of the demand for luxuries. In its more obvious and quantitatively important aspect, fashion serves as a means of demonstrating command over current, as opposed to former, output. In its less obvious, qualitative and organizationally decisive effect, it serves to demonstrate command over such current means of production as are needed to accomplish changes in design for decorative purposes. Changing the design of commodities is expensive because of the imperfect mobility of the factors and it is just this consideration which makes fashion demand economically unique. As is equally true with respect to necessities, we do not at present possess adequate means of measuring the portion of demand which depends on luxurious or fashionable purposes, but there are strong reasons for supposing it to be very great. Whatever this magnitude, we must expect to find within it extreme inelasticity of product demand (unity or less than unity) save in the short run, as economists have long, if uneasily, suspected. If the economist comes to admit into his deliberations the actively rarity-minded consumer which fashion theory requires, the discipline may well undergo a readjustment of quasi-Copernican proportions.

NOTES

Source: *The Quarterly Journal of Economics*, 75(3) (Massachusetts Institute of Technology, 1961), 376–98.

Professor Edward H. Chamberlin's editorial suggestions concerning an earlier version of this paper were most helpful. I am also indebted to Professors Charles N. Henning and Philip J. Bourque for comments and to Miss Lois J. Wallace for invaluable assistance in the course of preparation. A substantial part of the research was carried out under a Ford Foundation fellowship. Responsibility for the views expressed and other statements are, however, the writer's alone.

1. For convenience, I have adopted the sense of the term *fashion* which denotes the entire process of behavior through which particular "fashions" succeed one another. For the social scientist it seems a more suitable word than style, since the latter does not so strongly suggest change and also possesses stronger normative connotations. I shall, however, speak of "fashion" and "style change" interchangeably.

2. Quentin Bell, *On Human Finery* (London: Hogarth Press, 1947), p. 12.

3. This statement is made on the basis of more than fifty interviews with persons involved in various phases of the dress trade including manufacturers, designers, retailers, consultants, journalists and others, carried out under a Ford Foundation Research Fellowship. On one occasion, when I asked a trade association research director to estimate the extent of fashion's impact on the business, he replied in so many words: "Thanks to fashion, this is an industry without statistics."

4. To illustrate: Karl Marx and Alfred Marshall, whatever their points of disagreement, were of one mind about fashion. Marx snarled at "the murderous meaningless caprices of fashion," which "consort so badly with the system of modern industry." (*Capital*, Part IV, Modern Library ed., p. 516. Cited Helen Everett Meiklejohn in "Dresses: The Impact of Fashion on a Business from *Price and Price Policies*, New York, McGraw-Hill, 1938). Marshall hoped for the day when "the evil dominion of the wanton vagaries of fashion would pass away." (*Principles of Economics*, London, Macmillan, 1940, p. 88, n. It is hard to believe that the echo of Marx's words was not in Marshall's mind as he wrote. It is no less revealing of nineteenth century attitudes that Veblen was just as contemptuous of fashion, explaining its shifts as recurrent reaction of distaste – in his own words, "aesthetic nausea" – to the excesses of "conspicuous waste."

5. For investigation into the possibilities of regularity and organization in fashion movements see Jane Richardson and A. L. Kroeber, "Three Centuries of Women's Dress Fashions: A Quantitative Analysis," *Anthropological Reco* V (Oct. 1940), 111–53 and Dwight E. Robinson, "Fashion Theory and Product Design," *Harvard Business Review*, XXXVI (Nov.–Dec. 1958), 126–38.

6. *Sartor Resartus and On Heroes* (London: Everyman's Library, 1908), p. 1.

7. As to history, Giulio Ferraro's stupendous *Il Costumo Antico E Moderno*, in thirty-two magnificently illustrated volumes, was published in Florence in 1823.

8. My attention was drawn to Hazlitt's essay by Quentin Bell's charming and lucid study of fashion in dress, *On Human Finery, op. cit.* I can think of no finer introduction to the theory of fashion than Bell's "slim volume," to which I must acknowledge a profound debt for its stimulation of my own thinking on the subject. For a valuable treatment written from a marketing standpoint the reader should consult Paul H. Nystrom's *The Economics of Fashion* (New York: Ronald Press, 1928). It should perhaps be acknowledged, however, that despite Nystrom's title he is far less concerned with the economic than with the social or institutional side of fashion. Cecil Beaton, in his *The Glass of Fashion* (New York: Doubleday, 1954) has provided a marvelously sophisticated review of fashion origination in the twentieth century. While these three books top my list of recommended readings in the field, other writers (beyond those mentioned below) who have contributed to it significantly include Max von Boehn, James Laver, C. Willet Cunnington, Iris Brooke,

Edmund Bergler, Agnes Young, and Joan Evans. Nor must we overlook the profound studies of style changes in the arts by men such as Jakob Burckhardt, Heinrich Wölfflin and Elie Faure.

9. A few perceptive value theorists with a philosophical awareness of the relativity of economic choice realize the importance of fashion. For example, Edward H. Chamberlin writes that "the style cycle is full of special problems and is certainly one of the most interesting and important aspects of the product as an economic variable." See "The Product as an Economic Variable," this *Journal*, LXVII (Feb. 1953), esp. 13–14. In an article in welfare theory, Jerome Rothenberg recognizes that fashion demands provide a strong exception to conventionally conceived demands. See "Non-Convexity, Aggregation, and Pareto Optimality," *Journal of Political Economy*, LXVII (Oct. 1960), esp. 449–53.

10. (New York: Macmillan, 1931), VI, 139–44.

11. *Ibid.*, p. 144.

12. *Ibid.*, p. 140.

13. *Ibid.*, p. 143. Cf. G. L. Kittredge in *Webster's New International Dictionary of the English Language* (Springfield, Massachusetts: G. & C. Merriarn Company, 1918): "'Fashion' – a term under which we include not merely the *fads* and whimsicalities of the moment, but certain larger and more impressive movements and tendencies."

14. *Are We Civilized* (New York: Harcourt, Brace, 1929), p. 159.

15. *The Psychology of Clothes* (London: International Psychoanalytic Library, 1950).

16. *Ibid.*, p. 15. The mere lust for variety receives scant mention as a motivational factor from writers on fashion. This is probably because the hypothesis is inconsistent with the conformity which is so evident in the behavior. If restlessness is significant anywhere it is in the motivation of the fashion-innovators, who are always highly individualistic.

17. It may also be noted that students of that rather amorphous field known as "consumer economics" are in full agreement with the foregoing analytical findings. See e.g., Hazel Kyrk's foundational study, *A Theory of Consumption* (Boston and New York: Houghton Mifflin, 1923), p. 269. To a remarkable extent study of the consumer has remained the province of women. Ruth Mack in her review, "The Economics of Consumption," in *A Survey of Contemporary Economics*, Vol. II, B. F. Haley (ed.), (Homewood, Illinois: Irwin, 1952), cites the following writers: Dorothy Brady, Geraldine S. DePuy, Janet A. Fisher, Rose D. Friedman, Elizabeth W. Gilboy, Alice C. Hanson, Elizabeth E. Hoyt, Day Monroe, Ruby T. Norris, Maryland Y. Pennel, Mary R. Pratt, Margaret G. Reid, Mabel A. Smith and Faith M. Williams.

18. This construction, sometimes referred to as the "trickle-down theory," has been questioned on the grounds that new fashions (as exemplified in the latest Paris imports) frequently turn up in low-priced apparel stores shortly after or occasionally even before their appearance in high-quality retail establishments. I have reviewed this question quite carefully in interviews with retail executives. My finding is that, "high fashion" departments of these stores are universally regarded as "loss leaders" and generally cater to well-to-do customers looking for bargains to fill out their wardrobes. For example, a well-known manager of one of these high fashion departments told me that her annual bonus was calculated on a basis of how small a loss her operation showed rather than on how large a profit. (Obviously, the volume of the operation must have been based on publicity and related criteria.) A deeper aspect of the problem is this: the true fashion leaders comprise a much smaller and more esoteric group than is commonly supposed.

They will have often lost interest in a designer by the time his name is known to the general public. The lag of vertical imitation between this esotery and others will be much greater than that between "the great vulgar and the small."

19. Like children in a gang crying "dibs" on this or that position before a game, the girls in an acquaintanceship develop a rather elaborate procedure to avoid the purchase of identical garments. That any self-expression which takes place is extremely qualified is suggested by the frequency of remarks among women such as "Why didn't I see that dress first?," or "Where *did* you get it?" or "Sally wanted it but the sales lady saved it for me!"

20. *The Oxford Universal Dictionary* (3d ed.; 1955). For material exemplifying the social and economic influence of taste innovators, see Dwight E. Robinson, "The Styling and Transmission of Fashions Historically Considered: Winckelmann, Hamilton and Wedgwood in the 'Greek Revival,'" *Journal of Economic History*, XX (Dec. 1960), 576–87, and N. McKendrick, "Josiah Wedgwood: An Eighteenth-Century Entrepreneur in Salesmanship and Marketing Techniques," *The Economic History Review*, Second Series XII (April 1960), 408–33.

21. See *Webster's New International Dictionary of the English Language* (2d ed., unabridged; Springfield, Massachusetts: G. & C. Merriam Company, 1961).

22. This probability is, of course, contingent upon the assumption that the demand in question is exercised by a reasonably homogeneous group of consumers. If, owing to secular changes, a large and distinctive income class becomes able to afford a type of commodity for the first time, then demand for it may increase markedly and for a long period before a point of saturation is reached.

23. In this connection it is interesting to reflect that not the least of the economic consequences of the automobile is that in addition to its having afforded cheaper and more efficient transportation than the horse it has also furnished a pretext for the display of possession of significant quantities of steel. A return to the knightly sport of jousting would have accomplished the same end only to a smaller extent. For a kind of disqualification of scarcity appeal quite distinct from bulk or weight we might consider the physiological inadvisability of personal ornament fabricated from scarce radioactive material such as uranium or plutonium. Yet human fortitude often will endure serious threats to bodily well-being to exploit the appeal of scarcity. Feminine adornment from Ubangi to Paris has in almost all periods and cultures offered striking examples of this disposition.

24. Demonstrability is not to be confused, of course, with Duesenberry's "demonstration effect," which has to do not with the implementation of display but with its effects. See James S. Duesenberry, *Income, Saving and the Theory of Consumer Behavior* (Cambridge, Massachusetts: Harvard University Press, 1949), pp. 27, 28.

25. The need for identification is precisely what gives such tremendous weight of advantage to those scarcities which have long been embedded in a cultural tradition. They evoke ready responses and possess, as it were by inheritance, the affective support which a mass advertising campaign could scarcely duplicate. A newly mined diamond, for instance, immediately enters into the kingdom of its gem family's prestige. The strength of this inertia gives warning that we must never underestimate how much the occident's relatively strong habituation towards changing tastes may have meant in furthering the cause of economic development.

26. For a working definition of current labor it will suit most analytical purposes simply to regard one year's time as its limits. In certain contexts, a year is merely an arbitrary division

in a continuum. In considering consumer behavior, however, this is not the case. A year is a cycle of seasons, and on that cycle consumer relations have been institutionalized. For example, the "social" year is divided into a number of accepted seasonal occasions upon which the fashionable woman is expected to reveal a new dress. There are other longer and subtler fashion periods which are outside of our present concern.

27. *Science and the Modern World* (New York: Macmillan, 1939), p. 126.
28. Vol. II, *op. cit.*
29. *Ibid.*, p. 54.
30. *Ibid.*, p. 150.
31. Cf. the interesting discussion by Peter Newman on Marshall's handling of the problem of long-run equilibrium. "The Erosion of Marshall's Theory of Value," this *Journal*, LXXIV (Nov. 1960), 587–601.

CHAPTER ELEVEN

From Gemstones to Jewellery[1]

ROLAND BARTHES

For a long time, for centuries, perhaps even millennia, the gemstone was considered to be essentially a mineral substance; whether it was diamond or metal, precious stone or gold, it always came from the earth's depths, from that sombre and fiery core, of which we see only the hardened and cooled products; in short, by its very origin, the gemstone was an infernal object that had come through arduous, often bloody journeys, to leave behind those subterranean caverns where humanity's mythic imagination stored its dead, its damned and its treasures in the same place.

Extracted from hell, the gemstone came to symbolize hell, and took on its fundamental characteristic: the inhuman. Like stone (and stones provided a large amount of gems), it was associated above all with hardness: stone has always stood for the very essence of things, for the irremediably inanimate object; stone is neither life nor death, it represents the inert, the stubbornness of the thing to be nothing but itself; it is the infinitely unchanging. It follows then, that stone is pitiless; whereas fire is cruel, and water crafty, stone is the despair of that which has never lived and will never do so, of that which obstinately resists all forms of life. Through the ages the gemstone extracted from its mineral origins its primary symbolic power: that of announcing an order as inflexible as that of things.

Nevertheless, humanity's poetic imagination was able to conceive of stones that were made to wear out, noble, venerable stones, which grew old and so were, despite everything, alive. As for the quintessential stone, the diamond, it is beyond time: never wearing, incorruptible, its limpidness forms the moral image of the most deadly of virtues – purity; in terms of substance, the diamond is pure, clean, almost aseptic; but whereas there are some purities that are tender, fragile (water for example), there are others that are sterile, cold, steely; for purity is life, but it can also be, by contrast, infertility, and the diamond is like the sterile son emerging from the deepest point of the earth, non-productive, incapable of rotting down, hence incapable of becoming the source of new life.

And yet, it seduces; hard and limpid, the diamond has a third symbolic quality: it glistens. Here it is incorporated into a new magical and poetic domain, that of the paradoxical substance, both lit up and stone cold: it is nothing but fire and yet nothing but ice. This cold fire, this sharp, shining object which is nevertheless silent, what a symbol for the whole world of vanities, of seductions devoid of content, of pleasures devoid of sincerity! For centuries, Christian humanity felt deeply (much more than we do today) the opposition between the world and solitude; thanks to its fire-like sparkle and its coldness, the diamond was this world, this abhorrent and fascinating order of ambition, flattery and disappointment, condemned by so many of our moralists – perhaps in order better to describe it.

And what about gold, which was also used to make gemstones? Though originating in the earth and in hell, arriving first as ore or as nugget, gold is a substance more intellectual than symbolic; it holds a fascination only within certain mercantile economies; it has no, or very little, poetic reality; it is only ever mentioned so as to show how this most mediocre of substances (a dull, yellowy metal) clashes with the importance of its effects. But as a sign, what power it has! And it is precisely the sign par excellence, the sign of all the signs; it is absolute value, invested with all powers including those once held by magic: is it not able to appropriate *everything*, goods and virtues, lives and bodies? Is it not able to convert *everything* into its opposite, to lower and to elevate, to demean and to glorify? The gemstone has long participated in this power of gold. And this is not all: owing to the fact that gold very quickly stopped being convertible or useful and so removed itself from any practical application, pure gold, whose usefulness was almost entirely self-referential, became superlative gold, absolute richness – here the gemstone becomes the very concept of *price*, it is worn like an idea, that of a terrific power, for it is enough to be seen for this power to be demonstrated.

There is no doubt that, fundamentally, the gemstone was a sign of superpower, that is of virility, and remained so for a very long time (after all, it is only recently and under the puritan influence of Quaker clothing, which is the origin of men's clothing today, that men stopped wearing gemstones). So why in our world has it been associated so constantly with woman, with her powers and her evil spells? It is because the husband very quickly delegated to his wife the job of showing off his own wealth (certain sociologists use this to explain the origins of fashion): the wife provides poetic proof of the wealth and power of the husband. Except that, as always with human society, a simple pattern is quickly invested with unexpected meanings, symbols and effects. Thus the primitive showing-off of wealth has been invaded by a whole mythology of woman: this mythology remains infernal, because woman would give everything to own gemstones, and man would give everything to own that very woman who wears the gemstones that she has sold herself for; with gemstones as the link, woman gives herself up to the Devil, the husband to the woman, who has herself become a precious, hard stone; and we must not assume that a symbolism of this sort, which is both prosaic, spiritual and, after all, naive, belongs only to the barbarous periods in Western history. The whole of the Second Empire in France (1852–1871) for example was intoxicated and panic-stricken by the power of gemstones, by this capacity to *induce* human Evil, which for so long had been almost a physical property of diamond and gold: Zola's *Nana* really is the grandiose and angry cry of a society destroying itself, or one might even say devouring itself, in two ways; woman is both a man-eater and a diamond-eater.

Such a mythology has not completely disappeared from our times: there are still fine jewellers, a world market in diamonds and thefts of famous gemstones. But their infernal aspect is clearly on the decline. First, because the mythology of woman has changed: in the novel, in films, woman is less and less the femme fatale, no longer the destroyer of men; she can no longer be essentialized, stopped from existing or made into a precious and dangerous object; she has rejoined the human race. And also gemstones, the great mythical gemstones, are barely worn nowadays; they are of historical value only, sterilized, embalmed and kept away from the female body, condemned to sit in a safe. In short, fashion – need I say more? – no longer speaks of the gemstone but only of jewellery.

Now fashion, as we know, is a language: through it, through the system of signs it sets up, no matter how fragile this may seem, our society – and not just that of women – exhibits, communicates its being, says what it thinks of the world; so, just as the gemstone basically expressed the essentially theological nature of ancient society, so jewellery today, as seen in shops and in fashion magazines, merely follows, expresses and signifies our times – having originated in the ancestral world of the damned, the piece of jewellery has in one word become *secularized*.

First and foremost this secularization has visibly affected the very substance of jewellery; it is no longer made from just stone or metal, but also fragile or soft materials such as glass or wood. Furthermore, jewellery is no longer routinely given the job of showing off a prize that is, so to speak, inhuman: you see jewellery made of common metal, of inexpensive glass; and when jewellery imitates some precious substance, gold or pearls, it is shameless; the copy, now a characteristic of capitalist civilization, is no longer a hypocritical way of being rich on the cheap – it is quite open about itself, makes no attempt to deceive, only retaining the aesthetic qualities of the material it is imitating. In short, there has been a widespread liberation of jewellery; its definition is widening, it is now an object that is free, if one can say this, from prejudice: multiform, multi-substance, to be used in an infinite variety of ways, it is now no longer subservient to the law of the highest price nor to that of being used in only one way, such as for a party or sacred occasion: jewellery has become democratic.

Of course, this democratization does not escape from new ways of conferring value. As long as wealth regulated the rarity of a gemstone, the latter could be judged by nothing but its price (that of its substance and of the work put into it); but once just about anyone could procure whatever they wanted, as soon as the work of art became a product, there had to be a way, in our democratic, but still differentiated, societies, of subjecting jewellery to another form of discrimination: and this is *taste*, of which fashion is precisely the judge and the keeper. So today we have *jewellery of bad taste*, and, rather paradoxically, what defines bad taste in a piece of jewellery is curiously that which was once the very sign of its prestige and of its magical qualities: namely its highest price; not only is jewellery that is too rich or too heavy now discredited but conversely, for expensive jewellery to have good taste, its richness must be discreet, sober, visible certainly but only to those in the know.

So what counts as good taste in jewellery today? Quite simply this: no matter how little it costs, the piece of jewellery must be thought about in relation to the whole outfit it accompanies, it must be subjected to that essentially functional value which is that of style. What is new, if you like, is that the piece of jewellery is no longer on its own; it is one term in a set of links that goes from the body to clothing, to the accessory and includes the circumstances for which the whole outfit is being worn; it is part of an ensemble, and this ensemble is no longer necessarily ceremonial: taste can be everywhere, at work, in the country, in the morning, in winter, and the piece of jewellery follows suit; it is no longer a singular, dazzling, magical object, conceived as a way of ornamenting and thus making woman *look her best*; it is now more humble and more active, an element of clothing which enters into an equal relationship with a material, with a particular cut or with another accessory.

So it is precisely its smallness, its finished look, its very substance as the opposite of the fluidity of fabrics, that makes the piece of jewellery part of fashion and it has become almost like the soul in the general economy of clothing: that is, *the detail*. It was inevitable that, in making taste into the product of a subtle set of functions, fashion would give more and more weight to the simple presence of one element, no matter how small and without regard for its physical importance; this gives rise to the highest value in today's fashion being placed on anything insignificant in size but which is able to modify, harmonize, animate the structure of a set of clothes, and it is called precisely (but from now on with a lot of respect) a *next-to-nothing*. The piece of jewellery is a *next-to-nothing*, but out of this next-to-nothing comes great energy. Often inexpensive, sold in simple 'boutiques' and no longer in the temples of jeweller's shops, available in a variety of materials, free in its styles (often including the exotic even), in short *depreciated* in the true sense of the word, in its physical state, the most modest piece of jewellery remains the vital element in getting dressed, because it underlines the desire for order, for composition, for intelligence. Analogous to those half-chemical, half-magical, substances which act all the more forcefully by virtue of their infinitesimal size, the piece of jewellery *reigns* over clothing not because it is absolutely precious but because it plays a crucial role in making clothing mean something. It is the *meaning* in a style which now becomes precious and this meaning depends, not on each element, but on the link between them and in this link it is the *detached* term (a pocket, a flower, a scarf, a piece of jewellery) that holds the ultimate power of signification. This is a truth that is not only analytical but also poetic: this great journey across centuries and across societies, from the gemstone to jewellery, is the very same itinerary that has transformed the cold and luxurious stones in the Baudelairian universe into those trinkets, pieces of jewellery and next-to-nothings in which Mallarmé could then enclose a whole metaphysics of the new power of Man to make the tiniest of things have meaning.

NOTES

Source: Translated by Andy Stafford. Andy Stafford and Michael Carter (eds) *The Language of Fashion* (Power Publication, 2006), 59–64.

1. Published in *Jardin des Arts*, 77 (April), 1961; *Oeuvres complètes* vol. 1, 911–14.

Part 3:
Fashion and Identity

CHAPTER TWELVE

Fashion: From Class Differentiation to Collective Selection

Herbert Blumer

DEFICIENCIES OF FASHION AS A SOCIOLOGICAL CONCEPT

This paper is an invitation to sociologists to take seriously the topic of fashion. Only a handful of scholars, such as Simmel (1904), Sapir (1931), and the Langs (1961), have given more than casual concern to the topic. Their individual analyses of it, while illuminating in several respects, have been limited in scope, and within the chosen limits very sketchy. The treatment of the topic by sociologists in general, such as we find it in textbooks and in occasional pieces of scholarly writing, is even more lacking in substance. The major deficiencies in the conventional sociological treatment are easily noted – a failure to observe and appreciate the wide range of operation of fashion; a false assumption that fashion has only trivial or peripheral significance; a mistaken idea that fashion falls in the area of the abnormal and irrational and thus is out of the mainstream of human group life; and, finally, a misunderstanding of the nature of fashion.

Fashion Restricted to Adornment

Similar to scholars in general who have shown some concern with the topic, sociologists are disposed to identify fashion exclusively or primarily with the area of costume and adornment. While occasional references may be made to its play in other areas, such casual references do not give a proper picture of the extent of its operation. Yet, to a discerning eye fashion is readily seen to operate in many diverse areas of human group life, especially so in modern times. It is easily observable in the realm of the pure and applied arts, such as painting, sculpture, music, drama, architecture, dancing, and household decoration. Its presence is very obvious in the area of entertainment and amusement. There is plenty of evidence to show its play in the field of medicine. Many of us are familiar with its operation in fields of industry, especially that of business management. It even touches such a relative sacred area as that of mortuary practice. Many scholars have noted its operation in the field of literature. Its presence can be seen in the history of modern philosophy. It can be observed at work in the realm of political doctrine. And – perhaps to the surprise of many – it is unquestionably at work in the field of science. That this is true of the social and psychological sciences is perhaps more readily apparent. But we have also to note, as several reputable and qualified scholars have done, that fashion appears in such redoubtable areas as physical and biological science and mathematics. The domain in which fashion operates is very extensive, indeed. To limit it to, or to center it in, the field of costume and adornment is to have a very inadequate idea of the scope of its occurrence.

Fashion as Socially Inconsequential

This extensive range of fashion should, in itself, lead scholars to question their implicit belief that fashion is a peripheral and relatively inconsequential social happening. To the contrary, fashion may influence vitally the central content of any field in which it operates. For example, the styles in art, the themes and styles in literature, the forms and themes in entertainment, the perspectives in philosophy, the practices in business, and the preoccupations in science may be affected profoundly by fashion. These are not peripheral matters. In addition, the nature of the control wielded by fashion shows that its touch is not light. Where fashion operates it assumes an imperative position. It sets sanctions of what is to be done, it is conspicuously indifferent to criticism, it demands adherence, and it by-passes as oddities and misfits those who fail to abide by it. This grip which it exercises over its area of operation does not bespeak an inconsequential mechanism.

Fashion as Aberrant and Irrational

The third deficiency, as mentioned, is to view fashion as an aberrant and irrational social happening, akin to a craze or mania. Presumably, this ill-considered view of fashion has arisen from considerations which suggest that fashion is bizarre and frivolous, that it is fickle, that it arises in response to irrational status anxieties, and that people are swept into conforming to it despite their better judgment. It is easy to form such impressions. For one thing, past fashions usually seem odd and frequently ludicrous to the contemporary eye. Next, they rarely seem to make sense in terms of utility or rational purpose; they seem much more to express the play of fancy and caprice. Further, following the classic analysis made by Simmel, fashion seems to represent a kind of anxious effort of elite groups to set themselves apart by introducing trivial and ephemeral demarcating insignia, with a corresponding strained effort by non-elite classes to make a spurious identification of themselves with upper classes by adopting these insignia. Finally, since fashion despite its seeming frivolous content sweeps multitudes of people into its fold, it is regarded as a form of collective craziness.

UNDERSTANDING THE CHARACTER OF FASHION

Nevertheless, to view fashion as an irrational, aberrant, and craze-like social happening is to grievously misunderstand it. On the *individual side*, the adoption of what is fashionable is by and large a very calculating act. The fashion conscious person is usually quite careful and discerning in his effort to identify the fashion in order to make sure that he is "in style"; the fashion does not appear to him as frivolous. In turn, the person who is coerced into adopting the fashion contrary to his wishes does so deliberately and not irrationally. Finally, the person who unwittingly follows a fashion does so because of a limitation of choice rather than as an impulsive expression of aroused emotions or inner anxiety. The bulk of evidence gives no support to the contention that individuals who adopt fashion are caught up in the spirit of a craze. Their behavior is no more irrational or excited – and probably less so – than that of voters casting political ballots. On its *collective side*, fashion does not fit any better the pattern of a craze. The mechanisms of interaction are not those of circular transmission of aroused feelings, or of heightened suggestibility, or of fixed preoccupation with a gripping event. While people may become excited over a fashion they respond primarily to its character of propriety and social distinction; these are tempering guides. Fashion has respectability; it carries the stamp of approval of an elite – an elite that is recognized to be sophisticated and believed to be wise in the given area of endeavor. It is this endorsement which under-girds fashion – rather than the emotional interaction which is typical of crazes. Fashion has, to be true, an irrational, or better "non-rational," dimension which we shall consider later, but this dimension does not make it into a craze or mania.

The observations that fashion operates over wide areas of human endeavor, that it is not aberrant and craze-like, and that it is not peripheral and inconsequential merely correct false pictures of it. They do little to identify its nature and mode of operation. It is to this identification that I now wish to turn.

Simmel: Fashion as Class Differentiation

Let me use as the starting point of the discussion the analysis of fashion made some sixty years ago by Georg Simmel. His analysis, without question, has set the character of what little solid sociological thought is to be found on the topic. His thesis was essentially simple. For him, fashion arose as a form of class differentiation in a relatively open class society. In such a society the elite class seeks to set itself apart by observable marks or insignia, such as distinctive forms of dress. However, members of immediately subjacent classes adopt these insignia as a means of satisfying their striving to identify with a superior status. They, in turn, are copied by members of classes beneath them. In this way, the distinguishing insignia of the elite class filter down through the class pyramid. In this process, however, the elite class loses these marks of separate identity. It is led, accordingly, to devise new distinguishing insignia which, again, are copied by the classes below, thus repeating the cycle. This, for Simmel, was the nature of fashion and the mechanism of its operation. Fashion was thought to arise in the form of styles which demarcate an elite group. These styles automatically acquire prestige in the eyes of those who wish to emulate the elite group and are copied by them, thus forcing the elite group to devise new distinctive marks of their superior status. Fashion is thus caught up in an incessant and recurrent process of innovation and emulation. A fashion, once started, marches relentlessly to its doom; on its heels treads a new fashion destined to the same fate; and so on ad infinitum. This sets the fundamental character of the fashion process.

There are several features of Simmel's analysis which are admittedly of high merit. One of them was to point out that fashion requires a certain type of society in which to take place. Another was to highlight the importance of prestige in the operation of fashion. And another, of particular significance, was to stress that the essence of fashion lies in a process of change – a process that is natural and indigenous and not unusual and aberrant. Yet, despite the fact that his analysis still remains the best in the published literature, it failed to catch the character of fashion as a social happening. It is largely a parochial treatment, quite well suited to fashion in dress in the seventeenth, eighteenth, and nineteenth century Europe with its particular class structure. But it does not fit the operation of fashion in our contemporary epoch with its many diverse fields and its emphasis on modernity. Its shortcomings will be apparent, I think, in the light of the following analysis.

Modernity and the Selection Process

Some years ago I had the opportunity to study rather extensively and at first hand the women's fashion industry in Paris. There were three matters in particular which I observed which seem to me to provide the clues for an understanding of fashion in general. I wish to discuss each of them briefly and indicate their significance.

First, I was forcibly impressed by the fact that the setting or determination of fashion takes place actually through an intense process of selection. At a seasonal opening of a major Parisian fashion house there may be presented a hundred or more designs of women's evening wear before an audience of from one to two hundred buyers. The managerial corps of the fashion house is able to indicate a group of about thirty designs of the entire lot, inside of which will fall the small number, usually about six to eight designs, that are chosen by the buyers; but the managerial staff is typically unable to predict this small number on which the choices converge. Now, these choices are made by the buyers – a highly competitive and secretive lot – independently of each other and without knowledge of each other's selections. Why should their choices converge on a few designs as they do? When the buyers were asked why they chose one dress in preference to another – between which my inexperienced eye could see no appreciable difference – the typical, honest, yet largely uninformative answer was that the dress was "stunning."

Inquiry into the reasons for the similarity in the buyers' choices led me to a second observation, namely, that the buyers were immersed in and preoccupied with a remarkably common world of intense stimulation. It was a world of lively discussion of what was happening in women's fashion, of fervent reading of fashion publications, and of close observation of one another's lines of products. And, above all, it was a world of close concern with the women's dress market, with the prevailing tastes and prospective tastes of the consuming public in the area of dress. It became vividly clear to me that by virtue of their intense immersion in this world the buyers came to develop common sensitivities and similar appreciations. To use an old but valuable psychological term, they developed a common "apperception mass" which sharpened and directed their feelings of discrimination, which guided and sensitized their perceptions, and which channeled their judgments and choices. This explains, I am convinced, why the buyers, independently of each other, made such amazingly identical choices at the fashion openings. This observation also underlines a point of the greatest importance, namely, that the buyers became the unwitting surrogates of the fashion public. Their success, indeed their vocational fate, depended on their ability to sense the direction of taste in this public.

The third observation which I made pertained to the dress designers – those who created the new styles. They devised the various designs between which the buyers were ultimately to make the choices, and their natural concern was to be successful in gaining adoption of their creations. There were three lines of preoccupation from which they derived their ideas. One was to pour over old plates of former fashions and depictions of costumes of far-off peoples. A second was to brood and reflect over current and recent styles. The third, and most important, was to develop an intimate familiarity with the most recent expressions of modernity as these were to be seen in such areas as the fine arts, recent literature, political debates and happenings, and discourse in the sophisticated world. The dress designers were engaged in translating themes from these areas and media into dress designs. The designers were attuned to an impressive degree to modern developments and were seeking to capture and express in dress design the spirit of such developments. I think that this explains why the dress designers – again a competitive and secretive group, working apart from each other in a large number of different fashion houses – create independently of each other such remarkably similar designs. They pick up ideas of the past, but always through the filter of the present; they are guided and constrained by the immediate styles in dress, particularly the direction of such styles over the recent span of a few years; but above all, they are seeking to catch the proximate future as it is revealed in modern developments.

Taken together, these three observations which I have sketched in a most minimal form outline what is significant in the case of fashion in the women's dress industry. They indicate that the fashion is set through a process of free selection from among a large number of competing models; that the creators of the models are seeking to catch and give expression to what we may call the direction of modernity; and that the buyers, who through their choices set the fashion, are acting as the unwitting agents of a fashion consuming public whose incipient tastes the buyers are seeking to anticipate. In this paper I shall not deal with what is probably the most interesting and certainly the most obscure aspect of the entire relationship, namely, the relation between, on one hand, the expressions of modernity to which the dress designers are so responsive and, on the other hand, the incipient and inarticulate tastes which are taking shape in the fashion consuming public. Certainly, the two come together in the styles which are chosen and, in so doing, lay down the lines along which modern life in this area moves. I regard this line of relationship as constituting one of the most significant mechanisms in the shaping of our modern world, but I shall not undertake analysis of it in this paper.

Fashion and the Elite

The brief account which I have given of the setting of fashion in the women's wear industry permits one to return to Simmel's classic analysis and pinpoint more precisely its shortcomings. His scheme elevates the prestige of the elite to the position of major importance in the operation of fashion – styles come into fashion because of the stamp of distinction conferred on them by the elite. I think this view misses almost completely what is central to fashion, namely, *to be in fashion*. It is not the prestige of the elite which makes the design fashionable but, instead, it is the suitability or potential fashionableness of the design which allows the prestige of the elite to be attached to it. The design has to correspond to the direction of incipient taste of the fashion consuming public. The prestige of the elite affects but does not control the direction of this incipient taste. We have here a case of the fashion mechanism transcending and embracing the prestige of the elite group rather than stemming from that prestige.

There are a number of lines of evidence which I think clearly establish this to be the case. First, we should note that members of the elite – and I am still speaking of the elite in the realm of women's dress – are themselves as interested as anyone to be in fashion. Anyone familiar with them is acutely aware of their sensitivity in this regard, their wish not to be out of step with fashion, and indeed their wish to be in the vanguard of proper fashion. They are caught in the need of responding to the direction of fashion rather than of occupying the privileged position of setting that direction. Second, as explained, the fashion-adopting actions of the elite take place in a context of competing models, each with its own source of prestige. Not all prestigeful persons are innovators – and innovators are not necessarily persons with the highest prestige. The elite, itself, has to select between models proposed by innovators; and their choice is not determined by the relative prestige of the innovators. As history shows abundantly, in the competitive process fashion readily ignores persons with the highest prestige and, indeed, by-passes acknowledged "leaders" time after time. A further line of evidence is just as telling, namely, the interesting instances of failure to control the direction of fashion despite effective marshalling of the sources of prestige. An outstanding example was the effort in 1922 to check and reverse the trend toward shorter skirts which had started in 1919 to the dismay of clothing manufacturers. These manufacturers enlisted the cooperation of the heads of fashion houses, fashion magazines, fashion commentators, actresses, and acknowledged fashion leaders in an extensive, well organized and amply financed campaign to reverse the trend. The important oracles of fashion declared that long dresses were returning, models of long dresses were presented in numbers at the seasonal openings, actresses wore them on the stage, and manikins paraded them at the fashionable meeting places. Yet, despite this effective marshalling of all significant sources of prestige, the campaign was a marked failure; the trend toward shorter skirts, after a slight interruption, continued until 1929 when a rather abrupt change to long dresses took place. Such instances – and there have been others – provide further indication that there is much more to the fashion mechanism than the exercise of prestige. Fashion appears much more as a collective groping for the proximate future than a channeled movement laid down by prestigeful figures.

Collective Selection Replaces Class Differentiation

These observations require us to put Simmel's treatment in a markedly different perspective, certainly as applied to fashion in our modern epoch. The efforts of an elite class to set itself apart in appearance takes place inside of the movement of fashion instead of being its cause. The prestige of elite groups, in place of setting the direction of the fashion movement, is effective only to the extent to which they are recognized as representing and portraying the movement. The people in other classes who consciously follow the fashion do so because it is the fashion and not because of the separate prestige of the elite group. The fashion dies not because it has been discarded by the elite group but because it gives way to a new model more consonant with developing taste. *The fashion mechanism appears not in response to a need of class differentiation and class emulation but in response to a wish to be in fashion, to be abreast of what has good standing, to express new tastes which are emerging in a changing world.* These are the changes that seem to be called for in Simmel's formulation. They are fundamental changes. They shift fashion *from* the fields of *class differentiation to* the area of *collective selection* and center its mechanism in the process of such selection. This process of collective selection represents an effort to choose from among competing styles or models those which match developing tastes, those which "click," or those which – to revert to my friends, the buyers – "are stunning." The fact that this process of collective selection is mysterious – it is mysterious because we do not understand it – does not contradict in any way that it takes place.

FEATURES OF THE FASHION MECHANISM

To view the fashion mechanism as a continuing process of collective selection from among competing models yields a markedly different picture from that given by conventional sociological analysis of fashion. It calls attention to the fact that those implicated in fashion – innovators, "leaders," followers, and participants – are parts of a collective process that responds to changes in taste and sensitivity. In a legitimate sense, the movement of fashion represents a reaching out for new models which will answer to as yet indistinct and inarticulate newer tastes. The transformation of taste, of collective taste, results without question from the diversity of experience that occurs in social interaction in a complex moving world. It leads, in turn, to an unwitting groping for suitable forms of expression, in an effort to move in a direction which is consonant with the movement of modern life in general. It is perhaps unnecessary to add that we know very little indeed about this area of transformation of collective taste. Despite its unquestioned importance it has been scarcely noted, much less studied. Sociologists are conspicuously ignorant of it and indifferent to it.

Before leaving the discussion of fashion in the area of conspicuous appearance (such as dress, adornment, or mannerism), it is desirable to note and consider briefly several important features of the fashion mechanism, namely, its historical continuity, its modernity, the role of collective taste in its operation, and the psychological motives which are alleged to account for it.

Historical Continuity

The history of fashion shows clearly that new fashions are related to, and grow out of, their immediate predecessors. This is one of the fundamental ways in which fashion differs from fads. Fads have no line of historical continuity; each springs up independently of a forerunner and gives rise to no successor. In the case of fashion, fashion innovators always have to consider the prevailing fashion, if for no other reason than to depart from it or to elaborate on it. The result is a line of continuity. Typically, although not universally, the line of continuity has the character of a cultural drift, expressing itself in what we customarily term a "fashion trend."

Fashion trends are a highly important yet a much neglected object of study. They signify a convergence and marshalling of collective taste in a given direction and thus pertain to one of the most significant yet obscure features in group life. The terminal points of fashion trends are of special interest. Sometimes they are set by the nature of the medium (there is a point beyond which the skirt cannot be lengthened or shortened [see Richardson and Kroeber, 1947; Young, 1937]); sometimes they seem to represent an exhaustion of the logical possibilities of the medium; but frequently they signify a relatively abrupt shift in interests and taste. The terminal points are marked particularly by a much wider latitude of experimentation in the new fashion models that are advanced for adoption; at such points the fashion mechanism particularly reveals the groping character of collective choice to set itself on a new course. If it be true, as I propose to explain later, that the fashion mechanism is woven deeply into the texture of modern life, the study of fashion in its aspects of continuity, trends, and cycles would be highly important and rewarding.

Modernity

The feature of "modernity" in fashion is especially significant. Fashion is always modern; it always seeks to keep abreast of the times. It is sensitive to the movement of current developments as they take place in its own field, in adjacent fields, and in the larger social world. Thus, in women's dress, fashion is responsive to its own trend, to developments in fabrics and ornamentation, to developments in the fine arts, to exciting events that catch public attention such as the discovery of the tomb of Tutankhamen, to political happenings, and to major social shifts such as the emancipation of women or the rise of the cult of youth. Fashion seems to sift out of these diverse sources of happenings a set of obscure guides which bring it into line with the general or over-all direction of modernity itself. This responsiveness in its more extended form seems to be the chief factor in formation of what we speak of as a "spirit of the times" or a *zeitgeist*.

Collective Taste

Since the idea of "collective taste" is given such an important position in my analysis of the fashion mechanism, the idea warrants further clarification and explanation. I am taking the liberty of quoting my remarks as they appear in the article on "Fashion" in the new International Encyclopedia of the Social Sciences V (1968:341–345).

> . . . It represents an organic sensitivity to objects of social experience, as when we say that 'vulgar comedy does not suit our taste' or that 'they have a taste for orderly procedure.' Taste has a tri-fold character – it is like an appetite in seeking positive satisfaction; it operates as a sensitive selector, giving a basis for acceptance or rejection; and it is a formative agent, guiding the development of lines of action and shaping

objects to meet its demands. Thus, it appears as a subjective mechanism, giving orientation to individuals, structuring activity and moulding the world of experience. Tastes are themselves a product of experience; they usually develop from an initial state of vagueness to a state of refinement and stability, but once formed they may decay and disintegrate. They are formed in the context of social interaction, responding to the definitions and affirmations given by others. People thrown into areas of common interaction and having similar runs of experience develop common tastes. The fashion process involves both a formation and an expression of collective taste in the given area of fashion. Initially, the taste is a loose fusion of vague inclinations and dissatisfactions that are aroused by new experiences in the field of fashion and in the larger surrounding world. In this initial state, collective taste is amorphous, inarticulate, vaguely poised, and awaiting specific direction. Through models and proposals, fashion innovators sketch out possible lines along which the incipient taste may gain objective expression and take definite form. Collective taste is an active force in the ensuing process of selection, setting limits and providing guidance; yet, at the same time is undergoes refinement and organization through its attachment to, and embodiment in, specific social forms. The origin, formation, and careers of collective taste constitute the huge problematic area in fashion. Major advancement in our knowledge of the fashion mechanism depends on the charting of this area. . . .

Psychological Motives

Now, a word with regard to psychological interpretations of fashion. Scholars, by and large, have sought to account for fashion in terms of psychological motives. A perusal of the literature will show an assortment of different feelings and impulses which have been picked out to explain the occurrence of fashion. Some students ascribe fashion to efforts to escape from boredom or ennui, especially among members of the leisure class. Some treat fashion as arising from playful and whimsical impulses to enliven the routines of life with zest. Some regard it as due to a spirit of adventure which impels individuals to rebel against the confinement of prevailing social forms. Some see fashion as a symbolic expression of hidden sexual interests. Most striking is the view expressed by Sapir in his article on "Fashion" in the first edition of the Encyclopedia of the Social Sciences VI (1931:139–141); Sapir held that fashion results from an effort to increase the attractiveness of the self, especially under conditions which impair the integrity of the ego; the sense of oneself is regained and heightened through novel yet socially sanctioned departures from prevailing social forms. Finally, some scholars trace fashion to desires for personal prestige or notoriety.

Such psychological explanations, either singly or collectively, fail to account for fashion; they do not explain why or how the various feelings or motives give rise to a fashion process. Such feelings are presumably present and in operation in all human societies; yet there are many societies in which fashion is not to be found. Further, such feelings may take various forms of expression which have no relation to a fashion process. We are given no explanation of why the feelings should lead to the formation of fashion in place of taking other channels of expression available to them. The psychological schemes fail to come to grip with the collective process which constitutes fashion – the emergence of new models in an area of changing experience, the differential attention given them, the interaction which leads to a focusing of collective choice on one of them, the social endorsement of it as proper, and the powerful control which this endorsement yields. Undoubtedly, the various feelings and impulses specified by psychologists operate within the fashion process – just as they operate within non-fashion areas of group life. But their operation within fashion does not account for fashion. Instead, their operation presupposes the existence of the fashion process as one of the media for their play.

The foregoing discussion indicates, I trust, the inadequacy of conventional sociological and psychological schemes to explain the nature of fashion. Both sets of schemes fail to perceive fashion as the process of collective selection that it is. The schemes do not identify the nature of the social setting in which fashion arises nor do they catch or treat the mechanism by which fashion operates. The result is that students fail to see the scope and manner of its operation and to appreciate the vital role which it plays in modern group life. In the interest of presenting a clearer picture of these matters, I wish to amplify the sketch of fashion as given above in order to show more clearly its broad generic character.

GENERIC CHARACTER OF FASHION

It is necessary, first of all, to insist that fashion is not confined to those areas, such as women's apparel, in which fashion is institutionalized and professionally exploited under conditions of intense competition. As mentioned earlier, it is found in operation in a wide variety and increasing number of fields which shun deliberate or intentional concern with fashion. In such fields, fashion occurs almost always without awareness on the part of those who are caught in its operation. What may be primarily response to fashion is seen and interpreted in other ways – chiefly as doing what is believed to be superior practice. The prevalence of such unwitting deception can be considerable. The basic mechanism of fashion which comes to such a clear, almost pure, form in women's dress is clouded or concealed in other fields but is none the less operative. Let me approach a consideration of this matter by outlining the six essential conditions under which fashion presumably comes into play.

Essential Conditions of Its Appearance

First, the area in which fashion operates must be one that is involved in a movement of change, with people ready to revise or discard old practices, beliefs, and attachments, and poised to adopt new social forms; there must be this thrust into the future. If the area is securely established, as in the domain of the sacred, there will be no fashion. Fashion presupposes that the area is in passage, responding to changes taking place in a surrounding world, and oriented to keeping abreast of new developments. The area is marked by a new psychological perspective which places a premium on being "up to date" and which implies a readiness to denigrate given older forms of life as being outmoded. Above all, the changing character of the area must gain expression or reflection in changes in that subjective orientation which I have spoken of under the term, "taste."

A *second* condition is that the area must be open to the recurrent presentation of models or proposals of new social forms. These models, depending on the given areas of fashion, may cover such diverse things as points of view, doctrines, lines of preoccupation, themes, practices, and use of artifacts. In a given area of fashion, these models differ from each other and of course from the prevailing social forms. Each of them is metaphorically a claimant for adoption. Thus their presence introduces a competitive situation and sets the stage for selection between them.

Third, there must be a relatively free opportunity for choice between the models. This implies that the models must be open, so to speak, to observation and that facilities and means must be available for their adoption. If the presentation of new models is prevented the fashion process will not get under way. Further, a severe limitation in the wherewithal needed to adopt models (such as necessary wealth, intellectual sophistication, refined skill, or esthetic sensitivity) curtails the initiation of the fashion process.

Fashion is not guided by utilitarian or rational considerations. This points to a *fourth* condition essential to its operation, namely, that the pretended merit or value of the competing models cannot be demonstrated through open and decisive test. Where choices can be made between rival models on the basis of objective and effective test, there is no place for fashion. It is for this reason that fashion does not take root in those areas of utility, technology, or science where asserted claims can be brought before the bar of demonstrable proof. In contrast, the absence of means for testing effectively the relative merit of competing models opens the door to other considerations in making choices between them. This kind of situation is essential to the play of fashion.

A *fifth* condition for fashion is the presence of prestige figures who espouse one or another of the competing models. The prestige of such persons must be such that they are acknowledged as qualified to pass judgment on the value or suitability of the rival models. If they are so regarded their choice carries weight as an assurance or endorsement of the superiority or propriety of a given model. A combination of such prestigeful figures, espousing the same model, enhances the likelihood of adoption of the model.

A *sixth* and final condition is that the area must be open to the emergence of new interests and dispositions in response to (a) the impact of outside events, (b) the introduction of new participants into the area, and (c) changes in inner social interaction. This condition is chiefly responsible for the shifting of taste and the redirection of collective choice which together constitute the lifeline of fashion.

If the above six conditions are met, I believe that one will always find fashion to be in play. People in the area will be found to be converging their choices on models and shifting this convergence over time. The convergence of choice occurs not because of the intrinsic merit or demonstrated validity of the selected models but because of the appearance of high standing which the chosen models carry. Unquestionably, such high standing is given in major measure by the endorsement and espousal of models of prestigeful persons. But it must be stressed again that it is not prestige, *per se*, which imparts this sanction; a prestigeful person, despite his eminence, may be easily felt to be "out-of-date." To carry weight, the person of prestige must be believed or sensed to be voicing the proper perspective that is called for by developments in the area. To recognize this is to take note of the importance of the disposition to keep abreast of what is collectively judged to be up-to-date practice. The formation of this collective judgment takes place through an interesting but ill-understood interaction between prestige and incipient taste, between eminent endorsement and congenial interest. Collective choice of models is forged in this process of interaction, leading to a focusing of selection at a given time on one model and at a different time on another model.

FASHION AND CONTEMPORARY SOCIETY

If we view modern life in terms of the analytical scheme which I have sketched, there is no difficulty in seeing the play of fashion in many diverse areas. Close scrutiny of such areas will show the features which we have discussed – a turning away from old forms that are thought to be out-of-date; the introduction of new models which compete for adoption; a selection between them that is made not on the basis of demonstrated merit or utility but in response to an interplay of prestige-endorsement and incipient taste; and a course of development in which a given type of model becomes solidified, socially elevated, and imperative in its demands for acceptance for a period of time. While this process is revealed most vividly in the area of women's fashion it can be noted in play here and there across the board in modern life and may, indeed, be confidently expected to increase in scope under the conditions of modern life. These conditions – the pressure to change, the open doors to innovation, the inadequacy or the unavailability of decisive tests of the merit of proposed models, the effort of prestigeful figures to gain or maintain standing in the face of developments to which they must respond, and the groping of people for a satisfactory expression of new and vague tastes – entrench fashion as a basic and widespread process in modern life.

The Expanding Domain of Fashion

This characterization may repel scholars who believe that fashion is an abnormal and irrational happening and that it gives way before enlightenment, sophistication, and increased knowledge. Such scholars would reject the thought that fashion is becoming increasingly embedded in a society which is presumably moving toward a higher level of intelligence and rational perspective. Yet, the facts are clear that fashion is an outstanding mark of modern civilization and that its domain is expanding rather than diminishing. As areas of life come to be caught in the vortex of movement and as proposed innovations multiply in them, a process of collective choice in the nature of fashion is naturally and inevitably brought into play. The absence or inadequacy of compelling tests of the merit of proposals opens the door to prestige-endorsement and taste as determinants of collective choice. The compelling role of these two factors as they interact easily escapes notice by those who participate in the process of collective choice; the model which emerges with a high sanction and approval is almost always believed by them as being intrinsically and demonstrably correct. This belief is fortified by the impressive arguments and arrays of specious facts that may frequently be marshalled on behalf of the model. Consequently, it is not surprising that participants may fail completely to recognize a fashion process in which they are sharing. The identification of the process as fashion occurs usually only after it is gone – when it can be viewed from the detached vantage point of later time. The fashions which we can now detect in the past history of philosophy, medicine, science, technological use and industrial practice did not appear as fashions to those who shared in them. The fashions merely appeared to them as up-to-date achievements! The fact that participants in fashion movements in different areas of contemporary life do not recognize such movements should not mislead perceptive scholars. The application of this observation to the domain of social science is particularly in order; contemporary social science is rife with the play of fashion.

The Societal Role of Fashion

I turn finally to a series of concluding remarks on what seems to be the societal role of fashion. As I have sought to explain, the key to the understanding of fashion is given in the simple words, "being in fashion." These words signify an area of life which is caught in movement – movement from an out-moded past toward a dim, uncertain, but exploitable immediate future. In this passage, the need of the present is to be in march with the time. The fashion mechanism is the response to this need. These simple observations point to the social role of fashion – a role which I would state abstractly to be that of enabling and aiding collective adjustment to and in a moving world of divergent possibilities. In spelling out this abstract statement I wish to call attention to three matters.

The *first* is a matter which is rather obvious, namely, that fashion introduces a conspicuous measure of unanimity and uniformity in what would otherwise be a markedly fragmented arrangement. If all competing models enjoyed similar acceptance the situation would be one of disorder and disarray. In the field of dress, for example, if people were to freely adopt the hundreds of styles proposed professionally each year and the other thousands which the absence of competition would allow, there would be a veritable "Tower of Babel" consequence. *Fashion introduces order in a potentially anarchic and moving present.* By establishing suitable models which carry the stamp of propriety and compel adherence, fashion narrowly limits the range of variability and so fosters uniformity and order, even though it be passing uniformity and order. In this respect fashion performs in a moving society a function which custom performs in a settled society.

Second, fashion serves to detach the grip of the past in a moving world. By placing a premium on being in the mode and derogating what developments have left behind, it frees actions for new movement. The significance of this release from the restraint of the past should not be minimized. To meet a moving and changing world requires freedom to move in new directions. Detachment from the hold of the past is no small contribution to the achievement of such freedom. In the areas of its operation fashion facilitates that contribution. In this sense there is virtue in applying the derogatory accusations of being "old-fashioned," "outmoded," "backward," and "out-of-date."

Third, fashion operates as an orderly preparation for the immediate future. By allowing the presentation of new models but by forcing them through the gauntlet of competition and collective selection the fashion mechanism offers a continuous means of adjusting to what is on the horizon.[1] On the one hand, it offers to innovators and creators the opportunity to present through their models their ideas of what the immediate future should be in the given area of fashion. On the other hand, the adoption of the models which survive the gauntlet of collective selection gives expression to nascent dispositions that represents an accommodation or orientation to the immediate future. Through this process, fashion nurtures and shapes a body of common sensitivity and taste, as is suggested by the congeniality and naturalness of present fashions in contrast to the oddness and incongruity of past fashions. This body of common sensitivity and taste is analogous on the subjective side to a "universe of discourse." Like the latter, it provides a basis for a common approach to a world and for handling and digesting the experiences which the world yields. The value of a pliable and re-forming body of common taste to meet a shifting and developing world should be apparent.

CONCLUSION

In these three ways, fashion is a very adept mechanism for enabling people to adjust in an orderly and unified way to a moving and changing world which is potentially full of anarchic possibilities. It is suited, *par excellence*, to the demands of life in such a moving world since it facilitates detachment from a receding past, opens the doors to proposals to to the future, but subjects such proposals to the test of collective selection, thus bringing them in line with the direction of awakened interest and disposition. In areas of life – and they are many – in which the merit of the proposals cannot be demonstrated, it permits orderly movement and development.

In closing, let me renew the invitation to sociologists to take fashion seriously and give it the attention and study which it deserves and which are so sorely lacking. Fashion should be recognized as a central mechanism in forming social order in a modern type of world, a mechanism whose operation will increase. It needs to be lifted out of the area of the bizarre, the irrational and the inconsequential in which sociologists have so misguidingly lodged it. When sociologists respond to the need of developing a scheme of analysis suited to a moving or modern world they will be required to assign the fashion process to a position of central importance.

NOTES

Source: *The Sociological Quarterly,* 10 (Blackwell Publishing, 1969), 275–91.

1. The recognition that fashion is continuously at work is, in my judgment, the major although unintended contribution of Simmel's analysis. However, his thesis that the function of fashion is the oscillating differentiation and unification of social classes seems to me to miss what is most important.

REFERENCES

Blumer, Herbert 1968 "Fashion." Pp. 341–345 in *International Encyclopedia of the Social Sciences* V. New York: Macmillan.

Lang, Kurt and Gladys Lang 1961 *Collective Dynamics.* New York: Crowell.

Richardson, J. and A. L. Kroeber 1947 "Three centuries of women's dress fashions: a quantitative analysis." *Anthropological Records* 5:111–153.

Sapir, Edward 1931 "Fashion." Pp. 139–141 in *Encyclopedia of the Social Sciences* VI. New York: Macmillan.

Simmel, G. 1904 "Fashion." *International Quarterly* 10.

———. 1957 "Fashion." *American Journal of Sociology* 62:541–558. (reprint).

Young, A. B. 1937 *Recurring Cycles of Fashion: 1760–1937.* New York: Harper & Brothers.

CHAPTER THIRTEEN

Why the Midi Failed

Fred D. Reynolds and William R. Darden

The success of fashions, not surprisingly, depends upon giving the consumer what she wants.

The substantial number of new product failures each year is frequently cited as the justification for exploring adoption and diffusion processes among consumers. Presumably, marketing planners with a greater understanding of the acceptance processes can more ably adapt their marketing programs to these processes and thereby increase their new product "batting averages."

Fine.

But a strange, empirical paradox has emerged: surprisingly little research has been devoted to the new products that *failed* to diffuse. What is the difference, if any? Are new products rejected simply because they are perceived negatively? Or, are the sources of information used by consumers as they move from awareness to rejection also different? How important are mass media compared to informal media in the rejection decision? Are opinion leaders more or less active than non-leaders in discussing rejected products?

To provide tentative answers to these and other questions, research was conducted to study the nature of information used by consumers in reaching their decisions to reject a new clothing style, the midi.

A search of the relevant literature uncovered no previous research on the rejection of new clothing styles. The review also indicated that relatively little research has focused on the diffusion of new styles.

In developing hypotheses, it was thus assumed that essentially no differences exist in the structure and function of information sources utilized by consumers in adoption and rejection processes. The assumption suggests that perceived characteristics of new styles, in part revealed by discussion, become significant factors leading to an adoption or rejection decision.

There are obviously many sources from which consumers can obtain information. In fashions, impersonal sources inform consumers of general fashion trends, new styles, merchandise availability, and detailed fashion instruction (King, 1965). Personal sources, while often complementary to impersonal sources, function as evaluative sources. Interpersonal sources are persuasive in that they provide other-reference on group norms for specific types of social activities. "Self," or a person's experience world including past decisions and perceived interrelationships among events, provides the decisional criteria for the current choice situation.

Source functions suggest that impersonal sources of information are most important at the awareness stage, and personal sources are most important at the evaluation stage in the rejection process (Rogers, 1962).

Because of the importance of interpersonal communication in diffusion, researchers have sought further understanding by exploring the concept of opinion leadership. Little is known, however, about the differential use of information sources among opinion leaders and non-leaders at the various stages of the adoption/rejection process.

Studies by Reynolds and Darden (1971) and by Summers (1970) have found that opinion leaders are more exposed than non-leaders to the mass media, particularly those media specializing in the area of the leader's influence. These findings suggest that impersonal, but fashion specialized information sources, are more important for opinion leaders than non-leaders at the awareness stage of the rejection process. Yet relatively little research has examined the question of source importance at the information stage of the adoption/rejection process.

Given the increasing importance of interpersonal communication after awareness, what is the role of the opinion leader in the transmission of information? Evidence shows that opinion leaders tend to transmit and receive word-of-mouth information to a greater degree than non-leaders.

These findings suggest that opinion leaders should engage in conversation about a new style to a somewhat greater extent than non-leaders. Also, opinion leaders should report self-initiated and friend-initiated conversations more frequently than non-leaders. Non-leaders, on the other hand, should report a disproportionate number of friend-initiated discussions.

SOURCES AND FUNCTIONS

If, as suggested, the structure and function of information sources are essentially the same for both adoption and rejection decisions, then the content of information as perceived by consumers becomes highly significant as to whether or not a new style will diffuse.

Arndt's study (1967) of the diffusion of a new brand of coffee supports the importance of perceived content. He found that favorable word-of-mouth exposure increased probability of purchase whereas unfavorable exposure decreased the probability. He also found that the word-of-mouth patterns tended to be exchanges of opinion rather than attempts by transmitters to control the purchasing actions of comment receivers.

Arndt's study suggests two fashion rejection hypotheses: (1) that the direction of word-of-mouth discussions is positively related to the adoption/rejection of a new style; and (2) that neither opinion leaders nor non-leaders view themselves as either influencing others or being influenced by others from style-related discussions.

THE STUDY

The data for this article primarily are based on a follow-up survey conducted as part of a continuing investigation of fashion diffusion at the University of Georgia. An initial survey of 300 Athens, Georgia, home makers was conducted during July 1970 to investigate several fashion topics including ex-ante fashion prediction about the midi. The analysis and interpretation of the original data indicated that the midi would be rejected.

The follow-up survey was designed to validate the prediction and, if validated, to investigate the rejection hypotheses formulated.

In May 1971, 116 of the original 300 respondents were randomly selected and interviewed in a telephone survey. Using a pretested questionnaire, responses were obtained from 103 persons, 94 of whom did not purchase the midi. The 13 non-respondents included two refusals and 11 persons who could not be contacted. Since the purpose of the study was to investigate rejection instead of discontinuance, the data for this report are based upon the 94 rejectors.

The stages of the decision process were put into questions as follows: (1) *Awareness:* "Where, or from whom, did you first see or hear about the midi?" (2) *Information:* "After you first heard about it, where or from whom did you get additional, more detailed information about it?" (3) *Evaluation:* "After you had enough information to know quite a lot about the midi, where or from whom did you get information that helped you decide whether or not to buy it for yourself?"

The designation of respondents as opinion leader or non-leader was based upon data obtained in the initial study (Reynolds and Darden, 1971). The proportion of opinion leaders was essentially the same, 18 per cent in the initial sample of 300 and 17 per cent in the follow-up sample of 94.

Multiple-choice questions were used to determine discussion direction frequency, etc., but an open-end question was used to elicit content of discussions about the midi.

INFORMATION SOURCES

Data in Table 1 show that impersonal sources were the main sources for awareness of the midi. Their importance declined consistently from awareness to evaluation; conversely, personal sources were most important at evaluation.

TABLE 1: Information sources at process stages

| Information sources | Stage in the rejection process | | | | | |
| | Awareness | | Information | | Evaluation | |
	No.	%	No.	%	No.	%
Impersonal						
Fashion Magazine	40	42.5	23	24.5	10	10.8
Newspaper	25	26.6	7	7.4	–	–
Television	21	22.3	19	20.2	2	2.1
Advertisements	1	1.1	2	2.1	–	–
Subtotal	87	92.5	51	54.2	12	12.9
Personal						
Friend	1	1.1	3	3.2	8	8.6
Relative	1	1.1	4	4.3	4	4.3
Store Employee	–	–	1	1.1	–	–
Visual	2	2.1	16	17.0	7	7.4
Self	–	–	–	–	62	66.7
Did not seek	–	–	17	18.1	–	–
Subtotal	4	4.3	41	43.7	81	87.0
Don't Recall	3	3.2	2	2.1	1	1.1
Total	94	100.0	94	100.0	94	100.0

Within the categories, fashion magazines were the most important impersonal sources at each stage of the rejection process. The consistency of one dominant source at each process stage was not found, however, for the personal sources. Self was reported to be the most important evaluative source. Interpersonal sources, however, were more important than impersonal sources at evaluation.

Fashion specialized sources were more important for opinion leaders than non-leaders at the awareness stage, as shown by the data in Table 2. Both newspapers and television programs were more important for non-leaders. It should be noted that opinion leaders reported only friends and relatives as personal sources of awareness whereas non-leaders reported only visual sources.

Table 1 also shows that 80 per cent of the respondents reported additional sources after awareness. The data also indicate that impersonal sources remain relatively more important than personal sources. Visual sources, however, reach their peak during the information stage. This suggests the importance of promotion devices such as store and window displays and fashion shows (the most frequently mentioned visual sources) for imparting fashion knowledge to consumers.

Table 3 shows the distribution of additional information sources. The proportions were approximately the same in each category for respondents who did not obtain information and for those who did. For those who reported additional sources, more opinion leaders consulted only one source, and more non-leaders consulted two or more sources.

TABLE 2: Awareness sources reported by opinion leaders and Non-leaders

	Opinion leader		Non-leader	
Information source	No.	%	No.	%
Impersonal				
Fashion Magazine	8	50.00	32	41.03
Newspaper	3	18.75	22	28.21
Television	1	6.25	20	25.64
Advertisement	1	6.25	–	–
Personal				
Friend	1	6.25	–	–
Relative	1	6.25	–	–
Visual	–	–	2	2.56
Don't Recall	1	6.25	2	2.56
Total	16	100.00	78	100.00

TABLE 3: Number of additional sources consulted

	Number of sources		
Category	1	2	3
Opinion Leader	76.92%	15.38%	7.80%
	(10)	(2)	(1)
Non-Leader	67.74%	29.03%	3.23%
	(42)	(18)	(2)

The relationship between additional search and self-confidence appears stronger, as indicated in Table 4. The tendency for non-leaders to seek additional information from a larger variety of sources appears to be a function of less self-confidence rather than of non-leadership. These findings suggest that additional search, while pervasive, is inversely related to self-confidence.

Table 5 shows the distribution of the number of midi discussions with friends. The data indicate that the topic was widely discussed and that there was a greater tendency for opinion leaders to engage in interpersonal discussions. The results, however, suggest that the lower level of fashion interest among non-leaders is not a sufficient deterrent to frequent discussion of a controversial and highly publicized style.

Table 6 provides supportive evidence for the hypothesis about discussion initiation. Of the 54 persons responding to the question, opinion leaders were more equally represented whereas a disproportionate number of non-leaders reported that a friend tended to initiate midi discussions. These findings suggest that opinion leaders tend to be more active as initiators of word-of-mouth communication and that non-leaders tend to perceive themselves as being primarily receivers of inter-personal information.

TABLE 4: Number of sources by self-confidence holding leadership constant

	Number of sources		
Category	1	2	3
Opinion Leader			
High Self-Confidence	100%	0%	0%
	(7)	(0)	(0)
Low Self-Confidence	50%	33%	17%
	(3)	(2)	(1)
Non-Leader			
High Self-Confidence	89%	11%	0%
	(17)	(2)	(0)
Low Self-Confidence	58%	37%	5%
	(25)	(16)	(2)

TABLE 5: Midi discussion frequency

	Frequency			
Category	5 or More	4 or 3	2 or 1	Not at All
Opinion Leader	62.50	12.50	18.75	6.25
	(10)	(2)	(3)	(1)
Non-Leader	37.18	23.08	30.77	8.97
	(29)	(18)	(24)	(7)

TABLE 6: Discussion initiators

Category	Self-Initiated	Friend-Initiated
Opinion Leaders	40%	60%
	(4)	(6)
Non-Leader	13.6%	86.4%
	(6)	(38)

Nevertheless, interpersonal communication is apparently as important for opinion leaders as for non-leaders at the evaluation stage. Data in Table 7 show only a slight tendency for non-leaders to report proportionately more interpersonal sources and self than leaders. Thus the data continue to support the notion of the pervasive importance of personal information sources for evaluative purposes.

INFORMATION CONTENT

One hypothesis derived from Arndt's study postulated a positive relationship between the direction of word-of-mouth content and style acceptance decisions. Since the respondents of our study were rejectors, it was expected that most would perceive

TABLE 7: Evaluation sources reported by opinion leaders and non-leaders

Information source	Opinion leader		Non-leader	
	No.	%	No.	%
Impersonal				
Fashion Magazine	2	12.50	8	10.26
Television	1	6.25	1	1.28
Personal				
Friend	1	6.25	7	8.97
Relative	1	6.25	3	3.85
Visual	1	6.25	6	7.69
Self	10	62.50	52	66.67
Don't Recall	–	–	1	1.28
Total	16	100.00	78	100.00

their midi discussions to be unfavorable. This was confirmed: of the 81 persons responding to the question, 76 or 93 per cent reported that the discussions were primarily unfavorable.

The data in Table 8 also provide supporting evidence on the perception of influence hypothesis. There appear to be few differences between opinion leaders and non-leaders in viewing themselves as being influencers or in-influencees in discussions of the midi. The respondents overwhelmingly said "no" to each question.

The grouping of the 233 negative comments related to the content of discussion about the midi produced the following themes:

Recurrent Theme

39 comments related to the recurrence of an old fashion. Women perceived the midi as a recurring style from yesteryear. They expressed a belief that the midi would make them feel "older" or "old fashioned"– a feeling incompatible with their life styles and/or, perhaps, youth value. This theme reflects a negative compatibility characteristic of the midi.

Economic Theme

17 comments related to the need for buying a "whole look." Women perceived a necessity to buy accessories to complement the look. This, they claimed, was too expensive. An economic disadvantage coupled with the perceived, in part, indi-visibility of the "whole look."

TABLE 8: Perceived influence

Category	Influencer		Influencee	
	Yes	No	Yes	No
Opinion Leader	13.3 (2)	86.7 (13)	6.7 (1)	93.3 (14)
Non-Leader	16.7 (12)	83.3 (60)	6.9 (5)	93.1 (67)

Mirror Theme

71 comments related to appearance of wearer as she saw "herself" in the midi. These women used comments such as "I am less feminine looking in it," "It isn't flattering," "My legs are too pretty to cover," "I am too short to look well in it," "I wouldn't look attractive in it," "It would look sloppy on me," and "It would make me look chubbier." Clearly, not the image these women would like to present to others. A factor of social visibility, negatively perceived.

Poor Design Theme

18 comments about design features excluding "length." These women perceived the design itself to be poor; i.e., heavy, bulky, uncomfortable, too few suitable fabrics for the style, too hot for the Southern summer, not versatile for daily wear, the unfinished look, and movement inhibited. Clearly a disadvantage for those who desire comfortable and versatile styles.

Fashion Prediction Theme: Risk Element

11 comments related to whether or not it would be accepted. These women apparently perceived greater risk in the midi than others. They were concerned about whether or not others would wear it and cause their own styles to become "obsolete" or "out of fashion." A perceived risk characteristic of the midi.

Fashion Prediction Theme: Fad Element

8 comments on the faddish nature of the midi. These persons perceived it as a fad; something "too shocking to stick;" much like the granny dress of a few years ago. A social visibility theme.

Other

69 comments too superficial to assign to a theme. The most typical were, "I just don't like it" and "length."

When the first comment reported was distributed by opinion leadership categories, the differences were apparent. Non-leaders, to a greater extent than leaders, reported Themes 1 and 4; leaders reported Themes 3 and 5. Non-leaders also provided proportionately more of the superficial responses, suggesting, perhaps, that they are less articulate in reporting their perceptions or that because of less interest they are less willing to articulate.

Table 9 presents the distribution of the four perceived characteristics of the midi as indicated by the non-superficial content themes. For non-leaders, incompatibility

TABLE 9: Perceived characteristics by opinion leaders and non-leaders

	Perceived characteristics			
Category	Compatibility	Visibility	Relative risk advantage	Risk
Opinion Leader	0	60.0	10.0	30.0
	(0)	(6)	(1)	(3)
Non-Leader	22.2	55.5	20.0	2.2
	(10)	(25)	(9)	(1)

and relative disadvantage were the important negative perceptions: risk and visibility were important for the opinion leaders.

DISCUSSION

In summary, this research found that the information sources used by consumers in fashion rejection are essentially the same as for the diffusion of an innovation. In addition, several findings related an antecedent condition, opinion leadership, to the differential use of information in the rejection process.

Overall results suggest the need for complementary media selection to stimulate awareness and interest in a new clothing style. Specialized fashion sources are useful for communicating with opinion leaders, but other forms such as television and local newspapers must serve this purpose for non-leaders. In essence, opinion leaders and non-leaders represent separate market segments for new styles and, given the short duration of the selling season, it is advisable to create awareness as early as possible for both segments even though the non-leaders may adopt later in the season than the opinion leaders. The skillful use of publicity is also underscored since it appears that widely-publicized styles are related to the frequency of word-of-mouth discussion.

Not only should complementary sources of information be selected to reach both leader and non-leaders, but the message content should also be differentiated for maximum appeal. The data also suggest that opinion leaders are more concerned with the personal aesthetics and frills of fashion than non-leaders. They are also resistent to highly visible frills that create high risk of current style obsolescence. Non-leaders, on the other hand, are more likely to respond to function appeals than to frills. They are concerned with the compatibility of new styles and their relative advantage over existing styles. In general, marketing communicators must develop messages that are related to the style characteristics important to the separate market segments for the best impact.

Finally, the midi failure points out that no amount of promotion will ensure the success of a new style whose design is incongruent with the characteristics desired by the markets. The consumer is still king.

NOTE

Source: *Journal of Advertising Research*, 12 (The Advertising Research Foundation, 1972), 39–44.

REFERENCES

Arndt, Johan. Role of Product-Related Conversations in the Diffusion of a New Product. *Journal of Marketing Research*, Vol. 4, August 1967, pp. 291–95.

King, Charles W. Communicating With the Innovator in the Fashion Adoption Process. *Proceedings* Fall Conference of the American Marketing Association, 1965, pp. 425–39.

Reynolds, Fred D. and William R. Darden. Mutually Adaptive Effects of Interpersonal Communications. *Journal of Marketing Research*, Vol. 8, November 1971, pp. 449–54.

Rogers, Everett M. *Diffusion of Innovations*, New York: The Free Press, 1962.

Summers, John O. The Identity of Women's Clothing Fashion Opinion Leaders. *Journal of Marketing Research*, Vol. 7, May 1970, pp. 178–85.

CHAPTER FOURTEEN

The Production of Belief: Contribution to an Economy of Symbolic Goods

PIERRE BOURDIEU

TIME AND MONEY

[. . .] Thus the various publishing houses can be characterized according to the distribution of their commitments between risky, long-term investments (*Godot*) and safe, short-term investments,[1] and, by the same token, according to the proportion of their authors, who are long-term or short-term writers. The latter include journalists extending their usual activity into 'current-affairs' books, 'personalities' presenting their 'personal testimony' in essays or memoirs and professional writers who stick to the rules of a tried and tested aesthetic (award-winning literature, best-selling novels, etc.).[2]

An examination of two publishing houses that are characteristic of the two poles of the publishing field, Robert Laffont and Editions de Minuit, will enable us to grasp the numerous aspects of the oppositions between the two sectors of the field. Robert Laffont is a large firm (700 employees) publishing a considerable number of new titles each year (about 200), overtly success-oriented (in 1976 it had seven prints of over 100,000 copies, fourteen of over 50,000 and fifty of over 20,000). This entails a large sales department, considerable expenditure on advertising and public relations (especially directed towards booksellers), and also a systematic policy of choices guided by a sense of the safe investment (until 1975, almost half the Laffont list consisted of translations of works already successful abroad) and the hunt for bestsellers (the list of 'famous names' with which Robert Laffont refutes those who 'refuse to recognize us as serious literary publishers' includes Bernard Clavel, Max Gallo, Françoise Dorin, Georges Emmanual Clancier and Pierre Rey). By contrast, Editions de Minuit, a small firm employing a dozen people, publishing fewer than twenty titles a year (by no more than about forty novelists or dramatists in twenty-five years), devoting a minute proportion of its turnover to publicity (and even deriving a strategic advantage from its refusal to use the lower forms of public relations), is quite used to sales under 500 ('P's first book, which sold more than 500 copies, was only our ninth') and print-runs under 3,000 (in 1975, it was stated that out of 17 new titles published in the three years since 1971, 14 had sold less than 3,000 copies and the other three had not gone beyond 5,000). The firm is always loss-making, if only its new publications are considered, but lives on its past investments, i.e. the profits regularly accruing from those of its publications which have become famous (e.g. *Godot*, which sold fewer than 200 copies in 1952 and 25 years later had sold more than 500,000 copies).

These two temporal structures correspond to two very different economic structures. Like all the other public companies (e.g. Hachette or Presses de la Cite) Laffont has an obligation to its shareholders (Time-Life in this case) to make profits, despite very substantial overheads, and so it must 'turn over' very rapidly what is essentially an economic capital (without taking the time required to convert it into cultural capital). Editions de Minuit does not have to worry about profits (which are partly redistributed to the personnel) and can plough back the income from its ever-growing assets into long-term undertakings. The scale of the firm and the volume of production not only influence cultural policy through the size of the overheads and the concern with getting a return on the capital; they also directly affect the behaviour of those responsible for selecting manuscripts. The small publisher, with the aid of a few advisors who are themselves 'house' authors, is able to have personal knowledge of all the books published. In short, everything combines to discourage the manager of a big publishing house from going in for high-risk, long term investments: the financial structure of his firm, the economic constraints which force him to seek a return on the capital, and therefore to think primarily in terms of sales, and the conditions in which he works, which make it practically impossible to have direct contact with manuscripts and authors.[3] By contrast, the avant-garde publisher is able to confront the financial risks he faces (which are, in any case, objectively smaller) by investing (in both senses) in undertakings which can, at best, bring only symbolically profits, but only on condition that he fully recognizes the specific stakes of the field of production and, like the writers or 'intellectuals' whom he publishes, pursues the sole specific profit awarded by the field, at least in the short term, i.e. 'renown' and the corresponding 'intellectual authority'.[4] The strategies which he applies in his relations with the press are perfectly adapted (without necessarily having been so conceived) to the objective demands of the most advanced fraction of the field, i.e. to the 'intellectual' ideal of negation, which demands refusal of temporal compromises and tends to establish a negative correlation between success and true artistic value. Whereas short-cycle production, like *haute couture*, is heavily dependent on a whole set of agents and institutions specializing in 'promotion' (newspaper, magazine, TV and radio critics) which must be constantly maintained and periodically mobilized (with the annual literary prizes performing a function analogous to that of fashion 'collections'),[5] long-cycle production, which derives practically no benefit from the free publicity of press articles about the prize competitions and the prizes themselves, depends entirely on the activity of a few 'talent-spotters', i.e. avant-garde authors and critics who 'make' the publishing-house by giving it credit (by publishing with it, taking manuscripts there and speaking well of authors published by it) and expect it to merit their confidence by refraining from discrediting itself with excessively brilliant worldly successes ('Minuit would be devalued in the eyes of the hundred people around Saint-Germain who really count if it won the *Prix Goncourt*') and thereby discrediting those who are published by it or praise its publications ('intellectuals think less of writers who win prizes'; 'the ideal career for a young writer is a slow one').[6] It also depends on the educational system, which alone can provide those who preach in the desert with devotees and followers capable of recognizing their virtues.

The total opposition between *best-sellers*, here today and gone tomorrow, and *classics*, best-sellers over the long run, which owe their consecration, and therefore their widespread durable market, to the educational system,[7] is the basis not only of two completely different ways of organizing production and marketing, but also of two contrasting images of the activity of the writer and even the publisher, a simple businessman or a bold 'talent-spotter' who will succeed only if he is able to sense the *specific laws* of a market yet to come, i.e. espouse the interests and demands of those who will make those laws, the writers he publishes.[8] There are also two opposing images of the criteria of success. For 'bourgeois' writers and their readers, success is intrinsically a guarantee of value. That is why, in this market, the successful get more successful. Publishers help to make best-sellers by printing further impressions; the best thing a critic can do for a book or play is to predict 'success' for it ('It's bound to be a runaway success' – R. Kanters, *L'Express*, 15–21 January 1973; 'I put my money on success for *Le Tournant* with my eyes closed' – Pierre Marcabru, *France-Soir*, 12 January 1973). Failure, of course, is an irrevocable condemnation; a writer without a public is a writer without talent (the same Robert Kanters refers to 'playwrights without talent and without an audience, such as Arrabal').

As for the opposing camp's vision, in which success is suspect[9] and asceticism in this world is the precondition for salvation in the next, its basis lies in the economy of cultural production itself, according to which, investments are recompensed only if they are in a sense thrown away, like a gift, which can only achieve the most precious return gift, gratitude (*reconaissance* – recognition), so long as it is experienced as a one-way transaction; and, as with the gift, which it converts into pure generosity by masking the expected return-gift which the synchronization of barter reveals, it is the *intervening time* which provides a screen and disguises the profit awaiting the most disinterested investors.

ORTHODOXY AND HERESY

The eschatological vision structuring the opposition between avant-garde and 'bourgeois' art, between the material ascesis which guarantees spiritual consecration, and worldly success, which is marked, *inter alia*, by institutional recognition (prizes, academies, etc.) and by financial rewards, helps to disguise the true relationship between the field of cultural production and the field of power, by reproducing the opposition (which does not rule out complementarity) between the dominated and dominant fractions of the dominant class, i.e. between cultural power (associated with less economic wealth) and economic and political power (associated with less cultural wealth), in the specific logic of the intellectual field, i.e. in the transfigured form of the conflict between two aesthetics. Specifically aesthetic conflicts about the legitimate vision of the world, i.e. in the last resort, about what deserves to be represented and the right way to represent it, are political conflicts (appearing in their most euphemized form) for the power to impose the dominant definition of reality, and social reality in particular. On the right, reproductive art[10] constructed in accordance with the generative schemes of 'straight', 'straight-forward' representation of reality, and social reality in particular, i.e. orthodoxy (e.g. par excellence, 'bourgeois theatre') is likely to give those who perceive it in accordance with these schemes the reassuring experience of the immediate self-evidence of the representation, i.e. of the necessity of the mode of representation and of the world represented. This orthodox art would be timeless if it were not continuously pushed into the past by the movement brought into the field of production by the dominated fractions' insistence on using the powers they are granted to change the world-view and overturn the temporal and *temporary* hierarchies to which 'bourgeois' taste clings. As holders of an (always partial) delegated legitimacy in cultural matters, cultural producers – especially those who produce solely for other producers – always tend to divert their authority to their own advantage and therefore to impose their own variant of the dominant world-view as the only legitimate one. But the challenging of the established artistic hierarchies and the heretical displacement of the socially accepted limit between what does and does not deserve to be preserved, admired and transmitted cannot achieve its specifically artistic effect of subversion unless it tacitly recognizes the fact and the legitimacy of such delimitation by making the shifting of that limit an artistic act and thereby claiming for the artist a monopoly in legitimate transgression of the boundary between the sacred and the profane, and therefore a monopoly in revolutions in artistic taxonomies.

The field of cultural production is the area par excellence of clashes between the dominant fractions of the dominant class, who sometimes fight there in person but more often through producers oriented towards defending their 'ideas' and satisfying their 'tastes', and the dominated fractions who are totally involved in this struggle.[11] This conflict brings about the integration in a single field of the various socially specialized sub-fields, particular markets which are completely separate in social and even geographical space, in which the different fractions of the dominant class can find products adjusted to their tastes, whether in the theatre, in painting, fashion or decoration.

The 'polemical' view which makes a sweeping condemnation of all economically powerful firms ignores the distinction between those which are only rich in economic capital, and treat cultural goods – books, plays or pictures – as ordinary products, i.e. as sources of immediate profit, and those which derive a sometimes very substantial economic profit from the cultural capital which they originally accumulated through strategies based on denial of the 'economy'. The differences in the scale of the businesses, measured by turnover or staff, are matched by equally decisive differences in their relation to the 'economy' which, among recently established smaller firms, separate the small 'commercial' publishers, often heading for rapid growth, such as Lattès, Laffont (as distinct from Robert Laffont), Orban, Authier or Mengès[12] and the small avant-garde publishers, which are often short-lived (Galilée, France Adèle, Entente, Phébus), just as, at the other extreme, they separate the 'great publisher' from the 'big publisher', a great consecrated publisher like Gallimard from a big 'book merchant' like Nielsen.

Without entering into a systematic analysis of the field of the galleries, which, owing to the homology with the field of publishing, would lead to repetitions, we may simply observe that, here too, the differences which separate the galleries according to their seniority (and their celebrity), and therefore according to the degree of consecration and the market value of the works they own, are replicated by differences in their relation to the 'economy'. The 'sales galleries', having no 'stable' of their own (e.g. Beaubourg) exhibit, in relatively eclectic fashion, painters of very different periods, schools and ages, (abstracts as well as post-surrealists, a few European hyper-realists, some new realists), i.e. whose greater 'accessibility' (owing to their more classic status or their 'decorative' potential) can find purchasers outside the circle of professional and semi-professional collectors (among the 'jet-set executives' and 'trendy industrialists' as an informant put it). This enables them to pick out and attract a fraction of the avant-garde painters who have already been 'noticed' by offering them a slightly compromising form of consecration, i.e. a market in which the prices are much higher than in the avant-garde galleries.[13] By contrast, galleries like Sonnabend, Denise René or Durand-Ruel, which mark dates in the history of painting because they have been able in their time to assemble a 'school', are characterized by a *systematic slant*.[14] Thus in the succession of painters presented by the Sonnabend gallery one can see the logic of an artistic development which leads from the 'new American painting' and Pop Art, with painters such as Rauschenberg, Jaspers Johns, Jim Dine, to Oldenburg, Lichtenstein, Wesselman, Rosenquist, Warhol, sometimes classified under the label Minimal Art, and to the most recent innovations of *art pauvre*, conceptual art and art by correspondence. Likewise, there is a clear connection between the geometric abstraction which made the name of the Denise René gallery (founded in 1945 and inaugurated with a Vasarely exhibition) and kinetic art, with artists such as Max Bill and Vasareley forming a sort of link between the visual experiments of the inter-war years (especially the Bauhaus) and the optical and technological experiments of the new generation.

WAYS OF GROWING OLD

The opposition between the two economies, i.e. between two relationships to the 'economy', can thus be seen as an opposition between two life-cycles of the cultural-production business, two different ways in which firms, producers and products *grow old*.[15] The trajectory leading from the avant-garde to consecration and the trajectory leading from the small firm to the 'big' firm are mutually exclusive. The small commercial firm has no more chance of becoming a great consecrated firm than the big 'commercial' writer (e.g. Guy des Cars or Cécil Saint-Laurent) has of occupying a recognized position in the consecrated avant-garde. In the case of 'commercial' firms, whose sole target is the accumulation of 'economic' capital and which can only get bigger or disappear (through bankruptcy or take-over), the only pertinent distinction concerns the size of the firm, which tends to grow with time; in the case of firms characterized by a high degree of disavowal of the 'economy' and submission to the specific logic of the cultural goods economy, the chronological opposition between the newcomers and the old-established, the challengers and the veterans, the avant-garde and the 'classic' tends to merge with the 'economic' opposition between the poor and the rich (who are *also* the big), the 'cheap' and the 'dear', and ageing is almost inevitably accompanied by an 'economic' transformation of the relation to the 'economy', i.e. a moderating of the denial of the 'economy' which is in dialectical relation with the scale of business and the size of the firm. The only defence against 'getting old' is a refusal to 'get fat' through profits and for profit, a refusal to enter the dialectic of profit which, by increasing the size of the firm and consequently the overheads, imposes a pursuit of profit through larger markets, leading to the devaluation entailed in a 'mass appeal.[16]

A firm which enters the phase of exploiting accumulated cultural capital runs two different economies simultaneously, one oriented towards production, authors and innovation (in the case of Gallimard, this is the series edited by Georges Lambrichs) the other towards exploiting its resources and marketing its consecrated products (with series such as the Pléiade editions and especially Folio or Idées). It is easy to imagine the contradictions which result from the incompatibility of the two economies. The organization appropriate for producing, marketing and promoting one category of products is totally unsuited for the other. Moreover, the weight of the constraints which management and marketing bring to bear on the institution and on ways of thinking tends to rule out high-risk investments, when, that is, the authors who might give rise to them are not already turned towards other publishers by the firm's prestige. (They may equally be discouraged by the fact that the 'intellectual' series tend to pass unnotice when they appear in lists in which they are 'out of place' or even 'incongruous' e.g. as an extreme case, Laffont's '*Ecarts*' and '*Change*' series.) It goes without saying that though the disappearance of the firm's founder may accelerate the process, it is not sufficient to explain a process which is inscribed in the logic of the development of cultural businesses.

The differences which separate the small avant-garde firms from the 'big firms' and 'great publishers' have their equivalents in the differences that can be found, among the products, between the 'new' product, temporarily without 'economic' value, the 'old' product, irretrievably devalued, and the 'ancient' or 'classic' product, which has a constant or constantly growing 'economic' value. One also finds similar differences among the producers, between the avant-garde, recruited mainly among the (biologically) young, without being limited to a generation, 'finished' or 'outdated' authors or artists (who may be biologically young), and the consecrated avant-garde, the 'classics'. [. . .]

NOTES

Source: *Media, Culture and Society,* 2(3) (SAGE Publications, 1980), 281–88 (extract).

1. Among the guaranteed short-term investments, we must also include all the publishing strategies designed to *exploit a backlist:* new editions, naturally, but also paperback editions (for Gallimard, this is the *Folio* series).

2. Although one must never ignore the 'moiré' effect produced in every field by the fact that the different possible structurations (here, for example, according to age, size, degree of political and/or aesthetic avant-gardism) never coincide perfectly, the fact remains that the relative weight of long-term and short-term firms can probably be regarded as the dominant structuring principle of the field. In this respect, we find an opposition between the small avant-garde firms, Pauvert, Maspero and Minuit (to which one could add Bourgois, if it did not occupy a culturally and economically ambiguous position, because of its link with Les Presses de la Cité), and the 'big' publishers, Laffont, Presses de la Cité and Hachette, the intermediate positions being occupied by firms like Flammarion (where experimental series coexist with specially commissioned collective works) Albin Michel and Calmann-Lévy, old, 'traditional' publishing houses, run by 'heirs' whose heritage is both a strength and a brake, and above all Grasset, once a 'great' publishing house, now absorbed by the Hachette empire, and Gallimard, a former avant-garde firm that has now attained the peak of consecration and combines back-list exploitation with long-term undertakings (which are only possible on the basis of accumulated cultural capital – le Chemin, Bibliothèque des sciences humaines). The sub-field of firms mainly oriented towards long-term production and towards an 'intellectual' readership is polarized around the opposition between Maspero and Minuit (which represents the avant-garde moving towards consecration) on one side, and Gallimard, situated in the dominant position, with Le Seuil representing the neutral point in the field, (just as Gallimard whose authors feature both in the best-seller list and in the list of intellectual best-sellers, constitutes the neutral

point of the whole field). The practical mastery of this structure, which also guides, for example, the founders of a newspaper when they 'feel there is an opening' or 'aim to fill a gap' left by the existing media, is seen at work in the rigorously topographical vision of a young publisher, Delorme, founder of Galilée, who was trying to fit in 'between Minuit, Maspero and Seuil' (quoted by J. Jossin, *L'Express*, 30 August 1976).

3. It is well-known in the 'trade' that the head of one of the largest French publishing houses reads hardly any of the manuscripts he publishes and that his working day is devoted to purely managerial tasks (production committee meetings, meetings with lawyers, heads of subsidiaries, etc.).

4. In fact most of his professional actions are 'intellectual acts', analogous to the signature of literary or political manifestos or petitions (with some risks, as well – consider the publication of *La Question*) which earn him the usual gratifications of 'intellectuals' (intellectual prestige, interviews, radio discussions, etc.).

5. Robert Laffont recognizes this dependence when, in order to explain the declining ratio of translations to original works, he invokes, in addition to the increased advances payable for translation rights, 'the decisive influence of the media, especially television and radio, in promoting a book': 'The author's personality and eloquence are an important factor in these media's choices and consequently in access to the public. In this respect, foreign authors, with the exception of a few international celebrities, are naturally at a disadvantage' (*Vient de paraître* – Robert Laffonts' monthly publicity bulletin – January 1977).

6. Here too, cultural logic and 'economic' logic converge. As the fate of Les Éditions du Pavois shows, a literary prize can be disastrous, from a strictly 'economic' point of view, for a young publishing house suddenly faced with the enormous investments required to reprint and distribute a prize-winning book.

7. This is seen particularly clearly in the theatre, where the classics market (the 'classical matinées' at the Comédie Française) obeys quite specific rules because of its dependence on the educational system.

8. The same opposition is found in all fields. André de Baecque describes the opposition he sees as characterizing the theatrical field, between the 'businessmen' and the 'militants': 'Theatre managers are people of all sorts. They have one thing in common; with each new show, they put an investment of money and talent at risk on an unpredictable market. But the similarity stops there. Their motivations spring from very different ideologies. For some, the theatre is a financial speculation like any other, more picturesque perhaps, but giving rise to the same cold-blooded strategy made up of the taking of options, calculated risks, liquidity problems, exclusive rights, sometimes negotiated internationally. For others, it is the vehicle of a message, or the tool of a mission. Sometimes a militant even does good business . . .' (de Baecque, 1968).

9. Without going so far as to make failure a guarantee of quality, as the 'bourgeois' writer's polemical vision would have it: 'Nowadays, if you want to succeed, you need failures. Failure inspires confidence. Success is suspect' (Dorin, 1973, p. 46).

10. Oh dear! All I do is reproduce what I see and hear, just arranging it and adapting it. Just my luck! What I see is always attractive, what I hear is often funny. I live in luxury and champagne bubbles' (Dorin, 1973, p. 27). There is no need to evoke reproductive painting, nowadays incarnated by the 'impressionists' who are known to supply the publishers specialising in reproductions of works of art with all their best-sellers (apart from the

Mona Lisa): Renoir (*Girl with Flowers, Le Moulin de la Galette*), Van Gogh (*L'eglise d'Auvers*), Monet (*Les coquelicots*), Degas (*Ballet Rehearsal*) Gauguin (*Peasant Women*) (information supplied by the Louvre, 1973). In the literary field, there is the vast output of biographies, memoirs, diaries and testimonies, which, from Laffont to Lattès, from Nielsen to Orban, provide 'bourgeois' readers with alternative 'real-life' experiences.

11. In literature, as elsewhere, full-time producers (and, *a fortiori*, producers for producers) are far from having a monopoly of production. Out of 100 people in *Who's Who* who have produced literary works, more than a third are non-professionals (industrialists, 14%; senior civil servants, 11%; doctors, 7% etc.) and the proportion of part-time producers is even greater in the areas of political writing (45%) and general writing (48%).

12. Among the latter, one could also distinguish between those who have come into publishing with explicitly commercial aims, such as Jean-Claude Lattés, who started as a press attaché with Laffont and originally saw his project as a Laffont series (Edition spéciale), or Olivier Orban (both of whom went straight for commissioned stories), and those who have fallen back on 'pot-boilers' after various abortive projects such as Guy Authier or Jean-Paul Mengès.

13. By the same logic, the discoverer-publisher is always liable to see his 'discoveries' seduced by richer or more consecrated publishers, who offer their name, their reputation, their influence on prize juries, and also publicity and better royalties.

14. As opposed to the Sonnabend gallery, which brings together young (the oldest is 50) but already relatively recognized painters, and to the Durand-Ruel gallery, whose painters are almost all dead and famous, the Denise René gallery, which stands in that particular point in the space-time of the artistic field in which the normally incompatible profits of the avant-garde and of consecration are momentarily superimposed, combines a group of already strongly consecrated painters (abstract) with an avant-garde or rear avant-garde group (kinetic art) as if it had momentarily managed to escape the dialectic of distinction which sweeps schools away into the past.

15. The analytical opposition between the two economies implies no value judgment, although in the ordinary struggles of artistic life it is only ever expressed in the form of value judgments and although despite all the efforts to distance and objectify, it is liable to be read in polemical terms. As I have shown elsewhere, the categories of perception and appreciation (e.g. obscure/clear or easy, deep/light, original/banal, etc.) which function in the world of art are oppositions that are almost universally applicable and are based, in the last analysis, through the opposition between rarity and divulgation or vulgarization, uniqueness and multiplicity, quality and quantity, on the social opposition between the 'elite' and the 'masses', between 'elite' (or 'quality') products and 'mass' products.

16. This effect is perfectly visible in haute couture or perfumery, where the consecrated establishments are able to keep going for several generations (e.g. Caron, Chanel and especially Guerlain) only by means of a policy aimed at artificially perpetuating the rarity of the product (e.g. the 'Exclusive concessions' which limit sales outlets to a few places which are themselves chosen for their rarity – the great couturiers' own shops, perfume shops in the smartest districts, airports). Since ageing is here synonymous with vulgarization, the oldest brands (Coty, Lancôme, Worth, Molyneux, Bourjois, etc.) have a second career, down-market.

CHAPTER FIFTEEN

Fashion Shapes: Film, the Fashion Industry, and the Image of Women

MAUREEN TURIM

Except for the opening scene of the officer's ball, the only women who appear in John Ford's *They Were Expendable* are a group of army nurses. In a film that otherwise concentrates on PT boat action in the Pacific battles of World War II, the presence of nurses provides a rationale for a romantic subplot between John Wayne and Donna Reed. Wayne repeatedly rejects the possibility of sexual interest in the nurses, using such phrases as, "Call them women? Who can look at anything in those potato sacks?" Somehow even a woman in uniform captures enough interest to receive an invitation to dinner at the hut-headquarters of the platoon. As Reed enters the hut to dine with the group of men, she pauses in front of a conveniently placed mirror, then (illegally) modifies her uniform by placing a lace handkerchief in her pocket, putting on a string of pearls and removing her cap and brushing her hair. She turns to face an appreciative Wayne, who proclaims, "Well, now you look like a woman."

It is through such scenes that Hollywood teaches us about being women and particularly the visual cues that indicate not only the distinctive traits of femininity, but many other specific connotations which we forcibly choose as we dress.

Watching innumerable film scenes wherein women's appearance not only indicates their character and class, but determines their actions, I have come to appreciate the shaping quality of fashion. Fashion molds human beings into visual designs which communicate consciously and unconsciously specific attitudes, values, and desires. Thus the punning title of this article, "Fashion Shapes," reminiscent of the puns used in fashion reporting and advertising.[1] But the shaping of the body through fashion is more than a pun, more than a metaphor. It is an ideological practice facilitated by various cultural mechanisms. My aim here is to begin to explore that practice and analyze those mechanisms.

THE FASHION INDUSTRY AND FILMS

In the United States the fashion industry's power to shape the image and self-images of women has been closely tied to the growth of the film industry and its use of fashion. Hollywood films, coupled with the wide distribution of women's magazines (including fan magazines devoted to stars and the screen world), have colluded with the garment and advertising industries to mold who we are and can become. Certainly this collusion cannot be described as a conscious plot to maintain patriarchy, capitalism, and imperialism and to oppress women. The dialectics of fashion are too complex and spontaneous. Changes in fashion through the twentieth century have brought enormous changes in the physical treatment and conceptualization of women's bodies. These transformations in the way women appeared were both influenced by and contributed to changing notions of womanhood. I want to keep in mind that if feminism emerges strongly in the America of the sixties and seventies, it is perhaps a by-product of some of the same cultural mechanisms that we could too quickly read as merely oppressive if we subscribed to the "fashion-as-capitalist-plot" explanation. Yet there is an overall conservatism to fashion. Although fashion gives expression to new impulses towards change and liberation, it also tends to reabsorb and assimilate such expressions to the alienated social conditions in which women live. The quest for profit in the fashion industry can exploit both the impulse for liberation and its reassimilation.

The growth of an indigenous American fashion industry coincides with the growth of the film industry. There were American costuming traditions prior to the twentieth century, most distinctively the craft and artisanal products of native Americans and pioneers. But fashion owes the greatest debt to European design, and specifically the highly developed industry of Paris, which until the late 1920s virtually dictated high fashion of the Western world. Looking back at the development of French fashion will help to show us what significant differences a mid-twentieth-century American fashion establishes, as Hollywood glamour replaces Parisian class and style.

Parisian *haute couture* was born in the midst of the Second Empire when Worth opened the first design house. Worth made the kind of elaborate gowns that previously could be made only by dressmakers.[2] In the Belle Epoque high fashion quickly became stratified as industry expanded the manufacture of the fashion house. The most expensive and richly decorated crinoline gowns of the period, fitted to a severely corseted bodice, could only be bought by the rich. Yet frills and flounces also marked the Sunday dress of the working class. Leisure time and class ascendancy became marked for women by the ability to adorn themselves as shining, floating billows sheltered by parasols.[3] In the United States this fashion was often ordered directly from Paris, but it was also copied by the American manufacturers emerging at the turn of the century. While these dresses had looser bodices and were both less frilly and more tailored than the French originals, they still retained connotations of grace and dignity. Known as the "Gibson Girl" style, these dresses and the innovative skirt and blouse ensembles were retailed in department stores and even mail order houses to middle-class and working women. Despite their more comfortable look, they continued to depend on the S-shaped corset. Thus, constriction remained the prerequisite for an image of dignity and respect.

The break with nineteenth-century modes and the emergence of a "modern" look occurred first in Paris, largely as a reaction to the constricting corset. The new styles rejected the unhealthy effects of corsets – deformed posture, bone structure, and organ alignment; and in so doing, they also moved away from the image of female frailty and passivity that corsets created. The designer credited with the transformation is Paul Poiret, whose dresses minimized formerly emphasized curves and eliminated molding undergarments. Not surprisingly, the new look coincided with the growth of the suffragist movement in the late teens. In fashion as in life, liberation was only partial; Poiret's "hobble skirts" had tight hemlines around the ankles, which constricted mobility.[4] Still, once established, the straighter lines remained dominant throughout the next twenty years. They are seen in Jenny's "little knee-length chemise" and Patou's flapper dress, dresses thought to emphasize mobility. Even though these styles were sometimes worn merely over slips, they often called for "brassiere and corset combined to flatten the bust and hips," necessitating their own form of forced shaping.[5]

American films of the teens and twenties did much to introduce the new *haute couture* lines to the mass American audience. They also interpreted these fashions by placing them in social and narrative contexts. Poiret's straight dresses were used as costumes for Sarah Bernhardt's *Camille*, made by Famous Players in 1912. Bernhardt's reputation in the "legitimate" theatre gave stature and legitimacy to this "art" film, while the play's own risqué narrative could be justified by the tradition of French theater and opera. Already a mixed artifact, a film like *Camille* adapted high culture for a mass audience.

With the emergence of the "flapper," popular culture and Hollywood film begin to absorb *haute couture*, but drastically transform it in the process. In Hollywood films of the early twenties, dress design helps represent new social behavior. Stars such as Gloria Swanson, Coleen Moore, Constance Talmadge, and Clara Bow act out various manifestations of the energetic and youthful new American woman. The new heroines could be salesclerks or coeds, but their main preoccupation is presented as a search for romance. They engage in this search in a certain style; modern romance and modern fashion become inseparable. As a result class is less fixed. The fantasy these narratives provide is that of class mobility facilitated by acquiring a look.

Fashion learned to profit from the fantasies and desires of all classes of women: while popular culture introduced working women to the ideals of high fashion, the fashion industry began marketing the same basic designs in various price ranges.

The careers of many designers can, however, illustrate this intermediary, trans-formational role of Hollywood designs for the fashion industry. The career of Adrian illustrates Hollywood's role in the growth of the American fashion industry and also the rise of American designers. After studying design at Parsons in New York and then Paris, Adrian became a costume designer on Broadway and then went to Hollywood to create the wardrobe for a Valentino film. His work at MGM began with the extravagant designs for Greta Garbo in *Woman of Affairs*. As Robert Riley, Adrian's biographer, noted, these designs closed the circle, bringing Adrian "back to New York's garment industry":

> Seventh Avenue designers and sketchers rushed to the Capitol Theatre to see Garbo's crepe coat and dress inlaid with Ombre bands; her slinky satin dinner gown with casual scarf tossed across her shoulders. But the costume that bugged their eyes was Garbo's slouch hat and loosely belted trench coat, entirely lined in bold plaid wool. These marvels of casual elegance were emblazoned in *Women's Wear Daily*, and plaid linings and trench coats appear in hundreds of showrooms.[6]

Although manufacturers offered to market his designs commercially, Adrian remained exclusively a Hollywood costume designer until 1940. At MGM he created not only Garbo's elegance and much period fantasy, but also the sophisticated suitings of Norma Shearer and Joan Crawford and the boudoir extravagance of Jean Harlow. Others translated these leads into American ready-to-wear. During the Second World War, however, Adrian opened Adrian Ltd. and became an exclusive supplier to the most expensive retailers coast to coast. It was Adrian who established the severe, padded-shoulder, slim-skirted suits with geometric detailing that have come to signify the forties.

Fashion newsreels were another form of combined consumer assault by the film and fashion industries. They began in the late teens as short documentaries of fashion shows, filmic versions of a fashion magazine. Some attempted to introduce narrative into the fashion display.[7] Later, as newsreels came to consist of a series of news reports, a section of fashion would be sandwiched betweeen news of the depression, the Spanish Civil War, or the negotiations with Hitler.[8]

Modern Merchandising Inc. offers an even more blatant example of Hollywood-fashion industry collusion. This firm, founded by Bernard Waldman in 1930, pro-duced ready-to-wear clothes labeled "Cinema Fashions," "Screen Star Styles," and "Cinema Modes."[9] The labels also named the movie stars who wore the originals and the films they appeared in. Even studios were named. Such arrangements reached a peak in the thirties and continued on that level throughout the forties and fifties. Thus, the working- or middle-class woman could purchase a fantasy of glamor in the form of a commodity.

Fashion could also become the subject matter of Hollywood narratives. *Fashions of '34*, directed by William Dieterle, contains fashion shows choreographed by Busby Berkeley. The film narrates the intrigues of an unscrupulous firm, Baroque Designs, whose owner steals high-fashion designs for bargain-basement copies. William Powell plays the sly entrepreneur who enlists the help of Bette Davis as a spy. As in other depression comedies, such illegal activity appears justified: these urbane crooks merely beat a dishonest system that the film ridicules. The witty hero and heroine out-hoax it by popularizing ostrich feathers after making a deal with an ostrich farmer. And like Hollywood itself, they also raid the past for fashion ideas. One of the Berkeley numbers features fashions based on images of Richelieu, Louis XIV, and Napoleon. What the film omits from its narrative is precisely Hollywood's role in this "borrowing" from French high culture. Hollywood could thus thematize the marketing strategies of the fashion industry without directly implicating itself in the pirating, scheming, and ideological image manufacture the films would depict.

Movies saluted a growing garment industry even more openly. Fashion shows and shopping sprees became standard episodes in films. There are memorable examples in *The Women* (1939), *Gentlemen Prefer Blondes* (1953), and *That Touch of Mink* (1962), where Doris Day acquires a complete new wardrobe at Bonwit Teller. While earlier films discreetly showcased a designer's work (as in Adrian's designs for *The Women*), the later films openly named and plugged specific designers and retailers. Remember Monroe's orgasmic squeal, "Tiffany's!," in the "Diamonds Are a Girl's Best Friend" production number?

FASHION NARRATIVES

Most fictional films are far less direct in the way they serve the fashion industry. Their more subtle use of fashion depends upon a process in which the viewer identifies with the fashion image. Identification can mean simply an affinity with a character or a given narrative situation. This affinity can foster a desire in the viewer to emulate the appearance of that character. This is not limited to positive role models. A woman can identify with Joan Crawford in *Possessed* (1947), because like Crawford's character she has felt the anguish of being jilted by a lover who saw her as a social and sexual inferior. This identification is situational. The correspondence between the narrative and the viewer's own life experience produces a feeling of empathy.

Other kinds of identification have to do with "imaginary" relationships between the subject and what is seen and heard. Viewers may accept as their own the point of view or "look" of the camera, and its "ear," the audial space created by establishing a center in sound recording. The viewer thus enters an apparent reality, a reality edited to appear seamless and whole. From this central vantage point the viewer may even enjoy an illusory feeling of omnipotence, illusory because it masks the absence of any real power to resist or modify this placement except by critical thought. The degree to which spectators accept the camera's eye and ear as their own, the degree to which they experience the film as pleasurable, frightening, funny, or exciting, is largely the degree to which they get caught up in its diverse pulls and forces on an unconscious level.

Viewers are therefore vulnerable psychologically. The happy ending which seals off danger gains its force as a release from this masterfully created vulnerability. Identification permits the situation in which the viewer is unconsciously open to such manipulation. When the viewer is a woman, this vulnerability may be compounded since, as Laura Mulvey has pointed out, the "look" of the camera is often male-identified: women are the objects to be looked at. Women are thus led to identify with a view that looks back on themselves in distorted and alienating ways.

But the happy ending is not the only way to "save" the viewer from psychological jeopardy. I suggest that another way, for women especially, is to identify not so much with the female character but with female bodies. In the context of the films these bodies are often images of power: they have the power to entice desire. Rendered vulnerable by the narrative, we are more than ever sensitive to images of bodies like our own: the sister-self. Precisely because cinema's heroines are so weak, alienated, and self-defeating, we seek in their very bodies any signs of strength. For women, then, the process of identification in film includes a seeking of power as a sense of self. The image of the other women becomes a way of imagining ourselves conquering the fears and anxieties the narrative fiction has just evoked in us.

Thus, films not only expose new fashions to a mass audience, they not only provide the fashion industry with a glittering showcase; because we see those fashions within a narrative context, films also invest fashions with unconscious attachments, connotations. This process, the narration of fashion, means more than the association of a style with a given story or fiction. It is a process that fuses the unconscious effects of film experience with the very lines and colors of clothing designs. Above all it creates in American women a deeply felt need to care about what they wear on their bodies in all social situations.

The collusion between Hollywood and Seventh Avenue thus goes deeper than I indicated above. Hollywood has helped create the very audience through which the fashion industry can operate, since it encourages women to displace their desires for self-hood onto the visual, onto images created through the use of commodities. Advertising, then, develops as the bridge between culture and industrial capitalism. Its relationship to culture is parasitical. Its references to art, literature, dance, and music mask and legitimate its commerical functions and direct the generalized desire for specific images onto specific brands of commodities. Film is the perfect host corpus from which the parasite of advertising can nourish itself. Advertising has merely to appeal to the consumer by evoking the narration of fashion pre-established by film culture.

Given that Hollywood films serve the fashion industry, what are the specific images they create for women? And what are the meanings and ideological consequences of these images? One important factor to keep in mind is that at any one moment various fashion tendencies coexist, providing a spectrum of moods and a panoply of fantasy types. Hollywood films can establish this range of difference within its narratives as oppositions, or as character differences within women as a group.

An amusing key to the standard Hollywood panoply is provided by an intriguing publication, dating from 1945, entitled *Bonomo "Original" Hollywood "Success Course": Health, Charm, and Personality Improvement*. Promising to reveal "the fascinating secret of triumphant womanhood," this self-help manual advises women to "dress a type, . . . particularly the woman who is not truly beautiful." Each type is exemplified by a famous star whose portrait becomes its emblem. There are six major types:

The Exotic Woman – Ilona Massey
The Outdoor Woman – Katharine Hepburn
The Sophisticate – Merle Oberon
The Womanly Woman – Greer Garson
The Aristocrat – Joan Fontaine
The Gamine – Betty Hutton

First the personality traits of each type are described, and then the way those traits find expression in fashion styles. The reader is urged to "note how consistently the stars follow the principles which we give you in costuming their roles."[10] Thus, the "womanly woman," who is "100 percent feminine," takes the "second role on the stage of life and stars in it." She is "gentle, affectionate, and tender," has a low voice "with lilting cadences," and laughs "readily and charmingly." Accordingly, she dresses in "wools with a soft bloom upon them (never harsh worsted), silks and rayons, . . . laces, flowered chiffons." "Slacks she does not even so much as consider," since she does "not go in seriously for sports." Conveniently, the guide shows us how to be the aristocratic type "on a very limited budget." The Outdoor Woman "will have a well-cut professionally made riding habit even if she has to concoct every other garment in her wardrobe with her own bare hands." No mention is made of a type called the "working woman." The practical suit or dress for the office, the slacks that might have been worn to the factory are subsumed in Hollywood fantasies and become "feminized" as aristocratic or outdoors costumes.

The whole panoply occasionally appears in a single film. In *Stage Door* (1937), the aspiring young actresses who share life in a New York boarding house display a range of fashions that indicate their diverse personalities and backgrounds. More often the types appear in oppositions, as in the typical contrast between the good and the loose woman, the loose woman being either a dowdy version of the exotic or a degraded version of the sophisticated, while the good woman is womanly, a gamine, or a straightforward and toned-down version of the aristocrat. In *Footlight Parade* (1933), the opposition is drawn between an honest, natural, down-to-earth Joan Blondell who wears a middy-pants sailor outfit and a pseudo-sophisticated gold-digger in aristocratic disguise. The stylistic opposition articulates a sexual competition for their boss, James Cagney. *Footlight Parade* also contains a typological transformation. The unfashionable, serious office girl, played by Ruby Keeler, becomes a star, glamor lead. As a backstage musical that deals specifically with behind-the-scenes office work, *Footlight Parade* aptly illustrates a favorite Hollywood fantasy: that fashion can turn everyday life into exciting drama. Even off-stage life is presented as costumed performance. At any moment a secretary may suddenly be discovered – if she is properly dressed – and whisked into the limelight to steal the show. Thus, the dull reality of routine factory or office work is effaced. Fashion's unspoken promise is to let each of us be a star.

In recent years the fashion industry has self-consciously revived this promise. Macy's in New York opened a special boutique specializing in fashions inspired by Hollywood, pastiches of Marilyn Monroe's fifties hourglass dresses hung side-by-side with imitation Garbo and Crawford. The only authenticity in this revival is the manner in which it recapitulates Hollywood's own formula for period costumes: although film costumes retain some historically authentic features, their overall lines have a look and an appeal that always coincides with the moment of the film's production. This is true even when the costumes leap into the realm of fantasy, as in Adrian's extravagant reworking of the eighteenth century for MGM's Marie Antoinette. For over ten years fashion has played with various "retro" trends which seem to be inspired by the success of *Bonnie and Clyde*, in which Faye Dunaway's dresses revamp thirties fashion for a contemporary market. These modifications similarly efface the distinct historical characteristics of all past fashion periods.

What then can we say of the significant fashion transformations which have occurred in the twentieth century as represented in Hollywood film? I will discuss three tendencies that pose particularly interesting problems: first, what I will call the "slit aesthetic," the play with exposure of flesh in a multitude of places and directions; then transvestite designs; and, finally, sportswear.

The development of the "slit aesthetic" was preceded by décolleté, the baring of the neck, shoulders, back, and breasts, common since the late seventeenth century. The elaborate drapings and embellishments of these gowns contrasted with and highlighted the areas of the wearer's flesh that were left nude. Thus, a fetishistic concentration of focus on the bared flesh, often increased by jewelry, became the culminating element of female dress.

Fetishistic design re-emerges in American fashion with the gradual withering away of a moral imperative to cover all surfaces of the skin, even at the seashore. Exposed skin signaled the "flesh trade" – burlesque or prostitution. As this attitude changed, the skin surface increasingly became an element of design, first in evening gowns, then in bathing suits, and finally even in street clothes. These designs used slits, cut-outs, and directional lines and clung tightly to the body. They came to dominate Hollywood costume design, signaling glamor and sexuality.

Made of shiny materials such as satin or silk, they reflect light and even become luminous light sources with the projected film image, attracting the gaze of the spectator and focusing desire. As it appears in film, the slit aesthetic does more than tell us that "this woman is attractive, sexual." The film makes us live that attraction.

The film's glance/object editing – the cutting back and forth between the gazing male and the female body he looks at – prompts viewers to participate in a fetishistic system that kindles desire for the object. The lines of the designs lead to breast and genitals and emphasize curved outlines. Sophisticated gowns may introduce asymmetry, bare a shoulder or deflect the gaze into abstract geometrics, but most often the gaze is actually directed into the center of the body, into the triangular regions of female sexuality.

In the context of specific films the "slit aesthetic" takes on varied moral connotations. Heroines wearing these exposed styles may be judged according to different notions about the propriety of such a self-conscious sexual gesture. Early films established a pattern. These tended to divide women into good – they did not follow fashion or use make-up – and bad – they did. D. W. Griffith's *The Painted Lady* (1908), is one of the early narratives that developed the opposition, but by *True-Heart Susie* (1915), the heroine decides to modernize her appearance in order to compete with the flapper who is about to steal her boyfriend. By the time of Griffith's *The White Rose* (1923), the heroine is fully transformed into the "painted" lady of modern fashion, and yet she retains audience sympathy through a naïve "fall" and a pregnancy that makes her an outcast. The "good" woman can follow fashion, but she will suffer from being taken as a "bad" woman. As late as 1928 in Murnau's *Sunrise*, the absolute opposition between good and bad women is enforced by an equally exaggerated costume opposition. The dichotomy remains in later films, but the notions of decorum and good taste are more subtle. At all times the fallen woman and the whore lurk as possible connotations within any fashion that accentuates the female body as sexual or exposes its skin.

In the thirties art deco softened and legitimated such blatantly sexual exposure with a patina of elegance. When the heroines of such films as *Swingtime* (1936) and *Design for Living* (1933) rise to fortune from their working-class backgrounds, they wear white satin gowns that reveal and accent bare skin. Wealth and elegance permit a display that otherwise indicates pornography. Yet such costume always signals a potential degradation of the wearer by a given observer. Any attempt to flaunt one's sexual body can invite disgust or even violent aggression.

Fetishistic fashion raises particularly difficult questions for black, Latino, and Asian women. Fashion and film have been and continue to be racist. The "exotic" woman given as a type played by white women is actually a mixture of styles borrowed from third-world cultures, taken to indicate mystery, eroticism, and a provocative threat of danger. Black women are even more narrowly typed than whites. They appear either as unfashionable servants and religious mammies or as foxy ladies of night life and the street. *Cabin in the Sky* (1943), a Minnelli musical with an all-black cast, contrasts the religious, plainly dressed Ethel Waters with Lena Horne's slinky, sexy temptress. Because racism views black sexuality as especially threatening, the black woman has an even greater likelihood of exposing herself to a pornographic and derogatory view once she wears revealing fashions.

Similarly, in *The Letter* (1940), where the "exotic woman" is an Asian (though actually played by a white actress, Gale Sondergaard), sexual mystery is taken as evidence of evil, even though the film's white heroine (Bette Davis) is the murderess – she kills her former lover, the Asian woman's husband. The film could have been a powerful exploration of colonial racism; instead Hollywood gilds the "Oriental" wife as an exotic bird and turns her into a blackmailer and revengeful murderess.

Clothes as signifiers of sexuality, as designs that manipulate desire, open up a question of power. The "slit aesthetic" presents a different notion of female strength and power than does the broad-shouldered business suit or well-put-together tailored ensemble. These latter styles command attention by extending the sculptural presence of the body or emphasizing the composure and self-possession of the wearer. In the "slit aesthetic" with its fetishistic treatment of the body, female power is exclusively sexual. In its shiny satin gown the body becomes a streamlined, gleaming object of desire. It also becomes an emblem of "modernity" and sexual freedom; in short, a fantasy that psychoanalysis terms the "phallic woman": the woman signifying sexual power. It is my position that the concepts of fetishism and of the phallic woman are both products of a phallocentric society which sees all desire in terms of the phallus specifically and the genitals in general. Any other focus is seen as displacement and aberrant. The terms are useful insofar as they describe historical conditions, but dangerous once granted universality. While they help us interpret the slit aesthetic, they also enforce a male point of view.

Nowhere is the "slit aesthetic" dramatized with more force than in the fifties film *Gentlemen Prefer Blondes*. Dorothy and Lorelei (Jane Russell and Marilyn Monroe) dress exclusively in the slit aesthetic. Their dresses are blatant roadsigns for a fetishistic gaze, all the more channeled by the loud color contrasts made possible by Technicolor. Their song and dance numbers borrow from burlesque, but the strip-tease is limited to tossing ermines out at the audience. Nudity is less the goal than accentuating the fetishistic clothes. The manipulative aspects of this fashion and the negative societal judgements it provokes are explored by the narrative; but in the end the burlesque queens are absolved of these connotations in the glory of a sanctifying double wedding – although their bridal gowns are as tightly cut as their other costumes. A film like this could thus legitimate this exaggerated sexual stylization for daily wear.

Transvestite costume in film is often tied to performance. A most intriguing example is Marlene Dietrich's appearance in a white satin tuxedo in *Blonde Venus* (1932), where in a Parisian night club she sings about sexuality in the most apathetic tones imaginable. Earlier in the film she appears as Helen Jones in skimpy burlesque costumes chanting about the hot voodoo in her blood; in her transvestite number she plays a man who can take or leave sex, having experienced all its pleasures. Her lines "Ça puisse m'épater," "Je trouve ça très bien," (that could excite me, I find it to my liking) are delivered with a sense of control and superiority which the male dress validates. She is saying that in no longer seeking to be womanly, she has left behind sexual vulnerability. Now she can use sex in a game of power. As a woman in the nightclub audience comments: "She came from South America and used man after man to get where she is." The next scene reinforces this image of an ambitious, sexually manipulative woman. Cary Grant, her former lover, comes to her dressing room in an attempt to reconstitute their affair. A slogan on her mirror reads, "He travels fastest who travels alone," as Helen, still dressed in her tux, places her arm around a female mannequin and says, "I'm not in love with anybody and I'm completely happy."

Within this narrative context transvestism means not only lesbian self-sufficiency from male attention, but also the power to attract women – Helen, after all has become an elegant man. But she does not actually cross the boundary between male and female; her transvestism rests on the hinge, held in balance by multiple forces. She is a mixture not so much of male and female characteristics, but rather of male and female homosexualities. Transvestism in this instance is a marked disguise, a costume that is the emblem of a more sophisticated, rarer approach to eroticism that seeks to pervert sexual typings and strict codes of difference. The film narrative quickly rushes to the destruction of this image, replacing its perversity with Helen's return to the home as an aproned wife and mother. Yet the unsanctioned fashion stands out for its powerful appeal and message of self-sufficiency and independence, even though dropped as inappropriate for an ongoing social fabric.

Connected to transvestism is androgyny, which gets a wider play in films. This sort of androgyny is almost always present in the characters portrayed by Katharine Hepburn. In *Sylvia Scarlett* (1935) she passes as a young boy so successfully that she fools her con-artist partner in panhandling, played by Cary Grant. He discovers her sex only by accident when he catches her in a dress worn in a private moment. Even in male clothing she does not actually cross the sexual boundary; her real appeal is that of a tomboy. In *Christopher Strong* (1933) male clothes go with her occupation of aviatrix. Dressed in trenchcoat and pants, she drives to the runway in a sportscar. Later, still in pants, she straddles furniture in her elegant sitting room, talking to her lover's daughter whose femininely coded fashion contrasts to her own. This film implies that women engaged in traditionally male occupations are creatures apart from other women. Hepburn may have a lover, but her male dress tells us that she is not womanly, unlike her lover's wife and daughter, and must therefore fend for herself. Her transvestism reaches into the realm of the exotic when she goes to a costume party in a shiny moth costume, a silver lamé jumpsuit complete with antennae. In its narrative context this moth signals a fundamental ambiguity. Like Dietrich's tuxedo, it characterizes the very possibility of women's independence as simultaneously attractive and repulsive. Independent women, as represented in these films, constitute the perfect rare love objects. Yet they represent impossible choices for others and therefore for themselves.

Is this attitude confined to the thirties or does it extend into current notions of female fashion? Surely androgyny and transvessm have been even more widely used in fashion in the last forty years. The forties broad-shouldered suit always flirted with a transvestite connotation, but since it was worn with a tight skirt, heels, and hat and molded itself to the body, the built-up shoulders rarely seemed to signify maleness. Rather, its sharpened and expanded physical presence suggests an abstract notion of power. Menswear fashion for women does recur with suits, ties, and pants, every detail "man-tailored." But in film such clothing seems tied to the ambiguous attitudes surrounding the transvestite image of the thirties, replaying, still, a troubled view of female independence.

The woman in pants and overalls does make a serious appearance in films made during World War II. *Tender Comrades* (1942) not only depicts its women defense-plant workers wearing work clothes as they operate fork-lifts and weld, but shows some of them wearing slacks at home. Since the film is orchestrated by the flashbacks of its heroine (Ginger Rogers) to her marriage before the war, there is a marked contrast between her feminine, frilly housedresses in the late thirties (albeit "incorrectly" shortened to forties knee-skimming lengths) and her practical pants of the forties. Once the war ends, pants again become rare, except in instances of sportswear, the next category of fashion that I will examine.

Sportswear first appeared as clothes designed specifically for participation in athletic activity. Prior to its development, women engaging in sports had to wear the same long skirts, corsets, and hats they wore on other occasions. The bloomers worn as a political gesture by feminists were never seriously accepted, even though they represented a practical alternative to skirts for bicycling and other sports. The riding habit, with its man-tailored jacket and breeches, was a breakthrough restricted to the elite who could afford this costumed activity. Films such as *Dark Victory*, *Suspicion*, and *Marnie* introduce their wealthy heroines in riding habits. The male-styled apparel in these films draws on the connotations of transvestism discussed earlier, that is, sexual ambiguity and a troubled view of female independence.

Hollywood stars did more to popularize sportswear off screen than on. It was rare to see characters in sports clothes until the fifties. However, publicity shots and fan magazine illustrations often show stars wearing resort wear, shorts, and pants. One of the stars photographed regularly in pants, Katharine Hepburn, finally got to make a film, *Pat and Mike* (1952), in which she wears pants throughout as a gym teacher turned professional golfer. The novelty of this dress for an adult woman in a film of this period is marked in an opening scene in which she changes from her schoolteacher's skirt to pants in her boyfriend's covertible. *Hard, Fast, and Beautiful* (1951), Ida Lupino's film about a mother's driving ambition for her daughter's tennis career, not only features tennis outfits throughout, but makes an issue of a star's endorsements of sportswear as illegal graft in amateur athletics. But when we keep in mind that both of these films date from the early fifties, it is clear how late the notion of the athletic woman dressed in appropriately designed clothing was accepted even in America.

The blue jean lost its coding as male attire by working its way through the teenage population. In the fifties it still had strongly male connotations when worn by an adult woman, as is evident in one of the few westerns in which a woman appears in jeans, *Johnny Guitar* (1954). Joan Crawford's jeans and holster mark Vienna as a woman outside, independent, to be desired and feared. They function in the same ways as the formal transvestite suits.

Why was sportswear integrated into film narratives so belatedly? Why does the image of the athletic woman only begin to appear in the fifties? Was Hollywood behind the fashion trends in this instance? Not if we remember that sportswear left the resort and became acceptable in daily life only in the late fifties. Until then women did not go downtown or do office work in pants. In fact, the rise of the athletic woman in films probably helped the public accept more casual and movement-oriented clothes. The same might be said of the subsequent rise of the teenage film with its corollary youth cult.

The tendency towards the casual and the comfortable has dominated the image of fashion for American women up until the last four years, when we witnessed an attempt to bring back the glamor of the thirties and forties and the campy extravagance of the fifties. Hopefully women will hold on to the gain made in the acceptance of sportswear, particularly as it concerns the health and strength of female bodies. Certainly it is the clothes that are being advertised and sold to us now that raise most directly the ideological questions underlying this analysis of image creation by Hollywood and the fashion industry.

The knowledge that the three industries in question, fashion, advertising, and film/ television, have all evolved into increasingly complex capitalist market forms forces us to recognize how overdetermined our desires for creative expression through fashion are at this point in history. We clearly exist in a network of consumer research and advertising campaigns. For those who calculate which discrete differences in design, quality, and signification we will purchase, the stakes are extremely high. The *New York Times* reported that the company marketing Gloria Vanderbilt jeans put six million dollars into their advertising campaign for that one product in a single year.

It is fascinating in this light to remember how Hollywood has held up fashion as an arena of free choice, of capitalist pleasure denied the gray, sexless, uniformed communist world. In *Ninotchka* (1939) Garbo played the part of a dully dressed Soviet envoy who, seduced by a Parisian count, is gradually brought around to appreciating the extravagance of fashion. Hollywood liked the narrative so much it remade it as a musical, *Silk Stockings*, (1957). Fashion is obviously deeply ideological; like other artistic expressions, it can be used as an emblem of selfhood and subjectivity, thereby involving us in contradictions basic to our society. As subjects, we express and choose ourselves through fashion even while the film and fashion industries seek to efface our subjectivity and render us as segments of a consumer profile – objects to be controlled.

NOTE

Source: *Socialist Review,* 71(13) (Radical Society Ltd., 1983), 78–96.

REFERENCES

1. The discussion of the semiotic system employed in the verbal descriptions surrounding fashion in magazine presentations is thoroughly analyzed by Roland Barthes in his book *Système de la Mode* (Paris: Éditions du Seuil, 1967), translated into English as *The Fashion System* (New York: Farrar, Straus & Giroux, 1983). In speaking of the style of fashion writing, he emphasizes a tendency toward pseudo-proverbial pronouncements and a play with rhyming (pp. 232–233). He states that such stylistic traits function similarly to intonation in language, setting a tone and connotations which present difficult problems for the analyst since they are evoked by what Barthes terms "suprasegmental traits." Barthes's major concern, semiotically, is different from my own in this paper, however; he is attempting to analyze extralinguistic codes as expressed through image and sound narratives, the Hollywood filmic form. Still, Barthes's analysis and Julia Kristeva's response to it in her article "Le Sens et la Mode," published in *Semiotika, Récherches pour une Semanalyse* (Paris: Éditions du Seuil, 1969) contain many arguments that are directly applicable to the analysis of fashion as presented in film, particularly as regards the latency of the signifier of fashion, which has the role of creating ideological alienation by distinguishing the artificiality of the relationship between signifier and meaning by presenting it as a neutral, fixed relationship. In other words, the connotations of femininity, sportiveness, elegance, etc. are all assumed to have some natural correspondence to certain traits, rather than being seen as a series of psychoanalytical and ideological associations developed historically in a culture.
2. Ruth Lynan, *Couture* (New York: Doubleday, 1972), p. 56.
3. There is an interesting discussion of this phenomenon in T. J. Clark's analysis of the social codes that appear in Impressionist paintings in France. James Lectures, New York University, Fall 1979.
4. Elizabeth Ewing, *History of 20th Century Fashion* (New York: Scribner, 1974), p. 72.
5. Ibid.
6. Bernadine Morris, "Norell," in Sarah Tomerline Lee, ed., *American Fashion* (New York: Quadrangle, 1975), p. 320.
7. Elizabeth Leese, *Costume Design in the Movies* (New York: Unger, 1976), pp. 9–16.
8. Ibid.
9. Margaret Farrand Thorp, *America at the Movies* (New Haven, Conn.: Yale University Press, 1939; reprinted by Arno Press, 1970).
10. *Bonomo "Original" Hollywood "Success Course: Health, Charm, and Personality Improvement"* (New York: Bonomo Culture Institute, 1945).

CHAPTER SIXTEEN

Other People's Clothes? The International Second-hand Clothing Trade and Dress Practices in Zambia

KAREN TRANBERG HANSEN

World-wide exports of second-hand clothing from North America and Europe have expanded rapidly in recent years, with spectacular import increases in sub-Saharan Africa over the last two decades. Such clothing is given many names in the countries that import it. It was called *Vietnam* in Kivu in the eastern part of the former Zaire in the 1970s, and *calamidades* in Mozambique in the 1990s. It is known by local terms that mean "dead white men's clothes" in Ghana, "died in Europe" in northwestern Tanzania (Weiss 1996:138), and "shake and sell" in Senegal (Heath 1992: 28).[1] In East Africa it is called *mitumba*, which is Swahili for "bale." In Malawi, it is *kaunjika*, which in Nyanja/Chewa means "to pick," while in Zambia *salaula* means in Bemba "selecting from a pile in the manner of rummaging."

The significance of these references to the West's clothing surplus depends on the case at hand and the economic and cultural politics of its time. What matters in Zambia is the way *salaula* names how people deal with clothing, selecting, and choosing garments to suit both their clothing needs and desires. Their concern with cutting a fine figure struck anthropologists in the past (Mitchell 1956; Richards 1969 [1939]; Wilson 1941–42) and their active preoccupations with clothing, style, and fashion continue to do so today. Because of the many influences on which clothing practices draw, Zambian dealings with clothing – both new and used, for of course they implicate

one another – offer a particularly rich case for exploring some of the complex interactions between the local dress scene and its insertion in a variety of larger contexts.

Clothing, style, and fashion are important topics of everyday conversation in
Zambia. The dressed bodies of persons of importance are the subjects of intense
scrutiny and comment, as is the appearance of casual bystanders. Above all else,
dress sensibilities in Zambia are visual and sensual. Created in performance, the
aesthetic effect of the dressed body is a particular *look* that people strive to produce.
The clothing competence they bring to bear on this process is extensive. Poor and
rich, women and men, adolescent and adult, they all want to look "outstanding,"
"unique," or "exclusive." The meanings of clothes do not inhere in the garments
themselves, but are attributed to them in ongoing interaction. That is to say that how
clothing is construed and how it matters has a lot to do with the context in which
it is worn. Even then, because individual dress practice does not always conform to
widespread norms, the body surface easily becomes a battleground where questions
about dress and its acceptability are tested.

On the pages that follow, I map out some of these processes in relation to Zambia,
pointing to complex dialectics between the local clothing scene and its location in a
larger context that includes other African countries, the West, Asia, and the mass media,
among many other things. I begin with history, hinting at enduring entanglements
between the second-hand clothing trade and current clothing consumption in the
Zambian case. Then I sketch some contours of the international second-hand clothing
trade and note some of its different dynamics across Africa. Next I turn to Zambia
and the clothing consumption practices that have arisen around the rapidly growing
import of second-hand clothing since the middle to late 1980s. I draw from research I
have conducted since the early 1990s on the entire circuit of the international second-
hand clothing trade from the point of sourcing in the West to the point where our
used garments arrive in Zambia and enter into a local dress universe in which their
meanings are redefined (Hansen 2000).

THE SECOND-HAND CLOTHING TRADE

In much of the West today, second-hand clothing makes up fringe, or niche, markets.
Income distribution, purchasing power, affordable mass-produced garments and
apparel, and concerns with fashion have reduced the need for large segments of the
population to purchase used clothing. But well into the nineteenth century, used
clothing constituted the effective market for much of the population except the very
rich. Still in many countries in the Third World today, where the cost factor is enormously important, second-hand clothing is both desired and needed. While grinding
poverty and deteriorating purchasing power as a result of prolonged economic
decline in most of the countries of sub-Saharan Africa since the 1970s help explain
why this region is the world's largest import market for the lowest-quality used
clothing, economics and poverty do not adequately account for the popularity of a

commodity like *salaula* in Zambia. As I point out briefly below, the history of the second-hand clothing system of provision feeds into and sharpens popular sensibilities of clothing consumption.[2]

Past and present, the export trade in used clothing has been closely linked to the costs of domestic garment manufacture in a process on which historians have begun to throw light (Lemire 1997; Perrot 1994; Roche 1996). A detailed historical tracing of this trade is difficult because of the very nature of second-hand clothing consumption, which tends to exhaust the material evidence of its own past through extensive wear. Until well after the beginning of ready-made garment production, clothes went through many lives, passed down, resold or exchanged for other goods, altered or mended, and resewn before they reached the final phase of their journey and were recycled as rags into paper. "The success of the second-hand clothes trade can only be commemorated," suggests the costume historian Madeleine Ginsburg, "by their absence from museum collections of material survivals. [But it] would be an injustice to pay a similar complement to its history, of interest in its own right and as an aspect of the garment history" (1980: 121).

By 1600, if not earlier, the second-hand clothing trade flourished in major European cities, concentrated in specifically located markets, stores, and pawnshops. The abandonment of guild regulations and sartorial dress rules increased the demand for fashionable clothing, much of which was satisfied from the second-hand clothing market (Lemire 1991a). Itinerant "old clothes men" traded across the countryside in a process through which garments continued to change hands (Lemire 1997: 75–93). From the mid-eighteenth century on, the availability of more affordable cotton and wool fabrics began gradually reducing home markets in second-hand clothing at the same time as early mass producing tailoring firms made new clothing more affordable (Lemire 1991b).

Like any other commodity in demand, second-hand clothing was sourced and traded across vast distances. By the first half of the eighteenth century, the Netherlands and London were centers for the wholesale trade in used clothes, with exports to Belgium, France, and South America. The export trade reached the colonies as well, including North America and Africa. By the late nineteenth century in Paris, reasonably priced ready-wear competed so effectively with second-hand clothes that the used clothing trade became limited to exports, especially to colonial Africa (Perrot 1994: 71).

The profitable potential of the second-hand clothes market in colonial Africa was seized after the two World Wars, when surplus army clothing was exported by used clothing dealers in America and Britain and on the Continent. The availability of army clothing and men's work clothing from the early production of ready-wear are among the reasons why the histories of second-hand clothing consumption in Africa are distinctly gendered. Men's greatcoats and jackets came first, and only in the inter-war period did women's wear begin to enter used clothing consignments for export. But the substantive growth of the African second-hand clothing export market is a phenomenon postdating the Second World War, a product both of supply and demand: a vast surplus of still wearable used clothing in the West, and growing desires and needs for clothes in Africa, where socioeconomic transformations catapulted more and more Africans into new markets as consumers.

THE CHARITABLE CONNECTION

Developments in the export trade in second-hand clothing since the Second World War have depended to a great extent on the clothing collection activities of major charitable organizations who supply both domestic and foreign second-hand clothing markets. The charities have a long, and changing, involvement with second-hand clothing. In both Europe and the United States at the end of the nineteenth century, philanthropic groups collected and donated clothes to the poor (Ginsburg 1980: 128). In the period after the Second World War, shifts in income distribution and growing purchasing power enabled more consumers than ever before to buy not only new, but more, clothes, including fashions and styles oriented toward specific niches, for example, teenage clothing, corporate and career dressing, and sports and leisure wear. Such dress practices produced an enormous yield of used, but still wearable clothes, some of which ended up as donations to charity.

Many charitable organizations began emphasizing store sales in the late 1950s, among them the Salvation Army, for which the sale of used clothing was the largest single source of income in the United States by the 1960s (McKinley 1986). The charitable organizations dominated the second-hand clothing retail scene in the 1960s and 1970s. During the 1980s, they were joined by a variety of specialist second-hand clothing stores that began to appear operating on a for-profit basis, with names, in the Chicago area, like Crowded Closet, Flashy Trash, Hollywood Mirror, Hubba Hubba, Bewitched, and Strange Cargo. Although most of the specialty resale stores cater to women, some stock garments for both sexes, and there are stores for children's clothing as well. Men's stores are beginning to appear – for example, Gentlemen's Agreement on the Upper East Side of Manhattan (New York Times, 14 December 1997, p. B14) and Second Time Around, in the middle of Boston's Newbery Street (Wall Street Journal, 20 January 1997, p. 1 and p. 6). Some stores operate on a consignment basis, selling "gently worn" designer clothes both for women and men; others source in bulk from commercial second-hand clothing vendors, or both.

Rarely featuring words like "used," "second-hand" or "thrift" in their names, most of these recent stores target specific consumers, for example, young professionals who may want high-quality clothes at modest prices or young people keen on retro and vintage fashion, punk, and rave styles (McRobbie 1989). There is a vigorous resale market for designer clothes in specialty stores whose customers buy designer labels to wear as "investment dressing," much as collectors buy art (New York Times, 4 June 1996, p. B11). And "thrift shopping" appears to have developed a new allure, providing pastime activity for vintage connoisseurs who are on the lookout for rare finds (New York Times, 28 September 1997, Travel section p. 27). Some of these businesses donate garments that do not sell well "to charity," and some also dispose of their surplus at bulk prices to commercial second-hand clothing dealers.

The charitable organizations are the largest single source of the garments that fuel today's international trade in second-hand clothing. Because consumers in the West today donate much more clothing than the charitable organizations can possibly sell in their thrift shops, the charitable organizations resell their massive overstock at bulk prices to commercial second-hand clothing dealers. While the spectacular increase in second-hand clothing exports to Africa since the mid-1980s has taken place alongside the growth of the international humanitarian aid industry, this export is less about charity than it is about profits. In fact, used clothing as outright donations in crisis and relief situations plays a very minor role in an export process that is overwhelmingly commercial.[3]

The second-hand clothing trade is an unusual industry with peculiar problems that arise from the uneasy relationship between "charity" and commercial interests and the ways that each of these is organized. In the West today, the second-hand clothing trade both in domestic and foreign markets is dominated by non-profit charitable organizations and private textile recycling/grading firms, often family-owned. Its financial side has largely eluded public scrutiny. Thriving by an ethic of giving in the West, the major charitable organizations look like patrons in a worldwide clothing donation project. Yet the major charitable organizations routinely sell a large proportion of their donated clothing, between 40 and 75 per cent depending on whom you talk to, to textile recyclers. Their extensive interactions with textile recyclers/graders add a commercial angle to their dealings about which there is little substantive knowledge. What is more, growing environmental concerns in the West in recent years have enhanced both the profitability and respectability of the rag trade and given its practitioners a new cachet as textile salvagers and waste recyclers.

From across the United States and northwestern Europe the textile recyclers/graders truck the used clothing they purchase in bulk from the charitable organizations to warehouses/sorting plants near major port cities. "Used clothing" includes not only garments but also shoes, handbags, towels, sheets, blankets, and draperies. The clothes are sorted by garment type, fabric, and quality before being compressed into bales. The standard weight is 50 kilograms; yet some firms also compress bales of much larger weights, usually of unsorted clothing. The clothes are often sorted under poor work conditions by poorly paid workers, some of whom are recent immigrants from countries where the clothes will be sold. The bottom quality goes to Africa, and medium quality to Latin America, while Japan receives a large portion of top-quality items, among which brand-name denim jeans and sneakers are in popular demand.

This sketch of some of the shifting contours of the second-hand clothing trade appears to explain its dynamics with reference to the history of clothing manufacture, first tailor-made and then factory-produced garments. But it is also, and in the longer haul, a cultural story about consumption and about the importance of clothing, both new and old, to modern sensibilities, embodying new social and cultural abilities to discriminate. In the process, clothing has become an important agent of social change (Martin 1994).

WORLD EXPORTS AND IMPORTS

The second-hand clothing trade constitutes an immense, profitable, but barely examined world-wide commodity circuit that exports millions of dollars' worth of used clothing abroad. It grew more than sixfold over the last one and a half decades, from a value of US $207 million in 1980 to US $1,410 million in 1995 (UN 1996: 60).[4] The United States is the world's largest exporter in terms of both volume and value, followed by Germany, the Netherlands, Belgium-Luxembourg, and Japan. Between 1990 and 1995 alone, United States world-wide exports of this commodity doubled, from a value of US $174 million to US $340 million (UN 1996: 60).[5]

The countries of sub-Saharan Africa are the world's largest second-hand clothing destination, receiving in 1995 close to one-fourth of total world exports, worth US $379 million, up from US $117 million in 1990 (UN 1996: 60). There are several Asian countries among the large net importers of second-hand clothing, including Pakistan, Singapore, India, and Hong Kong. The large importers include such Middle Eastern countries as Syria and Jordan, as well as Malaysia and several countries in Latin America. Sizeable exports go not only to developing countries but also to Japan, the Netherlands, and Belgium-Luxembourg, which all engage in both import and re-export of this commodity.

African used-clothing markets undergo quick changes not only because of civil strife and war but also because of legislation guiding the entry or prohibition of second-hand clothing imports. Monetary policies affecting exchange rates and the very availability of foreign exchange influence the ability of local wholesalers to import. Some countries have at one time or the other banned imports, among them the Côte d'Ivoire, Nigeria, Kenya, and Malawi. Some countries have restrictive policies, for example South Africa, which only allows import of second-hand clothing for charitable purposes rather than for resale. Some small countries like Benin, Togo, and Rwanda before its civil wars, are large importers and active in transshipment and re-export. And although second-hand clothing imports are banned in some countries, there is a brisk transborder trade in this commodity.

AFRICAN SECOND-HAND CLOTHING MARKETS

Second-hand clothing exporters need local knowledge not only about the political climate, import rules, tariffs, and currency regulations but also about clothing consumption practices in the various African countries. Some exporters have lived in Africa, and those who have not make on-site visits to familiarize themselves with local clothing markets. From the African end, wholesalers feed back information to their contacts in North America and Europe about which garments do and do not sell well.

Exporters need to reckon with considerable regional variation in Africa's clothing markets. In Muslim-dominated North Africa, for example, used clothing constituted only 7 per cent of total garment imports in 1980 compared to 33 per cent in sub-Saharan Africa (Haggblade 1990: 508–9). Tunisia is an exception to this with large imports, probably due to long practices of re-export (van Groen and Lozer 1976).

Local dress conventions differ in terms not only of religious norms but also of gender, age, class, and region, informing cultural norms of dress practice and influencing what types of garments people will wear and when. Briefly, in several countries in West Africa, distinct regional dress styles that are the products of long-standing textile crafts in weaving, dyeing, and printing today co-exist with styles of dressing introduced during the colonial period and after. In Nigeria and Senegal, for example, second-hand clothing has entered a specific niche. Although people from different socioeconomic groups, not only the very poor, now purchase imported second-hand clothing and use it widely for everyday wear, Senegalese and Nigerians commonly follow long-standing regional style conventions on important occasions, dressing with pride for purposes of displaying locally produced cloth in "African" styles (Denzer 1997: 10–12; Heath 1992: 21, 28). This is much in contrast to Zambia, where such textile crafts hardly existed and where people from across the socio-economic spectrum except at the very top are dressing in the West's used clothing. What is more, people in Zambia have been wearing Western-styled clothing since the early twentieth century, in fact for so long that they have made it their own. As a result, references to the West are not very helpful when explaining local dress conventions. Last but not least, there are invented dress "traditions." In Mobuto Sese Seko's Zaire, for example, the "authenticity" code forbade men from wearing Western coats and ties and women from wearing jeans. His successor, President Laurent Kabila of the Democratic Republic of the Congo, is conservative in matters of women's dress. One of his first edicts after assuming power in 1997 was to ban women's wearing of jeans and miniskirts (*The Post*, 22 July 1997, p. 10).

THE *SALAULA* MARKET IN ZAMBIA

Zambia's second-hand clothing trade dates back to the colonial period, when imported used clothes reached Northern Rhodesia – as Zambia was called then – from across the border with the Belgian Congo, now the Democratic Republic of the Congo. Direct importation of this commodity was prohibited in Zambia during the first decades after independence in 1964. When restrictive import and foreign exchange regulations were relaxed in the middle to late 1980s, the second-hand clothing trade grew rapidly. The name *salaula* came into use at that time.

Second-hand clothing consignments destined for Zambia arrive by container ships in the ports of Dar es Salaam in Tanzania, Durban in South Africa, and Beira in Mozambique, from where they are trucked to wholesalers' warehouses in Lusaka, the capital. Lusaka is the hub of the *salaula* wholesale trade, though some firms have up-country branches. At the warehouse, marketeers, vendors, and private individuals purchase bales of *salaula*. They in turn distribute and sell their goods in urban and rural markets, hawk them in the countryside, and transfer them in rural exchanges in return for produce, goats, chicken, and fish. Today, in Zambia's urban and provincial markets, the *salaula* sections are many times larger than the food sections. *Salaula* is also sold from private homes in urban middle- and high-income residential areas, and some traders bring second-hand clothing to city offices and institutions like banks to sell on credit to employees who receive monthly paychecks.

The explosion of Zambia's *salaula* market has provided an income source for traders and created ancillary economic activities in repair, alteration, and support services for many others, including mature women and men, and a growing number of out-of-school youth, especially young men. In effect, in Zambia's declining economy, the *salaula* trade has created work opportunities for people who never held formal-sector jobs and for retrenched employees from both the public and private sectors. It also serves as a sideline for people who are seeking to extend their meagre earnings from jobs elsewhere. But above all, the *salaula* trade has made a profusion of clothing available from which dress-conscious consumers can purchase just the garments they want. "Watch Lusaka," suggested one writer. "All who are gorgeously attired mostly get their clothes abroad." Lusaka's so-called boutiques, he went on "have become rather like museums . . . neither Lusaka's Cairo Road nor the Kamwala shopping area is the place to look. You have a better chance at the second-hand clothes dealer, the flea market or even the city centre market dealer who jaunts between Lusaka and Johannesburg" (*Times of Zambia*, 26 August 1995, p. 4). He might have added what people in Zambia readily will tell you, namely that "three-fourths" of the population "shops from *salaula*." My survey observations about clothing consumption practices across class in Lusaka in fact confirm that popular impression.

ZAMBIAN CLOTHING PROFILES

What influences consumers in Zambia when they go about acquiring *salaula*? There is much more at stake in buying *salaula* than a mere exchange of cash, or barter, for clothes. Just as wholesalers of *salaula* are selective when ordering clothing consignments from the West to retail in local markets, so are consumers in their purchase of garments. Vital dimensions of the demand side are cultural taste and style matters. Indeed, consumption is hard work that may be understood through the practices and meanings consumers bring to bear on how they acquire and use things (de Certeau 1988: 30–1).

When shopping from *salaula*, consumers' preoccupations with creating particular looks are inspired by fashion trends and popular dress cultures from across the world. Negotiating both clothing needs and desires, consumers are influenced by a variety of sources when they purchase garments. They draw on these influences in ways that are informed by local norms about bodies and dress. Above all, clothing consumption implicates cultural norms about gender and authority. Local notions of what to wear when and how to present the dressed body construct dress practice in Zambian terms that influence how people dress in garments from *salaula*. Clothing consumers speak of these terms in the language of tradition. Because this is a made up tradition, it is subject to change. That is why the normative terms for how to dress delineate rather than determine how people dress, leaving room for idiosyncratic and provocative dress practices as well.

To flesh out the normative aspects of Zambian dress practice I asked the persons I interviewed to describe both a well-dressed woman and a well-dressed man and to explain what made people look not well-dressed. These questions followed discussions of their favorite types of clothes and what they did not like to wear and why.[6] In fact, the two sets of questions complemented one another. The descriptions of well-dressed persons were remarkably uniform across the different residential areas in which I interviewed, constituting what amounts to a culturally dominant notion of how to dress – in effect, a dress code. Questions about hairstyles, makeup, and accessories supported these notions as well. Only in *apamwamba* (a Nyanja term, meaning literally "those on the top") households and women-headed households with ample economic means were these notions occasionally challenged. Some young adults also challenged, or wanted to challenge, these norms that circumscribed their clothing desires.

The composite clothing profiles of a well-dressed woman and a well-dressed man have much in common. The adult dress profile of both sexes is tidy, with smooth lines and careful color coordination. It is loosely fitting rather than tight. "Too many" different garments, colors, and fabrics distort the smooth profile, making the person look dishevelled, and drawing undue attention to the dressed body. Women's moderate use of jewelry and make-up, and the hairstyles of both sexes enhance the total look to make it appear natural rather than artificial. In short, dress should complement the body structure and display it to its advantage.

For both sexes, these formal dress profiles convey notions about respectability and maturity, and of being in charge. Regardless of urban or rural residence, the accepted notion of how to dress makes adult men insist on suits, ties, long-sleeved shirts, and when of a certain age, hats for their public ensemble. Leather shoes, not boots, sneakers, or sandals, mark the man as properly put together. And irrespective of occupation and location, adult women insist on skirts below the knee, short-sleeved loose blouses or dresses, on top of which a *chitenge* (a wrapper of colorful printed cloth) can be worn if necessary and, when of a certain age, headscarves; shoes with heels, not sandals, and certainly not sneakers, are part of their ensemble in public. But on the matter of how to present the dressed body the clothing profiles of women and men differ significantly. Women must cover their "private parts," which in this region of Africa includes their thighs. This means that dress length, tightness, and fabric transparency become issues in interactions with men and elders both at home and in public.

The active concern with cutting a good figure on Zambian terms is evident in the hard work of *salaula* consumption. That work includes shopping in the market, where consumers gather information on the availability of specific garments/styles and screen and sort products while they skillfully work their way through the piles of *salaula*, checking both for quality and style. They turn garments inside out to examine if the sewing is neat and whether there are rips or other flaws in the fabric. But the work of consumption extends far beyond the market. A well-dressed person is well-kempt herself, and her clothing is well kept. Producing the smooth, tidy clothing profile involves processes that easily escape the gaze of the casual observer or traveler, who sees *salaula* only as the West's cast-offs. The desire to be well turned out, even if the garments are second-hand, makes clothes-conscious Zambians insist on immaculate ensembles whose elements are carefully laundered and ironed. For this reason, the faded and torn jeans that are part of *salaula* bales imported from the United States are particularly unpopular. The desire to look spick and span prompts careful scrutiny of fabric quality to ascertain that colors of printed fabrics will not run in washing. Fading in sunlight is an issue as well. Most households do their laundry in cold water using strong detergents containing bleach, and clothes are usually hung up in the sunlight to dry. This is why color fastness and fabric quality are important issues in identifying clothes that are durable and will keep their good looks. And everyone pays great attention to shoes, commonly carrying a piece of cloth under the waist of a *chitenge* wrapper in their handbags or their pockets to remove Lusaka's dust when entering public buildings and private homes.

The attraction of *salaula* to clothing-conscious Zambian consumers goes far beyond the price factor and the good quality for money that many of these garments offer. Above all, *salaula* makes available an abundance and variety of clothes that allow consumers to make their individual mark on the culturally accepted clothing profile. But the fact that we can identify Zambian terms for acceptable dress does not mean that everyone dresses alike. Nor does the desire to dress in "the latest" produce passive imitation and homogeneity. It is precisely the opposite effect consumers seek to achieve from *salaula* and that they find missing from much store-bought clothing: uniqueness. What they want are clothes that are fashionable rather than common. One of the women I interviewed in a high-income area put it this way when explaining why she shopped from *salaula:* "I don't want to wear what everyone else is wearing." "Clothes from *salaula* are not what other people wear," said another woman, explaining why they are viewed as "exclusive."

The desire for uniqueness, to stand out, while dressing the body on Zambian terms, produces considerable variations in dress in public workplaces and offices. Women never wear the same dress to work every day, according to their own reports, but rotate their garments and make new combinations of dresses and skirts. Their rotation occasionally includes dresses in a cut and style that in the West might be considered to be cocktail or evening wear. They may wear a *chitenge* dress to work as well, something rarely seen in the 1980s. In some banks and private firms, women wear suited uniforms, but have a "free dress" day once a week when they dress with their own sense of style.

Men work hard to achieve uniqueness in clothing presentation, too. Suits are worn in Zambia across a much wider range of the white-collar and civil service ranks than in the midwestern United States, for example. Civil servants rotate their immaculately kept suits, including older suits that wear the marks of time but always are crisply pressed. Young male bank tellers and clerical workers vary their suited look by wearing different types of shirt, tie and handkerchief combinations. Some men also wear jewelry, such as necklaces, tie-pins, bracelets, and rings, which they rotate. In fact men's suits are worn so commonly in Lusaka's downtown that, unlike in Harare, in neighboring Zimbabwe, you hardly ever encounter an adult Zambian man wearing shorts in public there.

Because notions of proper dress are context-dependent, their constraining effects may be temporarily put aside. This is the case on the urban disco and evening entertainment scene, which in the 1990s often displayed miniskirts and tight and transparent women's garments. Men who attend such events dress in designer jeans and trousers. And some could very occasionally be seen wearing the very high-waisted trousers inspired by Zairean rumba musicians. Specially styled jackets go with such trousers, adorned with a variety of inserted contrastive fabric or special collar, button, and pocket details. The majority of those who can afford to attend such events are of *apamwamba* background, the only group, as I suggested above, with an effective choice in the clothing market.

Last but not least, both play, idiosyncrasy, and pragmatics enter into how some people dress. I met many young men trading in the *salaula* markets who enjoyed dressing in a striking manner in garments they took a liking to. Examples include one young man who wore what looked like a hospital orderly's white uniform topped by a pink *peignoir*. Another young man dressed proudly in a church elder's purple gown. Dress practices such as these are not so much deliberate attempts to develop personal style distinctions as they are examples of the playfulness of young men who relish dressing up and showing off. This attitude of delight is also evident in the red nail polish that some young male street vendors paint on some, or all, of their fingers. "It looks good, we like it," they will tell you. What is more, the Zambian clothing scene is full of what to the Western eye may appear as unorthodox or incongruous styles, such as men wearing combinations of women's clothing, including coats, sweaters, and shorts, and women wearing men's dust coats and jackets. Such dress practices do not represent deliberate cross-dressing, but reflect the differential availability of women's and men's seasonal garments in the *salaula* consignments. Such clothing efforts are pragmatic aims at combining, for example, cold weather garments or work clothes from what is available from *salaula*.

CHITENGE WEAR

The cultural constraints on Zambian women's dress practices are far more pronounced than those on men, who can create the smooth, continuous line enveloping their bodies to perfection from the combination of suit, shirt, and tie. Although Anne Hollander's work is inspired by clothing in Western art, some of her arguments resonate with widespread clothing sensibilities in Zambia. Her recent book emphasizes the enduring appeal of the suit in creating the "perfect man" (Hollander 1994: 92). She suggests that women's dress always makes a strong, almost theatrical, visual claim, while men's tailored suits set the real standard (1994: 8). Zambian women's commentaries on male and female clothing practice acknowledge such a difference almost in the same terms. Indeed, they complain that men have a much easier time dressing. In addition to being concerned with quality issues, color coordination, fit, and the right accessories, women have to worry about decency and respectability in dress. Yet there is one clothing platform where women take safe dress conventions in their own hands and develop them to the fullest. This is the two-piece *chitenge* outfit, the postcolonial creation of a women's national dress "tradition" that continues to take on new shapes, influenced in particular by Zairean and West African clothing trends. By contrast, West African-inspired loose gowns and print shirts have not appealed to Zambian men.

In the 1960s and 1970s, the *chitenge* suit consisted of a wrapper or plain skirt with a minimally tailored, short-sleeved, matching top and at times a headscarf. When the local textile factories still produced *chitenge*, their lines included not only colorful patterns but also commemorative designs, prints to promote for instance wildlife conservation or immunization, and announcements that made them into wearable political billboards (*New York Times*, 26 November 1989, section XX, p. 6 and p. 26). Women commonly then, as they still do today, wrapped lengths of *chitenge* cloth on top of a skirt or dress when working around the house or in the fields, traveling by public transportation, shopping in the public markets, or spending long waiting periods – for example on hospital grounds – and when attending overnight wakes and funerals. The most widespread use of *chitenge* is for carrying infants on the back. The *chitenge* holds bundles, serves as blanket when people sit on the ground, and has many other usages. As a constructed garment, the *chitenge* suit gradually became more elaborate during the 1980s. It has now evolved into a fashion that holds the ample breasts and hips that fit so uneasily into ready-made clothing and many of the dresses in *salaula* markets.

During the middle to late 1980s *chitenge* outfits were simple skirts or wraps and tops of printed fabric, at times with contrasting ribbons sewn around necks and sleeves; tie-dye became common then, often locally produced by West African women who taught Zambian women the technique; tie-dye was sewn up into loose garments, including trouser and top combinations, often with West African-styled embroidery around necks, sleeves, and edges. This may have been influenced by the feminization of the men's two-piece outfit of trousers and oversized tops that was popular in Nigeria in the late 1980s (Bastian 1996). The trouser and top profile changed during the first half of the 1990s to skirts and tops of printed cloth or tie-dye with marked waistlines, peplums, increasingly elaborate, built-up sleeves supported by interfacing, and with collars, necklines, and fronts embellished by contrasting material, buttons, ruffles, or smocking. There were several types of skirts to choose between: plain wrappers, double wrappers, and Tshala Muanas, pencil-tight skirts reaching below the knee with a long slit in front, named after a popular Zairean singer. In 1997, the latest style was inspired by West African dress and locally referred to as "Nigerian boubou."[7] This style consisted of huge flowing gowns of single-colored fabrics, damask or damask weave imitations with elaborate embroideries in contrasting colors and with accompanying built-up headgear. *Chitenge* fashions will no doubt continue to change, as their popularity rises or declines in interactions with pan-African and global clothing trends. By 1999 in fact, the "boubou" was not much in evidence. The preferred *chitenge* outfit that year featured a straight skirt with a slit (worn in front or back) and a big sleeved blouse with a variety of trimmings. Perhaps in Zambia, as has been suggested for Kenya, this "global African dress signifies not tradition but modernity . . . [that constructs] an elusive and ambiguous . . . national identity" (Rabine 1997: 163).

"You can do so many things with *chitenge*," explained one of the teachers who kept account of her household budget and clothing expenditures for me. Her wardrobe consisted largely of *chitenge* outfits in some of the different styles I just described and only a couple of "European-styled" two-piece outfits. *Chitenges* are much more comfortable to wear, she argued, than dresses and skirts "where you have to worry about belts and matching blouses." Wearing *chitenge* is closely related to income, in that the price of fabric and the tailor's charges might be too high for many low-income consumers. A *chitenge* suit in 1995 easily cost K35,000 (more than the average monthly wage of a domestic servant) when the price of fabric, trimmings, and labor were added up and more, if the suit was highly embellished. This is why the self-reported ratio of "European-styled" to *chitenge* wear by low-income householders in my survey was heavily skewed toward the "European" end, which in this case means predominantly *salaula*. No one here claimed to wear only *chitenge*, although some women had one or two outfits that they wore on special occasions. In the high-income areas, by contrast, a small proportion of residents reported wearing only *chitenge*. Others wore *chitenge* with some regularity, and reported owning many suits. But "European-styled" clothing, which includes a high proportion of *salaula*, is the most widespread dress style here too.

Some women will tell you that they do not like *chitenge* outfits at all. Once pushed, they will explain that their dislike has to do with size, or "body structures" in the local dress language, meaning that they are "too" thin. Because of the body size factor, age plays into this preference as well, and young adult women do not in fact agree on whether or not they like *chitenge* fashions. "They do make big women look nice," said one young woman; whereas another complained that *chitenge* dresses only are for "old" women.

A good deal of clothing competence is entailed in purchasing attractive *chitenge* fabrics and identifying tailors who are able to deliver a finished product to the satisfaction of customers. Discriminating customers considered the *chitenge* fabric produced by the two formerly state-owned firms, Kafue Textiles of Zambia and Mulungushi Textiles until the early 1990s, to be of poor quality and unattractive design. Those who could afford it paid expensively on the black market for Dutch wax prints and *chitenges* brought across the border from Zaire and Burundi. The evaluation of *chitenge* depends not only on the attractiveness of the design but also on how well the fabric will keep after washing. Some *chitenges* contain a lot of starch and some have colors that run. In fact, *chitenge* dresses may not be very durable, which is one reason they have less appeal at the low-income level. Their short life is a product of mediocre fabric, frequent washing with strong detergents, and constant ironing,[8] often with a heavy charcoal iron, as many Zambian homes in the low-income areas are not electrified.

The increased availability in recent years of imported *chitenge* fabrics from India and Pakistan with attractive designs at more affordable prices and superior quality to those that used to be manufactured locally has helped to make *chitenge* fashions part of many more women's wardrobes than in the 1970s and 1980s. Office workers and teachers wear them to work, as do bank clerks on their "free dress" day. Above all, *chitenge* outfits are worn on formal visits and special occasions such as weddings and "kitchen parties" (bridal showers), where they are displayed proudly by mature women who have the body to carry them.

CLOTHING, GENDER, AND POWER

What Zambians describe as their dress "tradition" is not a static mold but an evolving set of practices in which different influences with various backgrounds are affecting one another, making it subject to variation over time as well as to resistance among some segments of consumers. Recent scholarship provides rich examples of the making and changing of "traditional" dress practices and their shifting cultural and political valuations (Ong 1990; MacLeod 1992). What is retained, borrowed or transformed in matters of dress depends a good deal on the cultural politics of its time. After Zambia's independence in 1964, the bush suit of colonial vintage with long trousers rather than shorts that the first president, Kenneth Kaunda, helped popularize as the safari suit came close to being considered men's traditional wear until the demise of the one-party state in 1991. The safari suit disappeared from the dress scene when the new president, Frederick Chiluba, chose to wear double-breasted suits with floral ties and matching handkerchiefs. Tailors got busy altering large-size single-breasted jackets into double-breasted jackets. Overnight, a new tradition of men's dress emerged, coinciding with the "new culture" associated with the opening up of both politics and economics.

Whether or not it has to do with politics, the general profile of the Zambian men's suited look has loosened up in the period during which I have paid close attention to dress practices. "Old people's styles are coming back," said one of the men I interviewed in 1997, no doubt thinking of the big trousers that were popular in the 1950s. The looser cut of men's suits today may in fact be influenced from the Zambian grass roots, by young male street vendors who since the early 1990s have been wearing looser and bigger clothes inspired by the American hip-hop and rap scene. Men used to insist on wearing shirts tucked in, well settled under their belts. Now not only street vendors wear their shirts loose, but also some white-collar workers. The loose shirt vogue has been legitimized by President Mandela, who, after taking office in South Africa in 1994, began wearing colorfully printed shirts, untucked, without jackets and ties, in public. "Mandela shirts" are often made of paisley-inspired print fabrics, and they are among the garments the suitcase traders bring back to Zambia from their shopping trips to South Africa.

Aside from the flourishing of *chitenge* fashions, less has changed in the realm of women's clothing, except perhaps for the sleeveless blouse and dress, which of late have become fairly widespread among younger consumers. But issues about women wearing short skirts and dresses, tight clothing, and trousers continue to agitate some segments of society. Young women's dressed bodies receive considerably more critical scrutiny than men's. This has been dramatized in Lusaka by intense reactions to repeated stripping incidents of young women wearing miniskirts in public throughout the 1990s. These sadly recurring events show that women's dress options in public settings where men are present are very circumscribed, and that challenge of what amounts to a dress code easily provokes men to verbal harassment and more. I have dealt with the miniskirt issue in some depth elsewhere (Hansen n.d.), and turn here to some examples of young men's dress practice.

If miniskirts, jeans, and dresses indexed young adult women's anxieties about their future possibilities and position in Zambia during the last half of the 1990s, so did suits and jeans for their young male age-mates, yet with different ramifications. Unlike young women, who carefully monitor the way they dress in public, young men like to draw attention to themselves, in different ways to be sure, depending on their socio-economic circumstances and regional location in Zambia's declining economy. For example, many young urban men close to secondary school graduation looked forward to wearing suits. Formal suits indexed their desire to lead adult, responsible, working lives, when as household heads they would become the men in charge. They were ambivalent about wearing jeans, which in their view too readily call forth the image of scruffy youths and street vendors, who are viewed in some circles as a threat to society's stability and security. Because I was curious about the evolving street vendor style scene and its influence on mainstream dress in Zambia, I explored it in more detail in 1997 through a brief survey of young men who stood out from the street crowd because of their dress and young entry-level civil servants, who were taken note of because of their sharp suits.[9]

The young street vendors were interviewed in public places where they work and relax, such as markets, streets, bus stops, and bars, while the young civil servants were interviewed in a basketball club. They ranged in age from 19 to 22; a few of them had completed grade 12, while the rest had dropped out of school earlier. The most striking observation, which complements my findings from interviewing *salaula* traders of this age-range in the markets, is that no one was married; most of them lived with their parents or guardians, intermittently helping out with household expenses; some of them lived in rented rooms they shared with friends who all were "in business," in one case the *salaula* trade in exchange for rural produce, and in another the suitcase trade to the south. They all preferred to dress in jeans styles. In addition to the style explanations I describe below, their preference for denim fabric has a clear practical reason. Jeans, one of them explained, "are durable; they are nice and easy to keep, especially by bachelors like me who have no one to look after our clothes."

What these young men did for their own pleasure was to dress up in public in variations on the baggy jeans look, several sizes larger than in 1995, and often wearing more than one set of clothes. The interviews did take place during the southern hemisphere's coldest months, when many people often wear garments on top of one another; yet the layered look was definitely in. In fact by 1999, the layered look had acquired a name of its own, *bombasa*, which had also inspired a new rap song (*Zambia Daily Mail*, 3 September 1997, p. 7). They did wear other styles. A couple of the young men wore oversize shorts, of the kind that hang down below the knee and were locally referred to as "hot pants." Unlike American rappers, whose brand name underwear is often visible underneath the layer of pants, these young men's underwear did not show. They all wore oversize tops, often with hoods. The preferred headgear had changed since 1995 from the baseball cap to knitted wool caps locally referred to as "headsocks," often with a pattern in multi-colored stripes, and occasionally a name or a logo. There were fewer hightop sneakers around than in 1995; the preferred footwear of the 1997 season was shoes with thick-treaded rubber soles leaving tractor-like imprints, called "galagata" (in Bemba, *ukukalakata* refers to walking with footwear that makes a noise). The young men often wore their shoes without socks. Several of them had an ear-ring in their left ear, one sported a nose-ring, and many wore bracelets.

These young men purchased their clothing from the "Zambia–Zaire" sections on the periphery of the city markets, where garments from "outside" were for sale; some used the tailor for special wear; and most of them scoured the *salaula* markets for just the right items. As one of them explained: "in *salaula* you will find things you can't believe how good they are." They readily pinpointed the inspiration of their style: friends from around town, local people that are admired, and foreigners. Foreign influences from a variety of sources enter through magazines, posters, music videos, television, and the cinema. Although a television set is far from being a common fixture in all households in Zambia's low- and medium-income residential areas, viewing it is often a shared experience that may include neighbors and friends. Many bars have TVs and VCRs. What is more, informal video parlors are appearing in the low-income areas where music videos draw an attentive audience, especially of young men. Clearly, young men such as these are exposed to multiple dress influences.

"I wear the big look because it is fashion," one of these young men said, while another explained that he liked to "move with time." "I don't like common clothes and imitations," said yet another. When shopping for clothes, these young men look for garments that will contribute to the overall creation of a particular style, in this case "the big look," rather than for brand-name items. Their dress style is far less glamorous than that of the *sapeurs* in Congo-Brazzaville, who, at least according to accounts prior to the recent civil war, celebrated appearance by parading expensive, upscale clothing they had obtained in Paris, proudly displaying *la griffe*, the label (Gandoulou 1989: 12–13). Like the women I described earlier, who wanted fashion and pieced their dress ensembles together from *salaula* to achieve what they considered to be uniqueness and exclusivity, these young street vendors strive for a particular look, and they also want fashion. And fashion does not mean homogeneity; while dressing almost alike, these young men in fact were hard at work on attaining "distinction," which is why they do not like "common clothes and imitations" but something that is "outstanding" and makes people look. "The big look," one of them said, "gives me confidence in myself."

The "big look" has been incorporated into the casual wear that young civil servants put on during weekends; and it has, as I noted earlier, affected the general suit profile. How young civil servants dress depends on the situation, and they have more choices than the street vendors. These young men, who ranged in age from 22 to 26, wore formal suits to work, and they liked them. They were all married with children, except for one who lived with his fiancée. Shopping from the same sources as the street vendors, they strive for the executive look, which they explained in terms fairly similar to those used by the street vendors. Clothes like these, one said, "make me look good and elegant and different from my age group. I don't like common clothes. Besides," he added, "ladies like nice clothes and I like to attract ladies." Two of these young civil servants spoke specifically about disliking "West African attire" with big, loose tops in bright colors and prints and simple pajama-like drawstring trousers underneath. Zairean-inspired high-waisted trousers of the Kind often worn by rumba musicians were not popular at all with any of these young men.

The "big look" the young street vendors work so hard to achieve through what they consider to be just the right combinations of clothes sometimes comes with an attitude that is inflected in language use and an intonation that has given them the name "yoo boys." "They are performing," said an elderly man who was commenting on the big look, "they want to identify differently from ordinary people. They can take these clothes off again." But even if these young men take their clothes off again, their life chances are not likely to improve considerably. Their dress style is not part of a subculture in the sense described by Dick Hebdige that sneers at mainstream dress conventions (1988). Instead, they dress to escape their own economic powerlessness, momentarily and vicariously; and so they put on clothes they equate with power and success. The young male secondary school students who spoke disparagingly about the street vendors' get-up fear ending up like them. Will they themselves after completing secondary school face unemployment and perhaps dead-end jobs, like the street vendors, who earn too little to set up households of their own? It is not in the least surprising that many of them liked suits, which, on their horizon, given the economic situation in Zambia, index formal employment, wages, household comforts, and the power that comes from being men in charge.

OTHER PEOPLE'S CLOTHES?

In everyday talk in Zambia, few would think of blaming the West for affecting clothing consumption whether new or old, and there is no suggestion of *salaula*'s being the flip side of Western fashion. In fact, people here rarely use the category "the West." Instead they talk about the "outside," which includes neighboring countries in the region, as well as Hong Kong and the United States. Or they invoke the "well developed countries" or "the donor countries." This is not surprising since, after all, in the post-colonial era, especially from the mid-1970s on, "development" has been the principal avenue through which "the West" has affected their lives. They also use terms that emerge in the context of specific encounters, for instance the United States, the United Kingdom or India. Their narratives employ changing idioms of time and place that are indicative of the varying types of exposure to the world beyond home among the generations who grew up prior to and after independence.

What the West is, above all, is an imagined place, associated with power, wealth, and an abundance of consumer goods that surpass most local products in quality and style. From it comes, for example, via American youth subculture, the hip-hop and rap-inspired style of young male street vendors in Zambia. Yet women's two-piece outfits are not American-derived, but influenced rather by British and South African fashions. Distinctions between Zambian styles and dress styles in America, Britain, South Africa, and elsewhere obscure dynamic relationships and influences that cross such boundaries, producing creative tensions that energize the everyday world of dress practice. There is a multiplicity of heritages at work here, with complex dialectics between local and foreign influences, and between what is considered to be "the latest" and what is current, in a reconfiguration process that generates distinct local clothing consumption practices.

The popularity of *salaula* as an element of dress practice in a developing country like Zambia offers interdisciplinary scholarship on dress and popular culture several important insights. First of all, dress conventions in Zambia are the outcomes of multiple interactions that engage style-conscious individuals with influences from many different parts of the world. Prominent in the dress practices I have described in this article are inspirations from across the African continent, particularly in women's dress, through processes that are establishing what is beginning to look like a pan-African fashion system in its own right. The second insight concerns matters of cultural taste and style that are embedded in a complex host of local social and cultural processes. These processes have worked themselves out differently across the generations, by class, and, as I have shown here, particularly by gender. This insight adds a startling twist to conventional assumptions about gender and dress that have tended to attribute late twentieth-century concerns with style and fashion to women. For in the case of Zambia, adolescent girls and adult women have far less scope for experimentation with clothing than men, for whom local society allows more room to move with fashion. And the last but not the least compelling insight arising from this study of second-hand clothing consumption is that being poor and being a discriminating consumer are not mutually exclusive.

ACKNOWLEDGMENTS

The original version of this paper was prepared for a theme presentation at the annual meeting of the International Textile and Apparel Association held at Santa Fe, 11–13 November 1999. I am enormously grateful to Mary Littrell for inviting me and to members and participants for their response. My revisions have benefited from the constructive input of Valerie Steele and members of her editorial board. The discussion draws on preliminary work I carried out in Zambia during the summers of 1992 and 1993, extensive field research and archival work conducted in Zambia, the southern African region, and Europe during the calendar year of 1995, continued work in Europe during the summer of 1996 and the spring and summer of 1997, and returns to Zambia during the summers of 1997 and 1999. The research has been supported by faculty grants from Northwestern University and awards from the Social Science Research Council (USA) and the Wenner Gren Foundation for Anthropological Research. Many of the points presented in this paper are developed in more depth in my book (Hansen 2000).

NOTES

Source: *Fashion Theory,* 4(3) (Berg Publishers, 2000), 245–74.

1. I thank Jacques Depelchin, Roger Sanjek, Kathie Sheldon, and Teodosio Uate for these insights.
2. In my book (Hansen 2000) I use the notion of a system of provision (Fine and Leopold 1993) to analyze the entire economic circuit of the second-hand clothing trade, beginning with production in the form of sourcing, distribution and exchange, and consumption. I also explore the changing history of this system, paying particular attention to its developments since the Second World War.
3. In recent disaster situations, some relief organizations have urged the public to give money rather than foodstuffs and used clothing. According to the Red Cross, such donations can impede relief efforts because of the time and cost involved in collection, sorting, transportation, storage, and distribution (*Tampa Tribune,* 30 October 1998, p. 3).

4. These statistics must be interpreted with many qualifications. There is a widespread tendency to underreport both the value and volume of shipments for export in order to reduce shipping costs and import tariffs. The main statistical source, the United Nations international trade statistics, are not complete. Not all countries report to the United Nations, and even if they report, they might undervalue the extent of trade. And when they exist, many import statistics are misleading because of extensive smuggling.

5. According to a specialist from the US department of commerce, that amount represents only what is shipped abroad in compressed bales, and does not include garments piled loosely in containers as filler or smuggled across the Mexican border. He estimated the total export to be double the official figure (*Plain Dealer*, 25 January 1998, p. 6H).

6. My approach to these questions was influenced by Rick Wilk's (1997) constructive suggestion that exploring what people "hate to" consume casts critical light on desire and preference.

7. The term *boubou* is used in Francophone African countries for women's tunic-like dresses. The reference to "Nigerian boubou" in Zambia is an example of the extent of cross-over inter-African influences in dress styles.

8. Larvae from eggs laid by *putsi* flies on wet laundry easily enter the skin of a person, producing a boil-like swelling. To prevent this from happening, local and expatriate women alike insist that all clothing that has been dried in the open must be carefully ironed.

9. Oscar Hamangaba conducted this exercise for me in 1997. Aside from exploring the source of these young men's clothing, he engaged them in conversation about why they dressed in this manner. He asked questions about their personal circumstances as well.

REFERENCES

Bastian, Misty. 1996. "Female 'Alhajis' and Entrepreneurial Fashions: Flexible Identities in Southeastern Nigerian Clothing Practice." In Hildi Hendrikson (ed.), *Clothing and Difference: Embodied Identities in Colonial and Post-Colonial Africa*, 97–132. Durham, NC: Duke University Press.

de Certeau, Michel. 1988. *The Practice of Everyday Life*, trans. Steven Kendall. Berkeley, CA: University of California Press.

Denzer, LaRay. 1997. "The Garment Industry under SAP with a Special Case Study on Ibadan." Unpublished paper presented in workshop on SAP and the Popular Economy. Development Policy Centre, Ibadan, Nigeria. August.

Fine, Ben and Ellen Leopold. 1993. *The World of Consumption*. London: Routledge.

Gandoulou, Justin-Daniel. 1989. *Dandies à Bacongo: Le culte de l'élégance dans la société congolaise contemporaine*. Paris: L'Harmattan.

Ginsburg, Madeleine. 1980. "Rags to Riches: The Second-Hand Clothes Trade 1700–1978." *Costume* 14: 121–35.

Haggblade, Steven. 1990. "The Flip Side of Fashion: Used Clothing Exports to the Third World." *Journal of Development Studies* 26(3): 505–21.

Hansen, Karen Tranberg. 2000. *Salaula: The World of Second-hand Clothing and Zambia*. Chicago: University of Chicago Press.

———. n.d. "Dressing Dangerously: Miniskirts, Gender Relations and Sexuality in Zambia." Unpublished manuscript under review.

Heath, Deborah. 1992. "Fashion, Anti-Fashion, and Heteroglossia in Urban Senegal." *American Ethnologist* 19(2): 19–33.

Hebdige, Dick. 1988. *Subculture: The Meaning of Style.* London: Routledge.

Hollander, Anne. 1994. *Sex and Suits: The Evolution of Modern Dress.* New York: Alfred A. Knopf.

Lemire, Beverly. 1991a. *Fashion's Favourite: The Cotton Trade and the Consumer in Britain, 1660–1800.* Oxford: Oxford University Press.

———. 1991b. The Nature of the Second-Hand Clothes Trade: The Role of Popular Fashion and Demand in England, *c.* 1700–1850." In CISST (ed.), *Per una storia della moda pronta: problemi e ricerche* (Atti del V Convegno Internazionale del CISST Milano, 26–28 febbraio 1990), 107–16.

———. 1997. *Dress, Culture and Commerce: The English Clothing Trade before the Factory, 1660–1800.* New York: St Martin's Press.

McKinley, Edward H. 1986. *Somebody's Brother: A History of the Salvation Army's Men's Social Service Department 1891–1985.* Lewiston, NY: Edwin Mellen Press.

MacLeod, Arlene E. 1992. "Hegemonic Relations and Gender Resistance: The New Veiling as Accommodating Protest in Cairo." *Signs* 17(3): 533–57.

McRobbie, Angela. 1989. "Second-Hand Dresses and the Role of the Ragmarket." In Angela McRobbie (ed.), *Zoot-Suits and Second-Hand Dresses: An Anthology of Fashion and Music*, pp. 23–49. London: Macmillan.

Martin, Phyllis M. 1994. "Contesting Clothes in Colonial Brazzaville." *Journal of African History* 35(3): 401–26.

Mitchell, J. Clyde. 1956. *The Kalela Dance.* Rhodes-Livingstone Papers no. 27.

Ong, Aihwa. 1990. "State versus Islam: Malay Families, Women's Bodies, and the Body Politic in Malaysia." *American Ethnologist* 17(2): 258–76.

Perrot, Philippe. 1994 [1981]. *Fashioning the Bourgeoisie: A History of Clothing in the Nineteenth Century*, trans. Richard Bienvenu. Princeton, NJ: Princeton University Press.

Rabine, Leslie W. 1997. "Not a Mere Ornament: Tradition, Modernity, and Colonialism in Kenya and Western Clothing." *Fashion Theory* 1(2): 145–68.

Richards, Audrey I. 1969 [1939]. *Land, Labour and Diet in Northern Rhodesia.* Oxford: Oxford University Press.

Roche, Daniel. 1996 [1989]. *The Culture of Clothing: Dress and Fashion in the Ancien Regime*, trans. Jean Birrell. Cambridge: Cambridge University Press.

UN (United Nations). 1996. *1995 International Trade Statistics Yearbook 1994. Vol. II: Trade by Commodity.* New York: United Nations.

van Groen, Barth and Piet Lozer. 1976. *La Structure et l'organisation de la friperie à Tunis.* Groupe d'études Tunis. Amsterdam: Université Libre Amsterdam.

Weiss, Brad. 1996. "Dressing at Death: Clothing, Time, and Memory in Buhaya, Tanzania." In Hildi Hendrickson (ed.), *Clothing and Difference: Embodied Identities in Colonial and Post-Colonial Africa*, 133–54. Durham, NC: Duke University Press.

Wilk, Richard. 1997. "A Critique of Desire: Distaste and Dislike in Consumer Behavior." *Consumption, Markets, and Culture* 1(2): 175–96

Wilson, Godfrey. 1941–42. *An Essay on the Economics of Detribalization, Vols 1 and 2.* Rhodes-Livingstone Papers nos. 5 and 6.

NEWSPAPERS

The Post (Zambia). 1997. Caution Kabila (editorial). 22 July, p. 10.

New York Times. 1989. Zambia's Social Fabric. 26 November, section XX, p. 6 and p. 26.

————. 1996. Glad Rags to Riches in the Resale Market. 4 June, p. B11.

————. 1997. Secondhand Souvenirs. 28 September, Travel section p. 27.

————. 1997. Big-Men's Wear, from a Stranger's Closet. 14 December, p. B14.

Plain Dealer. 1998. America's Old Clothes Finding Homes Abroad. 25 January, p. 6H.

Tampa Tribune. 1998. Red Cross Needs Cash to Help after Georges. 30 October, p. 3.

Times of Zambia. 1995. Wanted: Quality Clothing in Zambia (by Samuel Ngoma). 26 August, p. 4.

Wall Street Journal. 1997. Second-Hand Rows: These Thrift Shops are Classy – and Doing a Booming Business. 20 January, p. 1 and p. 6.

Zambia Daily Mail. 1999. "Nasty D" Makes Debut Performance. 3 September, p. 7.

Part 4:
Fashion and Aesthetics

CHAPTER SEVENTEEN

To Cut is to Think

GERMANO CELANT

To cut is to think and to see. Ever since modern art first posited itself as a manner of making, based on the activities of the hand and eye and aimed at constructing a thing-in-itself, the formal and constructive experience of all things has changed. It has gone from the imitation of reality to the construction of reality: art as an autonomous act of knowing. The Cubists, with Pablo Picasso and Georges Braque, were the first to cut out images, disarranging and rearranging them in order to forge new relationships with the object seen and experienced. They sank their scissors into surfaces and images to give direct form and consciousness to an art that, having exhausted and destroyed the representation of reality, created an autonomous reality of its own: a new object that did not interpret the thing, but constructed and produced it.

Cutting up and organizing forms and figures, images and materials, on a surface and in space, was a radical process that changed one's manner of perceiving reality and constructing a new existence. The first modern conceptions of design, photography, graphic art, fashion and cinema spring, in a practical as well as linguistic sense, from Cubism and its cuttings.

Cutting structures language, but also clothing. It is an intervention into the traditional conventions of representing and seeing a body or thing, and thereby produces a new sensation. The cut of the scissors is like the click of a camera or the whirr of a movie camera, like a stroke of the pencil or paintbrush: all these acts decisively isolate a form or representation, marking a surface that generates a reality.

The cut puts an end to the traditional representation of the image, dissolving it and then restoring it as a testimony to the artist's vision and understanding. In this light, the cut confers meaning, and its use unites artists, photographers, designers and tailors, who cut their visions from the magma of their materials, whether these be color or bronze, fabric or film, metal or wool, wood or canvas.

In the history of modernism the cut is an important mechanism that contributes to the crisis of foundations. If reality and nature can be traversed, simultaneously, from different angles and perspectives, the claim to knowing the truth becomes indeterminate and relative. And if the artistic process involves cleaving and delimiting appearances so that they may be read, then the cut is its soul. It becomes the intimate, sensitive interpreter that can concretely define reality. The cut is the soul of clothing. It severs the endless thread of a garment as the simple container and portrait of the human figure and transforms it into a creative act, a language that builds new objects.

The thinking spawned by the Cubist cut opened up an infinite universe. It even insinuated itself into people's interpretation of the world. It ignores the worlds hardness and absoluteness so that it can make and unmake its representation, subjecting it to a whirlwind of furtive, momentary meanings that shun all mummified order.

Futurism, a few years after Cubism, was the first modern art movement to dramatize the logic of an art that cuts and severs, truncates and traverses, clips and separates, chops and facets, crosses and intersects. And the first to make it a weapon of action – of concrete and philosophical action, political and ideological action – theoretical and artistic action, sculptural and painterly action. Its goal was not the formalism of a visual philosophy, but an actual intervention into the world of experience in all its linguistic manifestations. This world had to be changed to fit the new mechanical sensibility: the *Futurist reconstruction of the universe.*

The assumption is that of a radical transformation, a change of skin, that would upset and sweep away every surface and every form of seeing and thinking, with no exception made for humanity's second skin, clothing, which itself was subject to cuts and transformations.

For Giacomo Balla, the desire to change skin, expressed in the *Antineutral clothing* manifesto (1914), is distinguished precisely by its cut from the earlier decorative proposals of such architects as Henri Van de Velde and Joseph Hoffman and designers such as Paul Poiret, who had made clothes printed with motifs of Raoul Dufy. While the former sought to rationalize and essentialize clothing – because by now it, too, played a part in the great industrial and social project – the Futurists seemed more interested in bringing disorder to the logic and communication of clothing. The changes they brought were based on the use of asymmetry, clashing colors, and juxtapositions of dynamic forms. These relationships were highlighted by fabric covered with geometric and iridescent motifs (1913), and by the elimination of certain parts or diagonal cuts shattering the concepts of unity and univocality in clothing.

If, in Futurism, clothing thinks and acts, being the result of a cut that synthesizes all the dynamics of eye and mind, of movement and action, in Sonia Delaunay's work, also in 1914, the garment becomes a harmony of colors and non-homogeneous materials differentiated by weave and hue. Delaunay's assemblage is based on the intertwining and simultaneous co-existence of fabrics created in 1912–13 from the grafting of several different cloths bearing a lively chromatic interrelationship between them. It is a montage of irregular forms and motifs, and reflects the paintings of both Sonia and Robert Delaunay. It does not alter the structure of clothing, nor break it apart in order to transform it, since it does not use a cut that is any different from what was customary at the time.

Indeed, if we follow developments through the twenties, her articles of clothing boast a vast range of compositional and chromatic variants that enrich the joy and surface of fashion, but do not affect it at all on the level of formal construction and design. Her goal in fact was to prove *The Influence of Painting on Fashion* (1926), so as to reassert the former's uniqueness and focus on surface.

The coincidence of the first and second skins in the work of the Russian Futurists was a way to absolutize a complete overlap between art and life. In 1913, Mikhail Larionov and Ilya Zadanevich asserted the coincidence between painting and the painting of the body, by painting their faces. It was an early example of a creative, eccentric, personalized use of make-up, later followed by the custom, as practised by Vladimir Mayakovsky, David Burljuk and others, of wearing black-and-yellow striped smocks and jackets during Futurist activities in numerous Russian cities. In this case the equivalence of flesh and fabric, of makeup and clothing, implied a further notion of fashion: the desire to identify the form of the garment with the anatomical perimeter, a tangency between inside and outside. The clothing thus becomes the body, a passage from same to same. The demand is for a constructive possession of one's own body. Where as Picasso had thought to cut it up into images, now one could decorate it and shape it. An awareness of sports played an active part in this sculpting of the flesh, so much so that Aleksandr Rodchenko, Aleksandra Ekster, and Varvara Stepanova, together with the fashion designer Lamanova, designed many athletic costumes and other sportswear in 1923.

If the flesh can think and be designed, then the phase in which its emptiness is transformed into fullness and its silence into a shout is not far off. In Surrealism, the body suggests obscure latent forces, turns desires and nightmares inside out. An imminent explosion threatens, the uncertain sensation that the body is about to disintegrate into thousands of pieces and splinters. Underlying the tearing away of the limbs is a lack of self-possession, and an equation of the body with an object that can be shattered and disassembled. As structural, structurable material, it can be subjected to cuts and cadencings, exchanges and expropriations, attributions and identifications.

In being subjected to a strategy of expropriation and de-personalization, the body can be placed under the sewing machine, as in Joseph Cornell's 1931 collage, or sexually sewn, as in Oscar Dominguez's *Electrosexual sewing machine*, 1943. It becomes at once object and anti-object, conscious and unconscious, nude and dressed, masculine and feminine: a locus of equivalence between unstable, aleatory significations.

The imaginary attributions affecting fashion in the age of Surrealism arise from the new relationship between the object and the body, which led to the creation of a new centaur-like figure, part animal, part human. Salvador Dalí's placement, as photographed by George Platt Lynes, of a lobster over the pubic area of a nude female model, not only "dresses" her, but also exalts the enigmatic, aggressive charge of her sexuality. It produces a linguistic shift in the role of the covering object, the garment, and reveals its secret erotic tension. Dalí uses an animal with sharp pincers, symbolizing scissors, to make a cut that creates an article of clothing, symbolizing libido and sex, pleasure and seduction. The spark produced highlights the act of clothing as a process regulated by desire. The violence of desire in the order of fashion is not lost on the Surrealists, who reintroduce it in luxury objects such as half-veils and fans, hats and silks, jewelry and belts, whose consonance with the sense of touch and opening, and with the acts of glimpsing and covering oneself, directly and indirectly suggests eroticism.

The metamorphosis of the thing and the clothed animal broadens a complex circuit of forms of identity. Fluidity among signs makes possible the disguise, the shift and simulation of a mobility between objects and images, things and bodies. The "transmutation" of a man's hat into a vulva, or the identification of a woman's head-dress as a breast (Man Ray, 1933), or the transformation of a shoe into a foot (René Magritte, *The red model*, 1935), or a shoe-shaped cap (Elsa Schiaparelli, *Shoe hat*, 1937), propose a metaphorical principle that engenders and destroys forms, dissolves them and brings them to life. The object and the body make love. The Surrealist cut is a bar that separates but also brings together fragments of bodies and reality in such a way that, by transforming one another, they may serve as metaphors of an active place from which it is possible to set in motion a sequence of bewildering, disruptive images in an interpenetration of conscious and unconscious, exterior and interior (Schiaparelli, *Tear-illusion dress and head scarf*, ca. 1937).

The recognition of the gaze in the anthropomorphic and sexual connotations of clothing is the very breath of fashion. It is an offered, fleeting siren, the sign of a troubling body whose dark seduction lives between the murky and the menacing, the fabular and the horrific, the orderly and disorderly. The famous inverted, symmetrical Man Ray photograph (*Untitled*, 1936) is an image of this body's endless variation, based on a game of mirrors that deceives to diversity because it is a simple representation.

Clothing remains the same, but produces multiple meanings, the true dynamic of fashion. Coco Chanel was the first to invent a figure-image: the "uniform," from whose matrix is organized – through changes of material and ornamentation, of length and accessories – the dream of a variability that satisfies the need for transformation, prolongs its existence, makes it a *perpetuum mobile*.

Starting in 1948, the effect of duplicity and bewilderment occurs in the encounter of form and formless, at the threshold of a propulsive, irrational energy of gesture that aims no longer to represent the scenery of a diffuse desire, but to represent the nascent event of a circumscribed tension. For Lucio Fontana, art is a vital action displayed as creative and anarchic power. It lives freely together with the rise of spatial and energy theories, and exalts behavioral dynamism. For this reason, its movement is related to the need to open new paths and universes of artistic knowledge: to break through and penetrate the black holes of space. The extraordinary emergence, in Fontana's works on paper and later in his paintings, of an unknown universe lying beyond the painted surface, set in motion a mechanism asserting the impalpable world of imagination, not the same world represented in the oneiric figurations of the Surrealists, but the concrete one experienced by anyone moving in the obscurity of the dark.

The desire – developed through the cuts and holes, the rips and crossings of the mono-chrome surface, which we also find in the clothes Fontana created in collaboration with Bruna Bini and the Fontana sisters – is to question the brushstroke-boundary, the plane joining and separating above and below, fabric and skin, clothing and nudity. Here the cut takes place in the fabric – black, yellow and silver – like his canvases, and reveals the material and fleshly inflow. The stroke of the blade or awl on the cloth is a dialectic between space and energy: the cut as spatial concept.

The garment, however, does not belong to a single series of objects, but rather participates in the universal display of things. More than a frontier between first and second skins, clothing can be seen as an interval or area of contact between body and surrounding space, place or tertiary system of difference and similarity to the social and cultural, architectural and visual, natural and visible environments.

Art never ceases to echo its context, to respond to it from a distance. It is as though it were forever seeking a complicity in order to produce a text that might reveal its hidden cause. Every art object, including articles of clothing, is the hidden meeting-point of artist and context. In 1952 in Paris, Ellsworth Kelly established a relation-ship of pure otherness between body and city. He freed clothing from all subjectivist demands and inscribed it in the universe of pure and primary elements. He transformed it into a structure that denies the different partitions of the body and turns it into a sequence of surfaces and colors, a repertoire of two- and three-dimensional geometry. Clothing became an occupation of space, a visual schema intervening in the chaos of the environment.

This perception of the garment in space became the concern, from a variety of perspectives, of the artists interested in pure visibility and those concerned with mass communications. Both groups are conscious of the occasional flux of life and events, but the former think it is possible to control and systematize them, while the latter seek to accept and integrate them. The strategy of the "before" interests such artists as Getulio Alviani and Paolo Scheggi, Max Bill and Gabriele De Vecchi, who attempt, in the area of body ornamentation ranging from garments to jewelry, to move about in the interstices between images or, so to speak, between the constituent models of the image, to subject the image to physical-mathematical effects. The investigation of the "after" is the concern of Pop and Neo-Dada artists such as Andy Warhol, Robert Rauschenberg, Arman, Daniel Spoerri, Yayoi Kusama and Christo, who seek an encounter between art and the mass-cultural context, that of consumer objects and advertisement. Both groups aspire to render manifest the meaning of the city as the preiconic matrix and iconic residue of a vision that encompasses design and use. Clothing is transformed into a magnetic surface that, like a three-dimensional camera, attracts things and signals, trademarks and objects, illustrations and quotations drawn from the everyday iconography of advertisement and television, comic books and movies. The garment becomes a secular shroud of mass idolatry, reducing the idol to an opaque, neutral outline to be worn ironically.

The imaginary map of places includes not only artificial nature, but natural nature as well, which knows no rules or procedures, but is full of free energies assigned principally to its physical and material components. Between 1966 and 1980, the pregnancy of natural materials – from the human organism to deserts to composites of flesh and bark, snow and wind, water and sand – emerges as the residual element of an environment yet to be discovered. With the advent of Land Art, Body Art, and Arte Povera, the attribution passed from the object to the factual significance of real things, as natural, vegetal and animal entities. These art forms are ways of intensifying the environment and are a far cry from any sort of objective, iconic, optical or popular apologia. They set themselves up as free, almost intuitive artistic processes in harmony with the focal nuclei of life. They are a kind of hymn to the banal, primary elements (air, earth, fire, water) and to the physical and mental fragment that works by minimal incidences and models of displacement. Now the cut of the scissors opens a fissure or hole in the earth's crust, delimiting a natural space. The garment becomes camouflaged in the environment and transformed into a burst of energy linked to the vitality of a tree or a fish, a squash or an epidermal excrescence, in the work of such artists as Piero Gilardi, Alighiero Boetti, Louise Bourgeois, Vito Acconci, Richard Tuttle, Franz Erhard Walther and James Lee Byars. In other instances the garment takes on a shamanistic character, serving to exorcize the presence of the social, represented by the chaos of politics and the invasiveness of the media, reducing it to a state of perfect organization. With Joseph Beuys and Nam June Paik, clothing is transmuted into a wizard's or barker's tool, subtended by a ritualism that aspires to embalm the forces of society and the reign of mass communication.

By the eighties, clothing's belonging to the realm of art is no longer a revelation, but a necessity, given that since 1950 fashion has become a global project for democratizing and aestheticizing appearance and self-presentation. What was once considered useless and frivolous, decorous and eccentric, has become the means to a search for identity, where what matters most are originality and constant change. The difference between art and fashion is tending to disappear, as if the cut that has defined the shape of both has actually succeeded, through a sequential process of collage, in superimposing and uniting the two. With Judith Shea, Rosemarie Trockel, Jana Sterbak and Jan Fabre, clothing has become a disturbing device – at once automaton and mannequin, statue and machine, dream and nightmare, delirious simulation and paranoid-critical scenery – while with Charles LeDray, Oliver Herring, Wiebke Siem and Beverly Semmes, it is transformed into the vector of an impulse to fantasy and marvel that revives the dream-logic of the garment as game and pleasure, life and spectacle, mask and disguise.

The magical instance of the cut that makes the garment has thus passed through all the various thresholds of artistic creativity. The time has now come for fashion to decipher its latent forces and desires and recognize itself as a free and original discipline, knowing full well that art will never lose sight of it, but only continue to respond with cuts and critiques.

NOTE

Source: *Art/Fashion* (Skira Editore, 1997), 21–26.

CHAPTER EIGHTEEN

Illuminations – Warhol in the 1950s

Richard Martin

By 1949, when Andy Warhol arrived in New York, the age of fashion illustration was over. Erwin Blumenfeld, Richard Avedon, and Irving Penn had their cameras clicking, and a new, arguably more authentic and arguably more intense, fashion imagery was dominant. A Blumenfeld face – even if abstracted to the elements and plane of an illustrator's abbreviation – on the cover of *Vogue*'s epochal January 1950 "Mid-Century" issue, and the Irving Penn covers that followed, plainly signaled that the era of the illustrators had ended. Even *Glamour*, the Condé Nast publication "for the girl with a job," in the parataxis of its cover, was primarily a magazine of the photograph, even when Warhol published his first work there in September 1949. On commission from its art editor, Tina S. Fredericks, Warhol contributed illustrations that are anomalous in an issue dominated by vivid color and black-and-white photographs. An eight-page insert, not on the smooth stock of the magazine but on a book paper, is dedicated to "What Is Success?" as analyzed and characterized by several writers. "Success," avowed Katherine Sonntag, "is a job in New York," whereas Marya Mannes argued that "success is the men who love you." In many ways, Warhol chose the former.

Ironically, many who have documented this first publication have noted the autobiographical forecast of "Success is a job in New York" without acknowledging the other option. Moreover, the diminutive figures on the ladders of success with which Warhol illustrated the article are little different from such juvenilia as his nose-picking portrait, even if outfitted with such swank accessories as a cigarette holder, seldom evidence of real style but only of haughty pseudo-style. In fact, Warhol's success in delineating and adumbrating fifties style was owed to his lack of sophistication, his rube-like willingness to accept the quasi-elegant as if it were the real thing. In this,

Hollywood met the Hudson: Warhol was a blissful follower and fabricator of the pseudo-elegant, an artist who could cover a fashion visage with jejune flowers and call it art, think it divine, and let us imagine whatever we might. Like Fran Dodsworth, the fame-seeking, frivolous wife in Sinclair Lewis's novel *Dodsworth*, Warhol was infatuated with style – fashion's or Hollywood's or camp's – however false that style might have been, and was even encouraged if the style seized on was a sham.

But Warhol's launch in New York, however astonishingly successful – for significant career as a commercial artist followed – was a venture in anomaly and reaction to mainstream fashion sensibilities, much as his art would later defy long-held contentions of modernism. The diffident but defiant artist of the sixties had long been foreshadowed by the illustrator of the fifties, who was promoting extravagance and precious sensibility in an era of fleeting, hard-glam modern fashion imagery. The *nostalgie de la soupe* of the later art is wholly anticipated in Warhol's pining memories of fashion illustration.

The first illustration of the *Glamour* insert, five shoes situated on rungs of ladders begins the ladder-of-success motif. Shoes had remained a specialty of the illustrator in many fashion magazines of the era since they were accessories and their analytical representation could assume the illustrator's license of scale even if juxtaposed with photographs whose scale is presumably authentic. Warhol's rust-colored images of pumps, here quite pedestrian, would later prance into fantasy. Through all the insert's illustrations, sweet sentiment prevails: Warhol coils the long cord of one of his recurrent telephones, affords a home-and-office image of typewriter in one hand and mop in another, and represents love proffered in a bouquet and manifest in drifting heart shapes. With the exception of the initial page devoted to the pumps, the illustrations appear chiefly at the margins, in the manner of medieval manuscript illuminations, as petty, if pretty, pictures.

The great tradition that Warhol knew and was, in a sense, condensing in the fifties was that of Erté and Vertès, earlier fashion artists whose sinuous lines and blots of color were not restricted to marginalia but commanded pages. Warhol's fashion ambition was akin to theirs. He did not aspire to make the diagrammatic little fashion drawings that accompanied patterns or co-ed and teen fashions; nor did he wish to be confined in the remaining sanctuaries of illustration in beauty and lingerie advertising and editorials – the photograph's absolutism being yet taboo in these intimate and idealized areas. Moreover, Warhol's great gift as a commercial artist was for inventory and evocation, not for direct representation of the product. Thus, in *Great Perfumes of France* (1959) for *Harper's Bazaar*, he uses the format of the flacon ten times, a model for his later repetitions without depletion of interest. Warhol sets each fragrance bottle up in taxonomy, as if counting off identical items in the manner of counting bottles, but also provides each its own interest, the actual shapes of the bottle being the visual distinction amid similarity. Illustration, in this waning moment, was being retained in the margins, literally and figuratively, for its facility in rendering easy-to-recognize details and accessories. Yet Warhol was ultimately not merely the delineator but the dreamer, the indefatigable, often reactionary optimist of fashion and glamour, however decadent, transparent, or passé.

His gloss of fantasy is most evident in a series of illustrations seen in Roger Rabbit tandem with Richard Avedon photographs in *Mademoiselle* (April 1955). The gamine Leslie Caron, on a movie poster, is transformed into the dreamer – with appropriate stars – of a Cinderella story. Inert fashion photographs said to be "inspired by M.G.M.'s *The Glass Slipper*," are plied into the narrative of *Cinderella* by Warhol's deft drawings. The impression of naiveté he often created is particularly effective in this suite of advertisements, linking otherwise unconnected, inchoate styles by the slender thread of a movie. Perhaps most beguiling is Warhol's use of text in the final image of the series, where it is played around descriptions of the dresses and garments on page 46. Here Warhol assumes the style of the artist-tyke: aptly illustrating a child's tale and narrating it with puerile script, including the handwritten footnote "also available in misses sizes," added in direct juxtaposition with the printed text. Warhol marshals his images, adding stars at the beginning and end, to convey enchantment to garments probably assembled under sweat-shop conditions. Without Warhol's effort to amuse and entertain, the tie-in of apparel and movie would be, at best, tendentious. Warhol imparts his mischief and magic as an illustrator to pre-existing images; he succeeds by dint of his indomitable faith in innocent illustration and in its ability to evoke a response from us, even as applied to a $70 ball gown.

Warhol's fashion vision is glamorizing and transformative, destined to take the "pretty maiden" in an "under $20" junior dress into an empyrean of fancy and imagination. What Warhol gives, he also takes. That is, he also seized from fashion its wonder of artifice and imagination. Later, the inspired *Vogue* editor Diana Vreeland would dub the category "allure," and Warhol himself would seek out Victor Hugo, Halston, Yves Saint-Laurent, Tina Chow, and Giorgio di Sant' Angelo for that aura of fashion essence in relation to which he had become both vampire and blood bank.

Warhol's role in fashion was, after all, his favored role in life: *flâneur* and observer, not maker. For other commissions in the fifties, Warhol used the narrative terseness and suggestion found in his fashion work. But distinctive to fashion was his vision of vignettes and taxonomies built on the principles of observations and visual delight. Much later, his *Who's Who in Holiday Hats* for *McCall's* demonstrated his ability to construct character out of fashion objects. Each hat becomes a distinct individual or type, Mary Poppins unmistakable for d'Artagnan, the chef's toque distinct from the tin soldier's braided cap. Characteristically, Warhol mingles memory and the contemporary: the sweet memory of hats in a millinery era that, by 1958, was beginning to cede its authority and ubiquity to new hairstyles and a casual, unaccessorized wardrobe, together with a contemporary reference to Marshal Dillon of television's "Gunsmoke" series. Multiplicity, in its repetitions and differences is especially rewarding in its fashion view.

After all, Warhol's fifties fashion subjects were not the couture of Dior or Balenciaga, the most demanding and the most significant fashion of the period. On the contrary, Warhol loved in fashion what was better than the ordinary, not supreme fashion art. A mock-up, a flacon, a touch of glamour would do. In *The Fifties*, David Halberstam recounts a very telling fashion story from 1958. The First Lady, Mamie Eisenhower, was told by Mollie Parnis, one of her preferred designers in New York, that Mrs. Richard Nixon had called to inquire about having clothing made for a state trip to Latin America. Mrs. Eisenhower replied, "No, no, dear, don't do that. Let the poor thing go to Garfinkel's and buy something off the rack." Parnis created stylish, but essentially middle-class to upper-middle-class clothing. These were not, in the vernacular, "Paris originals" but homegrown American in style. But even as Mrs. Eisenhower displayed her scorn for Mrs. Nixon, she recognized the hierarchy in fashion. Even a Mollie Parnis dress was a dream to some. Today, when Giorgio Armani, Donna Karan, and Ralph Lauren are household names, it is hard to recall the out-of-reach elitism of fifties' fashion. The sensible American woman did not realistically aspire to the Evins shoes Warhol conjured. They were icons beyond the average consumer's grasp. Warhol conspired to concoct the extravagant in fashion objects; his parvenu ignorance of good taste inspired him to a tantalizing vulgarity comprising both exuberance and theatricality.

Essential to Warhol's style in the fifties is a now hard to recreate, even harder to remember, sense of awe and amazement about objects better than the ordinary. Thus, the "holiday hats" of *McCall's* are little more than caricatures, but they are metaphors of the magical and the charismatic, rendered schematic and simple, but still Yahweh-like approximations, substitutes for the unspeakable name of glamour and fashion.

What is *High-Heeled Shoe* (1950s) but a Platonic shoe compounded of any and all fetishes and icons of foot and shoe, configured to a starlet's dainty shoe, Mrs. Lydig's unique shoes, and Cinderella's fictitious shoe? In the fifties, when the global distribution of luxury products was still a trickle compared with the flood of luxuries in the eighties and nineties, which has resulted in a far more cavalier attitude toward previously privileged styles, Warhol could still render the shoe as archetypal luxury. In his shoe personifications, he presented not only the radiant shoe but a luminary's biography as well, making icon and celebrity coalesce. His *Eight Shoes* (1950s) is more than the view of the bottom of a closet. Significantly, they are so archetypal as not to be pairs but individual shoes. Each is willfully different, from the insistently high lace-up to the variously decorated insouciant pumps. *This Is the Well-Heeled Look of Fashion* (1955), for his client I. Miller, sets heels of Byzantine splendor and monumentality as fan shapes seen consistently from center back. This architectonic series, unusual for Warhol, is consistent with his side and interior views of shoes, in seeing them as sculpture, but here with an element of abstraction. Thus, the garment as artifact played a role for Warhol. The artist who would later codify the most ordinary objects as icons of American art had long before discovered the iconic presence of fashion objects.

Warhol as fashion illustrator must be distinguished from others in the field. René Gruau (b. 1910), for example, a primary image-maker for Dior, allows partial representation to arise suggestively from the plane of the paper. Gruau created many familiar images indivisible from the Dior identity. For the fragrance Miss Dior, Gruau captured the ineffable, animalizing character of scent in a 1948 image of a woman's elegant hand placed languorously and seductively on a leopard's paw, a sure sign of beauty and the beast in concupiscent combination. Gruau's 1949 illustration for Miss Dior is also synecdochic: a more civilized gloved hand holding an open fan – another flirtation, but this time with mystery rather than with an identifiable animal. Gruau's sanctioned images for Miss Dior are the quintessence of fashion illustration, metaphor and message extracted from fashion, even when as intangible as a fragrance. Warhol's *Leg's in Red High Heels* (1950s) perhaps comes closest to Gruau's sensibility, suggesting an ideal trough a body implied by a part that is both anonymous and exemplary. Isolation of a part promotes the probity of line, allowing the drawing an enhanced aestheticism surpassing physical description.

Gruau's commercial and cordial imagery for Dior is in opposition to Warhol's tongue-in-cheek *Miss Dior* (1955), a drawing related to a Bonwit Teller window display. Here, the artist's campy, sardonic wit is his agency of abbreviation and identification, but it is clearly very far from Gruau's ingratiating corporate image. Warhol is scarcely disarming and certainly not disingenuous, but he is profoundly different. Warhol's *Miss Dior* is not a corporate signifier but an escutcheon with interior logos and stars, *encadrement* with tape measure, a top note of fundamental Warhol shoe, and pendant mermaid-maidens. With the fleur-de-lis and French flags, Miss Dior is proclaimed. And it is no accident that after 20 inches or so, a section of the tape measure disappears from the image, only to return to the count at the very end with "68" and "69," the last surely a gibe on a sexual configuration, though both "68" and "69" must be read upside down and backward. One doubts that Gruau would have slipped into a Dior image even the smallest hint of sexuality. As the art historian Donna de Salvo has shrewdly pointed out, Warhol's *Carnet de Bal by Revillon* (1959) incorporates into the window installation an amusing reference to Matisse's *Dance*, a few blocks away in the Museum of Modern Art as well as a wish list of dance partners. The careless fifties viewer unaware of hidden persuasion in advertising might let these campy personal references pass unnoticed, yet the cognoscenti (a very fifties usage) might roar with laughter and smug approval.

Moreover, the whole Warhol image conspires to "out" Dior, as we might say in the nineties. The profile of Dior himself, rendered in a most serious Hockneyesque semi-Egyptian style, is now emblazoned Miss Dior, less the fifties fashion "dictator" than art's Rrose Sélavy. Few would have openly discussed Dior's effeminate homosexuality in the fifties; Warhol portrays it.

Fashion was, as many have noted, a relatively safe world for homosexual men in the fifties, even as McCarthyism and homophobia raged elsewhere and even in comparison with the world of the fine arts in New York. Warhol's own sense of security may have allowed him to "out" Christian Dior; his sense of insecurity may have made him want to claim allies, especially in a form that, overt as it is, may have been too oblique for most in the fifties. Some spectators, enthralled by the pageantry and power of Dior, could merely have seen in Warhol's deception the mind of the creator, a flattering most Warholian combination of dress form, scissors, pins, sewing machine, and needle and thread, along with the Eiffel Tower, defining fashion as his métier and mental process. A banner made by a queen for a queen might have been little noticed as such and instead deferred to as a fashion/fragrance likeness.

Where else in the fifties could have existed the fey, gold-leafed fetish objects Warhol made, suggestive for Cornellian keepsakes while partaking of the racket in celebrity relics? In fact, their transition in the later fifties into boy drawings demonstrates the close connection that Warhols made among his arenas of alert and blissful, eyes-closed survey; fashion, Hollywood, and homosexual imagination and desire. As the art historian Trevor Fairbrother has proved, gay visual culture of the fifties fed into Warhol's highly successful commercial work and ultimately fed off it. These harbingers of commonplace icons are fashion souvenirs that offer value-added associations and the possibility of infinitely reflecting on the ordinary. Warhol's Midas used in the fifties are about a luxury associated with the gold of traditional manuscript illumination, but also the luxury gold used in 1950s printing. As the design critics Ellen Lupton and Abbott Miller have rightly pointed out, Warhol the technician was keenly aware of the processes of reproduction; he is the paladin artist for the Age of Mechanical Reproduction.

The gold drawings demonstrate the style ideals of Warhol's fifties work. Warhol was indubitably familiar with Charles Demuth's *I Saw the Figure 5 in Gold* (1928) in the Metropolitan Museum of Art. While Demuth's gold is not gold leaf and is only referential, the painting's title and visual allusion to the poet William Carlos Williams are akin to Warhol's portraits through shoes. Moreover, Demuth was a gay artist whose semiexplicit and explicit images were well known in reproductions and legend in the New York gay world of the fifties; Warhol saw size 5 in gold, again and again.

A gold shoe, *David Evins* (c. 1956), celebrates the shoe's designer. The designer of expensive shoes was renowned in New York (he and his wife were significant social figures of the time), but his work would probably have been unfamiliar to anyone not acquainted with New York society or expensive footwear. On the other hand (or leg), cognate drawing from about 1956 named after Za Za Gabor (*sic*) and Kate Smith hallow women of national recognition through television and media. His *Christine Jorgensen* (1956), depicting a pair of shoes seen from above, celebrates an early transsexual. Interestingly, Warhol's first great cultural encounters were with Hollywood and fashion; from there, and only after practice in rendering and exalting those cultures, did he attempt consumer popular culture. If Demuth had been able to express a gay man's allowable affection for a poet in *I Saw the Figure 5 in Gold*, then surely Warhol could express his admiration for a gaudy Memphis singer in *elvis Presely* (sic) (c. 1956).

Warhol effectively made a transition, beginning in 1955, from his commercial work for I. Miller to a personally resonant body of work, one that reflected his idiosyncratic sense of desire in objects and in fashion and media celebrities. The gold drawing of the mid-fifties move from fashion to bibelots and boys. The male *Fashion Figure* (c. 1955) is expressed in prosaic, reproduction-oriented ink and tempera, and with a commercial indifference. By 1957 gold takes the place of tempera, and Cocteauesque sensuality begins to supplant the impassivity of the earlier work. But these gold drawings in seriatim, ostensibly superficial artifacts touching on an ostensibly superficial world, are, of course, the matrix of Warhol's thinking. In the fifties, their whimsy and literary references, especially *A la Recherche du Shoe Perdu* (1955), haunted the obvious objects, implying literary affiliations. In *To all my Friends* (c. 1956), the shoes refer not only to the illustrious but also to personal friends.

And there always was deeper, more penetrating vision, even if that, too, was diagrammatic. One leitmotif of Warhol's work of the fifties was the X-ray-like phrenology evident in *Miss Dior*, but also seen in such works as *Female Head*. Where did Warhol get this idea of the divided and dissected brain? Advertising and the modest graphics of movie magazines (*Photoplay* and the other forties' and fifties' 'zines that Warhol adored and collected) often represented the mind in such a pattern of "ideas" visible within the head. Likewise, an untitled (1950s) all-Warhol exquisite corpse of a business card, sweetly combined with a corset, sets virtuoso "ideas" into a tattoo of clients and possibilities on the woman's body.

Furthermore, the discipline of commercial art fostered Warhol's ability to capture identity in adumbrated forms and linear brevity in a manner carried into his personal drawings of the fifties and thereafter into other work. His *James Dean* (c. 1955) renders the Cocteauesque diagram of the head lying as if asleep, conveying both desire for the handsome star and the fact of his death. In simple gestures, the signs of love and death are given: the overturned death car smashed into a wall (anticipating the *Disasters*); a memorializing tree sprouting heart-shaped leaves; and the line of Dean's sternum into neck referring both to anatomy and a cross. The fashion work of the fifties had valued the truistic: hearts, stars, and flowers that conveyed emotion. Thus, in *Madame Rubinstein* (1957), a pen-and-ink portrait is given grace and sentiment by the flower that serves doubly to suggest a feminine favor and the scented, elegant world of beauty and makeup.

In the sixties, Warhol was drawn to new endeavors. Art history, history, and our fascination have already guaranteed that the new vocation was a success and more than just a job. Nonetheless, fashion and his commercial roots in the fifties would inhabit the Warhol enterprise for the remainder of the artist's life. A follow-the-dot fifties advertisement, *Andrew Geller Shoe*, would inspire later work. The iconic potency of objects that Warhol discovered in fashion artifacts would send him from specialty stores to supermarkets, from New York culture to popular culture. The later success was predicated on commercial imagery. Warhol's life was, as it were, a ladder, rungs of which could all bear names from the fifties: commercial graphics, an assimilated Hollywoodism, fashion, beauty indeed or in sham, the beauty industry, and a coy, safe, gay professional culture.

NOTE

Source: Mark Francis and Margery King (eds) *The Warhol Look* (Hachette Book Group, 1997), 70–77.

CHAPTER NINETEEN

The Golden Dustman: A Critical Evaluation of the Work of Martin Margiela and a Review of *Martin Margiela: Exhibition (9/4/1615)*

CAROLINE EVANS

For this exhibition the fashion designer Martin Margiela worked in collaboration with a microbiologist on a show that was tailored to the museum space. Fashion, art and science came together in a strikingly poetic installation, one that transcended the expository and sometimes pedestrian way that fashion can be displayed in museums. The show was an important retrospective of his work so far, as well as an inspiration in itself. This seems a good moment to reflect, not only on the exhibition, but also on some other elements of Margiela's work in a more extended piece of writing than a review usually permits. I would like to take this opportunity to speculate specifically on Margiela's use and transformation of second-hand clothing in the field of high fashion, and to think in general about the transformations and reversals he effects with this material.

1

Margiela's eighteen earlier collections have featured a distinctive use of materials, deconstructions and reproductions. His predilection is for the abject – as epitomized by the second-hand or recycled – the cut-up and the one-off. Two forties dresses are cut up and spliced together to form one asymmetrical dress. A 1950s ball gown is cut down the front and worn open as a long waistcoat. The lining of a 1950s cocktail dress is exactly reproduced as a contemporary dress; the original lining of the same dress is photographed inside out and then screen printed on to a new dress. The tailor's dummy is recreated in linen canvas as a waistcoat, so that foundation becomes outerwear, the body becomes the dress. Over it Margiela shows a "study" for the half front of a draped dress in silk chiffon – chiffon that would normally be pinned to the Stockman dummy. Although he makes the chiffon study wearable with elastic bands and corset bones, it nevertheless gestures to a garment that remains forever unfinished, like a deconstructed work in progress. Elsewhere dolls' clothes are meticulously scaled up to human dimensions, so that jeans have surreally large zippers, cardigans huge stitches and unwieldy poppers to fasten them. Military socks are partially unpicked and stitched together again as jumpers, the heels used at the breast and elbows to ensure a snug fit.

The questioning spirit behind these designs is equally evident in Margiela's fashion shows. He has explored the alternatives to the glitz of a Paris catwalk in a series of shows that approximate more to fine art installations and performances. They have been held in derelict urban spaces such as car parks, warehouses and wasteland; in them models move anonymously through the crowds. Two shows take place simultaneously, one black-clad, one white. Or, rather than a show, seven women of different ages are filmed in black and white Super 8 wearing the clothes in the course of their daily lives. Or, nine presentations take place simultaneously, in six different cities. The Rotterdam exhibition was Margiela's first solo museum show; but all his fashion shows have been unconventional and have had more in common with contemporary fine art practice. His work, at the heart of the supposedly conventional *business* of Paris fashion, is in fact much more experimental and "cutting edge" than that of many contemporary artists who use fashion motifs in their work. Margiela, like Rei Kawakubo of Comme des Garçons, seems able to work experimentally and to succeed commercially at the same time.

For this exhibition, held in a museum of art and design, Margiela chose to recreate from each of the eighteen collections one design in white, which was then saturated with agar, a growing medium, and sprayed with either green mold, pink yeast, or fuchsia or yellow bacteria. After this the eighteen garments were "hothoused" in specially constructed timber and polythene greenhouses to enable the molds and bacteria to grow. Afterwards the temporary greenhouses remained in the garden of the museum like discarded husks, their polythene doors flapping in the wind. The "9" of the exhibition title refers to the nine years over which Margiela has presented eighteen collections; the "4" to the four days it takes the bacteria to grow; and the "1615" to the total hours the exhibition would be on view.

The experiment, and the show, are precisely detailed in the exhibition catalog, which is both an exemplary bit of cataloging (unusually informative and detailed for a contemporary installation, let alone for a fashion exhibition) and a very desirable object, reproducing as it does much of Margiela's aesthetic in its white, clothbound cover, its spectral typeface, which mimics the lost definition of over-photocopied texts, its fashion photomontages, its spindly line drawings, its empty pages for readers' notes and spare color photographs of molds and bacteria. What the catalog cannot show, however, is the boldness of the installation, which was tremendously elegant both in concept and in execution. The exhibition space itself, a modernist glass and steel pavilion of 1991 by Hubert-Jan Henket, was left entirely empty; the eighteen mannequins were ranged along the external glass wall like melancholy ghosts, their textiles given new life, fluttering in the breeze, paradoxically revivified by the deathly process of mold and decay. This *coup de théâtre*, the empty space from which we peered out at the models who in turn faced us, was the first of many reversals in a show that was full of complexity, visually breathtaking and intellectually rich.

The clothes were displayed on standard Stockman's dummies with legs but no heads or feet. The clothes were simply put on them and next to the base of many of them a pair of Margiela's trademark "Tabi" ankle boots, painted white, were arranged, slightly to one side of the figure. No effort had been made to simulate a human being, yet the mannequins evoked a ghostly presence: benign sentinels in their tattered, second-hand clothes, they brought the past into the present, just as the museum brings the outside into the interior, the rippling water outside reflecting moving patterns on to the ceiling. The green of the gardens is a counterpoint to the inorganic interior: beyond the windows the trees waved in the breeze, and before us the mannequins' garments drifted gently in synch.

The lyricism of the display worked particularly well in the context of Dutch modernism, and of the particularly high standards of design in architecture and graphics that prevail in Dutch cities. This beautiful museum space of pale grey and silver, glass and metal, was delicate enough to let these mute figures speak. Clad in tones of washed-out cream and buff, their bright fuchsia bacteria and green molds (which gestured to the colors of the park land beyond) had been bleached by exposure to sun and wind. We saw glimpses of darker mold in the fissures and recesses under reveres and jacket hems, in the crevasses of cuffs and the drift of a skirt. When first exhibited the garments were still wet and the molds very much fluffier; over two months time weathered them, flattening texture and color to leave a mottled tracery on the surface of the cloth by early August.

Margiela's deconstructions tend to make his clothes look completely modern. In this installation, however, there were curious and unexpected historical resonances. Many of the styles were surprisingly Napoleonic, adding to the ghostly impression of a troop of people from a previous age: a pea jacket, thigh boots, Empire line dresses, the deconstructed evening dress commuted into a gently rotting sash. A more Victorian connotation was evoked in the fifties ball dress, worn over a man's singlet and denim jeans painted white. Tattered, moldy, blowing gently in the breeze, there were shades here of Miss Haversham, given a new and unexpected lease of life.

The Tabi boots looked surprisingly goatish, cloven hooves imported from a different symbolic system.

Many of the garments looked like old clothes disinterred from a rusty trunk, hung up to air, spotted with mildew and mold, with their encrusted canvas or matted fur. Little drifts of furry mold like soft clouds had accumulated on jumpers; spots of bacteria traced patterns on ancient jackets. The textile artists Christopher Leitch and Stephanie Sabato have cultivated molds as a form of fabric printing, even making up the cloth into simple garments, and Reiko Sudo has used rust to similar ends (Schoeser 1995). Margiela, however, rather than using cloth as a blank canvas upon which to grow his moldy traces, used mold and bacteria as a final process, layering them upon garments that were already saturated with complex historical meanings. The two forties tea gowns, taken apart and stitched together as one dress, reappeared here, their already dissonant patterns of rose prints juxtaposed with gauze and net overlaid by a pattern of yellow bacteria, a false patina of age grown in a few days on fifty-year-old dresses. One could make a connection here with the work of the contemporary British computer artist William Latham, who "grows" organic forms on the computer, using the dynamics of natural systems. Latham's work also interferes with the processes of time and nature as he uses a simulation of evolution to create synthetic life. He refers to the artistic process of creation on the computer as being

> like gardening . . . I select, breed, and marry. There are no morals in my evolutionary computer world. I "kill," "mutate," "use incest" and "slaughter" families of sculptures; in fact the more subversive the techniques, the more interesting the sculptural forms. . . . I think the analogy of a gardener trying to breed the perfect rose for a flower show is close to what I am doing. But I am the creator as well. I can go behind the scenes and change the underlying rules of this synthetic nature and then back out as the gardener. What is fundamental to my work is that the evolutionary system is based on my imaginative ideas (Morgan 1993: 88 and 91).

Likewise, Margiela changes the rules of time, 'grows' something old overnight (the molds), makes something new and modern (the deconstructed dress) out of old things, and then layers one on top of the other. Similarly, the cream jumper reconstructed as a high fashion item from old army socks reappeared in this exhibition, now mottled brown and spotted with greyish drifts of furry mold.

2

Many of Margiela's "raw materials" are fashion detritus when he starts with them: second-hand or army surplus clothing is the commodity form with the lowest exchange value in the fashion system. Second-hand clothing has historically been associated with low economic status and class; the second-hand clothes trade clothed the poor long before there was a ready-to-wear industry. At least from the eighteenth century onwards it dealt in "need and aspiration" (Ginsburg 1980: 101). As the nineteenth century progressed, and despite a thriving trade in second-, third- and even fourth-hand clothing, "secondhand clothes became in working class myth-ology . . . a symbol of poverty and lower class oppression and patronage" (ibid.: 128). Most humiliatingly, they were a type of charity to be endured as enforced "gifts" from an employer to a servant, often with the trimmings stripped off to render the clothes more suitable to the humbler station of their new owner (ibid.: 129).

Margiela, in another of his reversals, gives new life to second-hand clothing and simultaneously repositions it at the top of a hierarchy of prestige. He converts it into something that has the highest status, not just in the art world, where cultural capital is all, but equally in the fashion world, where economic capital is not insignificant. Walter Benjamin discusses the low social and economic status of the nineteenth-century Parisian rag-picker, a product of the Industrial Revolution, who figures in Baudelaire's poem *Le Vin des Chiffoniers* ("The Ragpickers' Wine"):

> When the new industrial processes had given refuse a certain value, ragpickers appeared in the cities in larger numbers. They worked for middlemen and constituted a sort of cottage industry located in the streets. The rag-picker fascinated his epoch. The eyes of the first investigators of pauperism were fixed on him with the mute question as to where the limits of human misery lay (Benjamin 1997: 19).

The rag-picker, like the prostitute, existed at the margins of society, "human rubbish thrown up by the struggle for existence conducted on principles of economic *laissez faire*" (Quennell 1964: 18). In Britain, too "the lowest and weakest of the citizens" of the newly industrialized city were the "scavengers, rag-pickers and pedlars" who inhabited the slums and rookeries of central London (ibid.). Benjamin goes on to comment on the analogy that Baudelaire made between the rag-picker and the poet – for which latter term we could as well substitute "artist" or, I would argue in this context, "fashion designer." Not, of course, that Margiela's status as a fashion designer is low: on the contrary. But his interest in scavenging and revitalizing moribund material is not dissimilar to that of Baudelaire's poet/rag-picker:

> Here we have a man who has to gather the day's refuse in the capital city [for Margiela, twentieth-century Paris, a fashion capital]. Everything that the big city threw away, everything it lost, everything it despised, everything it crushed under foot, he catalogues and collects. He collates the annals of intemperance, the *capharnaum* (stockpile) of waste. He sorts things out and makes a wise choice; he collects, like a miser guarding a treasure, the refuse which will assume the shape of useful or gratifying objects between the jaws of the Goddess of Industry" (Charles Baudelaire, quoted in Benjamin 1997: 79).

Margiela converts the low status of second-hand clothing into the high status of a one-off fashion piece for the jaws of the Goddess of Fashion, the "Goddess of appearances," as Mallarmé called her (Flügel 1930: 137). And when he makes

T-shirts out of plastic carrier bags and waistcoats of broken crockery he converts urban waste and detritus into something of rare value (some such items have just been acquired by the Museum Boijmans Van Beuningen in Rotterdam as part of their permanent collection). Charles Dickens' *Our Mutual Friend* (1985), first published in 1865, starts with the inheritance of a dust heap and tells the tale of its inheritor, Boffin, the Golden Dustman. The dust heaps that towered over suburban London in the nineteenth century were a lucrative business, often employing a considerable number of people. Almost every kind of material, however abject, had a value in the nineteenth century. Margiela's re-use of contemporary "rubbish" such as broken shards and plastic carrier bags marks him out as a kind of "Golden Dustman" of the fashion world, converting base material into gold. The transformation of dust to gold is not just fanciful but has historical antecedents. Henry Dodd, a nineteenth-century owner of a great dust-yard in Islington, London, known to Dickens and a possible prototype for Boffin, the Golden Dustman, is said to have given his daughter a wedding gift of a single dust-heap, which afterwards fetched £10,000 (see Stephen Gill's note 3 in Dickens 1985: 898).

Like Boffin's, Margiela's creative transformation of such "abject" materials as old clothes, plastic bags and broken crockery is also an economic transformation. Although he uses the techniques of the avant garde his practice, like that of the Golden Dustman, is rooted firmly in commerce: the buying and selling of clothes. In Margiela's case it is Paris fashion, the status of which, even in the nineteenth century, was as exalted as that of the rag-picker was debased. Yet both ends of the fashion spectrum are, and were, ruled alike by what Baudelaire calls "the Goddess of Industry."

One could take the analogy between the rag-picker and the artist further in an analysis of the locations of Margiela's previous fashion shows. An interest (such as his) in derelict urban spaces has specific historical associations with the rag-picker/poet of nineteenth-century Paris. Hal Foster has argued that the rag-picker figures in texts and images concerning urban *dérives*[1] and derelict spaces (Foster 1993: 134). The spaces in which Margiela has shown include:

- the *Café de la Guerre*, an old theatre with wooden benches (October 1988)
- an area of wasteland in Paris's 20th *arrondissement* (October 1989)
- a warehouse corridor (March 1990)
- a vast, empty covered car-park near Barbès in the north of Paris (October 1990)
- the metro station *Saint Martin*, out of use since 1939 (October 1991)
- the sales depot of the Salvation Army (March 1992)
- simultaneous shows in a disused hospital in Montmârtre and an old house in Pigalle (October 1992)
- an empty supermarket (October 1993)

- a former Paris Metro company workshop for electric motors, and also Margiela's current showroom (March/September 1994)
- the auditorium of the Théâtre de la Potinière, Paris (October 1994)
- a red circus tent in the Bois de Boulogne (March 1995)
- la Maison de Mutualité on the Left Bank (October 1995)
- an old dance hall in the 17th *arrondissement* (March 1996)
- three sequential shows at, respectively, La Java, at Belleville, an abandoned covered market; Le Gibus, at République, the glass-covered loading bay of a vast building; and Le Ménagerie de Verre at Parmentier, a 1930s dance school (March 1997).

At the 1992 collection held in the sales depot of the Salvation Army the invited public sat on the furniture amid racks of used clothing. The venue is not dissimilar to Mayhew's description from 1851 of the Old Clothes Exchange in London, a space 100 feet by 70 "to which the collectors of the cast-off apparel of the metropolis bring their goods for sale" (Quennell 1964: 209). The Victorian space was full of old clothes: "cloth, corduroy, woollen cords, fustian, moleskin, flannel, velveteen, plaids . . . coats, great-coats, jackets, trousers, and breeches" (ibid.: 211). Compare this to Margiela's collection as it is described in the catalog to this exhibition:

> Everything is either black or in dark tones. T-shirts are fitted, skirts are flared, made from pantyhose and worn over creased knitwear. 1970s leather overcoats are reversed and worn as tunics or long dresses with a high neckline, they are crossed over at the back. Transparent plastic protective covers for clothing are molded to shape on a tailor's dummy with 'scotch tape' and worn as dresses. There is also a "priest" soutane worn as an overcoat as well as oversized washed crêpe and satin dresses worn over thick sweaters (Museum Boijmans Van Beuningen, Rotterdam 1997: (b) 81).

In the Victorian space a purchaser, wholesale or retail, might buy either "a single hat, or an entire wardrobe, or a sackful of shoes" (Mayhew, in Quennell 1964: 109). Contrast him with Margiela's discerning, urbane, fashion-literate late twentieth-century customer, sitting amidst the cast-offs, contemplating their carefully crafted fellows, brought back to life by the designer's transformations.

If Margiela chooses to work with old clothes it may be because they have a "grain," a patina, that cannot be simulated. It is their forgotten history that he brings back to life, although one can only guess at what that history might be. Mayhew's speculation from 1851 shows that he too was intrigued by the possible narratives embedded in these garments:

> . . . it is curious to reflect from how many classes the pile of old garments has been collected – how many privations have been endured before some of these habiliments found their way into the possession of the old-clothes man – what besotted debauchery put others in his possession – with what cool calculation others were disposed of – . . . what was the clothing which could first be spared when rent was to be defrayed or

bread to be bought, and what was treasured until the last – in what scenes of gaiety or gravity, in the opera-house or the senate, had the perhaps departed wearers of some of that heap of old clothes figured – through how many possessors . . . had these dresses passed, or through what accidents of "genteel" privation and destitution – and lastly through what necessities of squalid wretchedness and low debauchery (Quennell 1964).

The warehouse full of old clothes contains a contradiction: what is, on the one hand, a tantalizingly obscure narrative is also, on the other, no more than a pile of smelly old clothes. Something of this contradiction was to be found in the artist Christian Boltanski's installation for the exhibition *Take Me I'm Yours*, at the Serpentine Gallery, London, in 1995. The gallery space was piled high with mounds of old clothes from which visitors filled a plastic bag (bought at the door for a nominal sum). Thus the artist turned the visitors to the exhibition into rag-pickers.

For all his transformations, Margiela's scavenging comes very close to that of the nineteenth-century poet/rag-picker: "marginal to the industrial process, . . . he too recovered cultural refuse for exchange value" (Foster 1993: 134–5). In a footnote to this statement Hal Foster asks, rhetorically, "Are postmodern *pasticheurs* any different from modernist *bricoleurs* in this ambiguous recuperation of cultural materials cast aside by capitalist societies?" (ibid.: 269). Here Foster makes explicit the connection between postmodern cultural practices and their early modernist counterparts in the newly industrialized city of the nineteenth century.

3

The rag and bone man picks over the meat and veg of the urban landscape, and what he finds is neither pretty nor fragrant. The molds and bacteria that Margiela uses in the Rotterdam exhibition have "abject" or base qualities also found in the most ancient of second-hand clothing. Mold connotes decay, decomposition, dilapidation, disintegration, rot, blight, mildew, waste. Bacteria (penicillin and blue cheese aside) are associated with disease and infection. There is, then, in Margiela's "living" dresses, which have been grown in the Rotterdam sun, a deathly and terminal element. Walter Benjamin, in his unfinished *Passagen-Werk* (his Arcades Project), conceives of fashion itself as both deathly and unreproductive: "the modern woman who allies herself with fashion's newness in a struggle against natural decay represses her own reproductive power, mimics the mannequin, and enters history as a dead object" (Buck-Morss 1991: 101).

Benjamin argues that fashion attempts to defeat, or transcend, death by making the inorganic commodity itself the object of human desire. Clothes mimic organic nature (for example the decorative use of fruit, flowers and feathers), whereas the living human body mimics the inorganic world (cosmetics with "satin" finishes, for example). Fashion "prostitutes the living body to the inorganic world . . . [and]

affirms the rights of the corpse over the living" (ibid.: 101 and 405). The frenetic pace of fashion change is an attempt to ward off the ageing process and stay the passage of time. In Margiela's work for the Rotterdam exhibition the mannequin remains the same, and it is the dress itself, rather than fashion, that changes rapidly, grows, assumes a life of its own. Not unlike the glove in Max Klinger's series of etchings of that name from the 1880s, the supposedly inanimate dress assumes an uncanny life of its own, becomes the gleeful protagonist on the inanimate dummy.

If, as Benjamin argues, fashion is profoundly inauthentic because it is profoundly inorganic, and anti-maternal, what sense can we make of Margiela's use of molds and bacteria in the Rotterdam exhibition? The mannequin (deathly specter, as Hal Foster argues in his text on surrealism and the uncanny), rather than the living woman, here *models* the organic, in the form of the molds, yeasts and bacteria. The mannequin cannot reproduce but the dress itself is weirdly fecund, having acted as the growing medium for the molds and bacteria. The living dress is worn by the tailor's dummy – another reversal of fashion, where the living woman wears inorganic fashion. Margiela "grows" decay in these designs, much as William Latham "grows" organic forms on the computer. They too are deathly, sterile and hybrid. But Margiela's work is not repulsive; rather, it is lyrical, evocative, poetical and melancholic. It signals an interest in decay that is more *fin-de-siècle* than forward-looking. It is compatible with a great deal of contemporary British styling and fashion design (images of decadence, decay and deathliness have figured in much British fashion photography of the mid-1990s, particularly in magazines such as *Dazed and Confused* and *The Face*). Historically it has its roots in the nineteenth-century city, and it connects particularly with Baudelaire's rag-picker, that most abject of figures; but Margiela's use of molds also chimes with more modern metaphors: metaphors of replication, contagion and simulation that permeate everyday life in the late twentieth century – the computer virus, the cyborg, and the decentered subject.

4

. . . the parody of the gaily decked-out corpse, the provocation of death through the woman . . . the bitter, whispered *tête-à-tête* with decay. That is fashion. For this reason she changes so rapidly, teasing death, already becoming something else again, something new, as death looks about for her in order to strike her down. (Walter Benjamin, cited in Buck-Morss 1991: 101).

Margiela grows mold and bacteria on his dresses, and gives a new, surprisingly regenerative, meaning to "the bitter, whispered *tête-à-tête* with decay." Here the inanimate mannequin sports the organic, living dress, in another of Margiela's reversals. But, in a final paradox, Margiela undoes these harsh associations, and brings the dress back to life in the form of a gentle ghost, reviving dead materials and lost traces, giving new life to old cloth, rewriting its history, and adding a benign twist to bleak associations. Here is decay without revulsion, a second chance, perhaps, for Miss Haversham.

NOTES

Source: *Fashion Theory*, 2(1) (Berg Publishers, 1998), 73–93.

1. *Dérive* translates literally as "drift"; but it has a specifically Situationist meaning. Primarily urban, and in its element in the great industrially transformed cities, *dérive* was one of several Situationist stratagems to disrupt and eventually dismantle the "spectacle" of capitalist society. It is part of a modernist tradition of an almost casual engagement with the city, and depends on chance and a degree of chaos. See G. E. Debord, "Theory of the *Dérive*" in L. Andreotti & X. Costa (eds), *Theory of the Dérive and Other Situationist Writings on the City*, Museu d'Art Contemporani de Barcelona: Barcelona, 1996. I am indebted for this definition to Calum Storrie's *The Delirious Museum*, 1996, as yet unpublished, completed for the Martin Jones Award, 1994 and the Royal Incorporation of Architects in Scotland.

REFERENCES

Benjamin, Walter. 1997. *Charles Baudelaire: A Lyric Poet in the Era of High Capitalism*, trans. Harry Zohn. London and New York: Verso.

Buck-Morss, Susan. 1991. *The Dialectics of Seeing: Walter Benjamin and the Arcades Project*. Cambridge, MA and London: MIT Press.

Dickens, Charles. 1985. *Our Mutual Friend*, ed. Stephen Gill. Harmondsworth: Penguin Books.

Flügel, J. C. 1930. *The Psychology of Clothes*. London: Hogarth Press.

Foster, Hal. 1993. *Compulsive Beauty*. Cambridge, MA and London: MIT Press.

Ginsburg, Madeleine. 1980. "Rags to Riches: The Second-Hand Clothes Trade 1700–1978." *Costume*, 14: 121–35.

Morgan, Jas. 1993. "William Latham: Gardener of Unearthly Delights." *Mondo 2000*, 9, 86–93.

Museum Boijmans Van Beuningen, Rotterdam. 1997. *La Maison Martin Margiela, Paris: (9/4/1615)*, trans. Ruth Koenig.

Quennell, Peter (ed.) 1964. *Mayhew's London: Being Selections from 'London Labour and the London Poor' by Henry Mayhew*. London: Spring Books.

Schoeser, Mary. 1995. *International Textile Design*. London: Laurence King.

CHAPTER TWENTY

Art, Fashion and Music in the Culture Society

Angela McRobbie

'I'm classically trained, though I've since broken all that down. But the training was important, otherwise you don't really know why you are doing something and it's just gratuitous . . .' (who does he think he is, Picasso?).

(Interview with Guido, hairdresser, *Independent on Sunday* 15/3/98)

The intention here is to explore some consequences of the 'aestheticisation of everyday life' from the viewpoint of Britain in the late 1990s, which various cultural theorists including Jameson (1984), Featherstone (1991) and Lash and Urry (1994) have described. This broad social process raises a number of questions. These include the changing meaning of art in such a context; the further implications of the breakdown between 'high and low culture'; the growth of creative labour markets; and the challenge to judgement on questions of cultural value. All four of these dimensions have recently become prominent and are seen when we explore the new cultural triumvirate; fashion, art and popular music, currently the subject of political attention by the Creative Task Force set up in July 1997 by the newly elected Labour government.

It is now almost fifteen years since Jameson argued that culture was the logic of late capitalism. More recently the German sociologist, Herman Schwengell, has proposed that we now live in a *Kulturgesellschaft*, Culture-Society (Jameson 1984, Schwengell 1991). All the more reason then to consider what has happened to culture after postmodernism. If both these writers are right, and culture now fires the engine of economic growth, it is not surprising that it becomes a key issue for government. As cultural phenomena seek global markets on the back of home-grown creative energies, and with 'culture becoming strategically linked to inward investment' (Ford and Davies 1998: 2), New Labour proclaims its enthusiasm for art, fashion and pop flying the flag for Britain. The image of 1960s Swinging London updated to a 1997 picture on the cover of *Vanity Fair* magazine featuring Patsy Kensit and Liam Gallagher in bed, draped in the Union Jack, and Naomi Campbell on the catwalk in a Union Jack dress designed by Alexander McQueen, shows what happens when cultural practices like fashion design and pop music get drawn upon a populist wave into promoting the national good abroad.

This kind of seemingly innocuous 'banal nationalism' (Billig 1995) strikes a discordant, uncomfortable note, especially for non-white people for whom ostentatious flying of the Union Jack in parts of London associated with racist activity signals a real threat to safety. The Union Jack flown outside Damien Hirst's *Quo Vadis* restaurant in Soho in London is a self-mocking signal that art nowadays is both commerce and tourism, and commerce itself is also art. It is a provocation to those he sees as part of the political correctness establishment and, as several writers have already pointed out, this gesture is in tune with the 'art offensive' of the young British artists. But seeing the world in terms of political correctness is in itself a mark of affiliation. It describes those who repudiate feminism, anti-racism and other similar movements as constraining, authoritative and almost bullying political practices (or else as simply dull and worthy).

The convergence of Damien Hirst's flag flying and New Labour's endorsement of the Cool Britannia initiative which emerged from the DEMOS report (the think tank with close links with new Labour) on re-branding Britain, represented an attempt to re-define culture and the arts away from their more traditional image as recipients of funding towards a more aggressively promotional and entrepreneurial ethos (Leonard 1998). They were to become 'more British', but for the international market. The rebranding was proposed on the basis of old Britain's image being out of date (John Major's 'warm beer and cricket') and in need of both modernisation and rejuvenation. But in this context Tony Blair's clumsy embracing of popular music, culminating in various photo-opportunities showing him shaking hands with Noel Gallagher, backfired when two months later, in April 1998, the *New Musical Express* ran a seven page special feature on how young musicians were disenchanted with New Labour policies. Gradually the media over-exposure of the ideal of Cool Britannia became unattractive to the kinds of figures which the government was hoping to use as examples of successful and creative British talent, and quietly the tag was dropped.

While the concerns of the Creative Task Force remain relatively opaque, a more detailed analysis of the culture industries is urgently required. Despite the interest in the cultural sector on the part of big business, the grassroots of cultural activity remains small scale. The upsurge of creative activity which has recently come to fruition on the art, fashion and music front has done so in the adverse economic circumstances of the Thatcher years. This may be the single most important feature which they share in common, that the designers, musicians and artists have all depended on Thatcher's Enterprise Allowance Scheme (EAS) and have all struggled to survive in the space between unemployment and self employment.[1] No records exist of the precise number of fashion designers, artists and musicians who were recipients of the EAS in the ten years of its existence from 1983 to 1993. However, various reports and studies all point to the important role it played in under-writing the early work of the young British artists (O'Brien, quoted in Harlow 1995), the expansion of the fashion design sector (McRobbie 1998) and the popular music industry. It is equally difficult to get a clear picture of how many people are employed in the culture industries as a whole, since that could embrace all communications workers, television and press, film, leisure and entertainment. Given this broad spectrum, figures vary wildly according to which categories of work are included although there is agreement on the expansion of the field and its overwhelming concentration in London (Garnham 1990; Pratt 1997).

Given the importance of the culture industries it is remarkable how under-researched they have been and it is the sparsity of research across the whole sector which accounts for the reported difficulties faced by the Creative Task Force in formulating policy. For example, with the introduction of the Job Seekers' Allowance in 1997, young musicians who depended upon the dole and eked out an impoverished existence for themselves while signing on until such a time as they might land a recording contract were, it appeared, now going to be forced into work. This, argued Alan McGee, a member of the Creative Task Force and owner of Creation Records, would mean the end of creative talent in Britain's music industry. Without the dole young musicians would not be able to write songs, rehearse, and hang about in the pub waiting for inspiration. Following a certain degree of uproar across the music press, the government surprisingly backed down. Behind the scenes a deal was set up which was intended to ensure that the talented would not be pushed out into work but would be placed on work experience placements in the music industry. With the fine details of this deal still to be published at the time of writing, the idea of young musicians having to perform to a panel of government-appointed experts as a sort of creative means-testing, to qualify for exemption from having to take a less creative job, seems somewhat unwieldy as social policy. Will there be enough placements to fill this demand? Is there not a stronger case to reintroduce some new version of the EAS for new recruits into the culture industries? After all, its track record is not so disastrous. Tricky was on an EAS scheme when he released his first record and there are plenty of other examples.

At present, policy is at best haphazard and cloaked in administrative mystery. At worst, it is publicity-led and seemingly thought up on the spur of the moment.[2] I would argue here that for policy makers some of the key issues will be: (a) how cultural activities which have historically depended upon state support can actually be capitalized. Is it possible to envisage a scenario where practising artists are not just self sufficient but are 'income generating'?; (b) how young people can be supported to create careers for themselves in these fields, where they move from poorly paid freelance work into sustainable careers, that is, how breadline existences can be turned into a business ethos; and (c) how public sector bodies which have traditionally supported artistic and creative activities can themselves be revamped in order to respond more directly and more imaginatively to changes in the cultural sector.

SENSATION: ART AS 'CULTURAL POPULISM'?

What exactly are these cultural changes? The *Sensation* exhibition held at the Royal Academy in London (18 September to 28 December 1997) demonstrates how the work of the 'young British artists' (including Damien Hirst, Rachel Whiteread, Mark Wallinger and the Chapman brothers, among others) is now phenomenally successful (300,000 visitors) and simultaneously less special. This new brand of art is no longer the prerogative of the élite, and this less special status warrants more attention. Not that we are witnessing a new democracy or a radicalization in the field of art. The young British artists distance themselves from all the art theory, the Marxism and post-structuralism which they may have come across at some point in their training. Tracey Emin's reported enjoyment of studying Marxism and feminism while at art college is touched with irony. The art work comprising the infamous tent in which she named everyone she had ever slept with owes more to the bawdy 'girls just wanna have fun' humour of *More!* magazine than it does to her feminist elders, Cindy Sherman or Mary Kelly.

There is, then, a rebuff to the seriousness of the political art and photography of the 1980s generation. A whole range of art magazines, galleries, cultural theorists and artists themselves are instantly forgotten. These include, for example, *Camerawork*, magazines like *Ten Eight*, influential cultural theorist Victor Burgin, and also the generation of black British artists whose work began to appear in galleries from the mid 1980s, such as Chila Burman, Mitra Tabrizian, Sonia Boyce, David Bailey, Keith Piper and film-maker Isaac Julien, all of whose worked engaged at some level with cultural theory, with questions of identity and with new ethnicities. In addition there is no sign of the whole wave of art work which developed in relation to the crisis of AIDS and HIV. Some critics, notably John Roberts, have argued that this disengagement with theory allows a new licentious and profane philistinism to emerge, particularly as the Jameson-inflected works of postmodern art have become over-institutionalized (Roberts 1998). The cynical, apolitical individualism, as well as the weary, not to say tawdry, disengagement of many of the pieces (Sarah Lucas' soiled mattress with phallic shaped fruit pieces casually thrown on top or, for that matter, Tracey Emin's tent) certainly says something about how art now perceives itself and where it also places itself. Acknowledging and even endorsing what Kobena Mercer has described as the 'vulgarity and stupidity of everyday life' (Mercer 1998), is casual, promiscuous, populist art which wishes to be repositioned inside the chat show world of celebrity culture, alongside the sponsorship deals, in the restaurants and at the very heart of consumer culture. This is art made for a prime-time society, where daytime television encourages the parading in public of private misfortunes ('My wife weighs 900 pounds' was the title of one Jerry Springer show broadcast on British television on 7 August 1998). Exposure and confession are recurrent themes in *Sensation*. The power of the popular media to penetrate every moment of our daily lives makes the tabloidisation of art inevitable.

It is tempting, but not entirely satisfactory, to explain all this on the grounds that art nowadays is simply good business and that these artists are 'Thatcher's children'. Liz Ellis has suggested that in this context the new art has reneged on all feminist achievements and shorn itself of all recognisable ethics, it is art as part of the political backlash (Ellis 1998). Convincing as this account is I would argue for a rather different approach to the young British artists. Ensconced inside the consumer culture, less lonely and cut off, the new art simply becomes less important, it downgrades itself, as an act of conscious bad faith. The *Sensation* exhibition did not require the usual quantities of cultural capital to enjoy it. It did not invoke cathedral-like silence. It self-consciously staged itself as shocking but was also completely unintimidating. In this respect art has come down from its pedestal, it has relieved itself of the burden of distance and of being expected to embody deep and lasting values. But, if not all art can be great and if there are more and more people seeking to earn a living as an artist, then this is a realistic, not merely a cynical, strategy. The new 'lite' art also means the blurring of the boundaries between where art stops and where everyday life commences. The singularity of art begins to dissolve. Is it a sculpture or a dress by Hussein Chalayan? Is the video by Gillian Wearing entitled 'Dancing at Peckham' effective because it isn't real art, just a small slice of urban life? Given the 'Nikefication' of culture, are the artists (most of whom emerged from Goldsmiths College in the early 1990s) literally 'Just Doing It'? Maybe they are simply making things based on ideas. And, in so doing, they are deliberately challenging the art world with its patrician critics and its lofty standards. In the late 1990s, instead of demystifying art (the traditional strategy of the left) the yBas are redefining it, repositioning it and, to use the language of New Labour, 'rebranding art' in keeping with what it means to be an artist today and how that cannot mean being pure about sponsorship and, consequently, very poor.

As students from more diverse backgrounds enter art school, Bourdieu's notion of the artist being able to stay poor in the short term thanks to some small private income in order to achieve success on the longer term is no longer appropriate (Bourdieu 1993a). There has to be some way of being an artist and making a living. We must also take into account the historical moment of the yBas. They have been brought up with their peers to venerate and value the conspicuous consumption of the 1980s, they are part of what Beck has called the 'me first generation' (Beck 1998). Few of the generation educated through the 1960s within the full embrace of the welfare society have really come to grips with the power which money and consumerism has over a younger generation. This new love of money crosses the boundaries of gender, class and ethnicity and, as Beck has also described it, is not incompatible with strongly expressed views about social injustice, poverty, the environment and human rights (ibid., 1998). Rather than be startled by the new commercialism in contemporary art we should therefore recognise how slow an older generation of social and cultural theorists have been to recognise this issue.

The experience of *Sensation*, the strangeness and the slightness, might therefore be enough and perhaps we need not expect more of art than this. Challenging, indeed confounding, critical judgement and thus freed from the burden of being classified in terms of great, good, mediocre or bad, there is a sense that there is nothing much to lose. (Some critics have referred to the self-conscious strategy of making bad art.) In an aestheticised culture art becomes another transferable skill. Train as an artist to become a DJ. Work nights in a club or bar and get a commission from the promoters to do an installation. Make a video, take photographs etc. Art can now be pursued less grandiosely. And considering that there are fewer traditional jobs to return to if all else fails, the yBas seem to be aware that ducking and diving is no longer the fate of unqualified working-class males but almost surreptitiously has crept up on us all. Sociologists have written extensively about the new world of work characterized by risk, uncertainty and temporary contracts. But their attention so far has not been focussed upon creative work. For this reason nobody has posed the question of how much art, music and fashion the culture society can actually accommodate. How many cultural workers can there be?

Although there is great diversity within the work of the yBas, there are a number of features which are common throughout. First, there is a generational revolt against the conviction and enthusiasm of their Marxist and feminist predecessors which has produced a marked anti-intellectualism in their work. Second, they relate to popular culture by simply adopting it wholesale, its gestures, language and identity, without attempting to explore it and then elevate it back into the art world and its circuits. Popular culture is staged 'post-ironically' as presentation rather than as representation, as if to reassure the viewer that there is absolutely nothing clever or complex going on here. These artists deliberately seek out the most downgraded forms, for example the 'Sod You Gits' headline of the 1990 piece of the same name by Sarah Lucas. This flat endorsement of popular culture and its transgressive pleasures describes a hedonism also connected with this particular 'tabloid loving' generation.

Even extreme or violent material remains devoid of social or political content or comment. *Sensation* exists in a generationally specific 'chill out' zone where, after the pleasure, thoughts of death and mortality make a seemingly inevitable appearance. But this is not marked by a sudden gravity. There is curiosity, a touch of morbidity (as in Ron Mueck's model of a miniature corpse carefully laid out, naked and still sprouting hair), but otherwise a casual interest in death and decay. This forges another link with the tradition of British youth cultures. Two pieces in *Sensation* reference the impact of punk. Marcus Harvey's *Myra Hindley* evokes Malcolm McLaren's 'God Save Myra Hindley' T-shirts, and Gavin Turk's *Pop* is, of course, a lifesize cross-breed of Sid Vicious and Elvis. While the explosive intensity of punk hurtled towards the violent deaths of Sid and Nancy, the yBas disavow such extremity. It is as if neither life nor death is really worth the effort of thinking about or reflecting upon.

The connection with youth culture leads to the third unifying feature which is the impact of rave and club culture and the effects of Ecstasy. The extension of bodily pleasures which underpins club culture also presents itself in the art, as does anti-intellectualism. The body is the focus of all attention and the mind is left to lag behind. There is something of the white, laddish 'off yer face' informality of rave lingo and the crude colouration of rave party flyers in a good deal of this work. The Chapman brothers' dolls have a drug-induced psychedelic and nightmarish quality about them and, inevitably, the DJ is the real artist and therefore the hero for the yBa generation.[3] But there is nothing novel in this, the veneration of the DJ is now subculturally the norm. As the title of the CD (August 1998) by the band Faithless indicates, 'God is a DJ'.

Fourth, and finally, there are the self-curating and promotional activities which the critics take as another mark of distinction of the yBas. From running their own shows to setting up shop (Tracey Emin and Sarah Lucas reportedly lived off the profits of their second-hand shop for a year), critics have seen all these as commercial strategies, which indeed they are. But these are also ways of getting work seen and commented upon, and getting off the dole and away from unemployment. This also locates the new artists in the do-it-yourself tradition of punk and its aftermath and in the enterprise culture of Mrs Thatcher. The enormous promotional energy involved in rave culture also serves as a model. Putting on a show is pretty much like doing your own club night. None of the pieces on show at the *Sensation* exhibition would be out of place in a club setting, from Whiteread's sepulchural baths, to Hirst's rotting cow's head, from the fleshy hugeness of Jenny Saville's canvases, to the Chapman brothers' mannequins with their grotesquely positioned sexual organs. And this is conveyed in the manner in which they are set out in the exhibition. Casually strewn, or simply jammed up close to each other, the anti-intellectualism of the ethos pervades the spatial organization of the show.

Overall this exhibition confounds most theoretical insights on the postmodern condition not so much by showing a 'waning in affect' as suggesting that there is nothing beyond affect, nothing but affect. In this sense, the yBas expose postmodernism by revealing the trust in theory to be a trust in the world, ultimately a kind of humanism. However, there are costs and the shallow life preferred by the yBas produces a scanty repertoire of themes. The overall 'liteness' is countered only by the literal heaviness of the work of the two most sophisticated yBas, Hirst and Whiteread. They each bring some primal belief in the sheer weight and solidity of (even decaying) matter and, by extension, a belief in sculpture itself. For them art provides some minimal core of value, for the rest, in a further subversion of the Duchamp tradition, it is virtually indistinguishable from anything else. The key issue in the long term might well be how long the yBas can afford to dispense with politics, history and theory. It would be surprising if, in the near future, questions of gender or ethnicity for at least some of the artists did not test to the limits the abandonment of commitment.

Yet even if the critics are often in agreement about the promotional dynamic of the yBas taking priority over a deep commitment to art, the work is nonetheless discussed. This may be the intention, to demonstrate (as did the holiday-making escapade staged by final year fine art students at Leeds University in June 1998)[4] that what art is depends upon what the critics and the media say it is. The key factor is the existence of taste groups, critical bodies who are all engaged in casting judgement and bringing the work into discourse, into language and into popular controversy. If this is then what really enervates art, the scale and volume of the talk is a sign of the privileged status of fine art. In fashion no such critical talk exists and in popular music, where it might be argued there is the greatest degree of creative activity occurring, there is also a less voluble and certainly less recognised set of intellectuals and critics whose judgement matters in the field of cultural capital.

FASHION DREAMS OF ART

An equally coherent story cannot be told about British fashion design as can be narrated about the yBas. If Bourdieu is right in his claim that words create things, then it is the absence of a substantial body of cultural intermediaries in fashion which accounts for its disembodied existence (Bourdieu 1993b). Despite individual designers becoming internationally famous there is nothing which binds them together as a movement other than their training in the British art schools, their commitment to conceptual rather than commercial fashion and their singular inability to stay in business. Unlike British trained artists or indeed pop musicians, fashion designers have never displayed a high degree of political engagement. Nor has there been any substantial theoretical tradition which has underwritten their practice. At best they have been seen outside the fashion media as an interesting part of popular culture, sometimes innovative or even revolutionary (as in the cast of Mary Quant) or as producing spectacular and theatrical displays of sartorial splendour (Galliano's shows). More often there is a kind of trivial image which reveals itself when, on occasion, mainstream broadsheet journalists make disparaging comments about the fashion design world. Despite this, the expansion of space given to fashion coverage in the national press, and the attention which figures like Galliano, McQueen, Westwood and McCartney attract, has boosted the self-image of this sector. If yBas are making art less special and more ordinary, fashion designers are insistent upon fashion being extraordinary. Their new confidence has allowed them to be even bolder in making claims for themselves as practising fine artists in the most conventional of 'art for art's sake' terms. They are encouraged in this respect by the fashion media who have also felt themselves to be the lesser partners in the world of the arts. But this coming of age, whereby fashion people now talk confidently in terms of minimalism, deconstruction and postmodernism, and fashion journalists proclaim figures like

Galliano and McQueen as geniuses, is problematic for the very reason that there is no known standard of judgement or criteria against which these claims can be measured. Almost nobody knows why Galliano is a genius. This is because there is virtually no developed language of art criticism (in the art history tradition) which would introduce and comment upon the work of young British fashion designers. There is a new journal, *Fashion Theory*, and there is a tradition of dress (or costume) history and, of course, a number of interesting monographs on dress (Harvey 1995) as well as the various feminist accounts of fashion. But this is a field where biographies of the great designers (often in the style of coffee-table books) has taken precedence over scholarly analysis. Unlike subcultural style, fine art fashion has been considered by only a tiny handful of writers (Evans and Thornton 1989; Wollen 1993).

There is also no sociological analysis about the distinction of this sector. As a result, when so many designers are forced out of business, there is very little response other than from fashion journalists who bewail the lack of investment but who otherwise are so used to this that it is almost a *rite de passage*, something young designers might almost expect to happen to them. Fashion designers in Britain are trained in the fine art tradition. This informs their identities and explains why they see their work ideally as pieces to be hung on the wall, and more reluctantly as items of clothing (McRobbie 1998). But, unlike fine artists, fashion designers must be able to follow their work into production. They must be able to produce a run of jackets. It is this which accounts for the high rate of bankruptcies and business failures. Even successful designers (with a few exceptions) actually have very small businesses, most with a turnover of less than £2 million (for example, Betty Jackson and Ally Capellino), and all the well-known British designers are now being supported (and, in effect, rescued) by deals with bigger companies to produce in-house lines.

The designers' situation is further aggravated by the differential economies at work in the fashion system. There is a huge disparity between the consumption of the fashion image and the consumption of its object (that is, we look but do not buy). This means that designers can be international names while still signing on and working at the kitchen table. This mismatch produces a series of dislocations and unevenness. Fashion design is a highly disorganized and disintegrated economy (Lash and Urry 1994). It is not the case that there is no market for the goods in the shops but that the high street intervenes in the space between the image on the page and the designer items in the shops, producing lower quality cheaper ranges. The market for the genuine article remains tiny. And, as Baudrillard would see it, the image overall remains more real than its object. Fashion economies as a result are almost virtual, or deferred economies. This is a field where nobody really seems to get paid even at the image industry end where the stylists, photographers and even the supermodels all work for exposure. Magazines like *The Face, i-D, Dazed, and Confused* and *Don't Tell It* rely on work which is in effect donated. The pay-off is the huge readership among the global image industry corporations who spot and then offer these underpaid British-trained cultural workers lucrative contracts, making the magazines function as job centres, or portfolios. Those working in this image industry are also products of the aestheticisation of society. Their priority is to make works of art. As the fashion editor of *i-D* says 'the page is art' (McRobbie 1998). Likewise, the stylists describe their work as 'image making'. The closeness of these fashion worlds, as well as the residual unconfidence on the part of its participants (including the fashion media) means that serious questions of cultural value and issues of judgement are sidestepped and replaced by euphoric assertions of greatness, genius and inspiration. These traditional vocabularies once again demonstrate the dislocated nature of fashion design as a cultural practice. While in almost every other part of the art world the boundaries appear to be breaking down and while, as various critics pointed out, *Sensation* marked a decisive shift for young artists into the field of popular culture, fashion in effect seeks a reconsolidation of the boundaries between high and low with fashion recognized in its rightful place in the cultural hierarchy.

Only more engaged debate, argument and scholarship can ease fashion design of its status panic. The designers ought to be eligible for Arts Council grants while, at the same time, the sector as a whole needs a much more effective industrial strategy. Designers like Hussein Chalayan should be entitled to Arts Council funding to show their collections on the catwalk as performance art. At the same time clearer thinking is required about the production and manufacturing side. It is the need to put a range of clothes into production which distinguishes fashion design from sculpture or installation work. In fact the obstacles to turning this into a more successful cultural sector are less unsurmountable than they frequently seem. Collaborative strategies to share expensive facilities, equipment and promotional services between designers under the auspices of urban regeneration schemes, the reintroduction of fashion centres and the provision of incentives to employ local direct labour rather than rely on anonymous chains of sub-contracted labour, are all feasible under a New Labour commitment.

'DEEP ANONYMOUS MURMUR'

When we turn our attention to the world of contemporary dance music (in particular, drum 'n' bass) the themes addressed in this book become particularly pronounced. Here is one of the clearest signs of the *Kulturgesellschaft* – the flow across the airwaves produces tracks that even the most avid listener is never likely to hear again (never mind write down who produced it so that he or she can actually buy it). So committed to experiment and improvisation are the 'junglist', or drum 'n' bass, musicians and DJs that they are frequently producing and playing tracks of which there is no record and no original. The commercial dynamics, the record deals and the whole political economy of this style of music remain elusive and undocumented. Only figures like Roni Size and Goldie have really registered in the public domain. This anonymous quality, where name DJs are known only to the various crowds who follow them around a number of different club locations, is connected with the music's primary identity as flow. Drum 'n' bass borrows from modern classical European, reggae, Hollywood and also Indian Bollywood soundtracks. Underneath all this is the dark and fast rumble of the distinctive booming drum and bass beat, across which echoes the intermittent scattergun, patois-influenced voice of the DJ (although often it is wholly instrumental). Whilst thudding out from specific points in the urban and domestic landscape, from car sound systems, black workmen's vans, the open windows of maisonnettes at four o'clock in the afternoon as 16 year olds get home from school, this is also a 'deep, anonymous, murmur' (Deleuze 1986).

Martin James defines drum 'n' bass as 'a combination of timestretched breakbeats played at approximately 160 beats per minute with bass lines lifted from reggae, running at 80 beats per minute and the metronomic 4/4 bass drum removed' (James 1996: xi). This is a speeded up reggae- and dub-influenced sound combined with frenetically fast drums from computer programmed sequences (thus beyond the humanly possible in performance terms) which also carries elements of the techno style of 'white' rave music, in particular stretches of swelling, deeply melodic sequences. However, live exposure to this music reveals its fully black aesthetic (McRobbie and Melville 1998). Listening to Grooverider, behind the decks, or to MC Nathan Haines it is possible to hear the full force of the improvised tradition of jazz, combined with the reggae sounds and toaster voiceover of the Jamaican dancehall, with the hip hop tradition of the rapper, now souped up by technological means to produce a thunderous and uniquely black and British underground sound. But there is no crude ethnic absolutism inscribed within this form, instead its openness and fluidity and serious, indeed scholarly, concern with the music celebrates the movement between the black, white and Asian mixes which is such a hallmark of this musical style. The DJs who form the inner circle around Goldie's *Metallheadz* label are young black and white Londoners. As Goldie said of fellow DJ Doc Scott, 'I seen niggers dance like they wouldn't ever dance before to this guy and nobody would believe that Scotty was blue eyes and long hair . . . He's got jet blue eyes and long hair to here.' (Goldie 1996: 41).

As 'Britart' flirts with the masses it could be argued that black British drum 'n' bass attempts to retain its own subcultural capital and underground exclusivity (Thornton 1996) by being forever ahead of the masses and the media. However, I argue that the relation maintained here between underground and mainstream is not so much a strategy of distinction, a game of culture, as a sign of aesthetic seriousness. It is about playing primarily for other musicians and DJs and also for the crowd which, in this case, is comprised not so much of fans as of fellow travellers. Such cerebral values are not typically associated with such a low culture form practised by otherwise unqualified young males ('inner city ghetto music' as Goldie has also called it). That is, the emphasis on what is special and unique about this music is not just a gesture of style, a pretence about not wanting to sell out, but a question of value. The elaboration of a distinctive artistic vocabulary is an expected bid for autonomy amongst any creative group but when it is from black culture and also a sector of black culture associated with poverty and social exclusion (Goldie grew up in care and in a series of foster homes) the complexity of this language is disregarded. So absorbed are these musicians, producers and DJs in what they are doing that, to an extent, the market and commercialization fades in importance.

The wild and noisy participative dynamics of the audience at 'jungle raves' of 1994, together with the extraodinary declarations of love, passion and commitment to the music from its followers, has produced a subcultural phenomena of exuberance and volume. As James writes 'the crowd would demand rewinds and when the MC shouted for them to make some noise the cacophony was deafening' (James 1996: 43). But the underground location and distinctive style and language means that only insiders from the DJ and dance music press comment upon it. On the part of Oxbridge-educated establishment critics drum 'n' bass remains a bewildering and confusing thing. In a recent two page profile of Goldie in the *Guardian*, Decca Aitkenhead failed to mention the music at all but was instead charmed by how 'he made up his own words' and 'claimed not to read' (Aitkenhead 1998: 3). This sense of being unable to place, locate or assess the artistic value of such work is both a mark of its otherness and also, as Bourdieu would say, of the unwillingness of the cultural legitimators to consider, never mind categorise as artists, those who exist at the far end of the social scale.

Of course there are boundaries which make access to this music difficult to outsiders. In particular there is a line that divides a generation of clubbers from those who dropped out in about 1986 when warehouse parties held in illegal spaces and hosted by DJs like Baz Fe Jazz or organised by anarcho-types like Mutoid Waste sowed the early seeds of rave. Now, in the late 1990s, it is striking how these new clubs also function as arts venues (rather like the old London Film-makers Co-operative). Most show films or slide shows during the course of the night. There is a real, tangible sense that what is happening inside these places is breaking new creative ground. For example, in one club, the 333 in London's Old Street, music evolves from week to week, from Jamaican-influenced drum 'n' bass to Asian tabla 'n' bass to Japanese taiko 'n' bass to 'eastern drum 'n' bass and, most recently (at least in my own experience), to something akin to drum 'n' drum. What is constant is the presence of rapturous audiences drawn from the entire metropolitan mix of London's young people.

I want, therefore, to invert the cultural hierarchy which still puts fine art at the top and this type of music at the bottom by suggesting a return to Gilroy's notion of 'black musical genius' (revised to take into account the more authorless nature of these particular musical forms), to the power of musical creativity as a lifeline of hope for black diasporic peoples, and to the complexity of this particular music whose own 'organic intellectuals' have forged an anti-essentialist aesthetic (black grooves on white rave–techno foundation) (Gilroy 1987, 1993). Contemporary dance music also tells us something about history and about the conditions of growing up and living in a mixed race urban culture and having some access to the creative potential of new technology in the form of the home or bedroom computer. This is cheap to produce music. It is a matter of 'taking the software and pushing the sound through the ringer backwards, just to see what it would do' (James 1996, p. 52) or again, to quote Goldie, 'We're joyriding technology, pushing it to the edge' (ibid: 53).

I am aware of the accusation of cultural studies romanticism and celebration or, worse, of 'middle youth voyeurism'. I am also aware of the dangers of returning to a mode which simply confers cultural value, but from a lower position, which says that this is great art. We need to ask, what it is we want or expect of art in a culturally saturated society? Is it possible to hold out for some idea of art when it is so thoroughly absorbed by, and integrated into, the field of popular culture? Does art simply become the new, serious, complex and interesting end of popular culture? Or is art the fiction which a particular form weaves around itself, its own distinctive 'rap'? Is it a matter of institutionalization and representation? Or am I arguing here that the art in dance music is also a type of politics, not in the overt sense, but in the sense that it writes and re-writes history in the collectivity of its style (The Roni Size Collective), and in its melting of the boundaries between black and white?

With the yBas we have seen a drift from the art world down towards the vulgar, cheap and tacky, a cynical, indifferent story about what I describe as merely liking pop, and doing self-consciously artistic things with it while avoiding the tedium of trying to be clever. The outcome is post-ironic. In contrast the music I have just described comprises a passionage, frenetic, quasi-private and urgent socio-historical dialogue, an equivalent to Afro-American hip hop, and an example of what Bhabha has called the 'uncontrollable innovations' of young black (and white) urban and disadvantaged populations (Bhabha 1998). However, the yBas still attract huge amounts of attention because what they do is still notionally art and supported by Saatchi. This makes it comprehensible to the middle-class critics who somehow create an appropriate vocabulary for debate (McCorquodale et al. 1998). As Bourdieu says, 'they create the creators' (1993a). Fashion exists as a weak shadow in comparison to both these voluble practices – it is hampered by its gendered, dressmaking history. However, instead of challenging this divide it has merely sought to emulate a fine art mode, as a kind of second best. It pays its respect to the street but needs the fine art tag to justify its presence. The only radical scholarship in the field of fashion comes from subcultural and feminist theory but the designers shy away from this type of connection as either too sociological or too political. This leaves its cultural intermediaries to be the journalists who for various reasons find themselves cloven to a vocabulary of approval (McRobbie 1998).

If academics and journalists have recently converged to write about yBas, and if fashion journalists have largely been responsible for the prominence and visibility of designers, the hidden and underground identity of drum 'n' bass music and its largely youthful following has meant that only a handful of writers, notably Sharma et al. (1996) and Melville (1997), have shown how it so clearly evokes the ideas of Stuart Hall and Paul Gilroy as an unwitting commentary upon and update of their work on 'new ethnicities' and the black Atlantic (Gilroy 1993; Hall 1992). There have been a few attempts to locate jungle and drum 'n' bass as Deleuzian forms 'Cubasing across bedroom studios . . . swerving through clubland . . . transmitting as cultural virus, pirate radio, illegal duplication . . .' (Ansell Pearson, quoted in McClure 1998: 184; see also Gilbert 1997; Hemmett 1997). But in none of the Deleuzian accounts is there any grounding in race and history, in the political economy of growing up at the edge of a de-industrial, post-employment society. Nor is there an engagement with the micro-economies of being a DJ or with what Harvey describes as the 'survival strategies of the unemployed' (Harvey 1989).

We are left then with a curious scenario in the 'Culture Society', with the breakdown of high and low culture being more apparent than real. Even when fine artists think they are not doing art, the critics, collectors and academics bring their own professional vocabularies to bear on the work and confirm that, yes, it is art. Fashion designers, in contrast, think that they are fine artists, giving rise to more than a few sniggers on the part of the culture critics (Glancey 1997; Johnson 1997). More generally they are seen as providing enjoyable visual spectacles, good copy for the front page. A touch of English eccentricity.[5] Meanwhile, the drum 'n' bass musicians are producing the most innovative and dynamic aesthetic in music since reggae, but there are so few black scholars, intellectuals and critics who have made their way up through the ranks of the academy or into journalism that there are virtually no voices of representation, never mind debate, except those that come from other, largely hidden, spaces.

Likewise, the economies underpinning these activities are more apparent, indeed virtual, than real. Apart from a few stars and celebrities at the top these are casualized, insecure occupations, more so than ever before. Yet increasingly there are no 'day jobs' to fall back on, especially for young black males. While this music can be seen as a soundtrack to the work of black intellectuals like Hall and Gilroy, it also describes a significant distance between the world of the black intellectual and that of the DJs running around London trying to make a living by creating clubs, setting up small labels and immersing themselves in creating new sounds from old sources. Should there be a dialogue between these musicians and people like Paul Gilroy, and on what lines would such a dialogue proceed? What would Goldie have to say to Gilroy? This is not to invoke some happy idea of intellectual and artistic community. Indeed, the small chance of such an encounter merely dramatizes the political reality where the resources of the university and art school system, made generously available to art students and fashion designers, remain foreign territory and an unknown and untapped resource for those who might derive the greatest benefit (despite living and working in the same city). The utopian space of the university as Edward Said has described it has not provided the haven for musicians like those mentioned above as it has done for generations of practising artists and also for fashion designers (in the guise of visiting teacher posts). This in itself is a clear sign of continuing inequalities reproduced through the rigidity of the cultural hierarchies of taste.

This music functions as a record of the lives of its producers. It is extraordinarily self-reflexive, continually redressing itself, telling and re-telling its own story. It combines elements of improvisation, uplift and utopia inscribed within its practice and performance (and described by Gilroy as part of a black Atlantic musical aesthetic) and also something newer, darker and different. A shot of fear, even terror, runs through the core of drum 'n' bass music. Virtually without voice or lyrics, except for the commands and commentary from the MC, there is also the underside of racial memory where there is no community, no protection, no security – only paranoia. Speed, physical force and vibration replace heart and soul. The energy and the danger also tells us something simple and direct about the sheer effort needed to make a living and forge some kind of future being black in the culture society.

NOTES

Source: *In the Culture Society: Art, Fashion and Popular Music* (Routledge, 1999), 3–21.

1. The Enterprise Allowance Scheme helped get people off the dole and into self employment by providing forty pounds a week for the duration of a year.
2. The operations of the Creative Task Force have remained obscure. At the time of writing no further documents or statements have followed press reports of a U-turn on the Job Seekers' Allowance.
3. During the summer of 1997 the ICA in London held a series of club nights hosted by artists-turned-DJs Jake and Dinos Chapman, Tracey Emin and Gillian Wearing.
4. In June 1998 as part of the final year degree shows a group of fine art students from Leeds University staged an elaborate hoax. The group work comprised an announced trip to Spain followed by a public return at the airport. The media predictably reported these events as a waste of taxpayers' money, at which point the students revealed that the trip had been to a local holiday resort. The 'art' was the media reaction.
5. English Eccentrics is the name of a London-based fashion label.

This article was first delivered as a lecture to students of the Fine Art Department, Glasgow School of Art, in December 1997.

REFERENCES

Aitkenhead, D. (1998) 'Dances With Wolverhampton', *Guardian*, 23 January 1998.

Beck, U. (1998) 'Cosmopolitan World', *New Statesman*, April 1998.

Bhabha, H. (1998) Lecture delivered at Stuart Hall Conference, the Open University, Milton Keynes, 14/15 May.

Billig, M. (1995) *Banal Nationalism*, London: Sage.

Blair, T, the Rt. Hon. PM (1997) 'Can Britain Remake It?', *Guardian*, 21 July 1997.

Bourdieu, P. (1993a) *The Field of Cultural Production*, Cambridge: Polity Press.

—— (1993b) *Sociology in Question*, London: Sage.

Deleuze, G. (1986) *Foucault*, Minneapolis: University of Minnesota Press.

Ellis, L. (1998) 'Do You Want To Be in My Gang?', *nParadoxa: An International Feminist Arts Journal*, vol. 1, pp. 6–14.

Evans, C. and Thornton, M. (1989) *Women and Fashion: A New Look*, London: Quartet.

Featherstone, M. (1991) *Consumer Culture and Postmodernism*, London: Sage.

Ford, S. and Davies, J. (1998) 'Art Capital', *Art Monthly*, no. 213, February, pp. 1–4.

Ford, S. (1998) 'The Myth of the Young British Artist', in D. McCorquodale *et al.* (eds) *Occupational Hazard: Critical Writing on Recent British Art*, London: Black Dog Publishing, pp. 130–42.

Garnham, N. (1990) *Capitalism and Communication: Global Culture and the Economics of Information*, London: Sage.

Gilbert, J. (1997) 'Soundtrack For an Uncivil Society: Rave Culture, the Criminal Justice Act and the Politics of Modernity', *New Formations*, no. 31, Summer, pp. 5–23.

Gilroy, P. (1987) *There Ain't No Black In the Union Jack*, London: Hutchinson.

—— (1993) *The Black Atlantic*, London: Verso.

Glancey, J. (1997) 'All Dressed up by the Queen of Frock 'n' Roll', *Guardian*, 18 July 1997, p. 18.

Goldie (1996) 'Goldie's Jukebox', *The Wire*, Issue 144, February 1996.

Hall, S. (1992) 'New ethnicities', in J. Donald and A. Rattansi (eds) *'Race', Culture and Difference*, London: Sage.

Harlow, J. (1995) 'Home is Where the Art is', *Sunday Times*, 17 December: 3.

Harvey, D. (1989) *The Condition of Postmodernity*, Oxford: Blackwell.

Harvey, J. (1995) *Men in Black*, London: Reaktion Books.

Hemmett, D. (1997) 'E is for Ekstasis', *New Formations*, no. 31, Summer, pp. 23–39.

James, M. (1996) *State of Bass: Jungle, the Story So Far*, Basingstoke: Boxtree Press.

Jameson, F. (1984) 'Postmodernism or The Logic of Late Capitalism', *New Left Review* 146, London.

Johnson B. (1997) 'Was Versace Really a Genius?', *Daily Telegraph*, 17 July, p. 21.

Lash, S. and Urry, J. (1994) *The Economy of Signs and Spaces*, London: Sage.

Leonard, M. (1998) 'Re Branding Britain', London: DEMOS.

McClure, B. (1998) 'Machinic Philosophy', *Theory, Culture and Society*, May, vol. 15, no. 2, pp. 175–85.

McCorquodale, D. Siderfin, N. and Stallabrass, J. (eds) (1998) *Occupational Hazard: Critical Writing on Recent British Art*, London: Black Dog Publishing.

McRobbie, A. (1998) *British Fashion Design: Rag Trade or Image Industry?*, London: Routledge.

McRobbie, A. and Melville C. (1998) 'Amblyssical Chords: Goldie's Saturnz Returns', *Village Voice*, 17 February, p. 68, New York.

Melville, C. (1997) 'Breakbeats and Metallheadz', MA Dissertation, unpublished, Goldsmiths College, London.

Mercer, K. (1998) Lecture delivered at Stuart Hall Conference, The Open University, Milton Keynes, May 14/15.

Roberts, J. (1998) 'Pop Art, the Popular and British Art of the 1990s', D. McCorquodale *et al.* (eds) *Occupational Hazard: Critical Writing on Recent British Art*, London: Black Dog Publishing, pp. 52–80.

Pratt, A. (1997) 'The Cultural Industries Sector: its definition and character from secondary sources on employment and trade, Britain 1984–91', Research Papers in Environmental and Spatial Analysis, no. 41, London School of Economics.

Schwengell, H. (1991) 'British Enterprise Culture and German *Kulturgesellschaft*', R. Keat and N. Abercrombie (eds), *Enterprise Culture*, pp. 136–51, London: Routledge.

Sharma, S., Sharma, A., and Hutnyk J. (1996) *Dis-orienting Rhythms: The Politics of New Asian Dance Music*, London: Zed Brooks.

Thornton, S. (1996) *Club Culture: Music, Media and Subcultural Capital*, Cambridge: Polity Press.

Wollen, P. (1993) *Raiding the Icebox: Reflections on Twentieth Century Culture*, London: Verso.

CHAPTER TWENTY ONE

Vionnet & Classicism

REBECCA ARNOLD

Classicism presents a façade of effortlessness. It demands a return to the essential elements of fashion design: body and textile. It is revered within western culture as an emblem of simple, natural truths, the beauty of geometric forms draped upon supple flesh, yet it takes considerable skill to create and wear. Beneath the smooth lines of classically inspired clothing is a complex web of elaborate construction techniques and contradictory meanings. To try to understand the values and beliefs with which we invest classically inspired designs, the work of early twentieth century couturier Madeleine Vionnet will be considered as a cipher, linking mythologies of classicism and modernism within a specific historical context. Her designs encapsulate the significance of classicism's influence on fashionable dress during the inter-war period, yet they also offer more subversive readings, which undermine stable interpretations of classicised design as timeless, democratic and 'pure'.

Madeleine Vionnet's training at a number of couture houses in both London and Paris taught her to favour the natural body as the guiding motif in any design and led her to develop her well-documented technique of draping specially woven double width fabric onto an 80cm high mannikin. This process emphasised her radical view of dressmaking, which focused on the body as a 3 dimensional whole, not a fractured vision of back, front, top, bottom. She had been taught to foreground the body while premiere at Callot Soeurs in the early 1900s. There, she watched one of the couture house's maitresses Mme Gerber, whose ability to perfect her designs and adapt them to the needs and tastes of each client was to influence Vionnet's later creations. At Doucet, where she moved in 1907 she was to display her avant garde view of fashion, becoming part of the triumvirate of couturiers, along with Chanel and Poiret, who were to construct a new form of fashion and beauty that heralded the concerns of the modern era. By discarding the corset and quite literally stripping away the superfluities of fashion and contemporary notions of respectability, Vionnet became part of the revolution in fashion, evoking a new form of femininity that spoke of freedom, independence and experimentation. For Vionnet, this new spirit was linked to a search for purity of form and artistic expression that sprang, at least in part, from a thorough exploration of classical design.

A silk crêpe dress of 1918–19 from the collection of the Musée de la Mode et du Textile in Paris's encapsulates many of Vionnet's main preoccupations. Betty Kirke, in her book Madeleine Vionnet of 1998, describes how its form is created by drapes and folds of fabric that in turn cling to and pull out from the figure, thus enhancing some features while masking others. The diagonal jabot points at the hemline of the dress echo those at the hem of the Greek chlamys or cloak which will be discussed later. The swathed cowl neckline falls like the chiton in deep folds that curve around the neckline providing a light-reflecting frame for the face. The dress is fluid and mobile, comprising a tube of crêpe hung diagonally so that it hovers around the body, touching but not moulding it. It wraps around the frame, a third armhole doubled over one side of the body helping to hold the garment in place and adding to its swathed effect. The dress is a bold statement of Vionnet's skills – her commitment to experimental construction techniques which challenged both the acceptance of western tailoring and the need for applied decoration to add interest to a design. It also reflected Vionnet's desire for an alternative vision of femininity that gave women the confidence to go without corsetry and the restrictive idea of woman as culturally constructed artefact that it evoked. For Vionnet the pre-eminence of a sensual form of femininity was crucial to her work. While other designers, like Chanel and Patou, looked to masculine dress as a means to visualise a stronger, more independent and, importantly, more modern version of feminine dress, Vionnet always focussed on the curves of women's bodies as the basis of any design. Even her daywear and tailleurs owe less to men's tailoring techniques than those of other designers. For her, modern femininity meant just that: feminine, not androgynous dress, which relied upon radical construction techniques to reassess gender roles rather than appropriating the symbolism of status and power inherent in masculine tailoring.

Vionnet had established her own house in 1912 and during the teens she focussed her attention on geometric forms, in particular the rectangle, as a basis of exploring her belief in paring designs down to their most essential forms. As Caroline Milbank Rennolds noted, 'Vionnet was called the Euclid of Fashion, and geometric shapes predominate in all her collections as decorative and functional devices.'[1] While such an approach may seem coolly aloof, the response to her garments had, from early on proved how revelatory this focus on fabric draped to the body was after centuries of seeing women only through the moulded mask of layers of restraining underwear.

While Vionnet was at the house of Doucet many of the vendeuses refused to show clients her designs, deeming them too risque and immodest with their revealing drapes and use of lingerie techniques such as rolltucked hems and fagoting decoration to disguise seams. It is no surprise that many of her clients were actresses and demimondaines, women who were already made dubious by their public lives and who favoured the inherent eroticism of dress that focussed on the body. Vionnet's work expressed the problems of femininity in a period of such rapid change and upheaval. As gender roles altered under the impact of the First World, women needed to renegotiate their relationship to public spaces; no longer closeted, literally within the domestic sphere, or metaphorically by restrictive clothing or rigid moral codes, younger women sought means to signal this change. Vionnet had been brought to the house of Doucet to add a youthful charge to its designs and began her career there by eliminating the heavy satinised black cotton dresses which all house models wore under the couture designs that they showed to customers. She was gradually peeling away the layers of stifling 19th century morality that had deemed no woman respectable who was not closed off from the world in corset and petticoat, her body a mysterious object encased in whalebone.

In this period of transition femininity was marked by ambiguity, likely to flip between seemingly contradictory ideas of public and private, moral and immoral. Classicism, the prism through which many designers were re-conceptualising the female form within a modernist context, was equally on the cusp. On the one hand it could be used by Mussolini as a right-wing vision of imperial dominance and military might through his appropriation of the imagery of Augustan Rome, yet on the other it provided a site for avant-garde experimentation, for example by Picasso. The mythologies circulating around classical source material, regarding its allegiance to transcendent ideals of pure mathematical form and eternal truths, ironically enabled it to be interpreted in radically different ways. In Vionnet's hands classicism provided a means to challenge and critique her own discipline, pushing at the boundaries of fashion by testing the limits of the classical ideal.

Other designers were also revealing the body through the lens of classical nudity. Mme Grès produced a series of finely pleated columns that were tucked and draped around the figure. But unlike Vionnet's work, her designs contained more structured underpinnings to sculpt and hold the figure within the fluid line of the light fabrics. They were images of classicism without the problematic display, albeit under a layer of crêpe, of naked flesh. While Grès's work was undoubtedly creative in its complex use of fabric, it did not represent the proto-feminist ideals that Vionnet's clothing explored. Both in her experimentation with the relationship between fabric and female body and with her advocacy of the rights of her (largely female) workforce, for whom she provided good working conditions and various benefits like paid holidays and medical care, Vionnet foregrounded feminine concerns.

Meanwhile Fortuny had followed a reformist line in his Greek inspired designs at the start of the century. They were symptomatic of a strand of dress that had run through the second half of the 19th century that sought an alternative to high fashion. Based on a healthier more natural form of dress, he built on ancient Greek ideals of beauty rather than the seasonal vagaries of haute couture. His Delphos gowns were worn by bohemians who recognised in his creations the ancient Greek peplos – a tube of fabric folded over at the neckline to produce a tunic effect at the top of the dress.

His dresses were rendered in various soft jewel tones, their slim-line forms slipping easily over the wearer's head – a far cry from the complex layers of most early 20th century clothing which required a maid's assistance to get into.

Fortuny's crinkled pleats paid homage to the effects produced in Greek costume where linen, wool, cotton and later silk were draped in folds against the body or finely pleated to cling to the skin. The basic garment for women's dress was the chiton, a simple tube of rectangular fabric fixed at the shoulders and then caught with bands at the waist and sometimes also the bustline. The peplos that Fortuny was so inspired by was a variation on the chiton, which added depth to the garment in its folded over top section. The various ways in which such drapery could be worn added nobility to the figure and emphasised the fabric's feeling of movement as it shifted around the body, constantly falling into new formations.

Anne Hollander in her book Seeing Through Clothes stresses the importance of imagery like this and the works of art it has inspired over the centuries, in creating a mythology surrounding the draping of the nude body. They have trained the viewer's eye to see the body as most harmonious when draped in cloth. Hollander writes:

'The nude body and draped cloth became essential elements of idealised vision; they came to seem correct for conveying the most valid truths of life, entirely through the persuasive force of their appearance in works of art rather than through the original significance attached to them in real life. The "natural" beauty of cloth and the "natural" beauty of bodies have been taught to the eye by art, and the same has been the case with the natural beauty of clothes.'[2]

It is this mythologising of Greek dress as "natural" that plays an important part in its appeal to Madeleine Vionnet and other designers, who like her saw classical dress as the most appropriate form to adopt and adapt in the first half of the 20th century. It represents an already legitimised reverence for the human body which was newly revealed in the fashions of the period and this indisputable heritage helped to deflect criticism from those who found the revealing nature of such fashions immodest. Vionnet's work seeks to weave new mythologies around the body, adding to the meanings that art has attached to the classical body, by linking her designs firmly into the contemporary modernist, rather than seeking to replicate classical dress precisely.

The other garment that was particularly influential on Madeleine Vionnet was the chlamys or cloak which consisted of a rectangle draped over the shoulders and allowed to flow vertically down the body creating dips and points at the hem. The importance of being able to wear such free form garments was significant in demonstrating the status of the wearer, since as Hollander points out:

'Sophistication, sexual allure, power and austerity could all be expressed by the style in which simple rectangles woven of different stuffs were disposed around the body.'[3]

The complex drapes made by this most minimal of garments and the need to move while keeping the chlamys in place heightened the dynamic tension between body and fabric. It also acts as a metaphor for the complex meanings that western culture attaches to the deceptively simple lines of classical dress.

It was not just fashion designers who were looking to ancient Greece for new modes of expression. The American dancer Isadora Duncan used the highly recognisable forms of Greek art and dress to create performances of revolutionary freedom and experimentation. In Paris in 1907 she appeared in classical tunic, bare legs and sandals, a lithe form that symbolised both the stripped down dynamism of modernity and the authenticity of ancient cultures. Her style represented both past and future. Her improvisational dance and draped body were emblematic of a period on the cusp of change – the classical reference point once again a means of imagining and authenticating the toned and revealed body that was to gradually emerge from the constricting fashions of the early 1900s and which was to come to dominate western fashion for the century to come.

For Madeleine Vionnet classicism was a starting point from which to create dramatically pared down forms that exploited the natural elasticity of the fabric to the full. Her designs were mobile, hanging free from the body anticipating each movement in their daringly simple shapes. One example from 1919–20 is notable for its use of rectangles of springy silk crêpe which drop on the diagonal from the shoulders, thus working on the bias of the fabric to produce a dress of geometric forms that appears sculptural and fluid as it pulls towards the curves of the wearer's body. Vionnet was known for her use of bias-cutting to increase the drape and movement of the fabric. While bias-cutting had existed before, in the 19th century its use had been restricted to trimmings, or the drapes of material had been fixed to an immobile lining. Vionnet used this technique to release the potential of the fabric and explore its relationship to the 3 dimensional forms of the body further. She said:

'My efforts have been directed towards freeing material from the restrictions imposed on it, in just the same way that I have sought to liberate the female form. I see both as injured victims . . . and I've proved that there is nothing more graceful than the sight material hanging freely from the body. I've attempted to create an element of balance in my material so that the lines of a dress are not marred by any movement, but emphasised.'[4]

In Vionnet's eyes, fabric had been limited by traditional cutting techniques, which literally restricted the female form, but were also symptomatic of woman's restricted role in western culture. By freeing the fabric she was also freeing the woman, enabling her body to be revealed and celebrated, unhampered by bourgeois notions of modesty and decorum. Like Isadora Duncan, expressive movement was the guiding motif and classicism the heroic prototype for a starkly modern image of femininity.

Bruce Chatwin, who interviewed Vionnet in 1973, three years before she died, spoke of the seriousness of Vionnet's commitment to her work. During her career fashion was still deemed a frivolous profession.

> 'But for Madame Vionnet, who was once penniless, couture is not a minor art. Like the dance it is an evanescent art, but a great one. She sees herself as an artist on the level of say, Pavlova. She was single-minded in the pursuit of perfection, and even her exemplary common sense is tinged with a streak of fanaticism.'[5]

He went on to recall the sparse modernist interior of her Paris apartment, saying,

> 'On [the fireplace] stands a photo of the Parthenon: a talismanic photo, for Madame Vionnet has always turned to classical Greece for inspiration.'[6]

This theme was continued in the new couture establishment in avenue Montaigne which she moved to in 1923. Frescoes by Georges de Feuve depicted mythical scenes alongside classicised renditions of women wearing her best selling garments, enabling her clients to measure themselves against heroic templates of perfected beauty. Models presented her designs in this brightly-lit salon, whose creation was overseen by M. Chanut, who found that

> 'What she wanted for the décor of her new, salon was the same as what she wanted for her clothes: the space should be harmonious and classically inspired? but modern.'[7]

Even the logo of her house expressed these themes in a simplified form – with a figure holding up a curving drape of fabric atop a classical column.

While the Vionnet dresses already discussed used classicism in an abstract way as a means to re-evaluate the space fabric creates around the body, some designs used Greek motifs in a more decorative manner. Genevieve Dufy, who worked for her after the first World War, recalled how Vionnet would make trips to the Louvre to study Greek vases and the couturiere discussed the influence these had on her work,

> 'I like to look at old costumes and fashions of times gone by, because of what they say about their times. They tell so much about their era and the people in it. My inspiration comes from Greek vases, from the beautifully clothed women depicted on them, or even the noble lines of the vase itself.'[8]

It is notable though that this interest in historical costume is never interpreted as nostalgic – partly because Vionnet's radical approach to construction methods continually broke new ground. But also because of our attitudes towards classicism – which is seen as a pure form, an eternal measure of excellence that transcends the period of its creation. Yet, surely there is a longing in this evocation of the past, a yearning for the ideals of balance, proportion, harmony and symmetry, which have themselves become mythologised in western culture. This cultural mythology reflects a desire to believe in stable 'golden ages' of the past as a means to find hope in the present. It is telling that classical reference points often resurface in periods of political and economic turmoil, for example in late eighteenth century France, and inter-war Europe in the twentieth century. While European artists and designers in the 1920s and 1930s sought to break with the past and find expression in the here and now, historicism played a role in reformulating contemporary representation, with classicism, as a signifier of the eternal, a key site for inventing a vision of newness.

An article from the Werkbund journal Die Form of 1930 emphasises the role of white, a key element of both classical and modern design in adding to a sense of the present, by stating that the white walls so favoured by modern architects,

'Expose any error and control any space. Furthermore, everything is being painted white because white establishes the sense of the present. White is the modern state of mind. It is both a colour and an organising principle of modern life. Something to be seen and a way of seeing.'[9]

The sweep of clear white fabric that dominates so many of Vionnet's designs may certainly be read in terms of control of both fabric and flesh, since, despite having freed the body from the restraint of the corset, there is still a sense of control of the self through exercise and diet to produce the requisite toned modernist body. Control is also implicit in the desire for pure geometrical rationality in Vionnet's work and that of modernist architects like Le Corbusier, who could be seen as searching for a controlled and contained representation of the body/home/workplace to mitigate against the impending crisis of the contemporary period. Classical whiteness therefore states allegiance to an all conquering eternal set of truths, yet inevitably reflects the present, fixing designer and designed object in their own cultural and historical context, as products of their time as well as creators of the way that period is viewed and interpreted.

Meanwhile Vionnet did not just use whiteness to refer to classical sources. Her 'Little Horses' dress of 1924, which was shown in the Musee des Tissus Madeleine Vionnet exhibition in Lyons in 1995, saw her integrate decorative embroidery – so popular in the twenties – with her usual rigorous exploration of new techniques. The dress is cut on the bias to add fluidity and lightness to the silhouette and normally applied embroidery would have weighed down the design, working against the diagonal cut of the fabric. Albert Lesage therefore developed a new technique to follow the bias grain and enable the dress to maintain the elasticity that Vionnet's construction methods required, covering the dress in tiny blue bugle beads that filled in the negative spaces of the design like a Red Figure vase. Cecil Beaton spoke of Vionnet's modernist view of classical source material during the twenties in his book The Glass of Fashion:

'When the fashionable silhouette was flat, Vionnet worked in the round, evolving a harmony between the supple curves of the feminine body and the hang of drapery that was to be fluted as a Hellenic column. She made a Greek dress in a way the

*Greeks could never have imagined; there was nothing archaic about her lines.
Everything Vionnet created had a cling or a flow, and women dressed by her were like
moving sculptures.'*[10]

While modernism spoke of standardisation in most areas of design, with mass-production sowing the seeds of a standardised body, Vionnet's couture was set firmly within the old world of individually fitted fashion. However, it also hinted at the standardised fashionable body that was to dominate the twentieth century with the designer's adoration of the lithe, toned figure that became the iconic, model ideal.

The bias cut was the foundation upon which Vionnet's design philosophy was built. It enabled her to smooth the link between structure and decoration, body and fabric to create a contained and unified image. The wearer's body was revealed and yet concealed by the smooth layer of spiralling fabric. As the thirties began, French couture began to feel the impact of the Depression – 1927 had been the peak year for couture sales but now the economic climate had radically changed and Vionnet predicted a shift towards the simpler styles that she had always favoured. From the early to mid 1930s she focussed more and more on white fabric. Her colour palette had always been fairly limited – indeed it was left to her assistant Marcelle Chaumont to add colours to her designs – but now white seemed strangely appropriate. White is associated in the west with purity, it speaks of cool statuary – a protective layer of classical imagery to idealise and mythologise the female figure.

The images which best encapsulate the importance and meaning of classicism within Vionnet's work are Hoyningen-Huene's 1931 photographs of her favourite model – Sonia dancing in silk crêpe romaine pyjamas, replicating the graceful moves of dancers depicted on Greek vases. Sonia was filmed dancing in this manner – her image preserved by 20th century technology as she recreated the spirit of classical antiquity. Anne Hollander has suggested that the advent of moving pictures irrevocably altered the way that clothing was perceived,

*'Women, once thought to glide, were seen to walk . . . The various dance crazes of the
first quarter of the century undoubtedly were an expression of this restless spirit, but its
most important vehicle was the movies.'*[11]

Film emphasised and enhanced the impact of movement on the relationship between fabric and body. In the footage of Vionnet's model Sonia, it is the fluidity of the material floating around her limbs that is most striking. What is also noteworthy is the way that Sonia seems to glow. The pale colour of her garments, the white of her skin and blonde hair transforms her into a glowing streak of light that inhabits the dark backdrop. Her form at times seems to have turned into an electrical current signalling movement and flux, as the fabric of her evening pyjamas settles and reforms constantly as she dances. The impact of such bright, white fashions and hairstyles was not lost on Hollywood, where screen stars like Jean Harlow were lit to maximise the glitter of their shiny white gowns, their pale skin and hair as shorthand for feminine allure and sexuality. The relationship between such filmic images and fashion in the thirties also tends to 'fix' such imagery in a particular period. While the dresses worn nod towards a timeless ideal of beauty and dressing, they capture the period's fascination with whiteness, at the aesthetic level of cinematography, reflecting what Hamman wrote above concerning white as a way of 'seeing', but also as a product of cultural unease about race, when whiteness was still an unproblematic marker of superiority and dominance.

Like the so-called 'goddess' dresses that Vionnet was making during the same period, the model becomes an ideal. Her smoothly made-up face and carefully curled blonde hair make her into a vision of sculptural perfection. Vionnet sought for 'true beauty' in her designs – an eternal or at least classical ideal that relied upon Platonic notions of proportion and wholeness. Each feature must be carefully balanced with the other – the harmony of facial and physical features extended and merged with the proportions of the dress. The model becomes the embodiment of an idea – an ideal of impossible perfection a dream of completeness – an invulnerable body with flaws smoothed away to construct an untouchable goddess of aloof physical unity.

There is a Roman myth that tells of Tuccia, a vestal virgin whose chastity is called into question. To prove herself she prays to the goddess Vesta and then goes to the river Tiber and dips her sieve in the water, filling it to the brim and then miraculously carrying the water back to the temple of Vesta as proof of her continence. As Marina Warner points out in her discussion of the iconography surrounding Tuccia in her book Monuments and Maidens,

'Tuccia's sieve, miraculously made whole by the power of her own wholeness, provides us with a symbol of ideal integrity, that puns on the semantics of virtue, and constitutes in itself a kenning on the inherent properties of goodness.'[12]

Warner goes on to show how this allegory has echoed down the centuries, with feminine virtue being repeatedly associated with notions of completeness. Women's bodies are seen as ambiguous, and made culturally and morally acceptable, only when they appear to be clean, smooth and impenetrable. Warner continues:

'Tuccia's sieve is an unsound vessel that becomes sound by a miracle, like the body of a woman, which, with its open orifices, dangerous emissions and distressing aptitude for change, can yet become preternaturally sound when representing the good.'[13]

During the 19th century this soundness was provided by the cuirass of the corset, which held in women's dangerous flesh, shielding the problematic natural body beneath a whale-boned layer that culturally defined the body with its unambiguous firm lines. The figure was therefore quite literally contained and made whole in order to denote the virtuousness of the wearer and assuage collective fears of the female body.

In Vionnet's designs the corset is discarded and the natural body revealed yet smoothed out and contained by a film of bias-cut fabric, a perfected second skin that makes the wearer's body once again miraculously complete. The reflective pale tones of the silk crêpe merges with her milky skin. She is a sculpture, an impenetrable whole. Yet Vionnet has added a warm sensuality to her figure, which although 'protected' by the completeness of her image speaks more of a celebration of femininity than fear of the realities of the female body. Vionnet's goddess dresses rephrase the allegory of Tuccia's sieve, by enabling the whole body to be free and to move – at once evoking ideals of the 'soundness', while at the same time making the figure a mobile plastic creation of flesh and fabric. The heroic, monumental image of the 'goddess dress' was evoked by other designers like Paquin, and imposing classical features provided backdrops for numerous fashion photographs of the thirties. Women were encouraged to use the classical proportions of the sculptures's faces as a measure of their own beauty. Mary G. Winkler commented, 'these images [in fashion magazines] are secularised remnants of a very ancient practice: the use of images as the foundation for self-reformation through empathy and emulation.'[14]

The face itself became a focus for the classicising trend. Fashion photographs and importantly, Hollywood, encouraged women to use make-up to perfect their features, to make them photogenic, ready for the spectator with cosmetics that could achieve far more natural effects than ever before. The mask-like decoratively made-up face of the previous decade was replaced by a coolly chic vision of 'natural' i.e. classical beauty that like the well-proportioned classical body was worn as an emblem of goodness.

Kate de Castelbajac sees this form of makeup as symptomatic of women's desire to present an image of control and calm to escape both the desperation of the Depression and also as a glamorous mask for the sense of confusion surrounding women's role in a period of economic and political crisis. De Castelbajac writes,

> 'This emotional need could be approached only by an idealised femininity, which planted the seeds of an obsession that would affect the appearance of women of the rest of the century. The ideas of 'looking good' and 'feeling good' became inextricably connected for the first time, and the identification of goodness with beauty is crucial to the understanding of thirties woman.'[15]

The bias cut required a slim toned body, which has become familiar as the standard model figure. As Madge Garland recalled,

> 'In fact, what the new fashion required was nothing less than a perfectly proportioned body with a naturally indented waist, small rounded breasts which needed no support, perfect shoulders, an absolutely flat back, and exceptionally slender thighs ending in extra long legs.'[16]

With underwear kept to the minimum, dresses like the one worn by Meredith Frampton's sitter in her 1935 painting in the Tate Gallery revealed the body to an unprecedented degree. The young woman shown wears a bias-cut dress of palest pink, the fabric hovering on the surface of her skin, revealing prominent hipbones and slim legs beneath its folds. Madeleine Vionnet stated that the bias cut was elastic enough to accommodate various body sizes, but as she noted in an interview for Marie Claire in 1937,

> 'I feel that my profession must enable me to bring out the best in the most varied types of women. Throughout my life I've always tried to be a 'doctor' of the female form. As such my aim has been to teach my clients to respect their bodies, to exercise and to have a disciplined approach to their health, discarding any items which might constrict and deform them.'[17]

During the 1930s numerous exercise programmes were devised to discipline and control the body, sculpting the muscles into the desired lean form. Nutritionists also produced diet regimes that were popular at health and beauty spas. Increasingly there was a need to produce a culturally acceptable idealised form that spoke of a healthy, that is to say carefully controlled intake of food, and exercised figure. Once again, there was a classical precedent to be followed. As Susan Bordo discusses in her book, Unbearable Weight,

> 'Aristocratic Greek culture made a science of the regulation of food intake, as a road to self-mastery and the practice of moderation in all things.'[18]

This creation of a public self that intimated a rational, perfected inner self spoke of status, spirituality and virtue. Once again we see the natural body being mastered to make it 'sound' and impenetrable, with firm muscles and toned skin. In the thirties slim bodies were equally symbolic of social and cultural value.

The body created rejected the continually changing silhouettes of the previous century and the corsetry that had artificially sculpted women's figures. The classical toned body was viewed as timeless, superior to transient fashion fads and, since control was invisible, with exercise and diet shaping the body from within, as a return to the 'natural'. Foucault linked the strengthening and controlling of the body through diet regimens and exercise to the development and care of the 'self'. Such practises, he argues, were developing during the Classical period and were grounded in moral ideas relating to power and control, of both the individual and the culture as a whole. In Care of Self he writes,

> 'This "cultivation of the self" can be briefly characterised by the fact that in this case the art of existence . . . is dominated by the principle that says one must "take care of oneself". It is this principle of the care of the self that establishes its necessity, presides over its development, and organises its practice.'[19]

Thus the need to attend to the body and produce a culturally acceptable exterior self is explicitly linked to the implied 'goodness' of the interior self. This again belies the suggested effortlessness and naturalness of the classicised body, since it is set within a complex set of moral and cultural processes.

By extension, there is a temptation to read the Vionnet clothes that we have been looking at as 'nude', since fabric and body appear as one. As Anne Hollander says, Vionnet and Mme Grès,

> 'Used fabric in a sculptural way, as if it were an extension of the mobile flesh, modelling it directly on the body to make a complete plastic and tangible composition.'[20]

Caroline Evans and Minna Thornton clarify this idea in Women & Fashion by saying,

> '[Vionnet's] dresses represent not so much a return to nature as an attempt to re-confront the raw material out of which women are (culturally) constructed, actively to mediate between nature and culture via the body and clothing. They are a brave attempt to underdetermine the female body.'[21]

Vionnet's work was certainly a radical departure from the complex layers that had comprised fashionable dress at the turn of the twentieth century and Vionnet herself asserted that her dresses were, 'not for fashion . . . I only like that which lasts forever.'[22]

This desire for an immortal form of clothing was clearly expressed in her 'goddess' dresses, photographed against classical pillars, a visual emblem of their timeless status. Dress/body/sculpture/architecture – become a cohesive whole.

It is significant that Vionnet's last collections before she closed her couture house on the outbreak of World War 2, drew upon early 19th century neo-classicism as a source. The high bustlines she showed evoked the austere rationality of that period's application of classical principles. Nikolaus Pevsner described neo-classical art and design of the first years of the 1800s as modernism's 'first chapter' and in this collection classicism becomes an expression of modernist intent once more. Modernist architecture had also seen a link to the purity of ancient forms. Le Corbusier praised such an influence as a means to strip down architecture, cleanse it of unnecessary decorative elements and construct timeless, perfect buildings, controlled and 'naked' with their stark white walls and geometric forms. Once again we return to this idea of nudity in relation to whiteness and clear lines. Mark Wigley, in his discussion of the use of white in modernist architecture comments on the contradictory reading of white walls as 'naked', saying,

> 'While everyone seems to be everywhere concerned with the beauty and purity of the naked body, modern architecture itself is not naked. From the beginning, it is painted white and this white layer that proclaims that the architecture it covers is naked clearly has an extraordinarily ambiguous role.'[23]

This recognition of the layer of meaning that supposedly 'pure' whiteness represents, whether created by paint or fabric is important in deciphering the complex meaning attached to Vionnet's work, in particular, as has already been shown, during the thirties when classical references and images of white could contain such extreme and opposite meanings. It must be remembered that as Wigley notes,

'The white wall is an item of clothing, authorised at once by modernity and the classical tradition, a recovery of the spartan puritan dress that befits the controlled nobility required in the face of mechanised life.'[24]

Both the modernist architect's buildings and Madeleine Vionnet's dress strive for nudity, for stripping away the transient elements of fashion and the search for a timeless form of design. However, both the classical sources that they explored and abstracted, and the whiteness with which they coloured their creations are themselves imbued with multiple layers of complex cultural meaning. They are linked to persistent western notions of whiteness in general as 'neutral', the 'norm', but as Richard Dyer discusses in his book, White,

'This way of conceptualising white as a hue, apparently the most objective aspect of colour, provides a habit of perception that informs how we think and feel about its other aspects. The slippage between white as a colour and white as colourlessness forms part of a system of thought and affect whereby white people are both particular and nothing in particular, are both something and non-existent.'[25]

It is therefore important to question our assumptions about classicism, considering it as a complex set of meanings that can potentially expose underlying fears concerning the status of gender, the body and of race. Both within the context both of western culture more generally but also within the specific historical period of the twenties and thirties when classicism became a key source for right-wing ideologies as well as avant-garde artists.

Madeleine Vionnet's work is a cipher of modernism and classicism united to create a form of design that speaks of both purity and control in a period of chaos. She constructed a space in which women could seek new means to define themselves, rethinking traditional ideas of femininity and modesty. She provided women with a form of dress that celebrated the female – making women into bearers of classical, but also importantly, modernist ideals. She managed to subtly subvert the predominantly masculine overtones of both classical art, by idealising a young female rather than male body, but also of modernism which tended to reject so-called 'feminine' traits of fashion and ornamentation, by injecting a strongly sensual femininity into all her garments. Her gowns may have been called 'goddess dresses', but they are never merely cold, untouchable icons. Her interest in the warm, living body beneath the fabric and the wearer's tactile experience of bias-cut garments hovering around the figure, militates against such distanced readings.

Her designs drew from the past but always looked to the future. Her revolutionary construction techniques and her rethinking of the relationship between body and fabric resonated through the 20th century, inspiring designers like John Galliano, Azzedine Alaia, Issey Miyake and Yohji Yamamoto. Vionnet's work gave women a sense of completeness; their bodies and clothing became a cohesive whole. They could feel confident in her designs, protected by the layer of fluid fabric that danced around their figures. Classical inspiration provided Vionnet with a means to foreground the body and its relationship to mobile fabric, enabling her to fulfil her decree that,

'If a woman smiles, her dress must also smile.'

NOTES

Source: *Madeleine Vionnet: 15 Dresses from the Collection of Martin Kamer* (Judith Clark Costume, 2001), 6 pages.

1. Millbank Rennolds, C., *Couture*, London: Thames and Hudson, p.163
2. Hollander, A, *Seeing through Clothes*, California: Yale, 1993, p.xiii
3. Hollander, ibid., p.5
4. Quoted in Marie Claire, May 1937, in Demornex, J, *Vionnet*, London: Thames & Hudson, 1991, p.137
5,6. Chatwin, B., *What am I doing Here*, London: Picador, 1990, p.86–8
7. Kirke, B, *Madeleine Vionnet*, San Francisco: Chronicle Books, 1998, p.119
8. ibid., p.41
9. Hamman, J.E., 'Weiss alles Weiss', Die Form, 1930, quoted in Wigley, M., *White Walls and Designer Dresses, The Fashioning of Modern Architecture*, Massachusetts: MIT Press, 1995, p.208
10. Beaton, C., *The Glass of Fashion*, London: Cassell, 1989, p.183
11. Hollander, op.cit., p.153
12. Warner, M., Monuments & Maidens, *The Allegory of the Female Form*, London: Vintage, 1996, p.242
13. ibid., p.254
14. Winkler, M.G., 'Model Women', Winkler, M.G., & Cole, L. B., (eds), *The Good Body, Asceticism in Contemporary Culture*, London: Yale, 1994, p.222
15. de Castelbajac, K., *The Face of the Century, 100 Hundred Years of Makeup & Style*, NY: Rizzoli, 1995, p.62
16. Garland, M., *The Indecisive Decade, The World of Fashion & Entertainment in the Thirties*, London: MacDonald, 1968, p.76
17. Quoted in Marie Claire, May 1937, in Demornex, op.cit., p.137
18. Bordo, S., *Unbearable Weight, Feminism, Western Culture, and the Body*, University of California Press, 1995, p.185
19. Foucault, M., The History of Sexuality: 3, *The Care of the Self*, Penguin, 1990, p.43–44
20. Hollander, A., *Sex & Suits, The Evolution of Modern Dress*, NY: Kodansha, 1994, p.134–5
21. Evans, C., & Thornton, M., *Women & Fashion, A New Look*, London: Quartet, 1989, p.118

22. Kirke, op. cit., p.41
23. Wigley, M., 'White Out: Fashioning Modern Architecture', Fausch, D., Singley, P., El-Khoury, R., Efrat, Z., *Architecture in Fashion*, NY: Princeton Architectural Press, 1994, p.172
24. ibid., p.238
25. Dyer, R., *White*, London: Routledge, 1997, p.47
26. Kirke, op. cit., p.14

CHAPTER TWENTY TWO

Paul Poiret's Minaret Style: Originality, Reproduction, and Art in Fashion

Nancy J. Troy

High-end fashionable clothing for women was developed and promoted in the late nineteenth and early twentieth centuries by French couturiers who regarded the commercial world with disdain and carefully constructed their personas as great artists or discerning patrons of the arts. For them, the banal and potentially degrading aspects of business were beneath the elite status to which they aspired. The most famous couturier-collector of the period, Jacques Doucet, was careful to segregate his business operations from the art-related activities he pursued at home. Paul Poiret presents a strikingly different paradigm of the couturier insofar as he openly incorporated the visual arts as well as diverse approaches to theatrical display in his efforts to sell expensive dresses and other products in the discreet and aestheticized environment of his Paris couture house. Unlike Doucet's arrangement, in which domestic and commercial environments were strictly segregated, Poiret's *hôtel de couture* was a business setting that often functioned more like a domestic space, as it did when he hosted extravagant costume parties where his wife circulated like a mannequin and his friends tried out his latest Orientalist styles, thus insuring that the difference between commercial and private activities would always be ambiguous. The precarious balance that Poiret strove to maintain after 1909 between an allegedly disinterested commitment to high culture and the demands of an increasingly complex, sophisticated, and diversified commercial enterprise was constantly being challenged, not only by rival couturiers, but also by changes in the couture industry and even by the success of his own fashions. This paper examines the ways in which Poiret's self-construction as an artist and his theatrical strategies of display were affected by the circumstances he encountered when, in the early teens, he began seriously to cultivate the American market for couture clothing by going to the United States to present his clothing to women there, rather than waiting for them to seek him out in Paris. Poiret's discovery that his work (like that of Callot Soeurs, Doucet, Paquin, the Maison Worth, and many other French couturiers) was being copied and his label counterfeited, evidently on a vast scale, exposed a serious challenge not only to the elite business of haute couture but also to its construction of originality on which its claim to elite status had always been based.

If in the realm of fine art the modern discourse of the copy was, as Rosalind Krauss argued in a ground-breaking essay of 1981, embedded within the very construct of the original,[1] the same could be said of the couture dress, which, despite couturiers' claims to the contrary, was never a unique original but rather a copy reproduced from a generic model and then adapted to the size and shape of the individual client. Yet despite the commonality of their discursive engagement with originality, couture dresses and works of fine art of course differ in many fundamental respects. Poiret always strove to collapse those differences, for example by equating the design of a woman's dress with the painting of her portrait. But when on the eve of the First World War he sought protection for his designs – and, not incidentally, for his status as an artist – under the provisions of American copyright law, he was forced to acknowledge the incompatibility of haute couture and fine art. Unlike French law, based on the concept of *droit d'auteur* which champions the inalienable intellectual and moral interests of the creator, American law has traditionally privileged the user. In the early twentieth century it refused to recognize in functional objects such as dresses the intellectual property rights reserved for works of art as products of the mind. Instead of reinforcing Poiret's claim to authorship as a creative artist, American law recognized only his right to commercial trademark protection of his couture label, and it thereby determined that his name signified his status as a businessman, not a fine artist.

The ways in which these conflicting identities were played out in France and America in 1913 will emerge as the subject of this paper. Its narrative incorporates a brief discussion of the status of authorship according to American law, but its broader focus is on issues of originality and reproduction – the professionally mounted theatrical production and its offshoot, the commercially staged fashion show; the authentic couture dress and its pirated copy. In order to get at these larger issues, I explore how the fashionable French theater functioned for Poiret (as it also did for other couturiers) as a particularly effective marketing tool not only in Paris but also in New York. As a case in point, I examine Poiret's involvement in *Le Minaret*, a three-act play by Jacques Richepin that opened in March 1913 at the Théâtre de la Renaissance, and six months later was reinvented as a fashion show and commercial vehicle in numerous American department stores.

As its title suggests, *Le Minaret* was a typical Orientalist fantasy involving "slaves, musicians, [and] eunuchs," that was set, according to the published text, "in the Orient of the Thousand and One Nights."[2] Its convoluted yet conventional story of romance and implied eroticism was launched by the decision of an old sultan that upon his death his harem should not be dispersed but instead his eight wives should be kept together, and they themselves should determine who would become their new master. A competition among the pretenders, initiated by the Grand Eunuch a month after the sultan's death, quickly eliminated all but three rivals. The story gained romantic appeal in the second act when, under the gaze of one of the wives disguised as a muezzin in the minaret overlooking the walled garden, the suitors appeared one after another to try to gain the favor of the inhabitants of the harem. The last act took place inside the sumptuous hall of the seraglio, where, after several complications and reversals in the plot, the various wives were united with their chosen lovers and a great celebration ensued.

Given the clichéd nature of the Orient represented in the play, which one critic characterized as "whimsical and rather conventional," it was understood that Richepin had no desire to present a work of theatrical realism but had opted instead for "pleasing and harmonious *tableaux*."[3] Accordingly, Ronsin's sets and Poiret's several hundred costumes – most, if not all, actually designed by his employees, Erté and José de Zamora – created what was described in the press as "a spectacle of the most delicious refinement. It is a feast for the eyes, a symphony of colors, a veritable dream of a Thousand and One Nights . . ."[4] The successful effort to harmonize the costumes with the sets and the lighting in terms of their colors as well as their design was interpreted as an "indication of a new kind of art, very superior in its distinction and its tact to that of the much heralded Ballet Russes,"[5] from which such efforts at coordination undoubtedly had derived a good deal of inspiration.

Poiret's fashions of this period were commonly identified with those presented in Ballets Russes productions such as *Schéhérazade*, and *Le Minaret* in particular was frequently compared with the Paris production of Max Reinhardt's *Sumurun*. Yet despite these foreign associations, and the fact that the play itself was entirely Orientalist in all its features, including the plot, the decors, and the costumes, *Le Minaret* was both produced and received as an expression of French nationalist sentiment. Indeed, in mounting the play, Cora Laparcerie, an actress, wife of Jacques Richepin, and manager of the Théâtre de la Renaissance, intended from the outset to avoid the alien sensibility that French audiences identified in *Schéhérazade* and *Sumurun*; the staging of *Le Minaret* was designed, she said, to present "a Persia [that is] more French, . . . a Persia of the eighteenth century, or almost."[6]

Laparcerie's success in familiarizing the foreign, in creating a representation of the Orient that Parisian audiences would find compatible with traditional *ancien régime* sensibilities, can be measured in the overwhelmingly positive responses of the critics, who praised both the sets and the costumes of *Le Minaret* for their relatively restrained and tasteful treatment of Oriental elements. This comes as something of a surprise almost a century after the fact, in light of what today still appear to be quite unusual, even radical or bizarre, features of the female actresses' costumes. Many of them included bouffant trousers topped by bodices whose projecting, wired hems, or hoops, encircled the wearers' hips, creating a "lampshade" effect that was visually striking on stage but highly impractical if adopted in real life, particularly when it came to costumes whose multiple hoops created a tiered effect. Described as "improbable, startling, glittering, flashing, so rich, so numerous that each entrance of the actresses was greeted with applause," the clothes were accompanied by "colossal aigrettes studded with precious stones, and corselets and turbans with large, delicate pearls" that one critic noted would be the financial ruin of any husband whose wife might mistake these for items that could be worn outside the theater.[7] Given the creative license and outlandish features of the costumes, "with their bouffant pantalons with metallic reflectors, their triple and quadruple wire hoops, their curved-toe Turkish slippers, their aigrettes like golden antennas,"[8] it is noteworthy that Poiret emerged with *Le Minaret* as the champion of what many critics identified as typically French values: "For once it was appropriate that the name of the couturier figured on the [cover of the] program and one could even say that M. Paul Poiret was the real triumph of the evening. Throughout the three acts he paraded before us creations of a very picant inventiveness and often of a most delicate taste: Persian costumes accommodated to the Parisian imagination, fabrics, furs, headdresses, whose color and mixture formed living and clever *tableaux*."[9]

The discourses of Frenchness that enabled an Orientalist play such as *Le Minaret* to be received as a work redolent of *ancien régime* French values also made it possible for Poiret to suggest that adaptations of his radical and extravagant costumes might be appropriate for the Frenchwomen in the audience. From the minute the play opened, Poiret used it as an opportunity to advertise his costumes to the members of the fashionable Parisian *haut monde* who, in the wake of the *Thousand and Second Night* fête held on the grounds of his couture house in June 1911, were mounting comparably lavish Oriental parties of their own, for which they of course required appropriate costumes. Indeed, the play's première furnished an ideal setting in which to publicize a line of women's clothing designed in what soon became known as the Minaret style. In the audience, outfitted in a costume as daring as the ones on stage – it was made of transparent red and violet chiffon and topped by a wide-brimmed lampshade hat, also in violet chiffon, with a fringe of pearls – Madame Poiret completed the theatrical illusion by appearing, according to one observer, "to be dressed to enter the scene."[10] Her presence in a lampshade tunic over bouffant trousers thus allowed for a seamless transition between the stage fantasy – itself verging on a fashion show – and the female consumers in the audience, those who attended the theater not simply to see the play or to be seen in the audience but also in order to scope out the latest fashions, the clothes they would like immediately to purchase for themselves. These women presumably experienced *Le Minaret* as a spectacle in which they might imaginatively take part, something Poiret's guests had literally been able to do when they attended his *Thousand and Second Night* fête, where Madame Poiret had also been dressed in a fringed lampshade tunic and bouffant trousers, setting an example for the Oriental costumes of all the other female guests at this and subsequent parties with the same theme. Thus, in the blurred boundaries between *Le Minaret* as a theatrical performance and a real-life event, an aestheticized production with aspirations to high culture on one hand and an opportunity for fashion marketing on the other, Poiret worked both with and against the upper-class privacy and elitism he claimed for his Orientalist costumes. He sought both to appeal to the *ancien régime* proclivities of his wealthy clients and to exploit the theatrical core of pre-war fashion, the way in which it mimicked contemporary theater as spectacle, by constructing women to be seen – often at the theater, even as they were in the act of seeing. One might further argue that *Le Minaret* exposed Poiret's contribution – if that is what it should be called – to the discourse of Orientalism in pre-War France as an effort to transpose this complex and value-laden cultural expression onto the commodity form by repeatedly confusing the distinctions between self and Other, producer and consumer, actor and audience, art and clothing, theater and real life.

When *Le Minaret* opened to rave reviews in Paris, Poiret insisted, as was the custom of all his colleagues in the couture business, that he had no interest whatsoever in the commercial implications of his theatrical and related activities. He declared at the time, "I invented the [Minaret] tunic for a Persian play to be worn in a Persian garden in a spectacular ballet. I was astonished when my patrons called me on the telephone the morning after the première and begged that I fashion them such a tunic for social occasions. Naturally, I complied . . ."[11] Indeed, he did much more than that; not content to wait passively for women to come to him, he determined to build a new and far broader clientele by maximizing the publicity surrounding *Le Minaret* and the dresses he made for the play. This resolution bore fruit six months after the Paris première, in September 1913, when Poiret himself orchestrated an extensive public relations campaign to accompany the introduction of dresses inspired by his Minaret costumes to the American market. This transatlantic effort was carefully planned to coincide with his own tour of major cities in the Northeast and Midwest, including New York, Philadelphia, Baltimore, Boston, Buffalo, Toronto, and Chicago, where he lectured extensively, accompanied by films and portfolios filled with photographs of his mannequins parading in the garden of his Paris *maison de couture*,[12] and he received members of the press in the commodious suites he occupied at luxury hotels. In New York, for example, Poiret made appearances at major department stores, including. J. M. Gidding, Gimbel Brothers, R. H. Macy, and John Wanamaker (all of them boasted about the presence of "The Famous Fashion Dictator" in their advertisements[13]); he addressed female students of "practical art" and what were known as "household arts" at the Horace Mann School of Teachers College at Columbia University, and at the Pratt Institute;[14] he lectured at Carnegie Hall under the auspices of the Société des Beaux Arts; and he spoke to reporters in a room of his suite at the Plaza Hotel that he transformed from a nondescript – if nevertheless luxurious – hotel interior into a small-scale version of his own *maison de couture*.

As Poiret toured the United States along with his Minaret costumes, showing off his wife, delivering his lectures, giving interviews, and dining as the guest of department-store executives, the couturier emphatically repeated the contention that his trip had nothing whatsoever to do with publicity. Two days after his arrival he declared to reporters "that he was 'very cross' at the advertisements that appeared in . . . newspapers exploiting his arrival. He said: 'I came to America on a social visit. I am merely a tourist. I think it is very bad form for my name to be used in a commercial sense just because I happen to be here . . .'"[15] The fact that his wife brought with her 100 outfits for a visit lasting less than a month should not, he insisted, be taken as proof that she was there to serve as his mannequin. "Nothing could be further from the fact. We will be here in this country three weeks. Mme. Poiret must wear clothes. That is the only purpose for which she has brought her costumes. She is not to act as my model."[16] Poiret's denial of any commercial intent, his disdain for advertising and publicity, was part and parcel of his self-construction as an artist and an aristocrat, an individualist who rejected fashion because it smacked of mass production: "Women are wrong to adopt one style regardless," he told a *New York Times* correspondent. "They are not all made alike. They are different. They should wear different gowns."[17] While stressing individualism and originality, however, he also was careful to distance himself from the reputation he had gained for stylistic extremism: "'Whenever there is anything sensational produced,' he said, 'people say "That is Poiret." Often it is something with which I have had nothing to do at all, out of character and beneath my style. So much that is outlandish has been credited to me that I have come to explain what my styles really are.'"[18] These, he said, could be described by two fundamental principles: simplicity and individuality. "Women must wear something simple, but personal or individual," he intoned. "It can be personal without extravagance. Simple things prove most original."[19] Thus Poiret sought to appeal to American clients interested in practical, functional clothes. While department stores were touting the extravagant and outlandish Orientalist costumes seen in *Le Minaret*, Poiret countered with the relatively demure clothes visible in his film and photographs, clothes that supported his rhetoric of simplicity much more credibly than did his most striking and critically acclaimed Minaret designs. Ultimately, this reversal functioned to drain away the force of the aesthetic differences between extravagant Orientalism and classical simplicity as these became discursive alternatives signifying not so much particular styles but rather the distinction and fashionable elitism so attractive to Poiret's wealthy client base. Seeking to retain that base but also to expand it, especially by appealing to the broad spectrum of American department-store patrons (who were no less drawn to distinction and fashionable elitism), the couturier made sure to explain to American women that simplicity was neither a path to uniformity nor the result of designing according to a formula: "The mode does not come from a theory; it is a sort of feeling. I feel the tendencies which

I cannot explain."[20] Steeping himself in the rhetoric of originality that characterizes modernist aesthetic discourse in general, Poiret appealed to the Romantic notion of the artist not as a mere artisan, or someone who had to hawk his own wares, but instead as a creator and a dreamer who pursued inspiration without any regard for commercial considerations.

The prohibition against mingling art with commerce was not Poiret's invention but was in fact deeply ingrained in art discourse. Intended to insure the elevated status of the artist, it was already inscribed in the mid-seventeenth-century statutes of the French Académie Royale de la Peinture et du Sculpture, whose members were forbidden to open a picture shop, display paintings in the windows of their houses or otherwise suggest any engagement in mercenary affairs.[21] Poiret always insisted on this ancient distinction and he spared no expense in his efforts to present himself as both an artist and an aristocrat who considered commercial matters to be beneath his dignity. Throughout his tour of North American cities, however, his actions belied the purity and disinterestedness that he consistently claimed for himself. During the few short weeks of his stay in the United States, where he was the guest of one department-store magnate after the next, he not only addressed thousands of potential clients in the lectures he delivered in hotel ballrooms and department store theaters, but he also closed deals with several American businesses, including a commitment to supply *Harper's Bazar* with a series of illustrated articles and an exclusive arrangement to provide "authoritative models" of blouses to Larrymade Waists.[22] Larrymade announced their arrangement with Poiret in *Women's Wear* in full-page, graphically arresting weekly advertisements in which they paired their trademark with the distinctive typography and imagery that Paul Iribe and Georges Lepape had designed for Poiret's Paris couture-house labels, stationery, and deluxe albums.[23] The department stores also made much of their association with the French couturier, often by trumpeting claims of having been the first to introduce Poiret's costumes from *Le Minaret*.

Advertisements, reports, photographs, and drawings published in newspapers and trade journals indicate that Gimbel's, Macy's, and Wanamaker's all installed special Oriental settings inspired by *Le Minaret* for the Fall 1913 fashion shows they mounted on their premises. The stores avidly competed with one another in adapting theatrical sets, props, and costumes from the Paris performance of *Le Minaret*. Macy's created a generic "Moorish Palace" on the eighth floor of its store, where the setting, "an arabesque mass of gold and red and green," occupied the greater part of the store's restaurant (an enormous space that could accommodate 2,500 people at a time[24]) and provided a focus for a raised promenade on which live mannequins paraded in fashion shows. Gimbel's and Wanamaker's went further, attempting to reproduce sets from the Paris production of *Le Minaret* in order to reinforce the authenticity of the Minaret-style dresses that were presented on the their stages – and sold in their Women's Gown Salons. The Fall fashion display that Wanamaker's mounted, entitled "In a Persian Garden," must have resembled an actual theatrical performance especially closely, because it was presented to the accompaniment of organ music in the vast auditorium of Wanamaker's New York store, which was capable of seating 1,500 people.[25]

Poiret's spectacular marketing campaign, which owed as much to the couturier as it did to the department-store owners who underwrote his American trip, proved to be enormously effective, although it differed markedly from the his customary practice, which was characterized by the privacy, intimacy, and elitism to which his personal clients were treated in Paris. The high visibility of the U.S. tour obviously responded to the particular conditions governing the merchandising of French fashions in North America, which took place in the public arena dominated by the large-scale department store rather than in the carefully controlled environment of the couturier's private *hôtel*. In the United States, Poiret's Orientalism as well as his classical simplicity would be seen not just by those wealthy women who could afford to travel to Europe and patronize his couture house in Paris but also, and more crucially, by a vast middle-class clientele.

In order to lure ever more customers while at the same time diversifying the class origins of their patrons, by the end of the nineteenth century American department stores, like their French counterparts, had expanded the scope of their merchandise to include more expensive items and improved their displays to appeal to more sophisticated customers. They also developed what *The Dry Goods Economist* described in 1903 as "spectacular methods of bringing people within their doors," including various kinds of free entertainment and culturally uplifting fare. "Very often these openings are held in the evening and partake of the nature of a reception, no goods being sold and visitors being treated as the guests of the concern."[26] It was, the author noted, a very effective, though also very expensive, form of advertising. Thus the department stores shared with Poiret some of the same strategies – though on a much larger scale and often without his commitment to stylistic modernism – of covering their marketing with a veneer of culture, or, in other words, promoting consumer interest and generating sales by means of theater, interior design, and the visual arts.

As Susan Porter Benson has pointed out, department stores like Wanamaker's were designed to be "palaces of consumption, schools for a new culture of buying."[27] By providing art exhibitions, restaurants with live music, lectures, and other cultural amenities as well as elaborate and often costly services in a spacious and luxuriously appointed environment, department stores conveyed to their clients the sense that consumption was not simply a means of addressing one's needs or even fulfilling one's desires, "but also a way of behaving that had links to class, particularly to urban gentility. The palace of consumption elevated prosaic goods and touched them with the aura of elegance while fostering a taste for luxury and encouraging the sale of finer goods."[28] In seeking the largest possible client base, department stores used art and theater to make ordinary objects appeal to a wide spectrum of potential patrons.

Poiret, on the other hand, stressed the high-end, luxury aspects of art and spectacle in order to build a relatively small, elite clientele through individual sales on the premises of his couture house in Paris; in coming to America, however, he entered the domain of the department store where art and especially theater operated more explicitly and on a much larger scale. As William Leach has pointed out, "The upper-class French trade . . . became an American mass market."[29]

Those who have written about the department store, whether in France or the United States, have frequently commented on the fact that theatricality of one sort or another is at the core of the shopping experience.[30] William Leach has described in detail the theatrical dimension of American department-store practices, pointing out that Orientalist themes – a pervasive feature of American popular culture – were among the most widespread merchandising vehicles because they provoked fantasies of sensuality and luxury that were particularly effective in the production of consumer desire. Leach relates the story of *The Garden of Allah*, a typically romanticized Orientalist novel published in 1904 by Robert Hichens, which was adapted for the stage in 1907 and eventually inspired three movies. Around 1910, this theme became the basis for numerous department-store productions. A spectacle mounted by Wanamaker's New York store in 1912 was by far the most lavish, with members of the cast of the Broadway play in Arab costume roaming through the store, not simply drawing attention to their own outfits but also encouraging clients to view similar gowns on the store's theatrical stage, where, to the strains of Oriental music played by a string orchestra, thirty mannequins modeled costumes said to have been inspired by Algerian designs.[31]

The effectiveness of just such machinations, enhanced by Poiret's active participation in them during his North American tour, had a direct and impressive impact on sales of his dresses in the United States. An article in *Harper's Bazar* noted that in the wake of Poiret's visit Americans had seen "a perfect avalanche of minaret or Poiret costumes."[32] According to an account of the Minaret style that appeared in the American trade journal, *Women's Wear*, "Already its extremist expressions have been shown by the leading stores in the largest American cities to thousands of women, and judging by the intent faces, the bated breath of the onlookers, the modes of Le Minaret, at least in modified form, are considered neither entirely ridiculous nor wholly impractical."[33] Within six months *Vogue* declared it "a safe wager that every woman in the land possessed at least one of [Poiret's lampshade] tunics during the past season."[34] This is obviously an exaggerated claim, but it nevertheless alerts us to a problem of which Poiret became acutely aware while touring the United States. As he went about denying any commercial interest in his visit, and indeed suggesting that as an artist he was above commerce altogether, he discovered to his great dismay that in the United States his exclusive dress designs were being copied for sale at cut-rate prices. The story was recounted eighteen months later in the pages of *Vogue*:

During his visit to America, Mr. Poiret was much astonished to see advertised in various shop windows Poiret gowns which he himself had never seen before. Needless to say, Mr. Poiret quickly identified these gowns as never having emanated from his establishment and the labels which were sewed in them as nothing but counterfeits of his original label. He immediately placed the matter in the hands of his attorney, who started an investigation which revealed the fact that not only were Poiret labels being imitated and sold throughout the country by a number of manufacturers, but the labels of other prominent couturiers were also being duplicated. In fact, it was discovered that quite a flourishing trade in these false labels had become well established in America.[35]

The widespread manufacture and use of false designer labels was hardly a secret, as is evident from an article entitled, "The Dishonest Paris Label," by Samuel Hopkins Adams. Published in *Ladies' Home Journal* in March 1913 (just over half a year before Poiret's arrival in the United States), the piece described precisely, according to its subtitle, "How American Women are Being Fooled by a Country-Wide Swindle."[36] In it, Adams reported that fraudulent labels were readily available in large cities such as Chicago and New York, where factories offered dozens of counterfeit labels from stock on hand, or a potential buyer could order new ones to be made up in a matter of days. In addition to those manufactured in America, a large number of genuine French labels were being imported and sewn into American-made garments, "some of which, however," Adams reported, "are legitimately used with the designation, 'copied after.' Deducting for this use, and allowing a moderate output for the factories in this country, a conservative estimate would indicate that not fewer than two million and a half hats, gowns and cloaks are on sale, under fraudulent labels, to the American public. It is one of the most extensive swindles of modern business."[37] Manufacturers, wholesalers, and retailers across the country and at all levels of the wholesale and retail industry participated in fraudulent trade practices; indeed, according to Adams, the number of honest labels was "almost negligible." Thus the overwhelming odds were that any woman in America who purchased a garment with a Paris label risked paying top dollar for a sham. Those who bought garments with Paris labels at what they must have known were impossibly low prices probably should have suspected that they were not getting genuine articles. "If our customers want the French-labeled goods," one label manufacturer told Adams, "we supply 'em. That's what we're in business for, to give 'em what they want . . . Any woman knows that she can't get a new Paris hat for twenty dollars. If she doesn't she's a fool, and she deserves to get swindled." When Poiret was informed that counterfeit copies of his house label had been sewn into headgear for which he was not responsible, he threatened to "turn the fullest punishment of the law upon those who offend in this manner." Since there were no legal remedies available to protect his clothing designs in America – a circumstance to which we will return shortly – Poiret's only recourse was to protect his label, which, he noted, "is now registered at Washington."[38]

It was not until six months after Poiret first complained of fraud, and well after he had returned from the United States to Paris, that he finally got some satisfaction when William Fantel of the Universal Weaving Company was found guilty of passing counterfeit trademark in the form of false labels and sentenced to a $50 fine or ten days in jail.[39] But most problematic instances of copying, particularly where clothes rather than labels were directly concerned, did not come to even a mildly satisfying conclusion such as this, nor were all of them equally clear-cut. At issue was a spectrum of practices that extended from outright fraud to legitimate copying, very little of which was regulated and for which there appear to have been few systematic rules. It is, for example, difficult to determine the status of copies advertised by some of Poiret's own commercial clients, including stores that prided themselves on introducing his Minaret style. The ambiguity of just what it was that department stores were selling points up the ways in which originality and reproduction were confounded in the fashion industry – and particularly in the language that department stores used in their ads. For example, J. M. Gidding used wording that made it unclear whether the store was selling original Paris models or American "interpretations" – or both: "Individual ideas from those famed couturiers, Poiret, Worth, Paquin, Premet, Callot, Cheruit, Bernard, Drecoll, Lanvin and others of equal note – The styles worn in Paris, Deauville, Trouville, Ostend, Brighton and other famous European resorts are at your very door in New York – The *uncommon* effects produced by the noted *style-originators* of the world . . . Our own exclusive interpretations of these new French modes form an interesting collection."[40] Another outlet which called attention to its genuine couture dresses also boasted, "Individual adaptations and Reproductions are assured. Chic style, perfect fit and superior workmanship at very moderate prices."[41] No mention is made in these advertisements of any authorization the stores might have obtained in order to sell their "adaptations" and "reproductions," and it is not stated whether they had paid a special price for the couture creations, one that could have included the right to make and market multiple copies of those garments. Such regulatory practices were only beginning to be put into place by the French couture industry during this period, and there is scant information about their nature and even less about the uniformity of their application. The fact that many American department stores seem to have acknowledged a distinction between authentic models imported from Paris and their own copies suggests that they were not guilty of the kind of dishonest copying and inclusion of false labels that Poiret discovered at the time of his visit to the United States. Nevertheless, Poiret's own experience, Adams's article, and the department stores' advertisements are only the tip of a very large mountain of evidence attesting to the serious problem that copying posed for Poiret and other French couturiers.

Copying, it is important to keep in mind, was inherent in the very structure of haute couture, according to which the couturier produces a model destined for reproduction and adaptation to the needs of individual clients. In practice, as soon as a model left the atelier of the couture house in order to be presented for sale, examples (what might be called "original copies") could be purchased by, and sent to, both high-end retail establishments and large-scale manufacturers abroad. Elite retailers would copy the couture example, with or without alterations, and sell that copy legitimately as a "reproduction" or "adaptation" of signature French haute couture. Most often these legitimate copies would not be made by the couturier or by another dressmaker in France but in the country of eventual sale, enabling the importer to avoid any taxes on the importation of finished goods as well as the high price that the couturier would demand for additional examples of his or her own models in order to support the creative work, skilled labor, and high-quality materials that were the hallmark of haute couture. The couturier also lost out on these resale arrangements when a design was purchased by a large-scale manufacturer who would typically use a carefully selected couture design as the basis for a series of garments made with cheaper fabrics, less costly decorative details, and inferior workmanship. Mass production and widespread distribution of inexpensive garments allowed the manufacturer to recoup costs with none of the risk that was assumed at the creative end of the industry. As a result, couturiers saw their markets diminishing; even when their designs were selling, someone else was reaping a much greater benefit than they. How much more difficult and complex the picture became when copying was done without any acknowledgment or compensation.

What all the agitation about copying in the press and among couturiers like Poiret suggests is that, just as his entrepreneurial dream became reality, at the moment that, as *Women's Wear* put it, every woman possessed at least one of Poiret's Minaret designs, the dream was turning into a nightmare of uncontrolled proliferation and consumption. Poiret was neither effectively overseeing the new developments in manufacturing and marketing, nor was he benefitting financially from them. It was as if the very strategies that he had successfully employed to position his clothes as unique creations and to put his name at the pinnacle Paris fashion – his self-construction as an artist and patron of the arts, a creative individualist operating above and beyond the debased world of business – had inadvertently encouraged the production of a profusion of examples destined for mass consumption, thereby effecting a popularization that simultaneously validated his fashionable status and destroyed his aspirations to elite culture. Thus the huge numbers of women who mobbed hotels and department stores in order to view Poiret's dresses testified at once to the success and to the failure of his couture enterprise. While American audiences were undoubtedly drawn by the theatricality of his fashion presentations, which marked both the high-culture ambitions and the broader commercial aspirations of Poiret and other French couture creators, these women constituted a mass audience, not the discrete individual clients who were in a position to sustain the elitism that continued to characterize Poiret's business practice, and haute couture generally, in Paris. The irony in this situation was that, especially in the American department store, Poiret embraced a vulgarized form of theater – the fashion show – in order to stave off a parallel vulgarization of haute couture. The compelling purpose was to marshall a form of expression that could be associated with high culture in the effort to protect haute couture as an art form from the menace of uncontrolled commerce.

At the same time, however, the theater was invoked precisely because it did appeal to such a broad audience and therefore assured that couture designs would reach a vast new clientele – precisely the circumstances that would ultimately compromise the elite status that was considered crucial to the viability of haute couture.

Poiret himself recognized that the discourses of high art would be no match for the forces unleashed by modern commerce. Compelled to do battle against copying and reproduction on a field that, in America at least, was structured in ways that benefitted industry rather than art, Poiret appealed to United States law by publicly threatening to "prosecute to the full extent of the law anyone who places a false label in imitation of my trademark on any article of merchandise." By invoking trademark law, which applied only to the couture label attached to his garments and not to any garments themselves, Poiret tacitly acknowledged the fact that American intellectual property law did not protect him against many types of design piracy, nor, indeed, did it accord him the status of creative and original artist to which he continually laid claim. Trademarks have nothing to do with originality, legal analysts have explained; they are "mere adjuncts or appurtenances of articles of trade" and as such they are distinct from the domain of copyright, which covers "things whose value in exchange resides in themselves, viz., works of literature, science, and the fine arts" where issues of originality and authorship do come prominently into play.[42]

As scholars of law and literature have pointed out, authorship is "a culturally, politically, economically, and socially constructed category rather than a real or natural one."[43] The modern concept of the author matured simultaneously with the capitalist system in the eighteenth century when copyright laws linked creativity and originality with the property rights of individual authors and artists.[44] In the United States, as Paul Goldstein has explained, early copyright law emphasized the interests of the consumer and allowed only a narrow scope of protection, largely to utilitarian products where personal creativity was at a minimum.[45] It was not until the middle of the nineteenth century that United States copyright law began seriously to concern itself with works of creative authorship as well, and only in 1870 did Congress revise the copyright law in order to embrace three-dimensional objects such as sculptures, molds, designs, and other works of fine art. Although a 1909 Copyright Act introduced a number of significant changes to American law, it did not cover utilitarian objects or functional designs of any kind.

American copyright law traditionally drew a sharp distinction between fine art on one hand and applied art or industrial design – anything functional or utilitarian in purpose – on the other; the former category was subject to copyright registration, while the latter was not.[46] Although the Copyright Act passed by Congress in 1909 seemed to weaken the distinction by omitting the term "fine" from the phrase "works of art" in stipulating what it covered, the Copyright Office, which was responsible for carrying out the regulations, specifically stated in 1910 that "[n]o copyright exists in . . . embroideries, garments, laces, woven fabrics, or any similar objects." Such utilitarian objects were relegated to the domain of design patent laws; these, however, had been developed to deal primarily with mechanical rather than aesthetic innovation. As a result, United States design patent laws were ineffective in protecting garments against piracy, if only because most articles of clothing lacked the kinds of innovative functional features that would enable them to rise to the level of protectable works of applied art. "The design patent statutes," Rocky Schmidt explains, "grant protection to 'a new, original and ornamental design for an article of manufacture.'. . . In order to be eligible for design patent protection, however, the design of an article of manufacture must be novel, non-obvious, original, ornamental, and meet the test of invention. Courts have consistently held that garment designs do not meet these requirements."[47] Moreover, the thorough search of existing designs, necessary in order to demonstrate that a candidate for design patent is indeed innovative, is far too lengthy to be practicable, since it generally exceeds what is called the "style life" of the garment, that brief period in which a new style retains its saleability as fashion.

Thus in contemplating how to go about protecting his designs from piracy in the American marketplace, Poiret discovered that he could not appeal either to copyright or to patent law. American copyright law refused to recognize his garments as works of art and thereby denied his status as an artist; with similar implications, American patent law failed to acknowledge that originality and invention were embodied in his work. The only recourse that remained was the protection of his trademark, the label that bore his name, which was also the name of his company. Although he had succeeded in making that name distinctive, in the eyes of the law, as a trademark it was neither creative nor original; it simply identified his business. Indeed, as Paul Goldstein has remarked, "If copyright is the law of authorship and patent is the law of invention, trademark is the law of consumer marketing."[48] In America, then, Poiret could lay claim neither to authorship nor to invention; United States law ignored his self-construction as an artist and as an inventor, according him status only as an entrepreneur – a designation he had always sought to avoid and repress.

Considering the market conditions that Poiret encountered in America encourages us to regard him as a symptom of the contradictory forces that shaped cultural discourse at a time when anonymous production was placing enormous pressures on the creative individual. Poiret's preoccupation with securing his identity as an artist while also developing a mass market for his clothes finds a parallel in the increasing value placed upon the trademark and brand name which by the end of the nineteenth century were enabling consumers to distinguish virtually identical commodities from one another in the marketplace for mass-produced goods. Similarly, Poiret's engagement with both Orientalism and classic simplicity suggests that these tropes did not belong to antithetical discourses, the one understood as transgressive and the other as sustaining traditional culture and class interests. Poiret deployed both Orientalism and classicism in a variety of contexts to position and promote his fashion statements as expressions of luxury and sumptuousness steeped in the cultural politics of a wealthy and aristocratic French elite; but he also directed these same fashion statements to the middle-class consumers who flocked to American department stores to see and to purchase modified adaptations of his most outrageous designs.

It was in the public arena of the American department store, as distinct from the private sphere of his artfully designed Parisian *hôtel de couture*, that Poiret confronted the conditions governing the merchandising of fashion in the mass market. There the multiple tangents of his trajectory through the world of fashion converged to expose the predicament of the individual artist in the face of mass production. In America he not only understood the danger that industrial production posed for haute couture, but he also began to come to grips with the fact that no aesthetic discourse, not even his self-construction as an artist, could protect him from the consequences of his own success as a purveyor of fashion. When Poiret sought to protect his designs as intellectual property, the law, instead of shoring up his status as an artist, forced him to acknowledge his identity as a businessman. After the First World War, when financial and commercial considerations gradually overwhelmed his artistic persona, Poiret not only surrendered his place at the crossroads of fashion and art, but he also lost control of his name to a corporation that took over his business and forced him out of his *maison de couture*. It is difficult to imagine any more potent image of the dissolution of the romantic ideal of the individual artist as genius under the pressures of commodity capitalism. That during the 1920s Poiret himself contributed to his own demise by continuing to spend vast sums of money to express his personal aesthetic vision and regain his stature as a dominant figure in the post-war fashion world makes his downfall not only poignant but also emblematic of the fate of the avant-garde artist committed to the values of individuality, originality, and authenticity. That the woman who took over his preeminent position, Coco Chanel, secured her success on the basis of couture clothes that projected an image of standardization and were favorably compared to mass-produced commodities suggests not so much the ways in which her "little black dress" differed from the exoticism and fantasy characteristic of Poiret's Minaret style, but rather that, like Poiret before her, but now in a fashion redolent with the values of conformity and reproduction, she found a means of representing the contradictory forces at work in modern culture.

ACKNOWLEDGMENTS

This paper is derived from a larger study, *Couture Culture: A Study in Modern Art and Fashion*, forthcoming from MIT Press. I am grateful to Richard Meyer, Andrew Perchuk, Wim de Wit, and especially Valerie Steele for their astute editorial comments and for their interest in my work. All translations are my own unless otherwise noted.

NOTES

Source: *Fashion Theory*, 6(2) (Berg Publishers, 2002), 117–43.

1. Krauss makes this point in her analysis of Auguste Rodin's sculpture in "The Originality of the Avant-Garde," and "Sincerely Yours," both reprinted in *The Originality of the Avant-Garde and Other Modernist Myths*, pp. 151–94. Cambridge, MA and London: MIT Press, 1985.

2. Jacques Richepin, *Le Minaret. Comédie en trois actes en vers*. Paris: Librairie Charpentier et Fasquelle, 1914.

3. Jules Delini, "Le Minaret de Jacques Richepin à la Renaissance." *Comoedia* (18 March 1913). Clipping in Bibliothèque de l'Arsenal, Paris, Rf. 70.593.

4. Paul Souday, "Renaissance: 'Le Minaret', comédie spectacle, en trois actes et en vers, de M. Jacques Richepin." Unidentified clipping (21 March 1913) in Bibliothèque de l'Arsenal, Paris, Rf. 70.593.

5. François de Nion, "Les Répétitions générales. Théâtre de la Renaissance – Le Minaret . . ." Unidentified clipping (20 March 1913) in Bibliothèque de l'Arsenal, Paris, Rf. 70.593.

6. Régis Gignoux, "Avant le rideau." Unidentified clipping (19 March 1913) in Bibliothèque de l'Arsenal, Paris, Rf. 70.593.

7. R. D., "Le Minaret: La Soirée." Unidentified and undated clipping in Bibliothèque de l'Arsenal, Paris, Rf. 70.593.

8. Louis Schneider, "Le Minaret – la mise en scène et les décors." Unidentified clipping (19 March 1913) in Bibliothèque de l'Arsenal, Paris, Rf. 70.593.

9. Guy Launay, "Répétition générale: au théâtre de la Renaissance, le Minaret" de M. Jacques Richepin, est avant tout une surprenante exposition de costumes." Unidentified clipping (20 March 1913) in Bibliothèque de l'Arsenal, Paris, Rf. 70.593.

10. Lise-Léon Blum, "Le Goût au théâtre." *Gazette du Eon Ton* 1, no. 6 (April 1913): 188.

11. Paul Poiret, quoted in Anne Rittenhouse, "The Prophet of Simplicity." *Vogue* 42, no. 9 (1 November 1913): 142.

12. Before his departure from Paris, Poiret had shown the film to about thirty guests at a "cinematograph dinner" described by a correspondent for *The New York Times* ("Poiret, Creator of Fashions, Here" [21 September 1913], sec. 7: 2).

13. This term appeared in an advertisement for Gimbel Brothers in *Women's Wear* (26 September 1913): 8.

14. See "Costumes: New York – Dates of Lectures to Be Given by M. Poiret." *Women's Wear* (24 September 1913): 1; "Paul Poiret Lectures." *Women's Wear* (26 September 1913): 1; "Teachers College." *Columbia Specator* 57, no. 4 (27 September 1913): 2. I am grateful to Andrew Perchuk for locating the last reference.

15. "Costumes: Paul Poiret Criticises the Commercialization and Capitalization of his Visit to this Country." *Women's Wear* (22 September 1913): 1.

16. *Ibid.*: 1, 7.

17. "Paul Poiret Here to Tell of his Art." *New York Times* (21 September 1913), sec. 1: 11.

18. "Costumes: New York – Dates of Lectures to be Given by M. Poiret." *Women's Wear* (24 September 1913): 1. The same passage is quoted in "Paul Poiret Here to Tell of His Art."

19. "Poiret Talks about his Art." *Women's Wear* (23 September 1912): 1, 9.

20. *Ibid.*

21. See Harrison C. White and Cynthia A. White, *Canvases and Careers: Institutional Change in the French Painting World* (1965; Chicago, IL: University of Chicago Press, 1993): 8 and 13, n. 6, where White and White cite L. Vitet, *L'Académie Royale*, p. 72. Paris: Levy, 1861.

22. For Poiret's arrangement with *Harper's Bazar*, see "Exclusive Poiret Costumes," *Harper's Bazar* 48, no. 5 (November 1913): 34.

23. For the Larrymade Waists advertisements, see *Women's Wear* (10, 17, 24, 31 October; 14, 28 November 1913), Retailers' Weekly Review Section.

24. Mica Nava, "Modernity's Disavowal: Women, the City and the Department Store." In Pasi Falk and Colin Campbell (eds), *The Shopping Experience*, p. 69. London: Thousand Oaks; New Delhi: SAGE Publications, 1977.

25. For a description of the fashion show, see Anna de Haven, "Costumes: The Wanamaker Presentation of Paris Fashions 'In a Persian Garden.'" *Women's Wear* (26 September 1913), sec. 4: 11–12.

26. "The Store Entertainment." *Dry Goods Economist* (18 April 1903): 33. On the complex issues raised by class difference in the context of the department store, see Susan Porter Benson, "Palace of Consumption and Machine for Selling: The American Department Store, 1880–1940." *Radical History Review* no. 21 (Fall 1979): 199–221.

27. Benson, "Palace of Consumption," 203.

28. Susan Porter Benson, *Counter Cultures: Saleswomen Managers, and Consumers in American Department Stores. 1890–1940*, p. 82. Urbana and Chicago, IL: University of Illinois Press, 1986.

29. William Leach, *Land of Desire: Merchants Powers and the Rise of a New American Culture*, p. 95. New York: Pantheon Books, 1993.

30. See Rachel Bowlby, *Shopping with Freud*. New York and London: Routledge, 1993, especially pp. 104–5; Kristin Ross, "Introduction: Shopping." In Émile Zola, *The Ladies' Paradise (Au bonheur des dames)*, pp. viii–ix. Berkeley, CA and London: University of California Press, 1992; and David Chaney, "The Department Store as a Cultural Form." *Theory Culture & Society* 1, no. 3 (1983).

31. Leach, *Land of Desire*, 108–11.

32. "In the World of Make-Believe." *Harper's Bazar* 50, no. 2 (February 1914): 12.

33. "The Style Influence of 'Le Minaret.'" *Women's Wear* (3 October 1913), sec. 4: 1.

34. "So Say the Paris Openings." *Vogue* 43, no. 9 (1 April 1914): 37.

35. "Copyrighting Clothes." *Vogue* 45, no. 3 (1 February 1915): 17.

36. Samuel Hopkins Adams, "The Dishonest Paris Label: How American Women are Being Fooled by a Country-Wide Swindle." *Ladies' Home Journal* (March 1913), repr. *Dress: The Journal of the Costume Society of America* 4 (1978): 17–23.

37. *Ibid.*: 18.

38. "The Specialty Shops." *Women's Wear* (14 October 1913): 1, 6. An identical article appeared three days later under a different title: "Poiret's Label." *Women's Wear* (17 October 1913): 3.

39. People vs. William Fantel, Docket Index, Minutes of Special Sessions, 5 August 1914–22 March 1915, 269. I am indebted to Rick Richman of the law firm of O'Melveny & Myers for making it possible for the legal research staff of their New York office, headed by Jo Cooper, to track down this case for me.

40. Advertisement for J. M. Gidding & Co., *The New York Times* (17 September 1913): 6.

41. Advertisement for Kurzman, *The New York Times* (24 September 1913): 5.

42. Herbert A. Howell, "The Print and Label Law." *University of Pennsylvania Law Review and American Law Register* vol. 70, no. 2 (January 1922): 95.

43. The phrase is Peter Jaszi's in "Toward a Theory of Copyright: The Metamorphoses of 'Authorship.'" *Duke Law Journal* (1991): 455–502; see also Michel Foucault, "What Is an Author?" trans. Josué V. Harari (1979). Repr. in Paul Rabinow (ed.), *The Foucault Reader*, pp. 101–20. New York: Pantheon Books, 1984. For my introduction to the wealth of issues that copyright law raises for understanding the status of the artist in the modern period, I am indebted to the work of Molly Nesbit: "What was an Author?" *Yale French Studies*, no. 73 (1988): 229–57; and "The Language of Industry." In Thierry de Duve (ed.), *The Definitively Unfinished Marcel Duchamp*, pp. 51–84. Cambridge, MA: MIT Press, 1991.

44. See Jaszi, "Toward a Theory of Copyright," 467.

45. Paul Goldstein, "Copyright," *Journal of the Copyright Society of the U.S.A.* 38 (1991): 116.

46. *Rules and Regulations for the Registration of Claims to Copyright*, Bulletin no. 15 (1910): 8, quoted in L. C. F. Oldfield, *The Law of Copyright* 2nd edn, p. 197. London, Sydney and Calcutta: Butterworth & Co, 1912.

47. Rocky Schmidt, "Designer Law: Fashioning a Remedy for Design Piracy." *UCLA Law Review* 30, no. 3 (April 1983): 867–8.

48. Paul Goldstein, *Copyright's Highway: From Gutenberg to the Celestial Jukebox*, p. 10. New York: Hill and Wang, 1994.

CHAPTER TWENTY THREE

Hollywood Glamour and Mass Consumption in Postwar Italy

STEPHEN GUNDLE

After 1945 the United States helped the war-torn societies of Western Europe progress from recovery to modernization, enabling them to achieve prosperity and political stability. It is not surprising, therefore, that analyses of Italy's transition to consumerism in the postwar period have ascribed much importance to the impact of the American example and American techniques. Although the history of this relationship has been extensively assessed in terms of diplomacy, politics, and economics, very little has been said about the way mentalities were altered, new desires were created, and material dreams were generated and managed. Sectoral studies of advertising, Marshall Plan propaganda, the impact of Hollywood, fashion, the popular press, and the star system all refer to the formation and diffusion of images of desirability, but they do not convey the systematic nature or purpose of the development of a repertoire of images of wealth, beauty, elegance, style, and sex appeal.

This article will show that the transformation of the Italian imagination can be explained by the concept of *glamour*. If properly employed, this undertheorized term can account for the particular seductive appeal that capitalism was able to take on in the early stages of mass consumption, helping it to bypass arguments about exploitation, imperialism, inequality, and alienation. Although glamour was part and parcel of the impact of the American model, Italy did not merely absorb an externally generated allure. Italian capitalism also gave rise to forms of enchantment of its own.

These were crucial in privatizing and materializing Italians' dreams and in providing Italy with imagery that could boost exports and services such as tourism.

GLAMOUR AND MODERNITY

Despite the vagueness of common usage, the etymology of *glamour* is reasonably clear. According to *The New Fowler's Modern English Usage* (1996) the word was originally Scottish. It was an alteration of the word *grammar*, which retained the sense of the old word *gramarye* ("occult learning, magic, necromancy"). *The Oxford English Dictionary* (1989) also highlights the word's Scottish origins and derivation from grammar, although this is indicated to mean magic, enchantment, and spells rather than necromancy and the occult. According to *Fowler's, glamour* passed into standard English usage around the 1830s with the meaning of "a delusive or alluring charm." For *Webster's Third New International Dictionary* (1961), *glamour* is "an elusive, mysteriously exciting and often illusory attractiveness that stirs the imagination and appeals to a taste for the unconventional, the unexpected, the colorful, or the exotic." In its secondary meanings *glamour* is said by *Webster's* to be "a strangely alluring atmosphere of romantic enchantment; bewitching, intangible, irresistibly magnetic charm; . . . personal charm and poise combined with unusual physical and sexual attractiveness."

Some observers have suggested that glamour is a timeless quality. Camille Paglia, for example, has asserted that Nefertiti was the first public figure to turn herself into "a manufactured being" possessed of "radiant glamour," and that glamour's origins date back to ancient Egypt.[1] Undoubtedly, modern glamour has a long and complex history that is beyond the scope of this article.[2] The concern here is with the meanings and associations that the term acquired in the 1930s, when it first entered everyday currency. From that time the world of illusion, mystery, seduction, and enchantment has been found largely in media representations. Glamour is also associated with commercial strategies of persuasion. Through consumer products people are promised instant transformation and entry into a realm of desire. This effect is achieved by adding colorful, desirable, and satisfying ideas and images to mundane products, enabling them to speak not merely to needs but to longings and dreams.

Glamour in the sense it is understood today – as a structure of enchantment deployed by cultural industries – was first developed by Hollywood. In the 1930s, the major studios, having consolidated their domination of the industry, created a star system in which dozens of young men and women were groomed and molded into glittering, ideal types whose fortune, beauty, spending power, and exciting lives dazzled the film-going public. Writing in 1939 about American film stars, Margaret Thorp defined glamour as "sex appeal plus luxury plus elegance plus romance." She asserted that "the place to study glamour today is the fan magazines," adding that:

Fan magazines are distilled as stimulants of the most exhilarating kind. Everything is superlative, surprising, exciting. . . . Nothing ever stands still, nothing ever rests, least of all the sentences. . . . Clothes of course are endlessly pictured and described usually with marble fountains, private swimming pools or limousines in the background. . . . Every aspect of life, trivial and important, should be bathed in the purple glow of publicity.[3]

Although glamour was forged in the rarefied climate of Southern California, it took shape at the intersection of political, social, and economic trends. During the Depression years it enabled privilege and inequality to continue and even flourish in countries suffering economic hardship. It did this by creating the simultaneous impression of distinction and accessibility, an effect achieved through spectacle, through an emphasis on new rather than inherited wealth, through the display of the pleasures of consumption over production, and through the use of femininity (with its particular associations with beauty, show business, and consumption) in place of the more obviously power-related quality of masculinity. Instead of envy and class hatred on the one hand and apathetic deference on the other, glamour fostered feelings of desire, aspiration, wonderment, emulation, and vicarious identification. In short, it fed individual dreams not collective resentments, ostensibly undermining class barriers while in fact reinforcing a hierarchy of status and money.

Glamour, it may be said, is the language of allure and desirability in capitalist society. Its forms change but it is always available to be consumed vicariously by the masses who see in it an image of life writ large according to the criteria of a market society. As a language it is a hybrid that mixes luxury, class, exclusivity, and privilege with the sexuality and seduction of prostitution, entertainment, and the commercial world. Aristocratic forms and styles persist within modern glamour; but without the beauty, color, and sexual enticements of the popular theater and high-class prostitution, the drama, dynamism, scandal, and feminine display that are central to glamour would be absent. Because glamour is dedicated to femininity and fashion as well as sex, show business supplies people, stories, modes, and avenues of mobility that are unique.[4] Historically, glamour also conveyed the air of scandal and sensuality that was so important in titillating middle-brow morality.

The highly polished, hyperbolic, and manufactured image that characterized the specificity of Hollywood glamour was not an original or even the first modern form of glamour, but it was the most readily recognizable and potent. Film was the only medium that gave rise to extended discussions of the phenomenon, and film studies is still the only field in which glamour has been evaluated seriously. Specialists including Richard Dyer, Laura Mulvey, and Annette Kuhn have concentrated on the images produced in movies and stills and have highlighted the importance of abstraction and standardization.[5] In an advanced industrial society in which movies and stars were produced for consumption like automobiles and refrigerators, glamour was a code of allure that required a person (usually a woman) to be fetishized as a fictionalized and surveyed object. It also entailed "deception, the interplay between appearance and reality, display and concealment, and ambiguity and role-playing."[6]

In the 1930s, as Neal Gabler has shown, Hollywood fiction entered the mainstream. What had been a vision of America shaped by newcomers and outsiders became the mythology of urban America.[7] As Americanism became inseparable from consumerism, glamour defined mentalities, behavior, aspirations, and patterns of consumption, as well as ideals of beauty.[8] Far from being the lingua franca of a melting pot, it became in the 1940s a powerful tool of American war morale and self-perception, as well as a weapon in America's arsenal against its enemies. The independent producer Walter Wanger was probably exaggerating in 1945 when he argued that America had won the war because it had Tyrone Power and Lana Turner on its side, whereas its enemies had only political figures; but the alignment of glamour and power was a seductive one that would serve the United States well in its efforts to persuade Europeans of the virtues of democracy and guide them toward a new model of modernization.[9]

Hollywood glamour was a potent force in Europe in the 1940s. People were dazzled by the beauty and sex appeal of the stars and delighted in imagining the dream world of prosperity and luxury that they inhabited. But there were filters that prevented Hollywood glamour from being accepted en bloc. Royalty and aristocracy occupied an important part of the space of glamour, cultivating a sense of loyalty and deference rather than just a desire to emulate. Moreover, many of the prerequisites of the development of American glamour, including national retail networks, department stores, modern advertising, and pronounced individualism, were absent. There were also domestic traditions of the representation of the desirable and the sexually alluring that reflected the class structure. Hollywood had the advantage of incorporating some of these, but its industrial model of glamour was often too big, too commercial, and too artificial to sustain the conversion of whole societies to new ways of thinking and behaving. Moreover, part of the intention of the European Recovery Program (ERP) and American policy in Europe was to stimulate European societies to develop their own mythologies of capitalism that would cut across, and ultimately displace, political ideologies. The case of postwar Italy provides a useful illustration.

AMERICAN GLAMOUR AND POSTWAR ITALY

Hollywood glamour arrived in postwar Italy through two means: film representations and magazine and newsreel images of American stars. By no means all American films were glamorous; the first to be shown, selected by the Allied forces' Psychological Warfare Branch, were largely propaganda films justifying the American war effort or, like Charlie Chaplin's *The Great Dictator*, satirizing the fascist regimes. Only with the advent of the big commercial films did viewers encounter the wealth, spectacle, and sexuality that communicated something new and that led them to expect more than just a life of hardship. It is probably misleading to refer to any single film in this context, but King Vidor's 1946 movie *Gilda* was undoubtedly important for the extremely potent image it offered of Rita Hayworth. Hayworth's star image had been forged by Harry Cohn's Columbia Pictures, and it presented an unusual mixture of hyperbolic, manufactured beauty, perfect fashioning, healthy physicality, vampish behavior, and innocence of spirit. As an image to be consumed, Rita-Gilda offered Italians a powerful taste of the American film industry. She filled the demand in postwar Italy for a dream of abundance and freedom. With her perfect figure, luxuriant auburn tresses, and the costumes of Jean Louis, she entranced a generation. Posters of the film were put up around Rome by the protagonist of *Ladri di biciclette* (1947), and Pier Paolo Pasolini produced a memorable account of the film's impact that later appeared in reworked form in his 1982 novella *Amado mio*. Gilda's easy sexuality, he wrote, "was like a shout of joy, a sweet cataclysm that brought down Caorle's cinema."[10] Gion Guida wrote in *Cinemoda*, "Gilda speaks a universal language that crosses all frontiers and enters into direct communication with the spectator by means of that special pass that is called *sex appeal*."[11]

Rita Hayworth represented the highest level of glamour that had yet been achieved, even in Hollywood. Born Marguerita Cansino, and of Mexican origin, she had undergone extensive remodeling to turn her into such a potent symbol of Americanism that her image was affixed by enthusiastic airmen to the first nuclear bomb to be dropped on Japan. The reaction to the film in Italy and the influence it had on the collective memory of Italians shows that they were ready to respond to it, even if the visual codes it employed were unfamiliar to most and even though it represented a precursor of social and economic developments rather than an integrated part of the development of a new industrialized imagination. Although Rita Hayworth's appeal was enormous and probably unique at the time, it should be seen in relation to the more general effects of the enormous quantity of Hollywood films that poured into Italy in the postwar years.

Hollywood films had been popular with the restricted audiences of the 1930s. Before the war a small number of stars had visited Rome to see the newly opened Cinecittà studios. From the late 1940s their visits became more regular and systematic, as American film production in Italy became routine following the introduction of protective legislation in 1947 and 1949. Although the impact of the films was significant and indeed crucial to the overall glamorous impression of the United States as the land of prosperity, sex appeal, and excitement, it was ultimately the arrival in Italy of the star lifestyle that had the greatest impact on the imagination, customs, and perceptions of glamour. The star lifestyle took on many forms, but it was always writ large, opulent, excessive, fantastic, and exciting in comparison with the daily lives of common people. Stars were, as Edgar Morin wrote in 1957, beautiful, euphorically happy, healthy, rich, untroubled, and leisured, at least in their publicity. Their love lives, weddings, houses, clothes, tastes, favorite haunts, and so on were of enormous interest.[12] Illustrated weekly magazines like *Oggi* and *Epoca*, which looked to *Life* as a model, conveyed these images to middle-class Italian families.

The Rome wedding of Tyrone Power and Linda Christian in early 1949 was a defining moment that attracted enormous press attention. Like everything associated with glamour, it was slightly unrespectable. Powers divorce from the French actress Annabella only became definitive on the day of the wedding, which was also ostentatious and, therefore, not in the best of taste. The journalist Ugo Zatterin recounted it in *Oggi* as though it were a publicity stunt. "Tyrone Power has acted in his second wedding," he wrote:

> At the start of the ceremony everything made the Church of Saint Francesca Romana resemble a Hollywood "studio." Mixed groups of people were making a dull, background noise, huge cables snaked between die golden chairs, flashes of neon lighting gave a white glow to the frescoes of the apse and, hidden among the white lilacs of the prie-dieu, two cold microphones were waiting to gather the fateful "I do" of Linda and Tyrone for the delight of radio audiences in Italy, France, Switzerland, and America. The "shoot" had been prepared in every detail. Since the altar did not lend itself well to the "visibility of the stalls," a substitute was set up at the foot of the statue of Saint Francesca. Even the little organ of the church was deemed inadequate for the musical accompaniment and another, much larger one was temporarily installed.

The spectacle also attracted the attention of the local population:

> The curious and noisy Roman crowd provided the mass audience. People perched with uneasy balance on the ruins surrounding the church, on the arches of the Colosseum and on the fallen pillars of the temple of Venus and of Rome. An entire "Celere" unit, Carabinieri on white horses whirling truncheons, tried to prevent thousands of uninvited spectators from spilling on to the bride and groom and the few genuine guests. An acute, high-pitched, almost hysterical yell from the thousand women stuck behind a gate was the "Action!" that began the shoot. Throughout the whole ceremony the voice of the priest and the solemn tone of the organ were overwhelmed by the distant shouting of the crowd and the closer whirring of the movie cameras.[13]

The wedding showed that American celebrities could be "adopted" by Italy, could be used for internal purposes, and could arouse enthusiasm, especially among the lower middle classes, although the lower-class element was also important. Accounts of the day in the newspapers identified schoolgirls, old women, and young workers among those present.[14] It gave the press something to talk about and helped fuel the development of a new type of celebrity photojournalism. In addition, it had certain political ramifications insofar as it was exploited by the elite for use against the Communist opposition. A Christian Democratic poster in the sharply fought 1948 election featured Power's image and proclaimed: "Even Hollywood stars are against Communism." A number of government ministers attended the Power-Christian wedding. Prime Minister De Gasperi appeared on the cover of *Oggi* on 16 January 1949 in the company of Linda Christian.

Hollywood stars had long enjoyed great social cachet in Europe, and their arrival in significant numbers after World War Two had the effect of partly opening up the closed world of the aristocracy. Indeed the stars' visibility in the press and dominance in such areas of traditional aristocratic prerogative as beauty and style led to a displacement of the old guard. This was especially marked in Italy, where the aristocracy was, in any case, weaker than in Britain or even France.[15] The arrival of a new, more attractive, and more public "aristocracy" in Rome created new centers of prestige and exclusivity, new rituals that drew in younger aristocrats, creating a new, more visible, and more open hierarchy of status. The old scenarios and palaces continued to serve a role, but the elite was more open and accessible, and it served as a focus not of deference or resentment but of emulation and dreams.

In the United States class images of European provenance were extremely useful in the 1950s. European refinement and sophistication could be marketed to a middle class that was seeking history and taste. Although the U.S. government had overridden the film industry's objections to Italian restrictions on the repatriation of movie profits in order to help the economic recovery of an ally, films set in Rome or Venice (or Paris or London) in fact proved highly marketable at home. They possessed enormous cachet, especially the big-budget productions that featured lavish scenery, beautiful people, elegant objects, and big stars. Hollywood studios proved adept not merely at representing European heritage but at appropriating it and remodeling it in their own terms. *Roman Holiday*'s fairytale story of the escape of "Princess Anne" (Audrey Hepburn) from the straitjacket of protocol has been seen as a bold attempt to annex the image of royalty. The Grace Kelly-Prince Rainier wedding in Monaco in 1956 was the climax of this process. Although nothing staged subsequently would eclipse the 1956 Monaco wedding, there were other significant marriages such as Rita Hayworths to Ali Khan and Dawn Addams's to Prince Vittorio Massimo in Rome. Such formal liaisons were proof that some parts of the aristocracy and even royalty were reinventing themselves through the glamour of Hollywood and that Hollywood could absorb older images of luxury and splendor.[16]

At a time of sharp political divisions, illustrated Italian magazines and newsreels provided star news over hard news, offering images of glamour as part of their recipe.[17] They learned to purvey a dreamworld that keyed in with other images of the West as Italy's destiny, America as a model society, new consumer products, Christian Democratic government, and scientific and technical progress. The magazines showed centers of old Italian elitism being taken over or invested once more with allure by a cosmopolitan elite that would shortly become the jet-set. Capri, Ischia, Portofino, and other locations were playgrounds of the rich and famous; but the undoubted center of it all was Rome's Via Veneto, with its cafés, hotels, restaurants, and night clubs. It was here that the celebrity photo-reporter was born.

The key elements of the new glamour were ostentatious wealth, especially of the new variety, and sex scandals. In the moralistic official climate of the 1950s, in which the Church was seeking to win support for the reimposition of conventional values, standards were rigid. Sex appeal was something unfamiliar in postwar Italy, since sex was either obvious (prostitutes) or very heavily masked (Italian actresses). In the cinema of the 1930s the entire weight of sexuality had been placed on the shoulders of a handful of home-grown femme fatales (Doris Duranti, Luisa Ferida, and Clara Calamai). The vast majority of actresses were sexless girls-next-door. Therefore, the routine association of sexual appeal with mainstream actors was perplexing. Articles appeared in the film press explaining what it was, and musical reviews joked about it in the Italianized *sessapiglio*. The separation of sexual appeal from commercial sex or sexual favors appeared improbable to Italians. Yet, with Hollywood stars, sex – occasionally illicit – and legitimate wealth seemed to go together. Even the saintly Ingrid Bergman had acquired a sexualized image when she arrived in Italy to begin a scandalous, adulterous affair with the director Roberto Rossellini.[18]

American stars were perfect consumers. In Hollywood fashion they were always beautiful, magnificently groomed, and well-coiffured. Moreover, they made themselves available for consumption by the public in films and images.[19] For many in postwar Italy such ideas were unfamiliar and odd. Star sponsorship of products was rare, and most entertainers led modest daily lives. Nevertheless, some indication of their economic role was perceptible to all: in the late 1940s magazines regularly printed Max Factor advertisements featuring Rita Hayworth as Gilda. Through her, Italian women were invited to participate in the beauty secrets that the Max Factor company had revealed to all American women, stars or not. Subsequently, other dimensions were added. Luxury cars and homes, together with leisure, enabled the new elite to offer a material extension of the dreams of the masses in the era of the economic recovery and the miracle.

In comparison to the prewar era all this was new. Only after the political and economic reconstruction of Italy was there a real possibility of developing the mass consumer market in Italy that was a premise of the deployment of glamour. Yet it remained the case that there was no equivalent of the term "glamour" in the Italian language, and there was some hostility to the abstract, standardized qualities it was seen to embody. The women's magazine *Grazia* regarded Hayworth as a vulgarized product of "a monstrous machine that renders everyone equal in appearance and taste."[20] The nearest Italian term, sometimes used in the press when it was felt that the foreign term would not be understood, was "fascino." But *fascino* did not convey the manufactured, exterior, or democratizing aspects of American glamour. Instead, it suggested an individual magnetism that was intrinsic rather than manufactured, and not at all commercial.

THE DEVELOPMENT OF ITALIAN GLAMOUR

In the postwar years, American glamour and artifice contrasted with Italian grittiness and authenticity. In *Roma città aperta* (1945) and other films of the time, elegance and luxury were associated with Nazi collaborators and/or sexual deviance. However, Italy soon developed positive models of glamour that were free of negative connotations. As shown below, Italian glamour could not have arisen without American glamour. It existed in relation to American glamour, and it was, in some respects, merely a version of American glamour with certain added features. The United States brought a widening, democratic influence to the Italian scene, a sense of the need to involve the masses in visions of excitement and plenty. Italian glamour developed as both a domestic adaptation of this lesson, taking account of local tastes and culture, and also as a special component of it, offering class products and images.

At the end of the war Italy had little to offer except a longstanding legacy as a land of beauty and high culture. The country had nearly been destroyed and was searching for self-discovery in cinematic Neorealism. It did, however, have an industrial base and was able to take advantage of the opportunities for development that were provided through the ERP. After autarky and war Italy was keen to reestablish contact with international currents and win export markets.

At a popular level the return of American glamour dovetailed with the proliferation of beauty contests and a more general ostentation of body. The use of beauty to get ahead was prime evidence of the influence of American commercial culture. It derived from the American cinema's emphasis on the female form, the pin-up culture that returning troops had brought with them, and indigenous associations of the body with leisure that in the 1930s had awkwardly coexisted with Fascism's political appropriation of women's bodies. Women and girls who entered beauty pageants usually aspired to fame and success; they had absorbed Hollywood's "me too" message, which encouraged the belief that anyone could make it. Unable to imitate the wealth or afford even modest consumer products invested with star aura, they turned instead to sex appeal and sought to display their own bodies.

Italian cinema could not compete with the sophistication, financial backing, and professional quality of its American counterpart, but it could offer plenty of feminine beauty, set against the backdrop of romantic Italian landscapes and lifestyles. For the foreign market Italy contributed significantly to the international pin-up culture that prospered so widely in the 1950s. Films ranging from the rice-field melodrama *Riso amaro* (Bitter Rice) to the working class potboiler *La donna del fiume* (Woman of the River) appealed to art-house spectators in English-speaking countries who found in the wild, dark women of Italian film a confirmation of the longstanding view of Italy as a primitive land of passion and waywardness. Since the early nineteenth century, foreign writers such as De Lamartine, Stendhal, and D. H. Lawrence had cultivated this impression. It found a further extension in the post-WWII writings of authors such as John Horne Burns and Joseph Heller.

The cult of Mediterranean beauty that prospered in Italian films in the 1950s owed something to the global success of neorealism, with its downbeat yet strong heroines and its rejection of the glamorous. But it owed more to the determination of Italian producers and directors to apply some of the lessons of Hollywood as they perceived them. These films were so successful that Hollywood turned increasingly to Italy for new exemplars of female beauty. Gina Lollobrigida, Sophia Loren, and others had the advantage of being less stylized than American actresses; they were physical rather than artificial. To American eyes, however, the Italians looked not like stars, but starlets, since in the United States only the latter exposed their flesh. Actor and director Vittorio de Sica confirmed this view when he declared, in poor English and causing much controversy, that "Italian beauties are all curves. . . . Their artistic capabilities really cannot compete with their physical qualities. It is very sad to say it, but the Italian film industry today tends mainly to highlight legs and showy, opulent bosoms."[21]

As the Italian starlets like Lollobrigida and Loren emerged and won Hollywood contracts, they underwent a process of refashioning. They became, in effect, absorbed into the styles and codes of Hollywood glamour. They adopted the low-cut gowns, perfect coiffures, statuesque qualities, poses and manners, and affluent lifestyles of the Hollywood stars with whom they entered into rivalry. For a brief period Lollobrigida and Loren were seen as direct competitors of Marilyn Monroe; some perceived them as much sexier, in a less innocent and more adult way. In many American films of this period Italian actresses played parts that called for them to be prostitutes (or ex-prostitutes) or to be otherwise sexualized. For some Italians, however, sexual allure was problematic. This was especially the case with Lollobrigida, who, ever since she had come in second in the Miss Italy contest of 1947, had been seen as a typical representative of young Italian womanhood. As Le ore wrote in 1954:

> According to the Americans, Gina's beauty is a special beauty. Everyone admits that it is "sexy," i.e., "provocative," but her fiercest supporters have defined her as a "typical Italian brunette," a definition that, understood in the traditional way, should rule out a "sexy" content; rather it is used to refer to types of women whose beauty is serene, pure, and a little ingenuous.[22]

In the mid-1950s Lollobrigida was the leading star of Italian cinema. She bought a pink stucco villa on the Via Appia antica and frequently appeared on magazine covers in full star regalia. She became something of an uncrowned queen, a national representative whose demeanor and mannerisms evoked admiration.[23] For Americans the glamorous image she and others offered was one of exotic Latin beauty. This had various commercial applications – for example, the Revlon Corporation tied the launch of its Fire and Ice product line to the Italian stars.[24] It gave Italy a material identity that also aided exports.

To foreigners, the Italian stars were undoubtedly glamorous. But, in fact, there was a significant difference between Italian and American stars. Silvana Mangano, who had been elected Miss Rome in 1946, was the first Italian star to come to the attention of the public solely through her alluring image. Mangano became known through a famous still photograph from *Riso amaro* in which she was wearing shorts in a rice field. Released as a promotional device because of the delayed launch of the film, the picture became an internationally celebrated pin-up. But Mangano never acquired in Italy the artificial appeal and manufactured beauty of Hollywood images. She was too specific and earthy, too individual and familiar. Moreover, she hated her sexy image and did everything possible to cast it off and assert her acting ability.

With reference to postwar Britain, Paul Swann and Jackie Stacey have separately argued that domestic stars were always seen as less packaged and less overtly sexual than the glamour queens of Hollywood.[25] The British stars had personality and talent rather than looks and were respectable and reserved. Only American femininity signified excitement and sexuality as well as luxury and abundance. Ordinary girls considered the American stars otherworldly and fantastic. Erica Carter makes some similar points in relation to Germany.[26] In Italy these differences also prevailed, but with important distinctions. Although Italian stars took on the trappings of glamour more eagerly than some British or German actors had, glamour did not become their defining feature. Moreover, Italian stars never seemed manufactured or artificial. They never became dehumanized or detached from the realm of the real.

In Italy at that time the body was not fully an object of narcissistic cultivation in a consumerized sense of self, although the female body was certainly subjected to a tendentially modern male gaze.[27] It was, rather, mainly perceived as geared to natural functions and to work. Italian stars were often bodies in landscapes – beautiful bodies that represented working bodies in real contexts: rice fields, lagoons, mountains. Piera De Tassis quotes Carlo Lizzani, who worked as a writer on *Riso amaro*, as saying that Mangano's body in the film assumed a presence and meaning not foreseen in the script. Her body was "offered up for viewing like a natural prodigy, a beautiful animal, or a beautiful tree."[28] Because Italy was not yet a fully industrial society, it found "star" qualities in men and women who were both recognizable and real: cyclists, boxers, and shapely women:

In Italy the talents and qualities that are celebrated are absolutely natural and spontaneous, the fruit not of research, study, or effort so much as gifts received at birth and cultivated spontaneously; and when they are suddenly revealed, they bring the individual to public attention, just like a stroke of luck or a lottery.[29]

Italians wondered about the polished, glossy images of Marilyn Monroe, but at least some commentators in Italy did not find her sexy. Her stylized sexuality was enticing, Oreste Del Buono conceded, "but beneath all the fuss there is the extremely unexciting reality of a small, chubby girl who is almost innocuous and rather dull. In the matter of *sex-appeal*, she certainly bears no comparison with our Mangano in *Riso amaro*."[30] Sex appeal was considered by Italians as something imported and curious, an American feature that was constructed rather than natural. Even in the mid 1950s the term glamour was scarcely used, though some efforts were made to try to understand what it signified in America. Glamour tended to be seen as something both alien and alienating, a product of "the orderly frigidity of appearances and social relations" in America.[31]

When Italian magazines depicted Silvana Pampanini and others in regal apparel, they did so not because the external manifestations of royalty had been taken over by the entertainment industry but because the myth of royalty still exercised considerable fascination for Italians. Lacking a studio system, Italy could not manufacture glamour except by imitation. The ersatz effects of the "white telephone" films in the 1930s gave way in the 1940s and early 1950s to an emphasis on one aspect of glamour – sex appeal – but the neglect of other aspects, including fashion and consumerism, which in America lent glamour a special appeal to women. Fashion spoke to their experiences and desires and provided a utopian element in the construction of images of the ideal self. In Italy this element evolved separately and followed a social trajectory different from that of cinema.

FASHION AND ARISTOCRATIC GLAMOUR

Italian fashion in the 1930s and 1940s was modest and provincial. The few fashion designers were little known except to their local clients. They used high-quality materials but lacked originality, adapting Parisian designs to the tastes and pocketbooks of their customers. Simonetta, Antonelli, Biki, Carosa, Galitzine, and others were considered professionals of good standing, but there was an abyss between them and the stars of the Paris scene – Chanel, Schiaparelli, and Dior. The latter were more creative, more artistic, and more original, and also more practical and modern in their efforts to relate fashion to the needs of a broad stratum of well-to-do women. An extreme example of the low standing of Italian fashion was offered in October 1948 when *Oggi* reported that the police had raided the Paris hotel where some Italian designers were staying during the autumn shows. The police arrested an Italian sketch artist who had copied the Dior collection without permission to sell at cut-rate prices to his Italian clients.[32]

The turning point came with the Power-Christian wedding in 1949. One of the great social events of the postwar period, it gave rise to massive publicity that also worked to the advantage of the Fontana sisters, who made Christian's wedding dress. As *Oggi* wrote:

> One hundred fifty meters of very fine tulle were used by a large Roman fashion house to create an original model with a bodice, a modest *decolletée* and a wide bell-shaped skirt, artistically pleated: this is Linda Christian's wedding dress. *Paillettes* and small pearls add precious touches to the splendid *toilette*. Known as one of the most elegant stars in Hollywood, fanciful in her tastes and impossible to satisfy in fittings, Linda is always arguing with the dress designers even though she is dressed in a fur coat and jewels worth sixty million Lire.[33]

Pictured by numerous magazines in the Fontana sisters' atelier, Christian provided testimony to the skill and quality of the work of Italian professionals.

Italian fashion had been decentralized and largely provincial before the war. In the early 1950s Italian executives made a serious attempt to unite it and promote it abroad by associating it with the traditional attractions of the Italian context. The idea was conceived by Giovan Battista Giorgini, a Florentine trader with excellent contacts among American department stores and the fashion press. The shows he organized in Florence from 1951 onward are conventionally seen as marking the attempt to break Italian fashions subordination to Paris and to promote it abroad, especially in America.[34]

The promotions emphasized the low-cost, fine-quality materials and simplicity of Italian design, but they also sought to confer an Italian identity on the work of the designers who took part in the shows. The shows drew attention to Italy's artistic and cultural heritage and to the elegance and traditional good taste of its aristocracy. Photographs of young aristocratic ladies wearing elegant clothes in the courtyards and corridors of Renaissance palaces appeared first in *Bellezza* and other Italian magazines and then in foreign ones. At times the models were depicted outside among the monuments of ancient Rome. Because Italian fashion lacked originality, the designers insisted on its image and its staging, highlighting "the triad of art-craft-aristocracy."[35] Lacking economic and political power, Italy's aristocrats, such as Pucci and Simonetta, acquired a new prestige abroad through the marketing of their aura.

Aided by organized promotional visits of young ladies and favorable press coverage, Italian fashion made an impression in the United States.[36] As Valerie Steele has argued, Italian fashion became known for its unusual shapes, bright colors, youthful verve, and playful feel.[37] Despite this improved image, Italy did not become a regular supplier of quantities of clothing to American department stores. Even boutique fashions such as Pucci's reached only a small clientele. They did, however, create a sense of desirability and prestige. Rich Americans who came to Italy did not pass up the chance to visit tailors and dress designers and acquire new wardrobes at reasonable prices. In the 1950s many major film stars took this route as Rome became an international center of film production. By the mid 1950s over 100 films a year – of which a significant proportion were American – were being shot in Italy. Audrey Hepburn, Ava Gardner, and Katherine Hepburn were among those who dressed in Italian fashions both on and off the screen. Films including *Roman Holiday* (1953), *Three Coins in a Fountain* (1954), and *Summer Madness* (1955) communicated an image of Italy as a land of beauty, charm, elegance, refinement, and nobility. For American stars and others, Italian glamour did not consist of buxom bodies but of class and elegance. Hollywood had always sought to expropriate aspects of European high culture; now Italy, too, was able to contribute to the elaboration of Hollywood glamour by lending it style and associations with history and leisure.

Fashion magazines and fashion pages in Italy paid little attention in the 1950s to Italian film stars like Lollobrigida and Loren. Instead they focused on noblewomen and aristocratic foreign stars such as Grace Kelly, Deborah Kerr, and Audrey Hepburn. It may seem strange that at the very moment when mass culture was taking off and consumerism was beginning to erode the old rigidity of the social hierarchy there should have been a flowering in Europe of images so evidently shot through with aloofness and elitist chic. Photographs of tall, slim, angular women, perfectly groomed and cool, proliferated in magazines and advertisements. Although these images were unapproachable for some women, they were not as removed from all as might be thought. First, as Erica Carter has pointed out in her analysis of German women's magazines, the images contained an emancipatory element by showing women acting in a confident and sophisticated way in public places, unencumbered by family and domestic duties.[38] Second, the magazines portrayed womanhood as fashion, taste, and consumerism – in other words, as a process involving pleasures. Third, things that were now coming within the reach of many – surplus spending, home comforts, domestic help (appliances in place of servants), beautification, and fashion – had previously been reserved for upper-class women. Fourth, images of models like Lisa Fonssagrives, and of some "class" film stars, actually "seemed accessible to every woman," as David Seidner has written. They offered grace, balance, and reserve, combined with a certain energy "that resonated in the subconscious of generations of women to whom [Fonssagrives's] appeal was irresistible." Such women appeared to be in control and true to themselves. Fonssagrives's "dance experience gave her a sense of theatre so that the elaborate costume never looked mannered or affected – a comfortable masquerade."[39]

The triumph of the "aristocratic type" confirmed the decline rather than the ascendance of the old upper classes, for it was not as substance that it acquired resonance but as mere image, a deracinated look. This image could be embraced by anyone of any background who possessed the right physique and bearing. The rise of this sort of image in Italy, associated with the haute couture model and later film actress Elsa Martinelli, was given further impetus by Lucia Bosè and a physically transformed Silvana Mangano, who showed that peasant culture and its associations with the fear of scarcity were being eclipsed.[40]

The influence of fashion culture and its centrality to the feminine consciousness were underlined by the way all Italian female stars became more elegant in the mid-1950s. Having won popularity with men by wearing flimsy, revealing costumes that exposed their shapely figures, Loren and Lollobrigida underwent a turn toward elegance in 1955–1956. The Neapolitan dressmaker Emilio Schubert, who catered to many foreign stars, brought a more refined look to Italian film costumes and contributed to the new image of Italy's stars by making spectacular gowns and dresses that they could wear for receptions, festivals, and premieres. These gowns and dresses were theatrical, geared to the demands of image. Schubert sought, while preserving the freshness and spontaneity of the stars, to transcend their early images.

He persuaded Lollobrigida, who had been "the typical good-looking Italian girl who doesn't really know how she wants to be or should dress" to cut her hair and become more sophisticated: "Once she had changed type, the clothes had to change, too. No more wide skirts; instead she'll have figure-hugging dresses; no more excessive simplicity; instead we'll have sumptuousness, richness, eye-catching qualities, folds, strass, white, black, pearls, and silver."[41]

Lollobrigida and Loren were well-placed to travel abroad to promote their films and, at the same time, to market a specific image of Italian craft and fashion. In Hollywood and more widely in the United States they would receive admiring comments for the richness and originality of their toilettes. They became objects of admiration and imitation on the part of women from a wide range of social classes the world over. Simultaneously different from and part of the star elite that defined and diffused the ideals of Hollywood glamour, they aroused interest and attracted attention.

THE "DOLCE VITA" CONNECTION

It was not just the Italian stars who traveled in the 1950s; the world also came to Rome. At the same time that the city underwent population growth and urban expansion, it became a fashionable city and a cosmopolitan crossroads for the international elite of the rich and famous. Vast numbers of film actors, directors, and support personnel acted as a magnet for hangers-on and for "movers and shakers." Rich playboys, idle aristocrats, and bored heiresses made Rome a vital point on their itinerary. The city became a hub for an international café society that evolved into the jet set in the 1960s. This cosmopolitan crowd provided a layer of social life that the city had never experienced before. On top of and alongside the conventional scene, there was another slice of society made up of the rich and the beautiful. For a period Rome became a combination of Paris and Hollywood, and certainly the place that gave rise to the most gossip and scandal as featured in some of the mainstream press along with the notorious scandal sheet *Confidential*.

For foreigners Italy had long possessed glamour. It presented an enticing image that incorporated beauty, sexuality, theatricality, wealth (as heritage), and leisure. In the years of the "dolce vita" this was given a new twist, as wealth acquired a contemporary, material connotation, and beauty and sexuality came to be associated with fashion and film. Many of the events that were covered by the world's press and were seen to typify the decadent hedonism of the life of the celebrity elite in Rome were not spontaneous; instead they were staged by press agents. These included Anita Ekberg's night-time dip in the Trevi Fountain in 1958 and a celebrated impromptu striptease performed at the Rugantino night club by Turkish model Aiché Nana. Still, the genuine conflicts that arose between celebrities and press photographers around the Via Veneto lent an air of authenticity to the phenomenon. Snapshots of illicit celebrity couples and of men kicking and punching photographers in the dead of night turned Rome into a center of a modern mythology whose characters included aristocrats and movie stars.[42] By the late 1950s the Italian lifestyle had become fashionable and desirable. The products of Italian design, like the Vespa, Fiat cars, and coffee machines, were no longer featured in films as amusing curiosities (as they had been in *Roman Holiday*) but were seen as stylish, as objects of status.

Federico Fellini's hit 1960 film, *La Dolce Vita*, offered a bittersweet portrait of a city and, by implication, a country that was caught in the whirl of success and celebrity. The film presented a staged reality, probably at a point when the city's status was already in decline, and wrapped it in a mythological aura. The film's exciting depiction of the Via Veneto (which was recreated in the studio) is said to have killed it off as a chic center by sparking an influx of tourists. According to Ugo Gregoretti, the film caused

> the whole world [to] imagine that Via Veneto was the center of forbidden pleasures. One evening a correspondent of the *Toronto Star*, a freckled "red-head," bumped into me in the street and asked me if I could give him the address of an "orgy." This was the climate; it was the impression that foreigners had acquired of the Via Veneto by this point. In a very short time everyone disappeared.[43]

But if the reality died, the image lived on. In the minds of the public worldwide, Rome was the city of sin and pleasure, of Liz Taylor, Ava Gardner, and Frank Sinatra, of elegance and night clubs, of Soraya, of aristocrats and Latin lovers, of fast cars and stylish intellectuals.

This image, perpetuated in American films and books, including Irwin Shaw's *Two Weeks in Another Town* (1960) and Tennessee Williams's *The Roman Spring of Mrs. Stone* (1961), provided Roman tourist industries and fashion houses with a resource that has lasted to the present day. Roman glamour became Italian glamour for the world. Throughout the 1960s the city was an adult alternative to London, the center of the new youth culture. Swinging Rome was not just classy but also dangerous in the popular imagination. The surface style and the bright, figure-hugging Brioni men's suits that preceded the flair of London and that featured in so many foreign television films and series of the period mixed stylishness with decadence and corruption.

Italian glamour combined sex and style for foreigners. Italy became an image to be consumed, to be bought into, and to be savored in small doses, by means of a film, a vacation, a meal in a restaurant, an item of clothing, or a domestic appliance. The press book for the U.S. release of *La Dolce Vita* encouraged exhibitors to set up tie-ins with local dress shops stocking Italian and continental clothes. Travel agencies and pizza parlors were also deemed suitable sites for window displays promoting the film. Department stores were a source of further such opportunities:

> The film's title lends itself to countless tie-ins with stores (in newspaper advertising and in store displays), since there is a certain snob appeal in a foreign title (particularly one that has received such tremendous advance exploitation) and the uninitiated discover

that there is an invitation to any number of products in the English translation. Sample copy: LA DOLCE VITA means THE SWEET LIFE. An air conditioner means a sweeter life for your family etc. . . . LA DOLCE VITA (The Sweet Life) is not to be missed at . . . theatre . . . . The Sweet Life is that much sweeter with . . . chocolates.[44]

This domestication of *La Dolce Vita* says more about 1950s American consumerism and its thirst for continental attributes than it does about Italy. Nonetheless, it was difficult to obscure the film's clear implication that Italy was not merely blandly picturesque but was also a site of scandal. The movie marked a transition in the way stars were perceived. In the United States studio publicity departments were accustomed to exercising complete control over the flow of news about stars, presenting flawless images that stressed their admirable qualities. In Rome, where there could be no such control, the stars seemed real and were often shown to be flawed. In addition, Rome in the late 1950s (the "dolce vita" reached a head in 1958) witnessed changes in the elite structure. After the aristocracy lost power, individual aristocrats who did not want to disappear were forced to reinvent themselves as personalities for consumption, like celebrities, or to become part of the alluring landscape of history, tradition, and palaces. In the world of image, where films and illustrated weekly magazines determined who was who, any old distinctions of status ceased to be meaningful. Celebrity, surface, and image triumphed. As had happened in the United States in the 1920s, publicity became an autonomous source of power.[45] Yet the simultaneous rise of Italian fashion and the development of Rome as a film capital meant that certain distinctions that applied elsewhere did not apply in Italy. "Here in Italy, glamour and elegance were born in the same historical moment, and still today they often overlap – just as they undoubtedly overlap with each other in the image people abroad have of a certain Italy," Italian *Vogue* wrote recently.[46]

TOWARD MASS CONSUMPTION

From the late 1950s to the early 1960s the profile of Italian society changed. The country became far more modern and urbanized, and the values and images of peasant culture, which only a few years earlier had been prevalent, took on a nostalgic, backward-looking air. What dominated the thinking of Italians was not the land and the seasons but the urban infrastructures, consumer goods, home comforts, and conveniences. In this context certain important changes occurred. The body ceased to be perceived in terms of the Catholic flesh/spirit dichotomy or the left's idea of it as a tool of work and became the object of care and attention.[47] This shift was reflected in a more modern idea of beauty and eroticism that no longer arose from the fixed relations of a static, rural society, but was, to some extent, free-floating in an American way. In the 1960s glamorous women were often featured in advertisements in Italy and for Italian products. Many of these, however, referred directly to an American lexicon. The "blondes" of Perroni beer and the elegant, illustrated glamour girls of Vespa scooters (replaced by actresses and live models in the mid-1960s) both bear witness to this. It was the American way of life that provided the framework of Italy's boom and that helped integrate the country.

Combined with this shift was a move away from archaic ideas of honor, shame, and sin. In the 1950s many film titles included the word *peccato* (sin), which simultaneously implied condemnation and titillation. *La Dolce Vita* was intensely controversial and in many ways a watershed.[48] On the one hand, the film was severely condemned by established and conservative opinion. The presentation of elite life in the eternal city as hedonistic was deemed subversive and dangerous. The hedonism itself was also condemned, particularly by religious spokesmen, as wasteful and immoral. Consumerism was not yet fully accepted as the predominant ethos in society, even though it was rapidly becoming the economic motor of the country.

On the other hand, the portrayal of the "sweet life" in magazines and its further mythologization on film provoked widespread fascination. Although the images had nothing to do with the way most Italians lived and had no direct effect on them, the spectacle of style, beauty, and consumption proved irresistible for many. Even the owners of small businesses, whose wealth was growing in the boom years, aspired to participate in nightlife, build Hollywood-style villas, and acquire expensive sports cars. *La Dolce Vita's*, emphasis on fashion (in particular, Anita Ekberg's costumes, based on the Fontana sisters' outfits for Ava Gardner, including her costumes for *The Barefoot Contessa*) reinforced a growing interest in fashion among both women and men. As early as 1953 *Oggi* increased its fashion coverage, although most space was still given to Paris. Many other Italians rushed to see the film because of the strong air of scandal associated with it. There is a brief episode in Pietro Germis satirical comedy *Divorzio all'italiana* (Divorce Italian-Style) that depicts the rush in provincial Sicily to see a film reputed to contain "orgies worthy of Emperor Tiberius."

The impact of the film signaled the end of the aristocracy as a class with a meaningful role in Italy. Instead of the aristocratic woman and her surrogate, known as the "aristocratic type," a more modern image of the elegant woman took shape. Elsa Martinelli passed seamlessly from one type to the other by jettisoning the stuffiness and rigidity characteristic of the 1950s. The modern, elegant woman – represented in *La Dolce Vita* by Anouk Aimée (Maddalena) – was not defined by conformity to social norms or by grace and poise but by autonomy, style, travel, and wealth. Women of any social class with the right looks and determination could take on this role; it was an option that could be pursued, not a birthright.

Among the lower and middle classes the great curiosity about monarchy that flowered in the immediate postwar years was not expunged, but there was a qualitative change. Royals no longer commanded deference or admiration in the way that Queen Elizabeth II did during her coronation in 1953. There was much greater interest in the exteriority of splendor. The change was apparent in the way the Iranian royal family acquired prominence in magazines in the early 1960s. In 1963, Soraya, the spurned wife of the Shah, who became the "sad princess" of the time, undertook her first screen test, arranged by Dino De Laurentiis. She passed without difficulty from court life to the nightclubs and the resorts of the jet set. In the same year Gina Lollobrigida visited the Shah in Teheran and escorted the readers of *Oggi* through the magnificence of the royal palaces. Although the actress made all the right deferential noises, it was apparent that she was being treated as an equal by the Shah and Farah Diba and that her clothes were just as interesting as the "enormous, stupendous rooms" of the palace.[49]

Within Italy, however, the provincial connotation remained. Foreign glamour, followed by domestic consumerism, was insufficient to eliminate a dimension of life that remained firmly rooted in family, community, and place. Italy gave rise to no domestic glamour in the full sense of the term. The techniques of glamour were often learned, mastered, and employed in designing and marketing products, but these took on truly glamorous implications only outside Italy.[50] Elegant clothes, fast cars, and luxury goods provoked desire abroad when combined with Italian natural settings, architectural achievements, and other aspects of the country. At home, though, even cars as romantic and overtly glamorous as Ferraris tended to be seen as products of a craft tradition – the substance counted more than the image. Even in the 1990s, Ferrari employed Sharon Stone and Ivana Trump in advertising to enhance the glamour of their cars.

CONCLUSION

In Italy celebrities eventually became part of the system of consumerism. They endorsed products and offered themselves as consumers and as objects of consumption. But they never truly acquired glamour. No one achieved the necessary separation from family, place of origin, and the familiar to become more than a pale imitation of American glamour. Television personalities always sought to highlight their down-to-earth qualities even while cultivating an appearance in line with international glamour. Yet the long-range influence of the American idea of glamour within Italy is evident not just in television but also in fashion, which was Italy's most successful export industry in the 1990s. Fashion has produced jobs, earnings, and image on a grand scale. Yet the imagery of fashion marketing is resolutely American and invariably refers back to Hollywood's golden age. Versace used supermodels who recalled the ice-cool blondes of the 1950s, while Giorgio Armani draws on the masculine tailoring of Hollywood in the 1930s and 1940s. Valentino and Dolce & Gabbana, designers for whom the domestic Italian market is less important, draw on images inspired by *La Dolce Vita* (the celebrated moment of Anita Ekberg's screen dip in the Trevi fountain – already a re-creation of a real-life stunt – was restaged by Valentino in 1996 with Claudia Schiffer in the place of Ekberg) and Neorealism. But this is Italian glamour for export. Italians made their transition to consumerism with the aid of American imagery. Over time they caught up and elaborated original and useful images of glamour for foreign consumption. These conferred a magical aura on the country that still functions to aid tourism and the sale of goods. But informing it all is an idea of American glamour that has never been matched or superseded, only reworked, repositioned, and reelaborated.

NOTES

Source: *Journal of Cold War Studies,* 4(3) (Massachusetts Institute of Technology, 2002), 95–118.

1. Camille Paglia, *Sexual Personae: Art and Decadence from Nefertiti to Emily Dickinson* (London: Penguin, 1992), pp. 67–68.
2. Some pertinent issues are considered in Reka C. V. Buckley and Stephen Gundle, "Fashion and Glamour," in Nicola White and Ian Griffiths, eds., *The Fashion Business: Theory, Practice, Image* (Oxford: Berg, 2000); and Stephen Gundle, "Mapping the Origins of Glamour: Giovanni Boldini, Paris and the Belle Epoque," *Journal of European Studies,* Vol. 29 (1999), 269–295. A fuller elaboration of these ideas will be presented in Clino Castelli and Stephen Gundle, *The Glamour System* (forthcoming).
3. Margaret Farrand Thorp, *America at the Movies* (New Haven: Yale University Press, 1939); quoted in Jeffrey Richards, *The Age of the Dream Palace: Cinema and Society in Britain 1930–1939* (London: Routledge, 1984), pp. 157–158.
4. For a case study, see Linda Mizejewski, *Ziegfeld Girl: Image and Icon in Culture and Cinema* (Durham, NC: Duke University Press, 1999).
5. Richard Dyer, *Stars* (London: BFI, 1979); Laura Mulvey, *Visual and Other Pleasures* (London: Macmillan, 1989); and Annette Kuhn, *The Power of the Image: Essays on Representation and Sexuality* (London: RKP, 1985).
6. Sybil DelGaudio, *Dressing the Part: Sternberg, Dietrich, and Costume* (Rutherford: Farleigh Dickinson University Press, 1993), p. 21.
7. Neal Gabler, *An Empire of Their Own: How the Jews Invented Hollywood* (New York: Anchor, 1989).
8. See Kathy Peiss, *Hope in a Jar: The Making of America's Beauty Culture* (New York: Metropolitan, 1998), chs. 4 and 5.
9. Walter Wanger, "America's Secret Weapon," University of Wisconsin-Madison, State Historical Society, Papers of Walter Wanger, Speeches, 36.58. See also Wanger, "Donald Duck and Diplomacy," *Public Opinion Quarterly,* Vol. 14, No. 3 (Fall 1950), pp. 443–452.
10. Pier Paolo Pasolini, *Amado mio* (Milan: Garzanti, 1982), pp. 191–192.
11. Gion Guida, "Gilda," *Cinemmoda,* 6 April 1947, p. 7.
12. Edgar Morin, *Les Stars* (Paris: Seuil, 1957).
13. Ugo Zatterin, "Matrimonio in technicolor per Tyrone il buono e Linda la bella," *Oggi,* 3 February 1949, p. 11.
14. For an analysis of the event as reported in the press, see Stephen Gundle, "Memory and Identity: Popular Culture in Postwar Italy," in Patrick McCarthy, ed., *Italy Since 1945* (Oxford: Oxford University Press, 2000), pp. 190–192.
15. For some perceptive observations on postwar Roman aristocracy, see Luigi Barzini, *From Caesar to the Mafia: Sketches of Italian Life* (New York: Doubleday, 1971), pp. 107–110.

16. For a more detailed examination of these issues, see Stephen Gundle, "Il divismo nel cinema europeo, 1945–60," in Gian Piero Brunetta ed., *Storia del cinema mondiale*, Vol. 1: *L'Europa*, Tome 1: *Miti, luoghi, divi* (Turin: Einaudi, 1999).

17. On the cultural clashes of the whole Cold War period, see Stephen Gundle, *Between Hollywood and Moscow: The Italian Communists and the Challenge of Mass Culture, 1943–91* (Durham: Duke University Press, 2000).

18. On this episode, see Stephen Gundle, "Saint Ingrid at the Stake: Stardom and Scandal in the Bergman-Rossellini Collaboration," in David Forgacs, Sarah Lutton, and Geoffrey Nowell-Smith, eds., *Roberto Rossellini: Magician of the Real* (London: BFI Press, 2000).

19. On the stars and consumerism, see Charles Eckert, "The Carole Lombard in Macy's Window," in Christine Gledhill, ed., *Stardom: Industry of Desire* (London: Routledge, 1991).

20. Ubis, "La Fornarina cede il passo a Rita Hayworth," *Grazia*, Vol. 404 (1948), pp. 22–23; cited in Marina Coslovi, "Il Glamour ci viene da Hollywood: 'L'immagine dell'America in una rivista femminile del dopoguerra," unpublished paper, n.d., p. 7.

21. Cited in Cinema Nuovo, "Lo scandalo delle curve," in Guido Aristarco, ed., *Il mito dell'attore: Come l'industria delta star produce il sex symbol* (Bari: Dedalo, 1983), p. 261.

22. Anonymous, "Lollo degli americani," *Le ore*, 6 February 1954, pp. 12–13.

23. See Reka C. V. Buckley, "National Body: Gina Lollobrigida and the Cult of the Star in the 1950s," *Historical Journal of Film Radio and Television*, Vol. 20, No. 4 (October 2000), pp. 527–547.

24. See Andrew Tobias, *Fire and Ice: The Story of Charles Revlon – The Man Who Built the Revlon Empire* (New York: Morrow, 1976), p. 122.

25. Paul Swann, *The Hollywood Feature Film in Postwar Britain* (London: Croom Helm, 1987); Jackie Stacey, *Star Gazing: Hollywood Cinema and Female Spectatorship* (London: Routledge, 1994).

26. Erica Carter, *How German Is She? Postwar West German Reconstruction and the Consuming Woman* (Ann Arbor: University of Michigan Press, 1987).

27. For a theoretical treatment of the male gaze, see Laura Mulvey, "Visual Pleasure and Narrative Cinema," in Laura Mulvey, *Visual and Other Pleasures* (London: Macmillan, 1989), pp. 14–26.

28. Piera De Tassis, "Corpi recuperati per il proprio sguardo," *Memoria*, Vol. 3, No. 6 (1982), p. 27.

29. Silvio Guarnieri, "Campioni e Dive" (1956), in Aristarco, ed., *Il mito dell'attore*, p. 49.

30. Oreste Del Buono, "Marilyn Monroe" (1953), in Aristarco, ed., *Il mito dell'attore*, p. 66.

31. Nadir Giannitrapani, "'Il glamour' nella società americana," *Cinema*, 15 November 1950, p. 174.

32. Ruggero Gilardi, "A Parigi i sarti italiani hanno conosciuto i poliziotti di Dior," *Oggi*, 3 October 1948, p. 7.

33. Errante, "Le ragazze svengono," *Oggi*, 3 February 1949, p. 11.

34. See Guido Vergani, "La Sala Bianca: nascita della moda italiana," in Giannino Malossi, ed., *La Sala Bianca: nascita della moda italiana* (Milan: Electa, 1992), pp. 23–86.

35. Sean Blazer, *Mercanti di moda* (Bergamo: Lubrina, 1997), pp. 32–33.

36. See Nicola White, *Reconstructing Italian Fashion: American and the Development of the Italian Fashion Industry* (Oxford: Berg, 2000).

37. Valerie Steele, "Italian Fashion and America," in Germano Celant, ed., *The Italian Metmorphosis 1943–1968* (New York: Guggenheim Museum Publications, 1994), pp. 498–499.

38. Carter, *How German Is She?* pp. 209–225.

39. David Seidner, "Still Dance," in Seidner, ed., *Lisa Fonssagrives: Three Decades of Classic Fashion Photography* (London: Thames and Hudson, 1997), p. 20.

40. See De Tassis, "Corpi recuperati," pp. 29–31. Mangano hated her youthful, sexy image and transformed herself into a thin, angular woman of poise and grace.

41. Michele Quiriglio, "Schubert veste le dive," *Cinema*, Vol. 9, No. 168 (16 June 1956), p. 288. See also Bonizza Giordani Aragno, ed., *Moda romana dal 1945 al 1965* (Rome: De Luca, 1998).

42. See Andrea Nemiz, ed., *Vita, dolce vita* (Rome: Network, 1983).

43. Cited in Sandro Giulianelli and Antonio Simbolotti, eds., *Via Veneto: Un mito e il suo futuro* (Rome: Quaderni di AU-Rivista dell'Arredo Urbano, 1985), n.p.

44. University of Southern California – Film Archives, Advertising, Publicity, and Promotion Material for *La Dolce Vita*: An Astor Release.

45. See Cleveland Amory, *Who Killed Society?* (New York: Harper, 1960), p. 143, for a discussion of what the author called "publi-ciety." See also Neal Gabler, *Walter Winchell: Gossip, Power and the Culture of Celebrity* (London: Picador, 1995), esp. p. 81.

46. Anna Gloria Forti and Antonella Amapane, "Glamour italiano," *Vogue (Italia)*, February 1995, p. 398.

47. Luisa Leonini, "Non mi vesto mi travesto," in Cesare Colombo, ed., *Tra sogno e bisogno* (Milan: Coop-Longanesi, 1986), p. 256.

48. On the impact of the film, see Stephen Gundle, "La Dolce Vita," *History Today*, Vol. 50, No. 1 (Januaty 2000), pp. 29–35.

49. Carlo Moretti, "Gina racconta: non credevo che lo scià fosse tanro giovanile e Farah così alta," *Oggi*, 28 March 1963, p. 26.

50. See Giannino Malossi, ed., *Volare: The Icon of Italy in Global Pop Culture* (New York: Monacelli, 1999).

CHAPTER TWENTY FOUR

Magic Fashion

Elizabeth Wilson

The starting point of Richard Martin's *Fashion and Surrealism* is Lautréamont's famous definition of beauty as: "the chance encounter of a sewing machine and an umbrella on a dissecting table." To illustrate this idea Martin uses two surrealist images of a woman being actually sewn, that is, created by a sewing machine. For Martin these disturbing images go to the heart of the fashion project, since "the fashion object, like the fashion machine, could be a most powerful force in the simultaneous deconstruction of the figure and remembrance of its presence that inevitably dwells in the garment" (Martin 1988: 15–16).

Each of the female bodies in Martin's chosen images, a painting by Oscar Dominguez and a collage by Joseph Cornell, appears passive and unmoved as she is fashioned by the machine. Such eerie detachment is a facet of that uncanny quality, which, says Hal Foster, "is central to Surrealism." He adds that the "surrealist uncanny" consists in part of a "confusion between the animate and the inanimate" (Foster 1993: xvii, 7), to which Martin also alludes in considering the relationship between garment and body. In the works by Dominguez and Cornell, the female figures are both living and inanimate, in suspended animation, at least. They purvey serenity rather than a sense of constriction. Yet they also recall Simone de Beauvoir's denunciation of fashion and beauty culture as the reduction of the living woman to a thing:

> Routine makes drudgery of beauty care and the upkeep of the wardrobe. Horror at the depreciation that all living growth entails will arouse in certain frigid or frustrated women a horror of life itself; they endeavour to preserve themselves as others preserve furniture or canned food. This negative obstinacy makes them enemies of their own existence . . . good meals spoil the figure, wine injures the complexion, too much smiling brings wrinkles, the sun damages the skin, sleep makes one dull, work wears one out, love puts rings under the eyes, kisses redden the cheeks, caresses deform the breasts, embraces wither the flesh, maternity disfigures face and body . . . spots, tears, botched

dressmaking, bad hair-dos are catastrophes still more serious than a burnt roast or a broken vase, for not only does the woman of fashion project herself into things, she has chosen to make herself a thing (de Beauvoir 1953: 512).[1]

To the confusion between the animate and the inanimate, the Surrealists added the confusion between the natural and the artificial. Both, as Martin demonstrates, are equally central to fashion, for garment and body are inseparable, neither complete without the other – or at least, some might argue that the naked body *is* complete, but the garment is certainly a mere shadow of itself until it is inhabited. Théophile Gautier remarked that: "In the modern age clothing has become man's second skin, from which he will under no pretext separate himself and which belongs to him like an animal's coat, so that nowadays the real form of the body has been quite forgotten" (Lehmann 2000: 40, quoting Gautier 1860: 5–6). This may be less true today than it was in 1860, but it is still clothes that make the body culturally visible, and, conversely, the clothes themselves are only complete when animated by a body. As Schiaparelli said: "A dress cannot just hang like a painting on the wall or like a book remain intact and live a long and sheltered life. A dress has no life of its own unless it is worn" (Schiaparelli 1954: 46).

Martin passionately defends the whole fashion enterprise in *Fashion and Surrealism* and, by aligning it with art, seemingly seeks to demonstrate fashion's cultural importance. For the surrealists, he argues, fashion became the "most compelling friction between the ordinary and extraordinary, between disfigurement and embellishment, body and concept, artifice and the real" (Martin 1988: 9). More – fashion, as understood by the surrealists, bears witness to the "insurrection art offers to daily life." Thus, for Martin, there exists a subversive element to fashion, or the "fashion arts," and fashion has depths and a profundity normally denied it.

Martin is equally concerned to defend surrealism from the charge, often leveled at it by sections of the art world, that in engaging with fashion and the advertising industry it was cheapened. For some critics, that surrealism proved amenable to the purposes of consumption proved its superficiality and lack of integrity. (Psychoanalysis, of course, proved similarly useful to PR and marketing, yet has escaped being denounced on that account.) Martin by contrast identifies the reason for surrealism's compatibility with consumer society and the arts of consumption: "it was precisely surrealism's ability to juxtapose the real and the unreal that made it a primary form for advertising and media expression . . . the simultaneity of an optical truth and its dreamed doppelganger could render the product enticing" (Martin 1988: 218).

Since the subject of *Fashion and Surrealism* is precisely the field in which they operated and may still operate together, it is not surprising – in fact it is almost inevitable – that Martin should emphasize the visual aspects of surrealism and the work of a second generation of surrealists, or artists influenced by the movement, such as Salvador Dali, Jean Cocteau, and Cecil Beaton. It was, after all, these artists who in the 1930s forged such a close relationship between fashion, popular media and commerce. Fashion magazines, advertisements, and window displays as much as film and photography, found a fertile source of inspiration in the surrealist movement. In consequence, display was transformed, as was advertising, and a new and more sophisticated and knowing environment was created for the "fashion arts."

Martin's concentration on the commerce and mass imagery of fashion nevertheless results in an overemphasis on the showmanship and also the playfulness of those such as Dali at the expense of a different, more literary tradition in surrealism, dominated by André Breton. Martin acknowledges obliquely that Breton was a difficult patriarch of the movement and broke with many of his followers, in particular Dali, whom he nicknamed with the anagram of the painter's name, Avida Dollars, alluding to Dali's showmanship and thirst for fame and celebrity. Breton by contrast was rigorously intellectual and principled and his work in many ways courted obscurity.

Both artists, however, were equal in the intensity of their preoccupation with the nature of the unconscious; but where – or so many argued, even at the time – Dali's efforts to introduce psychoanalytic symbolism and concepts into his art resulted in an all too conscious and knowing intellectual vulgarity, Breton pursued his sense of the Marvellous by journeying into "an uncharted conceptual terrain," using the "disorienting signposts" of somnambulism, hypnotism, and the occult "on a voyage 'to the end of the Unknown to find the new!'" (Lomas 2000: 70, quoting Charles Baudelaire, « Le voyage »).

In Richard Martin's account, the worlds of fashion and surrealism act upon each other to produce a conscious and witty, albeit subversive, sense of style, and sometimes shock and outrage. In Breton's world, objects, including garments, acquire a more obscure significance.

Although he was a resolutely avant-garde and intellectual writer, Breton's interest in fortune-telling, clairvoyance, hypnotism, and the Tarot connected him to a mass popular audience, for "superstition" and a fascination with the occult are rife in the allegedly "secular" societies of the West. Garments play a role in these shadowy realms.

In the summer of 2001 the Croatian tennis player Goran Ivanisevic, unlikely winner of the Wimbledon championship that year, provided a striking example. Sportspersons, like actors, are prone to superstition, perhaps because of the emotional risks any performer takes in subjecting her or his skill to an audience, but Goran's exploits were extreme by any standards. Not only did he display an extraordinary range of superstitious behavior; he also almost appeared to make a fetish of his own body, celebrating each successive unexpected victory in the tournament by stripping off his shirt and parading across the court bare-chested. At his victory parade in Split he stripped right down to his underpants to display his conqueror's body. Meanwhile his shirt, tossed into the crowd after every match, presumably became a mascot or fetish for the lucky spectator who caught it.[2] At the same time, his ironic off-court commentary on his own exploits demonstrated an element of disavowal as he spoke openly of his three personalities: good Goran, bad Goran and emergency Goran. In fact, he was well on the way to becoming a thoroughly surrealist personality in his mingling of the real and the imaginary. Did he, for example, really believe that God interrupted his tennis match against Tim Henman with a thunderstorm, in order to enable him to turn round what seemed to be a losing situation and beat the British "white hope"?

Other tennis players have from time to time developed superstitions surrounding articles of clothing. Billy Jean King, for example, had a "lucky dress" that had to be worn for particularly important matches. Nor is it surprising that dress should be involved in personal superstitions, since garments are so closely associated with the self, and perhaps particularly with the bodily identity of a performer. Such superstitions, however, are not the exclusive property of performers. For many, perhaps most of us, articles of clothing not only affect our mood and self-perception, but not infrequently acquire quasi-magical properties and meanings.

The British psychoanalyst Donald Winnicott developed a theory of the infant's relationship to a special "garment." He noted how many toddlers have a special object, often a blanket or shawl or sometimes a scarf or even part of a dress belonging to the mother, which they have to have with them at all times. Winnicott's name for this "security blanket" was the "transitional object." He argued that it symbolizes the mother and the mother's body – the infant clings to this symbol or metaphor of the mother as she gradually separates physically and emotionally from this first symbiotic relationship. Thus the piece of material or garment stands in for the mother during the transition from complete dependency to relative autonomy (Winnicott 1971). Walter Benjamin implies a similar association between clothing and the mother–child relationship when he writes of "what the child . . . discovers in the pleats of the old material to which it clings while trailing at its mother's skirts" (Benjamin 1999: 79). Garments, once they have been worn, come to have a residue. They take on qualities of the wearer and of the occasions on which they were worn. Their feel and smell come to represent memories, conscious and unconscious. They are far from being simply functional adjuncts to the body, or even a language of communication, although of course they are that too, but take on symbolic significance in ways of which we are not always even aware.

In his superstitious behavior, Goran Ivanisevic exposed a central feature of magical beliefs when focused on an object. The idea of "luck" is intimately related to the idea of "chance." A "lucky" outcome imbues the object that is believed to have contributed to it with an element of fate, converting chance into its opposite. On the first occasion a particular tennis ball was struck to make a winning shot, or a garment worn in a match that was won, it had been chosen by chance, but retrospectively it is imbued with the fortunate outcome so that now the choice of that garment or tennis ball rather than any other seems to show the "hand of God." It is in this way that a chance object becomes a fetish object – and fetish objects are, of course, highly magical.

This is no less true in contemporary secular society than in the traditional societies of old. It is simply that today a different ritual holds sway: today it is fashion that "prescribes the ritual according to which the commodity fetish demands to be worshipped" (Benjamin 1973: 166).[3] The society of the commodity demands the novelty of the continually changing, so that the fashion cycle is particularly resonant in the society of capitalist consumption, where exchange value defeats use value and where "the reciprocal and fixed relations between social groups are dismantled, and commodities function increasingly as signs organising value and desire" (During 2001: 279). This is often taken to mean simply that designer clothes and "labels" become straightforward status symbols, but it implies much more than that: garments, like other objects, can take on imagined and/or subjectively experienced properties that go far beyond the flaunting of wealth or refined taste. It is *because* we live in a society dominated by capital and consumption that we commandeer material goods for the symbolic expression of values remote from materialism. This includes ideas of a superstitious, magical and spiritual nature. The objects expressing or embodying them become something like secular fetishes.

Magic, witchcraft, paganism, and superstitious practices are in any case only the residues of older religions crushed by monotheism, besides which Christianity itself incorporated numerous features of pagan belief. Until the late sixteenth or early seventeenth century, moreover, magic and science were similar, and beliefs that today seem fanciful or magical, such as astrology, were part of the educated person's picture of the universe and its working (Thomas 1971: *passim*).

A like mingling and confusion between Christianity and paganism is to be found in the history of the fetish. Very briefly, the idea of the fetish arose in "a mercantile intercultural space created by the . . . trade between cultures so radically different as to be mutually incomprehensible, that is the European slave trade with West Africa" (Pietz 1985, 1987, 1988). It is a hybrid, belonging to neither culture. The term originates from the Portuguese and from the period when Portuguese traders were active on the West African coast. These Roman Catholics brought ideas of witch-craft, superstition, and idolatry to the objects and practices they encountered. In the seventeenth century the Dutch, Protestants, ousted the Portuguese. For them the fetish and related phenomena represented a chaotic irrationalism. To cut a long story short, a complex cultural encounter eventually led to the Enlightenment view of the fetish as an example of false values and superstitious delusions. These blocked reason and were misunderstood as miraculous events whose origins lay in the natural world.

Thus the fetish emerges in the same period as the commodity form, and it became and important rhetorical an theoretical idea in the writings of the foremost theorist of commodization, Karl Marx. For Marx, capital itself was a kind of fetish and political economy an "a-theological religion of everyday life" in a secular society that is fundamentally irrational.

He developed the concept of commodity fetishism to describe and explain the way in which, as in a religion, a human product acquires a life of its own. However, whereas in anthropological fetishism the fetish bestows power on the owner or wearer, in Marx the fetishization of the commodity involves the disempowerment and alienation of the human actors.

Marx spoke of the fetishism of the production process, but objects of consumption, including of course garments, are also fetishized, taking on a meaning far beyond their use value. They are thus like figures of speech or metaphors. But above all (Gammon and Makkinen 1994: 445–6):

> what the different types of fetishism have in common, is the process of disavowal . . . objects in our culture take on meanings that connect them to, or stand in for, other meanings and associations: but the connection is lost or partially denied as a consequence of the fetishism. Through the use of the fetish the practitioner is able to contrive to believe the false while also knowing that it cannot be true.

The fetishism of articles of clothing and body parts is most usually discussed in relation to sexual fetishism (Steele 1996), and for the surrealists the conjuncture of dress and the body could certainly become intensely erotic, as the surrealist Hans Bellmer, for example, indicated (Mundy 2001: 41, quoting Bellmer 1947: 111):

> I wonder if I will wear the tight seamless trousers made of your legs . . . and do you think I will, without swooning prematurely, button over my chest the heavy and trembling waistcoat of your breasts? As soon as I am immobilised beneath the pleated skirt of all your fingers . . . you will breathe in me your perfume and your fever.

However, I suggest that the fetish, including fetish garments, may also stand in for other, more nebulous, desires: for power, for social affirmation, for spiritual certainty, as well as, of course, as Marx brilliantly demonstrated, representing the machinery of capitalism.

Theodor Adorno, analyzing astrology and occultism, saw popular superstitious practices as alienated, yet, like neurotic symptoms, they have their own rationality; they perform a function of compromise between situations in which individuals are powerless yet desire to feel they have some control. The still pervasive, classical liberal view of the unfettered individual and his freedom is incompatible with the paranoid, bureaucratized world we live in, Adorno argues, but quasi-magical beliefs provide some kind of defense in this world. At the same time he notes the irony and disavowal characteristic of our attitude towards astrology and other beliefs, an intellectual attitude he describes as one of "disoriented agnosticism" (Adorno 1999: 116). Yet alienated forms of belief nevertheless express real and genuine yearnings, for something beyond the organized sciences, which, as Adorno says, "do not cover the universality of existence."

This was also Breton's view, but he went much further than Adorno, since he rejected the view that the fetish was only an aspect of false consciousness or alienation, albeit one with a defensive function. For Breton and the surrealists the fetish bore a relationship to their concept of the Marvellous. The Marvellous came about as the marriage of what they called convulsive beauty and objective chance. Thus chance encounters, unexpected places, and found objects all exemplified the Marvellous. Their accidental occurrence or the unexpected manner in which the surrealist became conscious of them invested them with the same sort of magical meaning as had been attributed to the fetish. In fact the found object was very similar to a fetish.

In *L'Amour fou* Breton defined chance as "the form making manifest the exterior necessity which traces its path in the human unconscious" (Breton 1992: 52). Engaged in an attempt to formulate what he termed "modern materialism" (see Cohen 1993: *passim*), a form of surrealist Marxism that would dissolve the distinction between the material and the ideal, he searched for an obscure third realm underlying both. Chance encounters and *trouvailles*, found objects, he sees as portents of or keys to this realm in which human subjectivity and external reality might be resolved of contradictions. The *trouvaille* contains repressed energies, but at the same time has the power to undo repression. Furthermore as a piece of the object world it connects that world with the psychic world of the individual.

Breton looked to psychoanalysis to bring a new dimension to Marxism, since one of its strengths is its insistence on the power of the irrational. Unlike Freud, though, he did not seek to reduce the sway of the irrational. On the contrary, he wrote that: "It is only by making evident the intimate relation linking the two terms real and imaginary that I hope to break down the distinction, which seems to me less and less well founded, between the subjective and the objective" (Breton 1992: 53).

There was an uncanny aspect for the surrealists to the dreams, chance encounters, and psychic states they privileged, in which dream/reality and animate/inanimate were blurred or confused. The relationship of dress to body is especially appropriate as a site for this blurring.

For the surrealists, the memories and associations stored in the folds of our garments constitute something more than alienation. Dress in modernity acts as a vehicle for the enchantment that Max Weber felt had been leached out of the world by the imperatives of bureaucratic rationalism. Dress became a largely unacknowledged conduit for the communication and symbolization of inchoate impulses and desires, and a blurring of boundaries.

Elsa Schiaparelli's designs in the 1930s exemplify this surrealist vision. Friendly with some of the surrealists and consciously influenced by them, her garments often derive their power and beauty from her exploration of the ambiguous, blurred boundary between body and garment, which hints at something darker and more uncanny beneath the playful surface (Evans 1999); Caroline Evans has demonstrated that far from forfeiting its claim to artistic seriousness by succumbing to the seduction of consumption, and becoming itself part of that seduction process, surrealism's engagement with fashion does not render it frivolous, but rather renders fashion serious.

Jean Baudrillard suggests something similar when he argues that psychoanalysis is anti-magical because it attempts to restore unconscious impulses to the realm of reason by way of interpretation. Seduction, by contrast, constitutes an anti-rationalist opposition to "all systems of production and interpretation," to all orthodoxies. It appears "as malefice and artifice," a black magic for the deviation of all truths, a game "with arbitrary rules and elusive rituals," and "to seduce is to die as reality and reconstitute oneself as illusion." This, Baudrillard suggests, is an aesthetic rather than a moral approach to life, and it is "what remains of a magical, fateful world." He suggests that fashion, which is "a passion for the artificial," is "a kind of fetish, an increasing excess of communication" (Baudrillard 1990: *passim*). This brings him momentarily, and perhaps surprisingly, quite close to Breton.

For Breton the magic find, the magic garment really can, if we analyze the source of its apparently chance attraction, unleash new energy, unchain our desires. The *trouvaille* or the fetish can act as a catalyst in transforming the individual's relationship to the world. It acts to redeem the non-sentient world and reenergize our relationship to it.

This is far from reducing fashion to play and parody. So far as fashion is concerned, this returns us to Richard Martin's observation that the fashion object could be a "powerful force" because of its power of memory and its subversive quality – insights whose promise, I would argue, is never quite fulfilled in *Fashion and Surrealism*.

Any attempt to explore the magical properties of dress may seem a puny and even trivial commentary on the unnerving world of consumption with its illusory and disorienting powers of enchantment. There is, of course, a powerful element of disavowal in the stereotypical popular dismissal of fashion as inherently trivial. It is disavowal because despite all that fashion scholars and critics may attempt to do in order to legitimate the study of dress, and despite a public that expresses its fascination by flocking to fashion exhibitions and following fashion ardently, at the same time the culture never ceases to subscribe to the dogma of fashion's silliness and unimportance. This is disavowal in action. The triviality of dress is the fetishized idea that makes it possible for us to continue – even as we denigrate it (in fact *because* we denigrate it) – simultaneously to indulge our fascination with it, and, further, constitute it as the vehicle for deeply significant ideas, aspirations, and feelings.

For the relationship of fashion to surrealism and thus to an aspiration towards the Marvellous addresses the way in which we strive to invest our lives with something of the magical. Over time our clothes accrue to themselves the residues of use and memory, residues of desire, of hope and occasion. It was in this sense that Benjamin perceived how fashion has accumulated within itself the "dream energy of society," which he felt had been leached out of so much of the cultural fabric of his time.

In the world of the surrealists the relationship between organic and inorganic, natural and artificial is a gap, or tear in the fabric of our experience, through which we may glimpse a different version of the world. It is moreover the very irrationality of fashion – its most often criticized aspect – that gives it significance. It bears witness that the magical is more than just the refuse, the useless rubbish of the rational Enlightenment world. Like surrealism, it still speaks to us today, affirming the autonomy of human desire at a time when not only our bodies but even those desires themselves are in danger of becoming wholly commodified, of being wholly colonized by consumer lifestyle. Fashion, the epitome of consumerism, is also its stealthiest critic, and in its obsession with what Freud referred to as the "refuse of the phenomenal world," of the disregarded, the marginal and everyday – including in this case, our garments – surrealism gives us hope, suggesting that there are still gaps in the apparent seamlessness of consumer culture through which we can escape into re-enchanted worlds.

NOTES

Source: *Fashion Theory,* 8(4) (Berg Publishers, 2004), 375–85.

1. Walter Benjamin echoes this thought in his ambiguous notes on fashion in *The Arcades Project*, perceiving a sinister side to fashion: "Every fashion stands in opposition to the organic. Every fashion couples the living body to the inorganic world. To the living, fashion defends the rights of the corpse. The fetishism that succumbs to the sex appeal of the inorganic is its vital nerve."
2. The curator of the museum at the All England Lawn Tennis Club is on record as saying that whether or not to wash garments that belonged to former champions is always an issue. Some curators argue that the bodily secretions of the athlete become part of the garment and should be conserved.
3. Since Benjamin's massive quantities of notes in *The Arcades Project* were translated into English they have become available to a much wider range of scholars, and because they are notes, they often have a gnomic or aphoristic quality or an ambiguity which makes it very tempting to insert them into one's own discourse – rather like the frill on the dress that Benjamin himself mentions in an especially famous quote, or like a piece of embroidery to embellish one's own pedestrian words with the imprimatur of the true artist. They are tempting especially because their very ambiguity somehow chimes with the ambiguity of dress or fashion itself. Like found objects, they are themselves almost – and sometimes literally, because many of them are quotations from other authors – literary *trouvailles*.

REFERENCES

Adorno, Theodor. 1999. *The Stars Look Down*. London: Verso.
Baudrillard, Jean. 1990. *Seduction*. Trans. Brian Singer. Montreal: New World Perspectives.
Beauvoir, Simone de. 1953. *The Second Sex*. Trans. H. M. Parshley. London: Jonathan Cape.
Bellmer, Hans. 1947. « L'Anatomie de l'Amour. » In *Le Surréalisme en 1947*. Paris: Exhibition Catalog, Galerie Maeght.
Benjamin, Walter. 1973. *Charles Baudelaire: A Lyric Poet in the Era of High Capitalism*. London: Verso.
——. 1999. *The Arcades Project*. Trans. Howard Eiland and Kevin McLaughlin. Cambridge, MA: Harvard University Press.

Breton. 1992. *Mad Love*. Trans. Mary Caws. Lincoln, NE: University of Nebraska Press.

Cohen, Margaret. 1993. *Profane Illumination: Walter Benjamin and the Paris of Surrealist Revolution*. Berkeley, CA: University of California Press.

During, Simon. 2001. *Modern Enchantments: The Cultural Power of Secular Magic*. Cambridge, MA: Harvard University Press.

Evans, Caroline. 1999. "Masks, Mirrors and Mannequins: Elsa Schiaparelli and the Decentred Subject." *Fashion Theory* 3(1): 3–32.

Foster, Hal. 1993. *Compulsive Beauty*. Cambridge, MA: MIT Press.

Gammon, Lorraine and Marje Makkinen. 1994. *Female Fetishism: A New Look*. London: Lawrence and Wishart.

Lehmann, Ulrich. 2000. *Tigersprung: Fashion in Modernity*. Cambridge, MA: MIT Press.

Lomas, David. 2000. *The Haunted Self: Surrealism Psychoanalysis Subjectivity*. New Haven, CT: Yale University Press.

Martin, Richard. 1988. *Fashion and Surrealism*. London: Thames and Hudson.

Mundy, Jennifer. 2001. "Letters of Desire." In Jennifer Mundy (ed.), *Surrealism: Desire Unbound*, pp. 10–54. London: Tate Publishing.

Pietz, William. 1985. "The Problem of the Fetish I." *Res* 9 (Spring): 12–36.

——. 1987. "The Problem of the Fetish II: The Origin of the Fetish." *Res* 13 (Spring): 23–47.

——. 1988. "The Problem of the Fetish III: Bosman's Guinea and the Enlightenment Theory of Fetishism." *Res* 16 (Autumn): 105–24.

Schiaparelli, Elsa. 1954. *Shocking Life*. London: J. M. Dent and Sons.

Steele, Valerie. 1996. *Fetish: Fashion, Sex and Power*. Oxford: Oxford University Press.

Thomas, Keith. 1971. *Religion and the Decline of Magic*. Harmondsworth: Penguin.

Winnicott, Donald. 1971. "Transitional Objects and Transitional Phenomena." In *Playing and Reality*, pp. 1–30. Harmondsworth: Penguin.

APPENDIX OF SOURCES

Grateful acknowledgement is made to the following sources for permission to reproduce material for these volumes.

VOLUME 1
Late Medieval to Renaissance

1. 'Costume and Fashion', *Fernand Braudel*
   Civilization and Capitalism, 15th–18th Century, 1 (HarperCollins, 1992), 311–33.
   Copyright © 1979 by Librairie Armand Colin. English translation copyright © 1981 by William Collins Ltd. and Harper & Row Publishers, Inc. Reprinted by permission of HarperCollins Publishers.

2. 'Fashion in French Crusade Literature: Desiring Infidel Textiles',
   Sarah-Grace Heller
   Désirée Koslin and Janet E. Snyder (eds) *Encountering Medieval Textiles and Dress: Objects, Texts, Images* (Palgrave Macmillan, 2002), 103–19.
   Published by Palgrave Macmillan, reproduced with permission of Palgrave Macmillan.

3. 'Art and Life', *Johan Huizinga*
   The Waning of the Middles Ages. A Study of the Forms of Life, Thought and Art in France and the Netherlands in the XIVth and XVth Centuries. Trans. F. Hopman, (E. Arnold & Co., 1924), 250–52, 270–74.
   Published by E. Arnold & Co.

4. 'The Medieval Aesthetic Sensibility', *Umberto Eco*
   Art and Beauty in the Middle Ages (Yale University Press, 1986), 4–16.
   Published by Yale University Press. Reprinted with permission.

5. 'Society and Festivals', *Jacob Burckhardt*
   The Civilization of the Renaissance in Italy (Phaidon/Allen & Unwin, 1878), 186–94.
   Published by Phaidon/Allen & Unwin.

6. 'Order and Fashion in Clothes: The King, His Household, and the City of
    London at the End of the Fifteenth Century', *Anne F. Sutton*
    Textile History, 22(2) (The Pasold Research Fund, 1991), 253–76.
    Previously published as the book *Fabrics and Fashion*, by The Pasold Research Fund. Reprinted
    with permission.

7. 'Summer: The Last Century', *Timothy Brook*
    The Confusions of Pleasure: Commerce and Culture in Ming China (University of California
    Press, 1998), 218–37.
    © 1998 Regents of the University of California. Published by the University of California Press.
    Reprinted with permission.

8. 'Between Clothing and Nudity', *Mario Perniola*
    Fragments for a History of the Human Body, Part 2 (New York: Zone Books, 1989), 236–65.
    © 1989 Urzone, Inc. Reprinted with permission.

9. 'Women and Sumptuary Law', *Catherine Kovesi*
    Sumptuary Law in Italy 1200–1500 (Oxford University Press, 2002), 111–32.
    Reprinted by permission of Oxford University Press.

10. 'The Upward Training of the Body from the Age of Chivalry to Courtly
    Civility', *Georges Vigarello*
    Fragments for a History of the Human Body, Part 2 (New York: Zone Books, 1989), 148–99.
    © 1989 Urzone, Inc. Reprinted with permission.

11. 'The Renaissance Beard: Masculinity in Early Modern England', *Will Fisher*
    Renaissance Quarterly, 54(1) (Renaissance Society of America, 2001), 155–87.
    Published by Renaissance Society of America. Reprinted with permission from The University of
    Chicago Press.

12. 'Appearances', *Georges Vigarello*
    Concepts of Cleanliness: Changing attitudes in France since the Middle Ages (Cambridge
    University Press, 1988), 78–89.
    © Cambridge University Press, reprinted with permission.

13. 'The Devil and His Striped Clothes: 13th–16th Centuries', *Michel Pastoureau*
    The Devil's Cloth: A History of Stripes and Striped Fabric (Columbia University Press, 2001), 7–32.
    Copyright © 2001 Columbia University Press. Reprinted with permission.

14. 'Venice and the Dress of Foreigners', *Stella Mary Newton*
    The Dress of the Venetians 1495–1525 (Ashgate Publishing, 1988), 132–44.
    © 1988 Ashgate Publishing. Reprinted with permission.

15. 'Costume and the Boundaries of Bodies', *Bronwen Wilson*
    The World in Venice: Print, the City, and Early Modern Identity (University of Toronto Press,
    2005), 70–132.
    Published by University of Toronto Press. Reprinted with permission.

16. 'Sewing Connections *Elizabeth Tudor, Mary Stuart, Elizabeth Talbot, and
    Seventeenth-Century Anonymous Needleworkers*', *Susan Frye*
    Maids and Mistresses, Cousins and Queens: Women's Alliances in Early Modern England
    (Oxford University Press, 1999), 165–82.
    Reprinted by permission of Oxford University Press.

17. 'Feathers and Flies: Aphra Behn and the Seventeenth-Century Trade in
     Exotica',   *Margaret W. Ferguson*
     Margreta de Grazia, Maureen Quilligan, and Peter Stallybrass (eds) *Subject and Object in
     Renaissance Culture* (Cambridge University Press, 1996), 235–59.
     © Cambridge University Press, reprinted with permission.

18. 'Clothing Provision and the Great Wardrobe in the Mid-Thirteenth Century',
     Kay Staniland
     Textile History, 22(2) (The Pasold Research Fund, 1991), 239–52.
     Previously published as the book *Fabrics and Fashion,* by The Pasold Research Fund. Reprinted
     with permission.

19. 'The Currency of Clothing',   *Ann Rosalind Jones and Peter Stallybrass*
     Renaissance Clothing and the Materials of Memory (Cambridge University Press, 2000), 17–33.
     © Cambridge University Press, reprinted with permission.

20. 'Gendered Space in Renaissance Florence: Theorizing Public and Private in
     the "Rag Trade"',   *Carole Collier Frick*
     Fashion Theory, 9(2) (Berg Publishers, 2005), 125–46.
     Published by Berg Publishers. Reprinted with permission.

21. 'The Economics of Clothing in the Late Seventeenth Century',   *N.B. Harte*
     Textile History, 22(2) (The Pasold Research Fund, 1991), 277–96.
     Previously published as the book *Fabrics and Fashion,* by The Pasold Research Fund. Reprinted
     with permission.

22. 'The Cost of Apparel in Seventeenth-Century England, and the Accuracy of
     Gregory King',   *Margaret Spufford*
     The Economic History Review, LIII(4) (Blackwell Publishing, 2000), 677–705.
     Copyright © 2000. Reproduced with permission of Blackwell Publishing Ltd.

23. 'Looks and Appearance',   *Baldesar Castiglione*
     Etiquette for Renaissance Gentlemen (The Book of the Courtier by Baldesar Castigloine,
     translated with an introduction by George Bull, Penguin Books 1967, Revised 1976)
     (Penguin, 1995), 9–11.
     Published by Penguin Books. Reprinted with permission.

24. 'Gesture, Ritual, and Social Order in Sixteenth- to Eighteenth-Century Poland',
     Maria Bogucka
     Jan Bremmer and Herman Roodenburg (eds) *A Cultural History of Gesture: from Antiquity to
     the Present Day* (Polity Press, 1991), 190–209.
     Published by Polity Press. Reprinted with permission from the author.

25. 'Prescribing Fashion: Dress, Politics and Gender in Sixteenth-Century Italian
     Conduct Literature',   *Elizabeth Currie*
     Fashion Theory, 4(2) (Berg Publishers, 2000), 157–77.
     Published by Berg Publishers. Reprinted with permission.

26. 'Masculine Apparel',   *Stephen Orgel*
     Impersonations: The Performance of Gender in Shakespeare's England (Cambridge University
     Press, 1996), 83–105.
     © Cambridge University Press, reprinted with permission.

27. 'To Fashion a Self: Dressing in Seventeenth-Century England', *Sue Vincent*
     Fashion Theory, 3(2) (Berg Publishers, 1999), 197–218.
     Published by Berg Publishers. Reprinted with permission.

28. '"Twisted" Poses: The *Kabuku* Aesthetic in Early Edo Genre Painting',
     John T. Carpenter
     Nicole Coolidge Rousmaniere (ed.) *Kazari: Decoration and Display in Japan 15th–19th Centuries*
     (British Museum Press, 2002), 42–49.
     Published by British Museum Press. Reprinted with permission.

VOLUME 2
The Eighteenth Century

1.   'The Cavaliers and the Parvenus as Imitators of the Court', *Werner Sombart*
     Luxury and Capitalism (Ann Arbor: The University of Michigan Press, 1967), 80–94.
     Published by The University of Michigan Press. Reprinted with permission.

2.   'Lord Chesterfield's Letters to His Son', *The Earl of Chesterfield*
     Lord Chesterfield's Letters to his Son, 2, 4th ed. (William Reeves, 1912), 27–30, 33–35, 47–49.
     Published by William Reeves.

3.   'Regrets on Parting with My Old Dressing Gown, *or, A Warning to Those
     Who Have More Taste than Money*', *Denis Diderot*
     Rameau's Nephew and Other Works, Translated by Barzun and Bowen (Random House, 1956),
     325–33.
     Published by Random House. Reprinted with permission from the editor.

4.   'Eros and Liberty at the English Masquerade, 1710–90', *Terry Castle*
     Eighteenth-Century Studies, 17(2) (The John Hopkins University Press, 1983), 156–76.
     © The John Hopkins University Press. Reprinted with permission of The John Hopkins University
     Press.

5.   'Freedom of Dress in Revolutionary France', *Lynn Hunt*
     Sara E. Melzer and Kathryn Norberg (eds) *From the Royal to the Republican Body. Incorporating
     the Political in Seventeenth- and Eighteenth-Century France* (University of California Press,
     1998), 224–49.
     © 1998 Regents of the University of Caliornia. Published by the University of California Press.
     Reprinted with permission.

6.   'The Purged Century', *Piero Camporesi*
     Exotic Brew: The Art of Living in the Age of Enlightenment (Polity Press, 1994), 36–45.
     Published by Polity Press.

7.   'Popular Dress', *Daniel Roche*
     People of Paris: An Essay in Popular Culture in the 18th Century (Berg Publishers, 1987),
     160–94.
     Published by Berg Publishers. Reprinted with permission.

8.   'Image–Object–Space', *Katie Scott*
     Art History, 28(2) (Blackwell Publishing, 2005), 137–50.
     Copyright © 2005. Reproduced with permission of Blackwell Publishing Ltd.

9. 'The Artistic Expression of *Iki*', *Kuki Shûzô*
    Translated by John Clark. Sakuko Matsui and John Clark (eds) *Reflections on Japanese Taste: The Structure of Iki* (Power Publication, 1997), 85–100.
    Published by Power Publication. Reprinted with permission.

10. 'Street Style: Dress in John Gay's *Trivia*', *Aileen Ribeiro*
    Clare Brant and Susan E. Whyman (eds) *Walking the Streets of Eighteenth-Century London: John Gay's Trivia (1716)* (Oxford University Press, 2007), 131–48.
    Reprinted by permission of Oxford University Press.

11. 'Nature and Artifice', *Georges Vigarello*
    Concepts of Cleanliness: Changing Attitudes in France since the Middle Ages (Cambridge University Press, 1988), 131–41.
    © Cambridge University Press, reprinted with permission.

12. 'Fleshing Out the Revolution', *Ewa Lajer-Burcharth*
    Necklines: The Art of Jacques-Louis David After the Terror (Yale University Press, 1999), 183–204.
    Published by Yale University Press. Reprinted with permission.

13. 'Consumer Behaviour, Textiles and Dress in the Late Seventeenth and Early Eighteenth Centuries', *Lorna Weatherill*
    Textile History, 22(2) (The Pasold Research Fund, 1991), 297–310.
    Previously published as the book Fabrics and Fashion, by The Pasold Research Fund. Reprinted with permission.

14. 'European Consumption and Asian Production in the Seventeenth and Eighteenth Centuries', *John E. Wills, Jr*
    Brewer & Porter (eds) *Consumption and the World of Goods* (Routledge, 1993), 133–47.
    Copyright (1993) Routledge. Reproduced by permission of Taylor & Francis Books UK.

15. 'Taxes upon Consumable Commodities', *Adam Smith*
    An Inquiry into the Nature and Causes of the Wealth of Nations, 2 (Oxford University Press, 1976), 869–74.
    Reprinted by permission of Oxford University Press.

16. 'The Queen and Her 'Minister of Fashion': Gender, Credit and Politics in Pre-Revolutionary France', *Clare Haru Crowston*
    Gender & History, 14(1) (Blackwell Publishing, 2002), 92–116.
    Copyright © 2002. Reproduced with permission of Blackwell Publishing Ltd.

17. 'The Production and Marketing of Populuxe Goods in Eighteenth-Century Paris', *Cissie Fairchilds*
    Brewer & Porter (eds) *Consumption and the World of Goods* (Routledge, 1993), 228–48.
    Copyright (1993) Routledge. Reproduced by permission of Taylor & Francis Books UK.

18. 'Developing Consumerism and the Ready-made Clothing Trade in Britain, 1750–1800', *Beverly Lemire*
    Textile History, 15(1) (The Pasold Research Fund, 1984), 21–44.
    Published by The Pasold Research Fund. Reprinted with permission.

19. 'Involuntary Consumers? Servants and Their Clothes in Eighteenth-Century England', *John Styles*
     Textile History, 33(1) (Maney Publishing, 2002), 9–21.
     Published by Maney Publishing www.maney.co.uk/journals/textile; http://www.ingentaconnect.com/content/maney/tex. Reprinted with permission.

VOLUME 3
The Nineteenth Century

1. 'Adolf Loos and the English Dandy', *Jules Lubbock*
    Architectural Review, 169 (1038) (EMAP, 1983), 43–49.
    Published by EMAP. Reprinted with permission.

2. 'The Treatises of Dandyism', *Rhonda K. Garelick*
    Rising Star: Dandyism, Gender, and Performance in the Fin de Siècle (Princeton University Press, 1998), 14–46.
    © 1998 Princeton University Press. Reprinted by permission of Princeton University Press.

3. 'The Invisible Flâneur', *Elizabeth Wilson*
    New Left Review, 1(191) (*New Left Review*, 1992), 90–110.
    Published by *New Left Review*. Reprinted with permission.

4. 'The Actress: Covent Garden and the Strand 1880–1914', *Christopher Breward*
    Fashioning London: Clothing and the Modern Metropolis (Berg Publishers, 2004), 67–95.
    Published by Berg Publishers. Reprinted with permission.

5. 'The Suffrage Response', *Joel H. Kaplan and Sheila Stowell*
    Theatre & Fashion: Oscar Wilde to the Suffragettes (Cambridge University Press, 1994), 152–84.
    © Cambridge University Press, reprinted with permission.

6. '*Tigersprung*: Fashioning History', *Ulrich Lehmann*
    Fashion Theory, 3(3) (Berg Publishers, 1999), 297–322.
    Published by Berg Publishers. Reprinted with permission.

7. 'The Love of Finery: Fashion and the Fallen Woman in Nineteenth-Century Social Discourse', *Mariana Valverde*
    Victorian Studies, 32(2) (Indiana University Press, 1989), 169–88.
    Published by Indiana University Press. Reprinted with permission.

8. 'The Exquisite Slave: The Role of Clothes in the Making of the Victorian Woman', *Helene E. Roberts*
    Signs: Journal of Women in Culture and Society, 2(3) (The University of Chicago Press, 1977), 554–69.
    © 1977 by The University of Chicago Press. Reprinted with permission via Copyright Clearance Center's Rightslink Service.

9. 'Dress Reform as Antifeminism: A Response to Helene E. Roberts's "The Exquisite Slave: The Role of Clothes in the Making of the Victorian Woman"', *David Kunzle*
    Signs: Journal of Women in Culture and Society, 2(3) (The University of Chicago Press, 1977), 570–79.
    © 1977 by The University of Chicago Press. Reprinted with permission via Copyright Clearance Center's Rightslink Service.

10. 'Reply to David Kunzle's "Dress Reform as Antifeminism: A Response to Helene E. Roberts's 'The Exquisite Slave'" (vol. 2, no. 3)', *Helene E. Roberts*
   Signs: Journal of Women in Culture and Society, 2(3) (The University of Chicago Press, 1977), 518–19.
   Published by The University of Chicago Press. Reprinted with permission via Copyright Clearance Center's Rightslink Service.

11. 'Fashion – Jewellery', *Marguerite de Ponty (Stéphane Mallarmé)*
   Mallarmé on Fashion: A Translation of the Fashion Magazine La Dernière Mode, with Commentary (Berg Publishers, 2004), 21–24.
   Published by Berg Publishers. Reprinted with permission.

12. 'Fashion', *Marguerite de Ponty (Stéphane Mallarmé)*
   Mallarmé on Fashion: A Translation of the Fashion Magazine La Dernière Mode, with Commentary (Berg Publishers, 2004), 51–53.
   Published by Berg Publishers. Reprinted with permission.

13. 'Consuming Kashmir: Shawls and Empires, 1500–2000', *Michelle Maskiell*
   Journal of World History, 13(1) (University of Hawai'i Press, 2002), 27–65.
   Published by University of Hawai'i Press. Reprinted with permission.

14. 'The Management of Colour: The Kashmir Shawl in a Nineteenth-Century Debate', *David Brett*
   Textile History, 29(2) (The Pasold Research Fund, 1988), 123–33.
   Published by The Pasold Research Fund. Reprinted with permission.

15. 'Sartorial Ideologies: From Homespun to Ready-Made', *Michael Zakim*
   American Historical Review, 16(5) (The University of Chicago Press, 2001), 1553–86.
   Published by The University of Chicago Press. Reprinted with permission.

16. 'Cheap Mass-Produced Men's Clothing in the Nineteenth and Early Twentieth Centuries', *Sarah Levitt*
   Textile History, 22(2) (The Pasold Research Fund, 1991), 179–92.
   Previously published as the book *Fabrics and Fashion*, by The Pasold Research Fund. Reprinted with permission.

17. 'Invisible Clothing', *Philippe Perrot*
   Fashioning the Bourgeoisie: A History of Clothing in the Nineteenth Century (Princeton University Press, 1994), 143–66.
   © 1994 Princeton University Press. Reprinted by permission of Princeton University Press.

18. 'Wool Cloth and Gender: The Use of Woollen Cloth in Women's Dress in Britain, 1865–85', *Lou Taylor*
   Defining Dress: Dress as Object, Meaning and Identity (Manchester University Press, 1999), 39–57.
   Published by Manchester University Press. Reprinted with permission from the author.

19. 'Materializing Mourning: Hair, Jewellery and the Body', *Marcia Pointon*
   Material Memories: Design and Evocation (Berg Publishers, 1999), 39–57.
   Published by Berg Publishers. Reprinted with permission.

20. 'Femininity and Consumption: The Problem of the Late Nineteenth-Century Fashion Journal', *Christopher Breward*
   Journal of Design History, 7(2) (Oxford University Press, 1994), 71–89.
   Reprinted by permission of Oxford University Press.

21. ''A Dream of Fair Women': Revival Dress and the Formation of Late Victorian Images of Femininity',   *Margaret Maynard*
    Art History, 12(3) (Blackwell Publishing, 1989), 322–41.
    Copyright © 1989. Reproduced with permission of Blackwell Publishing Ltd.

22. '*Femme Fatale*: Fashion and Visual Culture in Fin-de-siècle Paris', *Valerie Steele*
    Fashion Theory, 8(3) (Berg Publishers, 2004), 315–28.
    Published by Berg Publishers. Reprinted with permission.

23. 'Sex and the City: Metropolitan Modernities in English History',   *Margot Finn*
    Victorian Studies, 44(1) (Indiana University Press, 2001), 25–32.
    Published by Indiana University Press. Reprinted with permission.

VOLUME 4
The Twentieth Century to Today

1. 'Dress as an Expression of the Pecuniary Culture',   *Thorstein Veblen*
   The Theory of the Leisure Class: An Economic Study of Institutions (George Allen and Unwin, 1925), 167–87.
   Published by George Allen and Unwin.

2. 'The Philosophy of Fashion',   *Georg Simmel*
   Simmel on Culture David Frisby and Mike Featherstone (eds) (SAGE Publications, 1997), 187–206.
   Copyright © (1997). Reproduced by permission of SAGE Publications, London, Los Angeles, New Delhi and Singapore.
   'Adornment',   *Georg Simmel*
   The Sociology of Georg Simmel Translated and edited by Kurt H. Wolff (The Free Press, 1950), 338–44.
   Copyright © 1950 by The Free Press. Copyright © renewed 1978 by The Free Press. All rights reserved. Reprinted with the permission of the Free Press, a division of Simon & Schuster Adult Publishing Group.

3. 'The Economic and Social Rôle of Fashion',   *Pierre Clerget*
   Annual Report Smithsonian Institution (Smithsonian Institution Scholarly Press, 1913), 756–65.
   Published by Smithsonian Institution Scholarly Press.

4. 'The Cerementing of the Gentleman',   *Gerald Heard*
   Narcissus: An Anatomy of Clothes (E.P. Dutton & Co., 1924), 122–31.
   Published by E.P. Dutton & Co.

5. 'The Predominance of Male Homosociality',   *J.C. Flügel*
   Men and their Motives: Psycho-Analytical Studies, with Two Essays by Ingeborg Flügel (Kegan Paul, Trench, Trubner & Co., 1934), 61–65.
   Published by Kegan Paul, Trench, Trubner & Co.

6. 'Epilogue on Trousers',   *Eric Gill*
   Clothes: An Essay upon the Nature and Significance of the Natural and Artificial Integuments Worn by Men and Women (Jonathon Cape, 1931), 186–97.
   Published by Jonathon Cape.

7. 'The Functions of Folk Costume in Moravian Slovakia: Introduction',
    Petr Bogatyrěv
    The Functions of Folk Costume in Moravian Slovakia (Walter de Gruyter, 1971), 33.
    Published by Walter de Gruyter. Reprinted with permission.

8. 'An Economic Interpretation of Women's Fashions',   *Paul M. Gregory*
    Southern Economic Journal, 14(2) (Southern Economic Association, 1947), 148–62.
    Published by Southern Economic Association. Reprinted with permission.

9. 'Themes in Cosmetics and Grooming',   *Murray Wax*
    The American Journal of Sociology, 62(6) (The University of Chicago Press, 1957), 588–93.
    Published by The University of Chicago Press. Reprinted with permission via Copyright Clearance
    Center's Rightslink Service.

10. 'The Economics of Fashion Demand',   *Dwight E. Robinson*
    The Quarterly Journal of Economics, 75(3) (Massachusetts Institute of Technology, 1961),
    376–98.
    © 1961 by the President and Fellows of Harvard College and the Massachusetts Institute of
    Technology. Reprinted with permission.

11. 'From Gemstones to Jewellery',   *Roland Barthes*
    Translated by Andy Stafford. Andy Stafford and Michael Carter (eds) *The Language of Fashion*
    (Power Publication, 2006), 59–64.
    French version published by Éditions du Seuil. © Éditions du Seuil, 1993. English translation
    published by Power Publication. Reprinted with permission.

12. 'Fashion: From Class Differentiation to Collective Selection',   *Herbert Blumer*
    The Sociological Quarterly, 10 (Blackwell Publishing, 1969), 275–91.
    Copyright © 1969. Reproduced with permission of Blackwell Publishing Ltd.

13. 'Why the Midi Failed',   *Fred D. Reynolds and William R. Darden*
    Journal of Advertising Research, 12 (The Advertising Research Foundation, 1972), 39–44.
    Published by World Advertising Research Center, www.jar.warc.com. Reprinted with permission.

14. 'The Production of Belief: Contribution to an Economy of Symbolic Goods',
    Pierre Bourdieu
    Media, Culture and Society, 2(3) (SAGE Publications, 1980), 281–88 (extract).
    © 1980 Academic Press Inc. (London) Limited. Reproduced by permission of SAGE Publications,
    London, Los Angeles, New Delhi and Singapore.

15. 'Fashion Shapes: Film, the Fashion Industry, and the Image of Women',
    Maureen Turim
    Socialist Review, 71(13) (Radical Society Ltd., 1983), 78–96.
    Published by Radical Society Ltd.

16. 'Other People's Clothes? The International Second-hand Clothing Trade and
    Dress Practices in Zambia',   *Karen Tranberg Hansen*
    Fashion Theory, 4(3) (Berg Publishers, 2000), 245–74.
    Published by Berg Publishers. Reprinted with permission.

17.   'To Cut is to Think',   *Germano Celant*
      Art/Fashion (Skira Editore, 1997), 21–26.
      Published by Skira Editore. Reprinted with permission from the author.

18.   'Illuminations – Warhol in the 1950s',   *Richard Martin*
      Mark Francis and Margery King (eds) *The Warhol Look* (Hachette Book Group, 1997), 70–77.
      Copyright © 1997 by the Andy Warhol Museum. By permission of LITTLE, BROWN &
      COMPANY.

19.   'The Golden Dustman: A Critical Evaluation of the Work of Martin Margiela
      and a Review of *Martin Margiela: Exhibition (9/4/1615)*',   *Caroline Evans*
      Fashion Theory, 2(1) (Berg Publishers, 1998), 73–93.
      Published by Berg Publishers. Reprinted with permission.

20.   'Art, Fashion and Music in the Culture Society',   *Angela McRobbie*
      In the Culture Society: Art, Fashion and Popular Music (Routledge, 1999), 3–21.
      Copyright (1999) Routledge. Reproduced by permission of Taylor & Francis Books UK.

21.   'Vionnet & Classicism',   *Rebecca Arnold*
      Madeleine Vionnet: 15 Dresses from the Collection of Martin Kamer (Judith Clark Costume, 2001),
      6 pages.
      Published by Judith Clark Costume. Reprinted with permission from the author.

22.   'Paul Poiret's Minaret Style: Originality, Reproduction, and Art in Fashion',
      Nancy J. Troy
      Fashion Theory, 6(2) (Berg Publishers, 2002), 117–43.
      Published by Berg Publishers. Reprinted with permission.

23.   'Hollywood Glamour and Mass Consumption in Postwar Italy',
      Stephen Gundle
      Journal of Cold War Studies, 4(3) (Massachusetts Institute of Technology, 2002), 95–118.
      © 2002 by the President and Fellows of Harvard College and the Massachusetts Institute of
      Technology.

24.   'Magic Fashion',   *Elizabeth Wilson*
      Fashion Theory, 8(4) (Berg Publishers, 2004), 375–85.
      Published by Berg Publishers. Reprinted with permission.